Dan'l Webster

Æt. 37.

[illegible] Miniature by Miss Goodrich now in the possession of
Miss E. Wadsworth Lee

THE

PRIVATE CORRESPONDENCE

OF

DANIEL WEBSTER.

EDITED BY

FLETCHER WEBSTER.

IN TWO VOLUMES.

VOLUME I.

BOSTON:
LITTLE, BROWN AND COMPANY.
1857.

RIVERSIDE, CAMBRIDGE;
STEREOTYPED AND PRINTED BY
H. O. HOUGHTON AND COMPANY.

DEDICATION.

I DEDICATE these volumes of the Private Correspondence of DANIEL WEBSTER to the memory of his Wife and the Mother of his children,

GRACE FLETCHER WEBSTER.

I desire, as far as possible, to associate her name with that of him whose early fortunes she shared, whose early labors she cheered, whose character she appreciated, whose distinguished position she adorned, and on whose lips, amid their last utterances, hung her beloved name.

FLETCHER WEBSTER.

PREFACE.

Four years have now elapsed since the death of Mr. Webster, on the 24th day of October, 1852. The literary executors appointed by his will, and the Editor of these volumes, some time after that event, made application, by public notice and private address, to his correspondents in this country and Europe for copies of his letters. That application was generally answered.

Within a year a considerable collection of letters was made. The numerous manuscripts in Mr. Webster's possession at the time of his death, were, when collected and cursorily examined, placed in the hands of Mr. William Thaddeus Harris, of Cambridge, to be assorted, and, as far as their nature admitted, alphabetically arranged.

Mr. Harris undertook this task with zeal, but, after a year of assiduous and methodical toil, it was interrupted by his lamented death, leaving its completion to other hands.

In 1854, the Editor commenced the examination and arrangement of such letters as were in his own possession; and in 1855, he received from the literary executors the copies of the letters forwarded in compliance with the application above alluded to, made with great labor and accuracy by George Ticknor, Esq., and the ladies of his family, and forming a very important and interesting portion of the contents of these volumes.

In preparing the correspondence for the press, from all these materials, the chief difficulty has arisen from the necessity of exercising a severe judgment in making selections.

Every letter of Mr. Webster had in it something instructive, entertaining, or characteristic, which caused its omission to be doubtfully and reluctantly decided upon, though such a result was repeatedly unavoidable, in order not to swell the volumes to an inconvenient size, or too much increase their number.

The same consideration caused the omission also from the present work of his early productions in prose and verse, his occasional contributions to periodicals, political essays, and those of his speeches, early and late, not contained in Mr. Everett's edition, all of which had been collected and prepared for publication.

The general events of Mr. Webster's life are sufficiently well known from the Biographical Sketch by Mr. Everett, prefixed to his edition of "The Works of Daniel Webster," and from the political history of the country for the last half century.

No complete and impartial biography of him can be written until after such a lapse of time as shall render possible an unbiased consideration of his public acts, and a fair judgment upon the political sentiments which he entertained.

These volumes may prove of value as a collection of materials for the composition of such a work; and it is hoped that they will not be without interest to the general reader as affording a view of Mr. Webster's private character, his habits of intercourse, modes of thought, affections, tastes, pursuits, amusements, and style of familiar correspondence. To give a just presentation of these characteristics, has been the object of the Editor.

Expressions of political opinion, of course, not unfrequently occur in his letters, but it is hoped that none may be found calculated to injure the feelings of the living or detract from the just reputation of the dead.

It would have been difficult, indeed, to have selected such passages, if it had been desirable.

His letters are distinguished by an absence of harsh epithets, or denunciatory remarks, and none of them need be withheld from the public out of consideration to the writer. He often observed, that he had made it a rule through life, to write nothing which he would not be willing to see in print the next morning, and a thorough examination of his letters has shown how rigidly he adhered to it.

The reader will remark that there are occasional long intervals of time between the dates of some of the letters, and of those which immediately succeed them. This arises partly from the necessity of selection, and partly from the inability to obtain letters which may have been written during these periods. There are numerous letters in existence from Mrs. Grace Webster, his wife, acknowledging letters from him. Two or three only of these last can be found.

Mrs. Julia Webster Appleton, his daughter, shortly before her death, destroyed all letters addressed to her, which were in her possession. A few left in the hands of friends, have been preserved.

The volumes contain some letters addressed to Mr. Webster. These are chiefly from his brother and early friends and relatives; from distinguished contemporaries, with whom he was intimate; from occasional foreign correspondents of eminence, or from those illustrious men, long since become historical personages, whose letters form connecting links between the late and preceding generations.

The Editor would do injustice to others as well as to his own feelings, if he should fail to acknowledge his indebtedness to many friends, for their aid in the preparation of these volumes.

To Mr. Everett, he is especially obliged, for an unvarying kindness from the commencement of the undertaking to its completion; for advice and suggestions, which his general acquaintance with public men and knowledge of public events, his long intimacy with Mr. Webster, his matured judgment and cultivated taste, rendered invaluable.

Professor Sanborn of Dartmouth College, has a large and admitted claim upon the Editor's gratitude, for interesting materials supplied by him, for his own contributions, and for his vigorous aid throughout a whole winter in the arrangement of the papers.

The letters to Mr. Fillmore, written by Mr. Webster, as Secretary of State, were copied from the originals, with Mr. Fillmore's permission, by Mr. G. J. Abbot, of the State Department, a gentleman who stood in confidential relations to Mr. Webster, and for whom he entertained a high regard.

To Mrs. Eliza Buckminster Lee the Editor is under a peculiar obligation, for the use of the "Autobiography;" a favor, he is aware, which would have been granted to no one but himself, and also for the sketch of the character of Mrs. Grace Webster, his mother.

To Mrs. Fletcher Webster, his wife, for her constant and cheerful encouragement, her ever ready and grateful assistance, he wishes to express his affectionate thanks; and to those lady relatives and friends, who have either furnished interesting materials or lightened and lessened his labors in their preparation, he offers his heartfelt acknowledgments.

FLETCHER WEBSTER.

MARSHFIELD, October 24, 1856.

AUTOBIOGRAPHY OF DANIEL WEBSTER.

INTRODUCTORY NOTE.

THE following Autobiography was written for Mrs. Eliza Buckminster Lee, and presented to her by Mr. Webster. It was written in 1829, though it extends only to 1817.

A few of the facts which it contains have been made public, or generally stated, on some occasions by Mr. Webster himself; but the manuscript has never been out of Mrs. Lee's control, nor been permitted to be used for any purpose other than a perusal by some particular friends.

On learning my purpose of preparing my father's correspondence for publication, Mrs. Lee, with impressive kindness, offered me this manuscript.

The amount of my indebtedness to her for this favor will be best estimated after the Autobiography has been read.

No change has been made in it except the omission of two quotations from Mr. Webster's DIARY, which, as the Diary itself is published in these volumes, are left out, to avoid repetition.

AUTOBIOGRAPHY.

My earliest ancestor of whom I possess at present any knowledge, was Thomas Webster. He was settled in Hampton, New Hampshire, as early as 1636, probably having come thither from or through Massachusetts, though he may have come by way of Piscataqua. From him to myself the descent may be found regularly recorded in the church records and town records of Hampton, Kingston, now East Kingston, and Salisbury.

The family is, no doubt, originally from Scotland, although I have not been able to learn how far back any Scotch accent was found lingering on our tongue. Probably enough, the emigrants may have come last from England. The characteristics of the personal appearance of the Websters are pretty strongly marked, and very generally found with all who bear the name in New England. They have light complexions, sandy hair, a good deal of it, and bushy eyebrows; and are rather slender than broad or corpulent.

Dr. Noah Webster, the author of the Dictionary, is a *vera effigies* of the race. Rev. Mr. Webster, now of Hampton, the large family in the county of Grafton, and the various remnants of the old stock still to be found in Kingston and its neighborhood, bear the same general appearance.

My uncles were formed and marked in the same manner. No two persons looked more unlike than my father and either of his brothers. His mother was a Bachelder, a descendant of the Rev. Stephen Bachelder, a man of some notoriety, in his time, in the county of Rockingham. This woman had black hair, and black eyes, and was, besides, as my father, who was her eldest son, has told me, a person of uncommon strength of character. I learn the same thing from the elderly inhabitants of Kingston. My father resembled, in complexion and appearance, his mother; his brothers resembled their father. Of my own brothers, only one had the Bachelder complexion; the others, three, ran off into the general characteristics belonging to the name.

My first clear and distinct recollection of my father's appearance was, when he was at the age of fifty. I think it was rather striking; he was tall, six feet, or six feet within a half an inch, erect, with a broad and full chest, hair still of an unchanged black, features rather large and prominent, a Roman nose, and eyes of brilliant black. He had a decisive air and bearing, partly the effect, I suppose, of early soldiership. My late brother, at the moment of his decease, was nearly of the same age, and most strongly resembled him; except that his hair had turned white; his eyes were larger, and not quite so black, and his mouth and teeth hardly as perfect. In subsequent periods, my father suffered much ill health from rheumatism, and other complaints, which a good deal changed his appearance. He was born at Kingston, now East Kingston, in 1739; the eldest son of Ebenezer Webster and Susannah Bachelder. His father was a farmer, as we somewhat improperly call persons of his condition; that is to say, he was a small freeholder, tilling his own acres with his own hands, and those of his boys, till they grew up to manhood, when they were to look out, in the country round them, for acres of their own to till.

After the age of twelve or fifteen, he lived several years in the family of Colonel Stevens, the most considerable person in the vicinity; and then, as Major Dalgetty would say, he took service in the troops raised in the Provinces to carry on the French war. His first engagement, I believe, was in Robert Rogers's company of Rangers. He was with the army of Gen. Amherst, when that commander made his way by Albany, Oswego, Ticonderoga, &c., into Canada. When Canada was conquered, his occupation was gone; but that event opened new scenes of enterprise, more pacific, but promising more permanent good, to those who had strong hands and determined purpose.

Previous to the year 1763, the settlements in New Hampshire had made little or no progress inward into the country, for sixty or seventy years, owing to the hostility of the French, in Canada, and of the neighboring Indians, who were under French influences. This powerful cause of repression being effectually removed by the cession of Canada to England, by the Peace of Paris in 1763, companies were formed, in various parts of New England, to settle the wilderness, between the already settled parts of New England and New York and Canada. Colonel Stevens, already mentioned, and other persons about Kingston, formed one of these companies, and obtained from Benning Wentworth, Governor of the Province of New Hampshire, a grant of the township of Salisbury, at first called Stevenstown. It is situated exactly at the head of the Merrimac River, and very near the centre of the State. My father joined this enterprise, and about 1764, the exact date is not before me, pushed into the wilderness. He had the discretion to take a wife along with him, intending whatever else he might want, at least, not to lack good company. The party *travelled out the road*, or path, for it was no better, somewhere about Concord or Boscawen; and they were obliged to make their way, not finding one, to their destined places of habitation. My father *lapped on*, a little beyond any other comer, and when he had built his log cabin, and lighted his fire, his smoke ascended nearer to the North Star than that of any other of his Majesty's New England subjects. His nearest civilized neighbor on the north, was at Montreal.

His story of this early settlement was interesting, at least, to me. The settlers, doubtless, suffered much. The mountainous nature of the country, the very long winters, with prodigious depth of snow, and the want of all roads to communicate with the country below, often induced great hardships. The settlement increased, and when the revolutionary war broke out, ten or eleven years after, the town contained nearly two hundred men capable of bearing arms. My father was their Captain, and he led them forth, with the other New Hampshire troops, almost every campaign. He commanded a company at Bennington, at White Plains, at West Point, at the time of Arnold's defection, &c. I have some little articles, the *spolia prœlii* of Bennington, which I keep, *honore parentis*.

The last time I ever saw Gen. Stark, he paid me the compliment of saying, that my complexion was like that of my father, and that his was of that cast, so convenient for a soldier, that burnt gunpowder did not change it.

I was born January 18, 1782. My father, by two marriages, had five sons and five daughters. I am the youngest son, and only surviving child. I have nephews and nieces, both of the whole and half blood; that is to say, sons and daughters of my brothers and sisters, of both my father's wives.

The year following my birth, my father removed from his first residence, which was a log house on the hill, to the river side, in the same town; a distance of three miles. Here, in the meadow land, by the river, with rough high hills hanging over, was the scene of my earliest recollections; or, as was said in another case, "Here I found myself." I can recollect when *it was* 1790; but cannot say that I can remember further back. I have a very vivid impression, indeed, of something which took place some years earlier, especially, of an extraordinary rise in the river. I remember how the deluge of rain beat, for two days, on the house; how all looked anxiously to see the river overflow its banks, how the waters spread over the meadows, how the boat coming from afar, on the other side of the river, was rowed up till it almost touched the door-stone. How Mr. G.'s great barn, fifty feet by twenty, full of hay and grain, sheep, turkeys, and chickens, sailed down the current majestically before our eyes, and how we were all busy preparing to fly to the mountains, as soon as our house should manifest a disposition to follow Mr. G.'s barn. I remember, or seem to remember all these things; I did indeed see as much of them as a child of five years could see, for I think it was in 1787, but still I am of opinion that my impression is from narrative, and not from remembrance of the vision. Plain, intelligible, and striking things of this kind, I have learned, make an impression on young minds in recital, which it is difficult afterwards to distinguish from actual personal recollection.

I do not remember when or by whom I was taught to read; because I cannot and never could recollect a time when I could not read the Bible. I suppose I was taught by my mother, or by my elder sisters. My father seemed to have no higher object in the world, than to educate his children, to the full extent of his very limited ability. No means were within his reach, generally speaking, but the small town schools. These were kept by teachers, sufficiently indifferent, in the several neighborhoods of the township, each a small part of the year. To these I was sent, with the other children.

When the school was in our neighborhood, it was easy to attend; when it removed to a more distant district I followed it, still living at home. While yet quite young, and in winter, I was sent daily two and a half or three miles to the school. When it removed still further, my father sometimes boarded me out, in a neighboring family, so that I could still be in the school. A good deal of this was an extra care, more than had been bestowed on my elder brothers, and originating in a conviction of the slenderness and frailty of my constitution, which was thought not likely ever to allow me to pursue robust occupation.

In these schools, nothing was taught but reading and writing; and, as to these, the first I generally could perform better than the teacher, and the last a good master could hardly instruct me in; writing was so laborious, irksome, and repulsive an occupation to me always. My masters used to tell me, that they feared, after all, my fingers were destined for the plough-tail.

I must do myself the justice to say that, in those boyish days, there were two things I did dearly love, viz: reading and playing; passions which did not cease to struggle, when boyhood was over, (have they yet, altogether?) and in regard to which neither the *cita mors* nor the *victoria læta* could be said of either.

At a very early day, owing I believe mainly to the exertions of Mr. Thompson, the lawyer, the clergyman, and my father, a very small circulating library had been bought. These institutions, I believe, about that time received an impulse, among other causes, from the efforts of Dr. Belknap, our New Hampshire historian. I obtained some of these books, and read them. I remember the Spectator among them; and I remember, too, that I turned over the leaves of Addison's criticism on Chevy Chase, for the sake of reading connectedly the song, the verses of which he quotes from time to time as subjects of remark. It was, as Doctor Johnson said in another case, that the poet was read and the critic was neglected. I could not understand why it was necessary that the author of the Spectator should take such great pains to prove that Chevy Chase was a good story; that was the last thing I doubted.

I was fond of poetry. By far the greater part of Dr. Watts's Psalms and Hymns I could repeat *memoriter*, at ten or twelve years of age. I am sure that no other sacred poetry will ever appear to me so affecting and devout.

I remember that my father brought home from some of the lower towns Pope's Essay on Man, published in a sort of pamphlet. I took it, and very soon could repeat it, from beginning to end. We had so few books that to read them once or twice was nothing. We thought they were all to be got by heart. I have thought of this frequently since, when that sagacious admonition of one of the ancients (was it Pliny?) has been quoted, *legere multùm non multà.*

I remember one occurrence, that shows the value then attached to books. The close of the year had brought along the next year's almanac. This was an acquisition. A page was devoted to each month, and on the top of each page were four lines of poetry; some moral, some sentimental, some ludicrous. The almanac came in the morning, and before night my brother and myself were masters of its contents, at least of its poetry and its anecdotes. We went to bed upon it; but awaking long before the morning light, we had a difference of recollection about one word, in the third line of *April's* poetry. We could not settle it by argument and there was no umpire. But the *fact* could be ascertained by inspection of the book. I arose, groped my way to the kitchen, lighted a candle, proceeded to a distant room, in search of the almanac, found it, and brought it away. The disputed passage was examined, I believe I was found to be in the wrong, and blew out my candle and went to bed. But the consequence of my error had wellnigh been serious. It was about two o'clock in the morning, and just as I was again going to sleep, I thought I saw signs of light in the room I had visited. I sprang out of bed, ran to the door, opened the room, and it was all on fire. I had let fall a spark, or touched the light to something which had communicated fire to a parcel of cotton clothes, they had communicated it to the furniture, and to the sides of the room, and the flames had already begun to show themselves through the ceiling, in the chamber above. A pretty earnest cry soon brought the household together. By great good luck we escaped. Two or three minutes more and we should all have been in danger of burning together. As it was, I think the house was saved by my father's presence of mind. While others went for water, he seized every thing movable which was on fire, and wrapped it up in woollen blankets. My maternal grandmother, then of the age of eighty, was sleeping in the room.

I recollect no great changes happening to me till I was fourteen years old. A great deal of the time I was sick, and when well was exceedingly slender, and apparently of feeble system. I read what I could get to read, went to school when I could; and when not at school, was a farmer's youngest boy, not good for much, for want of health and strength, but was expected to do something. Up to this period, I had no hope of any education beyond what the village school-house was to afford. But now my father took an important step with me. On the 25th day of May, 1796, he mounted his horse, placed me on another, carried me to Exeter, and placed me in Phillips Academy, then and now under the care of that most excellent man, Dr. Benjamin Abbott. I had never been from home before, and the change overpowered me. I hardly remained master of my own senses, among ninety boys, who had seen so much more, and appeared to know so much more than I did. I was put to English grammar, and writing, and arithmetic. The first, I think I may say, I fairly mastered between May and October; in the others I made some progress. In the autumn, there was a short vacation. I went home, stayed a few days, and returned at the commencement of the quarter, and then began the Latin grammar. My first exercises in Latin were recited to Joseph Stevens Buckminster. He had, I think, already joined college, but had returned to Exeter, perhaps in the college vacation, and was acting as usher, in the place of Dr. Abbott, then absent through indisposition.

It so happened, that within the few months during which I was at the Exeter Academy, Mr. Thacher, now judge of the Municipal Court of Boston, and Mr. Emery, the distinguished counsellor at Portland, were my instructors. I am proud to call them both masters. I believe I made tolerable progress in most branches which I attended to, while in this school; but there was one thing I could not do. I could not make a declamation. I could not speak before the school. The kind and excellent Buckminster sought, especially, to persuade me to perform the exercise of declamation, like other boys; but I could not do it. Many a piece did I commit to memory, and recite and rehearse, in my own room, over and over again; yet when the day came, when the school collected to hear declamations, when my name was called, and I saw all eyes turned to my seat, I could not raise myself from it. Sometimes the instructors frowned, sometimes they smiled. Mr. Buckminster always pressed, and entreated, most winningly, that I would venture; but I could never command sufficient resolution. When the occasion was over, I went home and wept bitter tears of mortification.

At the winter vacation, December, 1796, or January, 1797, my father came for me, and took me home. Some long-enduring friendships I formed in the few months I was at Exeter. J. W. Bracket, late of New York, deceased, William Garland, late of Portsmouth, deceased, Gov. Cass, of Michigan, Mr. Saltonstall, and James H. Bingham, now of Claremont, New Hampshire, are of the number. In February, 1797, my father carried me to the Rev. Samuel Wood's, in Boscawen, and placed me under the tuition of that most benevolent and excellent man. It was but half a dozen miles from our own house. On the way to Mr. Wood's, my father first intimated to me his intention of sending me to college. The very idea thrilled my whole frame. He said he then lived but for his children, and if I would do all I could for myself, he would do what he could for me. I remember that I was quite overcome, and my head grew dizzy. The thing appeared to me so high, and the expense and sacrifice it was to cost my father, so great, I could only press his hands and shed tears. Excellent, excellent parent! I cannot think of him, even now, without turning child again.

Mr. Wood put me upon Virgil and Tully; and I conceived a pleasure in the study of them, especially the latter, which rendered application no longer a task. With what vehemence did I denounce Catiline! With what earnestness struggle for Milo! In the spring I began the Greek grammar, and at midsummer Mr. Wood said to me: "I expected to keep you till next year, but I am tired of you, and I shall put you into college next month." And so he did, but it was a mere breaking in; I was, indeed, miserably prepared, both in Latin and Greek; but Mr. Wood accomplished his promise, and I entered Dartmouth College, as a Freshman, August, 1797. At Boscawen, I had found another circulating library, and had read many of its volumes. I remember especially that I found Don Quixote, in the common translation, and in an edition, as I think, of three or four duodecimo volumes. I began to read it, and it is literally true that I never closed my eyes till I had finished it; nor did I lay it down for five minutes; so great was the power of that extraordinary book on my imagination.

Of my college life, I can say but little. Though death has made great havoc in our class, some yet live who were intimate with me; especially Mr. Bingham, before mentioned. Rev. Mr. Jewett, of Gloucester (Sandy Bay); Rev. Mr. Tenny, of Weathersfield; Rev. Thomas Abbott Merrill, of Middlebury; Judge Fuller, of Augusta; Mr. Farrar, of Lancaster; Judge Kingsbury, of Gardiner, and several others of the class, are still living.

I was graduated, in course, August, 1801. Owing to some difficulties, *hæc non meminisse juvat*, I took no part in the commencement exercises. I spoke an oration to the Society of the United Fraternity, which I suspect was a sufficiently boyish performance.

My college life was not an idle one. Beside the regular attendance on prescribed duties and studies, I read something of English history and English literature. Perhaps my reading was too miscellaneous. I even paid my board, for a year, by superintending a little weekly newspaper, and making selections for it, from books of literature, and from the contemporary publications. I suppose I sometimes wrote a foolish paragraph myself. While in college, I delivered two or three occasional addresses, which were published. I trust they are forgotten; they were in very bad taste. I had not then learned that all true power in writing is in the idea, not in the style, an error into which the *Ars rhetorica*, as it is usually taught, may easily lead stronger heads than mine.

I must now go back, a little, to make mention of some incidents connected with my brother, Ezekiel Webster. He was almost two years older than myself, having been born March 11, 1780. He was a healthy, strong-built, robust boy. His intellectual character, as it afterwards developed itself, was not early understood, at least in its full extent. He was thought to have good sense, but not to have, and perhaps had not, great quickness of apprehension. The older brothers were married and settled. My father's plan was that this brother should remain with him. This was the domestic state of things, when I went to college in August, 1797. But I soon began to grow uneasy about my brother's situation. His prospects were not promising, and he himself saw and felt this, and had aspirations beyond his condition. Nothing was proposed, however, by way of change of plan, till two years after. In the spring of 1799, at the May vacation, being then Sophomore, I visited my family, and then held serious consultation with my brother. I remember well when we went to bed, we began to talk matters over, and that we rose, after sunrise, without having shut our eyes. But we had settled our plan. He had thought of going into some new part of the country. That was discussed and disagreed to. All the *pros* and *cons* of the question of remaining at home were weighed and considered, and when our council broke up, or rather got up, its result was that I should propose to my father, that he, late as it was, should be sent to school, also, and to college. This, we knew, would be a trying thing to my father and mother, and two unmarried sisters. My father was growing old, his health not good, and his circumstances far from easy. The farm was to be carried on, and the family taken care of; and there was nobody to do all this, but him, who was regarded as the main stay, that is to say, Ezekiel. However, I ventured on the negotiation, and it was carried, as other things are often, by the earnest and sanguine manner of youth. I told him that I was unhappy at my brother's prospects. For myself, I saw my way to knowledge, respectability, and self-protection; but as to him, all looked the other way; that I would keep school, and get along as well as I could—be more than four years in getting through college, if necessary, provided he also could be sent to study. He said at once he lived but for his children; that he had but little, and on that little he put no value, except so far as it might be useful to them. That to carry us both through college would take all he was worth; that for himself he was willing to run the risk, but that this was a serious matter to our mother and two unmarried sisters; that we must settle the matter with them, and if their consent was obtained, he would trust to Providence, and get along as well as he could. The result was, that, in about ten days, I had gone back to college, having first seen my brother take leave of the meadows, and place himself in school, under a teacher in Latin. Soon afterwards he went to Mr. Wood's, and there pursued the requisite studies, and my father carried him, with me, to college in March, 1801, when he joined the then Freshman class.

Being graduated in August, 1801, I immediately entered Mr. Thompson's office, in Salisbury, next door to my father's house, to study the law. There I remained till January following, viz: January, 1802. The necessity of the case required that I should then go somewhere and gain a little money. I was written to, luckily, to go to Fryeburg, Maine, to keep school. I accepted the offer, traversed the country on horseback, and commenced my labors. I was to be paid at the rate of three hundred and fifty dollars per annum. This was no small thing, for I compared it not with what might be before me, but what was actually behind me. It was better, certainly, than following the plough. But let me say something in favor of my own industry; not to make a merit of it, for necessity sometimes makes the most idle industrious. It so happened that I boarded, at Fryeburg, with the gentleman, James Osgood, Esq., who was Register of Deeds of the then newly created County of Oxford. He was not *clerical*, in and of himself; and his registration was to be done by deputy. The fee for recording at full length a common deed, in a large fair hand, and with the care requisite to avoid errors, was *two shillings and three pence.* Mr. Osgood proposed to me that I should do this writing, and that of the two shillings and three pence for each deed, I should have one shilling and sixpence, and he should have the remaining nine-pence. I greedily seized on so tempting an offer, and set to work. Of a long winter's evening I could copy two deeds, and that was half a dollar. Four evenings in a week earned two dollars; and two dollars a week paid my board. This appeared to me to be a very thriving condition; for my three hundred and fifty dollars salary as a school-master was thus going on, without abatement or deduction for *vivres.* I hope yet to have an opportunity to see, once more, the first volume of the Record of Deeds, for the County of Oxford. It is now near thirty years since I copied into it the last "witness my hand and seal;" and I have not seen even its outside since. But the ache is not yet out of my fingers; for nothing has ever been so laborious to me as writing, when under the necessity of writing a good hand.

In May of this year, (1802,) having a week's vacation, I took my quarter's salary, mounted a horse, went straight over all the hills to Hanover, and had the pleasure of putting these, the first earnings of my life, into my brother's hands, for his college expenses. Having enjoyed this sincere and high pleasure, I hied me back again to my school and my copying of deeds. I stayed in Fryeburg only till September. My brother then came to see me, we made a journey together to the lower part of Maine, and returned to Salisbury. I resumed my place in Mr. Thompson's office, and he went back to college.

At Fryeburg, I found another circulating library, and made some use of it. I remember to have read, while at Fryeburg, Adams's Defence of the American Constitutions, Mosheim's Ecclesiastical History, Goldsmith's History of England, and some other small things. I borrowed Blackstone's Commentaries, also, and read, I think, two or three volumes of them. Here, also, I found Mr. Ames's celebrated speech, on the British Treaty, and committed it to memory. From September, 1802, to February or March, 1804, I remained in Mr. Thompson's office, and studied the law. He was an admirable man, and a good lawyer himself; but I was put to study in the old way, that is, the hardest books first, and lost much time. I read Coke Littleton through, without understanding a quarter part of it. Happening to take up Espinasse's Law of Nisi Prius, I found I could understand it, and, arguing that the object of reading was to understand what was written, I laid down the venerable Coke *et alios similes reverendos*, and kept company for a time with Mr. Espinasse and others, the most plain, easy, and intelligible writers. A boy of twenty, with no previous knowledge on such subjects, cannot understand Coke. It is folly to set him on such an author.

There are propositions in Coke so abstract, and distinctions so nice, and doctrines embracing so many conditions and qualifications, that it requires an effort, not only of a mature mind, but of a mind both strong and mature to understand him. Why disgust and discourage a boy, by telling him that he must break into his profession, through such a wall as this? I really often despaired. I thought I never could make myself a lawyer, and was almost going back to the business of school-keeping. A friend has recently returned to me a letter, written by me to him, at that time, showing my feelings of despondence and despair. Mr. Espinasse, however, helped me out of this, in the way I have mentioned; and I have always felt greatly obliged to him.

I do not know whether I read much, during this year and a half, beside law books, with two exceptions. I read Hume, though not for the first time; but my principal occupation with books, when not law books, was with the Latin Classics. I brought from college a very scanty inheritance of Latin. I now tried to add to it. I made myself familiar with most of Tully's orations, committed to memory large passages of some of them, read Sallust, and Cæsar and Horace. Some of Horace's odes I translated into poor English rhymes; they were printed; I have never seen them since. My brother was a far better Latin scholar than myself, and in one of his vacations we read Juvenal together. But I never mastered his style so as to read him with ease and pleasure. At this period of my life I passed a great deal of time alone. My amusements were fishing, and shooting, and riding; and all these were without a companion. I loved this occasional solitude then, and have loved it ever since, and love it still. I like to contemplate nature, and to hold communion, unbroken by the presence of human beings, with "this universal frame, thus wondrous fair;" I like solitude also as favorable to thoughts less lofty. I like to let the thoughts go free, and indulge in their excursions. And when *thinking* is to be done, one must of course be alone. No man knows *himself* who does not thus, sometimes, keep his own company. At a subsequent period of life, I have found that my lonely journeys, when following the court on its circuits, have afforded many an edifying day.[1]

Before proceeding to note some events which happened in 1804, I ought to say, that it would not have been possible for us to have got along, had it not been for the small income derived from my father's official situation. As soon as the war

[1] The argument in the Dartmouth College case was mainly arranged, during a journey on professional business from Boston to Barnstable and back. John Adams's speech was composed, not in Philadelphia, in 1776, but in Massachusetts, in 1826, in a New England chaise. The address for Bunker Hill was, in great part, composed in *Marshpee Brook; Testibus, Johanne de Trutta et F. W. puero.*

of the Revolution was over, and the pursuits of peace returned, he was elected into such public offices as it might be supposed he was qualified to fill. His qualities were integrity, firmness, decision, and extraordinary good sense. His defect, the want of early education. He never saw the inside of a school-house, in the character of a learner; and yet the first records, or some among the first, of the town of Salisbury, are in his handwriting. What he knew, he had taught himself. His character was generous and manly, and his manner such as gave him influence with those around him. Early and deeply religious, he had still a good deal of natural gayety; he delighted to have some one about him that possessed a humorous vein. A character of this sort, one Robert Wise, with whose adventures, as I learned them from himself, I could fill a small book, was a near neighbor, and a sort of humble companion for a great many years. He was a Yorkshire man; had been a sailor; was with Byng in the Mediterranean; had been a soldier; deserted from the garrison of Gibraltar; travelled through Spain, and France, and Holland; was taken up afterwards, severely punished, and sent back to the army; was in the battle of Minden; had a thousand stories of the yellow-haired Prince Ferdinand; was sent to Ireland, and thence to Boston, with the troops brought out by Gen. Gage; fought at Bunker Hill, deserted to our ranks, served with the New Hampshire troops in all the succeeding campaigns, and at the peace, built a little cottage in the corner of our field, on the river's bank, and there lived to an advanced old age. He was my *Isaac Walton.* He had a wife, but no child. He loved me, because I would read the newspapers to him, containing the accounts of battles in the European wars. He had twice deserted from the English king, and once, at least, committed treason, as well as desertion, but he had still a British heart. When I have read to him the details of the victories of Howe, and Jervis, &c., I remember he was excited almost to convulsions, and would relieve his excitement by a gush of exulting tears. He finally picked up a fatherless child, took him home, sent him to school, and took care of him, only, as he said, that he might have some one to read the newspaper to him. He could never read himself. Alas, poor Robert! I have never so attained the narrative art as to hold the attention of others, as thou, with thy Yorkshire tongue, hast held mine. Thou hast carried me many a mile on thy back, paddled me over, and over, and up and down the stream, and given whole days, in aid of my boyish sports, and asked no meed, but that, at night, I would sit down at thy cottage door, and read to thee some passage of thy country's glory! Thou wast, indeed, a true Briton.

My father was of such consideration among his neighbors, that he was usually in such public employment as they had to bestow. He was a member of the Legislature, and a Senator; and about the year 1791, I think, appointed a judge of the Court of Common Pleas for the county. This place afforded three or four hundred dollars a year, a sum of the greatest importance to the family. He lived just long enough to witness my first appearance, and hear my first speech in court.

In the winter of 1804, it had become necessary for either my brother or myself to undertake something that should bring us a little money, for we were getting to be "heinously unprovided." To find some situation for one or the other of us, I set off in February, and found my way to Boston. My journey was fortunate. Dr. Perkins had been in the instruction of a school, in Short street:[1] he was about leaving it, and proposed that my brother should take it. I hastened home, and he had just then finished a short engagement in school-keeping, at Sanbornton, or was about finishing it, it being near the end of the winter vacation; and he readily seized the opportunity of employment in Boston. This broke in upon his college life, but he thought he could keep up with his class. A letter, stating the necessity of the case, was sent to the authorities of the college, and he went immediately to Boston. His success was good, nay great; so great, that he thought he could earn enough to defray, in addition to debts and other charges, the expense of my living in Boston, for what remained of my term of study. Accordingly, I went to Boston, in July, to pass a few months in some office. I had not a single letter, and knew nobody, in the place to which I was going, except Dr. Perkins, then a very young man, and like myself struggling to get on. But I was sanguine, and light-hearted. He easily persuades himself that he shall gain, who has nothing to lose, and is not afraid of attempting to climb, when, if he fail in his first step, he is in no danger of a fall. Arrived in Boston, I looked out for an office, wherein to study.

[1] Now Kingston street.

But then, as I knew none of the legal gentlemen, and had no letter, this was an affair of some difficulty. Some attempts to be received into a lawyer's office failed, properly enough, for these reasons; although the reminiscence has since sometimes caused me to smile.

Mr. Gore had just then returned from England, and renewed the practice of the law. He had rooms in Scollay's building, and as yet had no clerk. A young man, as little known to Mr. Gore as myself, undertook to introduce me to him! In logic, this would have been bad. *Ignotum per ignotum.* Nevertheless it succeeded here. We ventured into Mr. Gore's rooms, and my name was pronounced. I was shockingly embarrassed, but Mr. Gore's habitual courtesy of manner gave me courage to speak. I had the grace to begin with an unaffected apology; told him my position was very awkward, my appearance there very like an intrusion, and that, if I expected any thing but a civil dismission, it was only founded in his known kindness and generosity of character. I was from the country, I said; had studied law for two years, had come to Boston to study a year more; had some respectable acquaintances in New Hampshire, not unknown to him, but had no introduction; that I had heard he had no clerk, thought it possible he would receive one; that I came to Boston to work and not to play; was most desirous, on all accounts, to be his pupil; and all I ventured to ask, at present, was, that he would keep a place for me in his office, till I could write to New Hampshire for proper letters, showing me worthy of it. I delivered this speech *trippingly* on the tongue, though I suspect it was better composed, than spoken.

Mr. Gore heard me with much encouraging good-nature. He evidently saw my embarrassment, spoke kind words, and asked me to sit down. My friend had already disappeared! Mr. Gore said, what I had suggested was very reasonable, and required little apology; he did not mean to fill his office with clerks, but was willing to receive one or two, and would consider what I had said. He inquired, and I told him, what gentlemen of his acquaintance knew me and my father, in New Hampshire. Among others, I remember, I mentioned Mr. Peabody, who was Mr. Gore's classmate. He talked to me pleasantly, for a quarter of an hour; and when I rose to depart, he said: "My young friend, you look as though you might be trusted. You say you came to study, and not to waste time.

I will take you at your word. You may as well hang up your hat, at once; go into the other room; take your book and sit down to reading it, and write at your convenience to New Hampshire for your letters."

I was conscious of making a good stride onward, when I had obtained admission into Mr. Gore's office. It was a situation which offered to me the means of studying books, and men, and things. It was on the 20th of July, 1804, that I first made myself known to Mr. Gore; and although I remained in his office only till March following, and that with considerable intervening absences, I made, as I think, some respectable progress. In August the Supreme Court sat. I attended it constantly, and reported every one of its decisions. I did the same in the Circuit Court of the United States. I kept a little journal at that time, which still survives. It contains little beside a list of books read.

In addition to books on the common and municipal law, I find I read Vattel, for the third time in my life, as is stated in the journal; Ward's Law of Nations, Lord Bacon's Elements, Puffendorf's Latin History of England, Gifford's Juvenal, Boswell's Tour to the Hebrides, Moore's Travels, and many other miscellaneous things. But my main study was the common law, and especially the parts of it which relate to special pleading. Whatever was in Viner, Bacon, and other books, then usually studied on that part of the science, I paid my respects to. Among other things, I went through Saunders's Reports, the old folio edition, and abstracted and put into English, out of Latin and Norman French, the pleadings in all his reports. It was an edifying work. From that day to this the forms and language of special pleas have been quite familiar to me. I believe I have my little abstract yet.

I remember one day, as I was alone in the office, a man came in and asked for Mr. Gore. Mr. Gore was out, and he sat down to wait for him. He was dressed in plain gray clothes. I went on with my book, till he asked me what I was reading, and coming along up to the table, I held out my book, and he took it and looked at it. "*Roccus*," said he, "*de navibus et naulo;*" "well, I read that book too, when I was a boy;" and proceeded to talk not only about "ships and freights," but insurance, prize, and other matters of maritime law, in a manner "to put me up to all I knew," and a good deal more. The gray-coated stranger turned out to be Mr. Rufus King.

On my aforesaid journal, " Some Characters at the Boston Bar, 1804;" they are drawings not worth preserving, but I quote what I find is written, at least a part of it, on one.[1]

* * * * * * * * * *

I will here transcribe one other thing from this little journal, the record of an occurrence which had entirely escaped my recollection. I copy the paragraph *verbum post verbum.*

" March 5th. This day, in one of the rooms of the State House, in presence of Isaac P. Davis, and Samuel A. Bradley, and Timothy Dix, Jr., I examined the letters to Callender from Jefferson. Mr. Dix told me he had often seen the signature of Mr. Jefferson, and, on being asked whether he doubted that Mr. Jefferson really signed the letters in question, he said he did not. I preserve this precious confession against time of need."

In March, 1805, I was admitted to practice in the Suffolk Court of Common Pleas. The practice then was for the patron to go into court, introduce the pupil to the judges, make a short speech, commending his diligence, &c., and move for his admission to the bar. I had the honor to be so introduced by Mr. Gore. I remember every word of his speech. It contained a prediction, which I firmly resolved, *quantum in me fuerit,* should not go entirely unfulfilled.

In January preceding my admission, I was the subject of a great honor. The clerk of the Court of Common Pleas for the county of Hillsborough resigned his place. My father was one of the judges of the court, and I was appointed to the vacant clerkship. This was equal to a Presidential election. The office had an income of fifteen hundred dollars a year. It seemed to me very great, and indeed it was so, *rebus consideratis.* The obtaining of this office had been a darling object with my father. Its possession would make the family easy, and he hastened to send me tidings that the prize was won. I certainly considered it a great prize, myself, and was ready to abandon my profession for it; not that I did not love my profession; and not that I did

[1] The "journal" referred to will be found in a subsequent part of this volume.

not hate the clerkship, and all clerkships; but simply from a desire to reach that high point of terrestrial bliss, at which I might feel that there was a *competency* for our family, myself included. I had felt the *res angustæ* till my very bones ached. But Mr. Gore peremptorily shut me out from this opening paradise. When I went to him, with my letter in my hand, to communicate the good news, he said it was civil in their Honors of the Bench, and that I must write them a respectful letter; that they intended it as a mark of confidence in me, and of respect, probably, for my father, and that I was bound to make civil acknowledgments. This was a shower bath of ice water. I was thinking of nothing but of rushing to the immediate enjoyment of the proffered office; but he was talking of civil acknowledgment and decorous declension. Finding my spirits, and face too, I suppose, falling, he found out the cause, and went on to speak, in a serious tone, against the policy and propriety of taking such an office. To be sure, his reasons were good, but I was slow to be convinced. He said, I was nearly through my professional preparation, that I should soon be at the bar, and he saw not why I might not hope to make my way as well as others; that this office was in the first place precarious, it depended on the will of others; and other times and other men might soon arise, and my office be given to somebody else. And in the second place, if permanent, it was a stationary place; that a clerk once, I was probably nothing better than a clerk, ever; and, in short, that he had taken me for one who was not to sit with his pen behind his ear. "Go on," said he, "and finish your studies; you are poor enough, but there are greater evils than poverty; live on no man's favor; what bread you do eat, let it be the bread of independence; pursue your profession, make yourself useful to your friends, and a little formidable to your enemies, and you have nothing to fear."

I need hardly say that I acquiesced in this good advice; though certainly it cost me a pang. Here was present comfort, competency, and I may even say riches, as I then viewed things, all ready to be enjoyed, and I was called upon to reject them for the uncertain and distant prospect of professional success. But I did resist the temptation; I did hold on to the hope which the law set before me.

One very difficult task remained, however, to be performed;

and that was to reconcile my father to my decision. I knew it would strike him like a thunderbolt. He had long had this office in view for me; its income would make him, and make us all, easy and comfortable; his health was bad, and growing worse. His sons were all gone from him. This office would bring me home, and it would bring also comfort and competency "to all the house." It was now mid-winter; I looked round for a country *sleigh*, (stage-coaches, then, no more ran into the centre of New Hampshire than they ran to Baffin's Bay,) and finding one that had come down to the market, I took passage therein, and in two or three days, was set down at my father's door. I was afraid my own resolution would give way, and that after all I should sit down to the clerk's table. But I fortified myself, as well as I could; I put on, I remember, an air of confidence, success, and gayety. It was evening. My father was sitting before his fire, and received me with manifest joy. He looked feebler than I had ever seen him, but his countenance lighted up on seeing his clerk stand before him, in good health, and better spirits.

He immediately proceeded to the great appointment, said how spontaneously it had been made, how kindly the Chief Justice proposed it, with what unanimity all assented, &c., &c., &c. I felt as if I could die, or fly; I could hardly breathe. Nevertheless, I *carried it through*, as we say, according to my plan. Spoke gayly about it; was much obliged to their Honors; meant to write them a respectful letter. If I could consent to record anybody's judgments, should be proud to record their Honors, &c., &c., &c. I proceeded in this strain, till he exhibited signs of amazement; it having occurred to him at length, that I might be serious in an intention to decline the office, a thing which had never entered into his imagination. "Do you intend to decline this office?" said he, at length. "Most certainly," said I. "I cannot think of doing otherwise; I should be very sorry, if I could not do better at present than to be clerk, for fifteen hundred dollars a year, not to speak of future prospects! I mean to use my tongue in the courts, not my pen; to be an actor, not a register of other men's actions. I hope yet, sir, to astonish your Honor, in your own court, by my professional attainments!"

For a moment, I thought he was angry. He rocked his chair,

slightly; a flash went over an eye, softened by age, but still as black as jet; but it was gone, and I thought I saw that parental partiality was after all a little gratified at this apparent devotion to an honorable profession, and this seeming confidence of success in it. "Well, my son, your mother has always said you would come to something or nothing, she was not sure which; I think you are now about settling that doubt for her." This he said, and never a word spoke more to me on the subject. I stayed at home a week, promised to come to him again as soon as I was admitted, and returned to Boston.

Being admitted to the bar, as already stated, in March, I went to Amherst, where the court was then sitting, and where my father was, and from Amherst to his own house. My design was to settle in practice at Portsmouth; but I determined not to leave my father, during his life. Accordingly, I took a room in the little adjoining village of Boscawen, and there commenced the practice of the law. My father lived but another year. He died in April, 1806, and lies in the burial-ground, in his own field, just at the turn of the road, beneath the shadow of a tall pine. Beside him repose my mother, my three own sisters, and Joseph, my youngest half brother. Alas! while the living all change, the tabernacle of the dead remains unaltered. To me, my little native village is now hardly known, but by its sepulchres. The villagers are gone; an unknown generation walk under our elms. Unknown faces meet and pass me in my own paternal acres. I recognize nothing but the tombs! I have no acquaintance remaining but the dead!

In May, 1807, I was admitted as attorney and counsellor of the Superior Court, and in September of that year, relinquished my office in Boscawen to my brother, who had then obtained admission to the bar, and removed to Portsmouth according to my original destination.

The two years and a half which I spent in Boscawen were devoted to business and study. I had enough of the first to live on, and to afford opportunity for practice and discipline. I read law and history; not without some mixture of other things. These were the days of the Boston Anthology, and I had the honor of being a contributor to that publication. There are sundry reviews, written by me, not worth looking up or remembering.

September, 1807, I went to Portsmouth, there to practise my profession. June 24, 1808, I was married.

I lived in Portsmouth nine years, wanting one month. They were very happy years. Circumstances favored me, at my first beginning there. Owing to several occurrences, there happened to be an unfilled place among leading counsel at that bar. I did not fill it; but I succeeded to it. It so happened, and so has happened, that, with the exception of instances in which I have been associated with the Attorney-General of the United States, for the time being, I have hardly ten times in my life acted as junior counsel. Once or twice with Mr. Mason, and once or twice with Mr. Prescott, once with Mr. Hopkinson, are all the cases which occur to me.

Indeed, for the nine years I lived in Portsmouth, Mr. Mason and myself, in the counties where we both practised, were on opposite sides, pretty much as a matter of course.[1] He has been of infinite advantage to me, not only by his unvarying friendship, but by the many good lessons he has taught and the example he set me in the commencement of my career. If there be in the country a stronger intellect, if there be a mind of more native resources, if there be a vision that sees quicker or sees deeper into whatever is intricate or whatsoever is profound, I must confess I have not known it. I have not written this paragraph without considering what it implies. I look to that individual, who, if it belong to anybody, is entitled to be an exception. But I deliberately let the judgment stand. That that individual has much more habit of regular composition, that he has been disciplined and exercised in a vastly superior school, that he possesses even a faculty of illustration more various and more easy, I think may be admitted. That the

[1] In illustration of this, the Editor will add an anecdote related to him by the late Eben. Chadwick, Esq., of Boston.

Mr. Chadwick said, "I used often to attend the court, when it sat at Portsmouth, on purpose to hear Mr. Mason and Mr. Webster, who were always on opposite sides, and engaged in all important cases. On one occasion the clerk was calling the docket, and the various counsel entering their names in the various suits; Mr. Mason and Mr. Webster answering for plaintiff or defendant in almost every one. At last a case was called, and I overheard the following conversation between them. Mr. Mason said, 'Webster, what side are you on in this case?' Mr. Webster replied, 'I don't know, take your choice.'"

original reach of his mind is greater, that its grasp is stronger, that its logic is closer, I do not allow.

My professional practice, while living in Portsmouth, was very much a circuit practice. I followed the superior court, in most of the counties of the State. It was never lucrative. There was a limit, and that a narrow one, beyond which gains could not be made from it. I do not think it was ever worth fairly two thousand dollars a year.

Business, too, fell off much, by the war; and, soon after that event, I determined on a change of residence.

I have never held office, popular or other, in the government of New Hampshire. My time was always exclusively given to my profession till 1812, when the war commenced. I had occasionally taken part in political questions, always felt an interest in elections, and contributed my part, I believe, to the political ephemera of the day. Indeed, I always felt an interest in political concerns. My lucubrations for the press go back, I believe, to my sixteenth year. They are or ought to be all forgotten, at least most of them; and all of this early period.

When I visited my father, from Boston, in January or February, 1804, a severe political contest was going on between Governor Gilman and Governor Langdon. The friends of the former, and they were my friends, wanted a pamphlet, and I was pressed to write one. I did the deed, I believe, at a single sitting of a winter's day and night. Not long ago I found a copy of this sage production. Among things of a similar kind it is not certainly despicable. It is called an "Appeal to Old Whigs." Like other young men, I made Fourth of July orations; at Fryeburg, 1802; at Salisbury, 1805; at Concord, 1806, which was published; and at Portsmouth, 1812, published also.

August, 1812, I wrote the "Rockingham Memorial." It was an anti war paper, of some note in its time. I confess I am pleased to find, on looking at it now, for I do not think I have read it in all the twenty years that have rolled by since I wrote it, among all its faults, whether of principle or in execution, that it is of a tone and strain less vulgar than such things are prone to be.

Before this period, I think in 1808, I had written the little pamphlet, lately rescued from oblivion, called "Considerations on the Embargo Laws."

In November, 1812, I was elected member of Congress; I took my seat at the extra session, May, 1813.

In August, 1814, I was reëlected. Of the little I did, and the little I said, while a member of Congress from New Hampshire, the amount is to be found in the history of the public proceedings of those times. I recollect some interesting occurrences, connected with important subjects, which I cannot narrate without refreshing my recollection of dates by reference to the journals. My efforts in regard to the banks, at different times suggested, and in regard to the currency of the country, I think were of some small degree of utility to the public. Other subjects were temporary, and whatever was done or said about them has passed away, and lost its interest. To these endeavors to maintain a sound currency, I owe the acquaintance and friendship of the late Mr. Cabot, who was kind enough to think me entitled to his regard.

In the session of 1815 and 1816, I also made the acquaintance of Mr. Francis C. Lowell. He passed some weeks at Washington. I was much with him. I found him full of exact, practical knowledge, on many subjects. At the same session, I made an acquaintance with our friend, Mr. Dwight,[1] or renewed and cultivated a slight one of longer standing. His friendship and advice very much influenced my subsequent resolution of coming to Boston, when I left Portsmouth. I balanced, at this time, between Boston and Albany, but finally settled to do what I soon did. I could carry my practice in New Hampshire no further; I could make no more of it; and its results were not competent to the support of my family. Having resolved on a change, I accomplished it at once. In June, 1816, I came over with my wife, to see about a house. On the 16th of August, I left Portsmouth forever, and the same day arrived, with my wife and children, at Boston. My children were then Grace and Daniel Fletcher. We stayed two or three weeks at Mrs. Delano's, and then went to housekeeping, in a house of Mr. J. Mason's, on Mount Vernon street.

I think I never went into court in New Hampshire again, except when I went down the following September in the Dartmouth College cause.

[1] The late Edmund Dwight Esq., of Boston.

When I moved to Boston, I had still one session to serve in Congress. Mr. Mason was a Senator at that time. We went to Washington in November with our families, and took lodgings together. But my wife and myself were called back by the illness of our daughter. We left Washington the first day of January and found her living. She died the 23d day of January. I returned to Washington soon after, mainly on account of business in court. On the rising of Congress and the court, I came back to Boston, and entered with diligence on the labors of my profession.

I have hurried over my residence in Portsmouth. There are incidents of no public concernment, yet interesting to me and mine, not mentioned. In December, 1813, I being gone to Washington, my house was burnt, in what is called the great fire. My wife and children had just time to escape. I had recently bought the house for six thousand dollars; its loss, with the loss of what was burnt in it, was no small matter. It was in no part insured.

THE END.

EZEKIEL WEBSTER.

INTRODUCTORY NOTE.

THE extraordinary intimacy and more than usual brotherly affection, which existed between Ezekiel and Daniel Webster, from the earliest moment to which their history can be traced, down to the time of the decease of the elder brother, is amply shown in their correspondence; and anything like the work contemplated by the editor, would be wanting, not only in completeness, but in proper sentiment, which should not contain a fit and affectionate notice of him.

Indeed, in addition to the dictates of his own sense of propriety and his affection, the editor feels it to be enjoined upon him, as far as lies in his power, to keep together the names and memories of the two brothers, when he considers the words of the dedication of his father's first volume of his works, to his nieces, from a desire, as he says, "that the name of my brother may be associated with mine so long as anything written or spoken by me shall be regarded or read."

Governed by these views, the editor applied to Professor Sanborn, of Dartmouth College, who was kind enough, in compliance with his wishes, to furnish him the following sketch of Mr. Ezekiel Webster.

BIOGRAPHICAL SKETCH

OF

EZEKIEL WEBSTER.

A FEW of the early letters of Mr. Webster, and his brother Ezekiel, have escaped the changes and accidents of more than half a century. These precious memorials bear the marks of age and decay. The manuscripts are worn and discolored, and their contents are deciphered with some difficulty, but the sentiments they contain are as fresh and vigorous as though they had been penned but yesterday. They breathe forth the warm affections of loving hearts, and reveal the manly opinions of earnest minds. A peculiar interest attaches to these letters. They relate to a very important period in the history of the writers. They show how these young students, by the home-bred virtues of industry and perseverance, forged their armor for the battle of life, and put on, at the very commencement of the struggle, that invincible panoply of good habits and correct opinions by means of which, in after years, they were enabled to achieve such memorable victories. The difficulties and trials, which they met and overcame, are precisely the same which lie in the path of every youth who depends on his own resources for his future success. A knowledge of the history of the first twenty years of a man's life is essential to the right appreciation of his subsequent career. During this period, the constitutional tendencies are manifested, the native endowments developed, and the moral character formed. The four years of a collegiate course subject every quality and faculty of the head and heart to the severest trial. It is generally conceded, that the moral and intellectual powers are fully and fairly exhibited during the process of education. Tried by this standard, the academic life of Daniel and Ezekiel Webster is a true index of their conduct and ability, as public men, in maturer years.

Ezekiel Webster was born in Salisbury, New Hampshire, April 11, 1780. The first nineteen years of his life were spent upon his father's farm. There, he faithfully performed all the labors and cheerfully submitted to all the hardships incident to the cultivation of a comparatively unproductive soil in a newly-settled country, and under a rigorous climate. By this he acquired that full, muscular development and majestic figure which, in later years, left upon all beholders the impression of extraordinary manly beauty. He was nearly six feet in height, finely proportioned, with a very commanding presence. Men now living, who knew him in the meridian of his manhood, speak with the highest enthusiasm of his personal appearance, his dignified deportment, and his winning countenance. A writer in one of our public journals, who knew him intimately, says: "The image of him that now presents itself is that of a magnificent form, crowned with a princely head, that in his last years was thickly covered with snowy hair. His complexion was just the opposite of Daniel's; and he was as conspicuous in that way, as the latter was in his. His countenance was open as the day; his heart was warm and affectionate; his manners kind and courteous." His brother, also, in a letter, written in 1846, says of him: "He appeared to me the finest human form that I ever laid eyes on. I saw him in his coffin; a tinged cheek, a complexion clear as the heavenly light."

There existed between these brothers a remarkable unity of opinion, sentiment, and affection. They were never known to disagree, upon any matter of importance, in youth, or manhood. They could say, with the utmost sincerity, what the Roman poet asserted of himself and his attached friend:

> "Fraternis animis quidquid negat alter et alter,
> Annuimus pariter vetuli notique columbi."

Almost every page of their long and frequent correspondence presents them as mutual helpers and advisers, in all the relations of life, both public and private. They loved each other with the intensity, fervor, and constancy of woman's devotion. They "took sweet counsel together," labored for their united welfare, and shared, in common, the fruits of their toil. The younger brother, because his slender frame could not bear the fatigues of a farmer's life, was consecrated to study. After enjoying for a time, the pleasures of intellectual effort and acquisition, he became anxious that Ezekiel should become the companion of his new and exciting pursuits. As they were united in sympathy and opinions, they desired to engage in the same professional employments. During a college vacation, when both were at home, they made the education of the elder brother the theme of their conversation, and laid their plans together for its accomplishment. One night, in particular, they passed in sleepless conference. Of their secret deliberations, and the results of them, Mr. Webster has given a very touching account in his autobiography. One affecting incident which he related to the writer, a few years before his decease, is there omitted. It is this. A family council was called. The mother's opinion was asked. She was a strong-minded, sagacious woman. She was not insensible to the merits of her sons. She saw the reasonableness of their request. She therefore decided the matter at once. Her reply was: "I have lived long in the world and have been happy in my children. If Daniel and Ezekiel will promise to take care of me in my old age, I will consent to the sale of all our property, at once, and they may enjoy the benefit of what remains after our debts are paid." This was a moment of intense interest to all the parties. Parents and children, as Mr. Webster himself declared, mingled their tears together and sobbed aloud at the thought of separation. The father yielded to the entreaties of his sons and the advice of his wife. Daniel returned to college, and Ezekiel took his scanty wardrobe in his hand, and sought, on foot, the scene of his preparatory studies.

He spent two terms at Salisbury Academy, in acquiring the rudiments of the Latin and Greek tongues; then, to avoid all unnecessary expense, he went to reside with Rev. Samuel Wood, of Boscawen, who was accustomed to board and instruct indigent students for a very limited compensation, ordinarily not exceeding one dollar a week. Mr. Webster's early acquaintance with books was very limited, because they were not to be found in the secluded retreat where he spent his boyhood. The Granite State, in its interior, scarcely presents a less attractive nook, than the place of his birth. The rough and forbidding aspect of the landscape has nothing about it to charm the eye or educate the taste. The society of the region had little to stimulate the intellect or develop the affections. A book was almost as rare as a nobleman or a coach. After the removal of Judge Webster to "Elms Farm," as it is now called, within the present limits of Franklin, the occasional visits of professional men, at his father's house, and the loan of a book, now and then, from the lawyer or pastor of the parish, gave to the young scholar a more elevated notion of intellectual culture and of refined society. But the young man who labors upon a farm till he nearly attains his majority, without the excitement derived from an association with educated minds and useful books, suffers greatly in comparison with those whose early years have been favored with opportunities of reading or listening to the thoughts of others. Such a student labors under a twofold disadvantage. He has neither intellectual stores, nor the power of acquiring them. He is obliged to learn both *how* to think, and *what* to think; to discipline his mind and to furnish it with the necessary impulse to independent effort.

The spirit and temper of the community, moreover, did not tend to foster a love of letters. The early settlers of that ungenial region were the enemies of liberal learning. They were as hostile to an aristocracy founded on such a basis, as to one of birth or wealth, and they deemed it wrong to elevate, by education, one member of a family to the comparative disparagement of the others. They believed that no young man, whose physical powers were adequate to the management of a farm or the defence of his country, should be allowed to enter a college. The pale and sickly boy might be devoted to learning, but the strong and vigorous should "abide by the stuff." In consenting, therefore, to the education of both his boys, and especially to that of the athletic and powerful lad, Ezekiel, Judge Webster acted in opposition to a well-known public opinion, and it required great moral courage to sustain him in doing so.

But the strongest objection after all, in the father's mind, to the departure of the elder son to school, was the want of means for his support. With his small farm, already encumbered by a heavy mortgage, it seemed to a mind deeply imbued with religion, as Judge Webster's was, almost like tempting Providence, to assume an additional burden in his old age. But the young men were ardent and hopeful, and to their brighter views of the future, his parental fondness and confidence induced him to yield, and he lived to have his declining years made happy by the result of his decision. Dr. Wood, who was the private tutor of both the sons, was distinguished for his rare Christian virtues. He was one of the excellent of the earth. During his long and successful ministry, at Boscawen, he fitted more than one hundred young men for college. Those who could not pay for their board immediately he trusted; and to some very indigent pupils, he forgave the debt. He was not an eminent scholar, though a lover of learning. He could appreciate genius, without feeling its fires in his own bosom. By his unwearied diligence and fidelity, he succeeded in making good scholars. He labored from principle, from an ever-present conviction that he must do all within his power to benefit the rising generation. It was the boast and glory of his life that he was the tutor of Daniel and Ezekiel Webster. He loved them as children; they honored him as a father. He rejoiced that, under Providence, he had contributed to their social elevation; and they esteemed it not the least of their blessings that their kind, generous, and godly teacher derived sincere pleasure from their success.

Ezekiel Webster, who afterwards, while he lived, sat under his theological instructions, was through life his warm friend and confidential adviser. He taught his children to reverence his gray hairs, and to esteem it one of their greatest earthly privileges that they were permitted to enjoy the religious counsels and witness the worthy example of this good man; and though he did not fully accord with all the doctrines inculcated by his venerable pastor, yet he never allowed others to assail him in his presence. He once replied, very pointedly, to a brother lawyer, who, after listening to one of Dr. Wood's sermons, took occasion to disparage the performance, that he "doubted his ability to appreciate him." Dr. Wood was no ordinary man. His heart ever beat with the warm pulsations of benevolence towards all men. He was an "Israelite indeed, in whom there was no guile." Ezekiel Webster, after spending about nine months under his tuition, entered Dartmouth College, in the spring of 1801. Notwithstanding the deficiency of his early education and his very limited preparation, especially for advanced standing, from the very beginning of his collegiate course, he took his position among the first in his class, and retained it to the day of his graduation. In the classics, he had no superior, if an equal. The earliest productions of his pen, now extant, show conclusively, that he had thoroughly mastered the elementary branches of an English education at the common school. The orthography, the grammatical construction, and even the punctuation, are entirely faultless. The tone of the thoughts they contain is manly, dignified, and serious. He never trifled, at any period of his life, nor allowed himself to be trifled with. His deportment always accorded with his instinctive convictions of propriety. He gave his whole soul to the duties before him, was always present in the lecture-room, and well prepared. By his unwearied devotion to study and his cheerful submission to the laws of the college, he won the lasting friendship of the faculty. One of them, Dr. Shurtleff, still survives to bear testimony to his superior scholarship and untarnished morals. The lapse of fifty years has not abated his admiration of the student or the man. He still remembers the marked ability with which he grappled with the difficulties of science, and the clearness, directness, and logical accuracy with which he solved the knotty problems of morals and metaphysics. Dr. Shurtleff also gave private instruction in theology. This was a voluntary exercise. Ezekiel Webster was an active and interested member of his class; and the professor now affirms, that there was no student in the college, at that day, whose intellectual powers he loved so well to put to the trial, or, to use his own words, "to push out into deep water," and none whom he always found so correct in his notions and so clear in his replies.

In the spring of his senior year, Mr. Webster found his longer residence in college impossible from want of funds. He then withdrew from his class, by permission of the faculty, and purchased the good-will of a private school in Boston, which he taught with great success till the following April. At the same time he pursued the studies of his class with reference to a degree at the approaching commencement, and taught an evening school for sailors, to eke out his scanty income. He was graduated in 1804, though he had been an actual resident in college only three years. His character is clearly evinced in the fixed and determined purpose which he early formed of securing the best education which his native State afforded, and by the decision, hopefulness, and perseverance with which he encountered the obstacles and endured the toil and self-denial essential to his intellectual and professional success. He taught district schools, during each winter of his abridged college course, and taught a select classical school, in Boston, for six months of his senior year, thus devoting nearly one half of all his time to the purchase of the privilege of studying during the other half. The necessity of this arrangement is explained in one of his letters to his brother. Notwithstanding these repeated interruptions of his studies, he earned a solid reputation as a scholar; and by his uniform integrity, sobriety, industry, and honorable deportment, secured the good-will of all who knew him. Many of the friendships which he formed in those years of trial and adversity, he cherished, with unabated warmth, to the close of life.

Mr. Webster commenced the study of law under the tuition of the late Governor Sullivan, then attorney-general of Massachusetts, and completed his course in the office of Parker Noyes, Esq., of Salisbury, N. H. He entered upon the practice of his profession in September, 1807, at Boscawen, where he continued to reside till his decease. His legal knowledge and moral worth soon became known, and acquired for him an extensive business. As a lawyer, he had few equals. He was a wise counsellor and an able advocate. After Daniel Webster removed from New Hampshire, Ezekiel Webster exhibited himself, more frequently, as a pleader of causes and a public speaker; but while his brother was practising in the same courts, his extreme modesty caused him rather to shrink from a comparison of their relative strength in forensic argument. He was never ambitious to excel as an orator. It was only the urgent appeal of duty or the imperative obligation of his profession that overcame his instinctive aversion to a crowd, and called forth his highest powers of eloquence. He never encouraged litigation; but on the contrary, used always his personal influence to bring about a private adjustment of most of the contested matters that originated in his own town. The disputes of his neighbors he generally settled, as did his father before him, by private advice. In youth, they confided in him as a friend; in mature manhood, they reverenced him as a father;

and there are many of his aged fellow-citizens, now living, who still keep his memory green, in their hearts, and speak of his loss in the mellowed tones of a sorrow, undiminished, if softened by years. He was a model lawyer, as he was a model man. In debate, he was dignified and courteous. His weapons were sound arguments clothed in simple, but elegant language. He never resorted to artifice, evasion, or false logic. His eloquence was earnest and effective. For many years, he was a member of one or the other branch of the state legislature; and in each, was as highly distinguished for his sound opinions, wise counsels, and powerful arguments, as for his well-defined and comprehensive views upon all the great interests of society. He was eminently qualified to take a leading part in public councils and to exert an effectual control over the minds and hearts of others. His political opinions were so enlarged and liberal, that he never allowed local interests to interfere with his firm support of the general welfare. He was educated a Federalist by his father, a Whig of 1776, of the old school, a soldier and an officer in the war of the Revolution, who inculcated upon his sons a profound respect for "the father of his country," and for his political opinions. They were old enough to remember the administration of Washington, and to form their own estimate of its merits. From the principles which he advocated, they never swerved. Mr. Ezekiel Webster's political sentiments amounted almost to religious convictions. They were the result of careful inquiry, calm consideration, guided and controlled by a strict regard for right and truth. He always maintained his opinions fearlessly, honestly, and eloquently, even when their defence brought upon him political proscription. He could tolerate no man who proved recreant to his professions, either in politics, morality, or religion, and put a proper estimate upon the changeling who regulates his creed by the voice of the multitude. His conscientious adherence to the unpopular principles of the Federalists left him, for many years, in the minority, in his own State, and effectually prevented his election to Congress, or his appointment to any post of honor or trust under the General Government.

Mr. Webster's private character and habits were thus delineated, at the time of his decease, by one who knew him intimately:—

"It was a remarkable feature of his character, that, in every relation of life which he sustained, his fidelity and benevolence were invariable. To his relatives and personal friends, his kindness was real and unceasing. He made no *professions* of good-will or attachment; in this respect he was peculiar. His *acts* were material and unequivocal demonstrations of a noble heart, and the memory of them will be cherished by numerous individuals, especially his younger and even distant relatives, as among their most precious and endearing recollections.

> "To *be*, and not to *seem*, was this man's wisdom—
> Reaping the fruits that in a rich mind grow,
> Whence sage advice and noble actions flow."

He was a practical and skilful farmer. Living in the country, enthusiastically attached to the healthful and virtuous pursuits of rural life, and the quiet, and happiness, and simplicity of domestic scenes, he was strongly inclined to be connected with and to cherish that great interest, which was the principal concern of his neighbors, the cultivation of the soil. He was the most active founder, a very efficient member, and subsequently the president of the Merrimac Agricultural Society. By exciting attention, in his vicinity, to improvements in the breed of animals, in fruits, grasses, grains, and the various valuable productions of the earth, and by examples of better modes of husbandry, in draining, reclaiming, and other agricultural processes, Mr. Webster sought to be useful, without regarding the expense to himself of what he foresaw to be ultimately serviceable to the farmer and to the community. His own farm, inherited from his father, became, under his care, one of the most improved and best cultivated, as it is one of the most pleasantly situated and valuable, in the county of Merrimac.

Most simple and temperate in his habits of life, his whole leisure from business was devoted to books. Reading was his luxury. His acquaintance with the ancient classics was far more extensive and accurate than is usually preserved, or indeed attained, by men so early and so constantly engaged in the pursuits of active life. With Latin authors, especially, his intimacy was uninterrupted. Indeed, the noble Roman spirit, the energetic brevity of expression, and the profound knowledge of human nature, which charmed him in some of these works, strikingly correspond to the great features of his own character and style.

History he regarded as an essential part of liberal knowledge, and necessary to professional and political distinction. That of our own country and of England, in particular, he studied with unwearied diligence and inexhaustible delight, not in the general and summary treatises only, but in the minutest details of biography, annals, and state papers. Early convinced of the essential imperfection of all abstracts and commentaries upon history, except as valuable and often splendid exhibitions of literary talent and taste, he was more and more fond, as he advanced in life, of tracing the great lines of human character, the leading motives and principles of human action, in the most precise and full details which the records of our race furnish.

He loved the established English classics, and would not admit that there is any thing in more modern productions which should lead us to forget Milton and Shakspeare, Clarendon, Sherlock and Taylor, Dryden and Pope, Burke and Johnson.

Of education, in all its branches, from our common schools to the college, of which he was for many years an efficient trustee, no man entertained more enlightened and just ideas, and no man felt a deeper interest in the subject. The flourishing academy in his own town grew up under his influence, and constantly felt his substantial aid and supervision.

The institutions of religion were cheerfully supported by him, their establishment recommended and encouraged wherever he had influence, and divine worship maintained in his family, and attended by him in public, with singular punctuality and propriety. His conviction of the truth, importance, and authority of Christianity, was unhesitatingly and habitually manifested on all suitable occasions. He left behind him, in his own handwriting, an interesting proof of his faith in Christianity, and of his judgment and belief as to what are its leading doctrines."

The following is an exact transcript of the manuscript alluded to, which was found, after his death, upon his office table.

"I believe there is one only living and true God, the maker of heaven and earth, the God and Father of our Lord and Saviour, Jesus Christ.

"I believe that Jesus Christ is the Son of God. That he came into the world, suffered under Pontius Pilate, was crucified, buried and rose from the dead, and ascended into heaven; and that he will come to judge the world at the last day. That God hath exalted him at his right hand, to be a Prince and a Saviour, to give repentance and remission of sins to those who call upon his name and have faith in him.

"I believe in the Holy Ghost, who is sent from God to guide, instruct, and comfort those, who devoutly and diligently seek to know and do the will of God.

"I believe that God created man in his own image, 'in the image of God created he him; male and female created he them.' And that our first parents transgressed the law of God, by eating of the forbidden fruit.

"I believe the Bible, containing the Old and New Testament, to be the word of God, written by holy men, inspired by him, whose doctrines we are bound to believe, and according to whose precepts we are bound to walk.

"I believe that there are many good men, and pious Christians, who do not think as I do, and that it is my duty to distrust my own heart; to entertain humble views of my own merits, and to exercise kind and charitable feelings toward those who differ from me in their religious opinions, and modes of worship, believing that God is no respecter of persons, but in every nation, he that feareth Him, and worketh righteousness, is accepted of Him.

"Omniscient God! Thou knowest all things. Thou knowest the frailties and infirmities of our natures; the weakness of our understandings and the perverseness of our hearts. If we are right we thank thee, and pray for thy grace, therein to abide stedfastly to the end. If we are wrong, impute it not, but have compassion on our ignorance and teach us the right way, and enable us to embrace it and walk in it. Whatever is erroneous in our belief, correct; whatever is amiss in our lives, reform; what is dark in our understandings, enlighten; what is weak, strengthen and support. Give us all needful knowledge, right tempers, and right feelings; and grant us the forgiveness of our sins, and acceptance with thee, through thy Son, Jesus Christ our Lord and Saviour."

Mr. Webster died on the 10th day of April, 1829, aged 49. The closing scene of his life strikes us as peculiar, and almost without a parallel. Instances of sudden death, it is true, have not been unfrequent; but there has generally been some precursor to impending dissolution, or some struggle with the mighty conqueror, after reason is dethroned, and the ultimate victory of the grave is rendered certain. The bar in our country would seem to have experienced their full share in this summary process of arrest by the king of terrors. Some of the noblest intellects which have ever enlightened and adorned this or any other country, have been in a moment scathed and withered, as by the lightning of heaven. The polished and eloquent Pinckney died in this manner; but he survived the blow several days, we believe nearly a week, after exhausting himself in a powerful argument. The erudite and accomplished Emmet, when attacked, was sitting at the table of the bar taking notes, and, when blasted by the stroke of death, his head fell on the table. He was removed alive from the court-house, and survived several hours. Mr. Webster was speaking, standing erect, on a plain floor, the house full, and the court, and jurors, and auditors intently listening to his words, with all their eyes fastened upon him. Speaking with full force, and perfect utterance, he arrived at the end of one branch of his argument. He closed that branch, uttered the last sentence, and the last word of that sentence, with perfect tone and emphasis, and then, in an instant, erect, and with arms depending by his side, he fell backward, without bending a joint, and, so far as appeared, was dead before his head reached the floor. *How unsearchable are the judgments of God, and his ways past finding out!*

The character of Mr. Ezekiel Webster, like that of his brother, will, however, be better displayed by his own writings than by any description or analysis by another; and they form, of themselves, the best eulogy upon his name and memory.

PERSONAL REMINISCENCES

OF

DANIEL WEBSTER.

INTRODUCTORY NOTE.

The following letters were written by Mr. Webster's early friends and classmates, in answer to specific inquiries respecting his student life, addressed to them soon after his decease, by Prof. E. D. Sanborn, who has kindly furnished them to the Editor for publication.

PERSONAL REMINISCENCES.

REV. E. SMITH TO PROF. SANBORN.

Pomfret, Vt., November 10, 1852.

Dear Sir,—Yours of the 10th instant was received last evening, and I hasten to reply. More than fifty years have elapsed since the events you allude to transpired; many facts, therefore, which would be interesting, are lost.

With respect to Daniel Webster's college life, his habits of study were good. He was a strict observer of order. His mind was too dignified to do otherwise. He never engaged in college disturbances. I should as soon have suspected John Wheelock, the President, of improper conduct as Daniel Webster. He looked with contempt on all lawless projects. I never knew him to waste the study hours. He was constant at the recitation, and always well prepared. He was peculiarly industrious. In addition to college studies, he read more than any one in his class. He read with great rapidity, and seemed to remember all. He would accomplish more labor, in a given time, than any one of his classmates. As a general scholar, Webster was good. He was not deficient in a single study. In composition and speaking, there was not his equal in the class. The truth is, that, by his thorough investigation of every subject and every study, while in college, by the aid of his giant mind, he rose to the very pinnacle of fame; and all he had to do was to sustain himself where he was, and fame would roll in upon him; and all his classmates have been compelled to look up high to see him, which I have ever been proud to do. As a debater in our society, he manifested the same talent and the same powers of intellect, in a degree, which he afterwards exhibited in public life. He was in the habit of writing his own declamations for the stage, though not required to do so, by the laws of the college. He was accustomed to arrange his thoughts in his mind in his room or private walks, and put them upon paper just before the exercise was called for. When he was required to speak, at two o'clock, he would frequently begin to write after dinner; and when the bell rung, he would fold his paper, put it into his pocket, and go in and speak with great ease. At one time, when thus writing, his windows being open, a sudden flaw of wind took away his paper, and it was last seen flying over the meeting-house; but he went in and spoke its contents with remarkable fluency. In his Sophomore year, I heard him speak a piece of poetry, before his class, which displayed great ingenuity. Every line ended in i-o-n. It was said to be his own composition. In his movements, he was rather slow and deliberate, except when his feelings were roused; then, his whole soul would kindle into a flame. I recollect that he used to commence speaking rather monotonously and without much excitement, but would always rise, with the importance of the subject, till every eye was fixed upon him. In social life, he was always pleasant and agreeable. His company was sought by all classes. He always attended public worship, on the Sabbath, and evidently felt that it was his duty to do so. Many idle stories have been circulated respecting Webster's tearing up his diploma. Of this I have no knowledge. I have no doubt that the report is false. I stood by his side, when he received his degree, with a graceful bow; and such was my connection with him, in our society affairs, that if he had destroyed it afterwards, I certainly should have known it. I think that he delivered two eulogies on deceased classmates; one in his Freshman, and one in his Senior year. The latter was published. As these appointments were made by his class, they show in what estimation he was held by them. His election by the faculty and citizens of Hanover, to deliver an oration on the Fourth of July, 1800, also indicates their opinion of his scholarship and attainments. I will only add that, in all his intercourse with students and townsmen, no one, then, presumed to bring a railing accusation against him.

Yours truly,

Elihu Smith.

HON. HENRY HUBBARD TO PROF. SANBORN.

Charlestown, November 15, 1852.

My dear Sir,—I regret that my absence from home has prevented an earlier answer to your letter of the 10th instant. With the greatest pleasure I shall comply with your request, as far as I am able to recall the facts connected with Mr. Webster's college history. I entered the Freshman class in 1799, at the early age of fourteen. I was two years in college with Mr. Webster. When I first went to Hanover, I found his reputation already established as the most remarkable young man in the college. He was, I believe, so decidedly beyond any one else, that no other student of his class was ever spoken of as *second* to him. I was led very soon to appreciate, most highly, his scholarship and attainments. As a student, his acquisitions seemed to me to be very extensive. Every subject appeared to contribute something to his intellectual stores. He acquired knowledge with remarkable facility. He seemed to grasp the meaning and substance of a book almost by intuition. Others toiled long and patiently for that which he acquired at a glance. As a scholar, I should say that he was then distinguished for the uncommon extent of his knowledge, and for the ease with which he acquired it. But I should say that I was more impressed by his eloquence and power as a speaker, before the society of which we were both members, than by his other qualifications, however superior to others. There was a completeness and fulness in his views, and a force and expressiveness in his manner of presenting them, which no other student possessed. We used to listen to him with the deepest interest and respect, and no one thought of equalling the vigor and glow of his eloquence. The oration which he delivered before the United Fraternity, on the day of his graduation is, I think, now on file among the records of that society. Whoever will read it, at this late day, and bring to mind the appearance of the author, his manner and power, during its delivery, cannot fail to admit that I have said no more of his eloquence than I was warranted in saying. The students, and those who knew him best and judged him most impartially, felt that no one connected with the college deserved to be compared with him at the time he received his first degree.

His habits and moral character were entirely unimpeachable. I never heard them questioned during our college acquaintance. I have written the honest convictions of my mind, the best feelings of my heart, respecting a man, now no more, who was distinguished as a scholar, in college, and equally distinguished, in his whole subsequent life, in every sphere and station which he was called to fill.

I am, Sir, very truly your friend,
HENRY HUBBARD.

MR. HILL TO PROF. SANBORN.

Hanover, N. H., November 25, 1852.

DEAR SIR,—I was a pupil of Daniel Webster while he taught the Academy at Fryeburg, in the winter and summer of 1802. During that short season, he gained the universal respect of both scholars and villagers; and the regret with which we parted with him is among my most vivid recollections of that period. The remarkable equanimity of temper which he ever manifested in school was a matter of common observation. Under all the vexations incident to such a school, not a frown was ever seen upon his brow. It was his invariable practice to open and close the school with extemporaneous prayer; and I shall never forget the solemnity of manner with which that duty was always performed. He delivered an oration on the Fourth of July of that year, and the only sentence which has not escaped my memory, related to the Constitution. It was this: "If the Constitution be picked to pieces, piecemeal, it is gone, as surely and as fatally gone, as though it had been struck down by one resistless blow."

Yours truly,
THOMAS P. HILL.

J. W. M'GAW, ESQ., TO PROF. SANBORN.

Bangor, November 16, 1852.

DEAR SIR,—Your favor of the 12th instant is before me, and I take great pleasure in giving you such reminiscences of my much honored friend, the late Hon. Daniel Webster, as occur to me.

It was not my good fortune to make the acquaintance of Mr. Webster, until he became a member of Dartmouth College; and then, I knew him only in his vacations. The office of Hon. Thomas W. Thompson, with whom I read law, was about twenty rods from Judge Webster's dwelling-house. Daniel called occasionally at the office, to spend a leisure hour with the late Parker Noyes and myself, who were fellow-students for nearly three years. On one of those occasions, Mr. Webster asked me if I saw and read the Dartmouth Gazette; and if so, what I thought of *Icarus*, whose productions sometimes appeared in that paper. My criticisms were more severe than just. Two or three years afterwards he informed me that he was the veritable *Icarus*. His victory over me was then complete.

Mr. Webster commenced the study of law in Mr. Thompson's office soon after I was admitted to the practice of my profession. My residence was at Fryeburg from January, 1801, to October, 1805. Mr. Webster came to that place in 1802, I think, to take charge of the academy. During his residence there, we boarded and roomed together. Nearly all our leisure hours were spent together. We read, conversed, walked, and had all our social amusements in company. Here was laid the foundation of that friendship, which, by his generous indulgence, has remained constant and uninterrupted till the time of his death, notwithstanding the very great changes which occurred in our relative positions, by reason of his constant elevation, from one grade of honor to another, till he attained a standing from which human greatness knows no progress. I will now attempt to relate some facts concerning Mr. Webster's early history, as he communicated them to me. The incident related by Mr. Everett, in his Memoir of Mr. Webster, respecting his elevation to a higher class, at the end of the first month at the Academy in Exeter, needs, I think, a little correction or explanation in order to present its most important bearing upon his future life. When his first term at Exeter was near its close, the usher said: "Webster, you may stop a few minutes after school; I wish to speak to you." When the other scholars had gone, the usher asked him whether he intended to return to the academy after the vacation. The answer indicated something like reluctance. It had not escaped the observation of the teacher, that Webster's rustic manners and unfashionable raiment had drawn upon him the ridicule of some of his associates, who in every respect, except habiliments and external accomplishments, were greatly his inferiors. The inference was justly drawn that the academy was in danger of losing an estimable and promising pupil, while it retained others who gave no promise of doing honor to that distinguished seminary. The usher, therefore, judiciously and kindly remarked to Mr. Webster, that he was a much better scholar than any in his class; that he learned more readily and easily than they did; and if he would return at the commencement of the next term he should be put into a higher class, and should no longer be hindered in his progress by those boys who cared more for play and dress than for solid improvement. "These were the first truly encouraging words," said Mr. Webster, "that I ever received, with regard to my studies. I then resolved to return and pursue them with diligence and with so much ability as I possessed." Probably the kindness and good judgment of the usher had an important influence upon the whole course of Mr. Webster's after life.

When Mr. Webster resided at Fryeburg, he had not attained to the full development of manhood. Neither the physical nor intellectual expression of his countenance had become so striking as in subsequent life. His cheeks were thin and his cheek bones prominent. There was nothing specially noticeable about him then, except his full, steady, large, and searching eyes. Nobody could see those eyes and ever forget their appearance or him who possessed them. His gentleness, modesty, and social habits won for him the good-will of his acquaintances and pupils. The reading of Mr. Webster, at Fryeburg, was chiefly English literature; such as Pope's Works, all of which he read at that time. He was much amused with the Dunciad. The Spectator, Tatler, &c., were among the books procured from a small village library. These were read aloud, alternately, by himself and room-mate. He read Blackstone's Commentaries when no company was present.

I never heard him speak of any embarrassments in his attempts at declamation, and think it could only have existed, while he was annoyed by idle and envious boys, at Exeter

Academy. At this period of his life, (1802,) Mr. Webster did not entertain any adequate expectations of his future eminence; or, if he had such expectations, they were entirely concealed, as appears from the following anecdote. Speaking of his future prospects in life, he remarked, that, if *ever* he should attain in his profession, to the standing of a certain young lawyer, whom he named, whose merit consisted more in an easy and ready mode of argument, than in sound learning, he, Mr. Webster, would have reached his highest elevation. The sincerity of this statement was questioned, on the ground that his scholarship in college had always been universally allowed to be of the highest grade, which was not true of the gentleman alluded to. "Ay," said he, "but the opinion of my scholarship was a mistaken one. It was overestimated. I will explain what I mean. Many other students read more than I did and knew more than I did. But so much as I read, I made my own. When a half hour or an hour, at most, had elapsed, I closed my book and thought over what I had read. If there was anything peculiarly interesting or striking in the passage, I endeavored to recall it and lay it up in my memory, and commonly could effect my object. Then, if in debate or conversation afterwards, any subject came up on which I had read something, I could talk very easily so far as I had read, and then I was very careful to stop. Thus, greater credit was given me for extensive and accurate knowledge than I really possessed." At other times, also, Mr. Webster made remarks indicating moderate expectations of his eminence in future life.

When Mr. Webster had been admitted to the bar, he attended, among other courts, those of Grafton county. A man who had once labored for Judge Webster was for some cause confined in jail, at Haverhill. While there, he murdered a fellow prisoner. He had engaged the late Hon. P. Sprague, a distinguished lawyer and advocate, to defend him. Mr. Webster went into the jail, during the session of the court, to see the prisoner, who had been a servant of his father. He was requested by him to render what aid he could to Mr. Sprague, at the trial. He consented to do so. The evidence of the prisoner's guilt was so palpable and conclusive, that Mr. Sprague refused to make an argument in his defence. In this emergency, the unpractised youth did not shrink from the duty; but the greatness of the occasion, to wit, the life or death of a human being, seemed almost to add inspiration to his native powers of mind. He made an argument of such wonderful force and ingenuity, that all who heard were astonished. The eminently learned and accomplished Judge Smith was then Chief Justice of the Superior Court of New Hampshire. He is said to have been more lavish of his encomiums upon the young advocate, than he had ever been known to be with regard to any other gentleman.

Such are a few of the incidents that occur to my mind respecting Mr. Webster's early life. Some of these you may possibly make use of in your eulogy of Mr. Webster.

Very sincerely and respectfully your friend and servant,

JACOB W. MCGAW.

REV. BROWN EMERSON TO PROF. SANBORN.

Salem, November 19, 1852.

MY DEAR SIR,—Time has obliterated many facts from my memory, relative to Hon. Daniel Webster, which might be interesting to the students of Dartmouth College. Having been with him for three years of his student life, and associated with him in the same literary society, the United Fraternity, I had an opportunity to know more of him than many others. You inquire respecting his habits of order, punctuality, and preparation for his recitations. On these points, some of the surviving members of his class can give you more particular information. As a classical and belles-lettres scholar, and as a speaker and debater, he stood far above all the other members of the college. Though young, he gave such unequivocal evidence of superior genius, that some, I recollect, predicted his future eminence. The powers of his mind were remarkably displayed by the compass and force of his arguments in extemporaneous debates at the meetings of our literary society. At that early day, the clearness of his reasonings, connected with his aspect and manner, produced an almost irresistible impression upon his hearers. His large, black, piercing eye, peering out under dark, overhanging brows; his broad, intellectual forehead; the solemn tones of his voice; the dignity of his mien, with an earnestness by which he seemed to throw his whole great soul into his subject, evincing the sincerity of his belief that the cause he advocated was that of truth and justice; all these created a power of eloquence which few could resist; and which, in the maturity of his life, neither judge nor jury could withstand, giving him success as an advocate, which, in our country, is without a parallel. I was not much acquainted with his brother Ezekiel; but I well remember his fine personal appearance, and that some then thought his talents superior to Daniel's.

With much respect and esteem, yours,

BROWN EMERSON.

MR. FARRAR TO PROF. SANBORN.

Derry, November 25, 1852.

DEAR SIR,—In answer to your inquiries, I give you my recollections of Daniel Webster's early life. I was in the class before him. Mr. Webster, Freeborn Adams, my brother William and myself, roomed at my father's house, during the first two years of his college course. Webster very early showed that he possessed talents of the first order. He was one of the best in his class as a linguist. He acquired knowledge with little labor. He read much. His memory was very retentive. By reading twenty or more pages of poetry, twice over, I have heard him repeat it almost verbatim. He was much in the habit of extemporaneous speaking. His favorite reading was general history and philosophy. He was a strict observer of the Sabbath, and a careful reader of the Bible and religious books. He possessed talents rarely found in union, a good judgment and a retentive memory. His social qualities were highly attractive. Even when a youth, he absorbed the attention of all present by his agreeable conversation. He was pleasant without ostentation. He enjoyed gunning and fishing; though he spent but little time in those recreations. When abroad on any excursion, a volume of poetry, from his pocket, would often engross his attention. During one of the last years of his college life, he was chosen orator for the Fourth of July, and delivered an oration before the Faculty and students of the college and the citizens of Hanover, which was published.

Yours respectfully,

GEORGE FARRAR.

REV. GEORGE T. CHAPMAN TO PROF. SANBORN.

Newburyport, January 25, 1853.

Dear Sir,—In answer to your favor of the 7th instant, I have to remark, that all my recollections of Ezekiel Webster are of a gratifying character. In the senior year, we occupied rooms opposite to each other, in a building directly north of the college. I am therefore enabled to state, from intimate personal acquaintance, that he was altogether exemplary in his habits and faithful in his studies. He had no enemies, and all were happy to be numbered in the list of his friends. Owing to his absence in teaching school, no part was assigned him at Commencement. But I have no doubt he stood high in the estimation of the college faculty; and although I should hesitate to pronounce him the first scholar in his class, it would be doing injustice to his memory to say that he was excelled by either of those who received the highest college honors on the day of our graduation. It has been recently stated, that he was particularly distinguished for his knowledge of Greek; but I cannot now recall the circumstance to mind; nor, in fact, make any discrimination as to relative proficiency in the several branches of study. He was deficient in none. He was good in all. Such, at least, is my recollection of the reputation he enjoyed. After leaving college, from all that I have heard, he obtained a greater degree of eminence, in the eye of the public, than any of his classmates; and when I revert to college days, after the lapse of almost half a century, all my recollections of what he then was, cause me to feel no surprise at the subsequent elevation which he attained.

Very truly yours,
G. T. Chapman.

MR. BINGHAM TO PROF. SANBORN.

Washington, D. C., November 25, 1852.

Dear Sir,—Your favor of the 12th instant, requesting facts respecting Mr. Webster's student life, was duly received. Your inference from the letters that you have seen from me to Daniel Webster, when we were boys together, "that there was a peculiar intimacy between us," was very justly drawn; although I have now scarcely the slightest recollection of what I may have communicated, in those letters of my youthful days, and at a time when, in consequence of that *intimacy*, we used to unbosom ourselves to each other, with all the ardor and confidence of true friendship. Our first acquaintance was at the academy, at Exeter, in 1796. I went there, in July of that year, and found him there. He was then a lad of about fourteen years, attending to English grammar, arithmetic, &c., always very prompt and correct in his recitations. He had an independent air and was rather careless in his dress and appearance, but showed an intelligent look. He did not join much in the plays and amusements of the boys of his age, but paid close attention to his studies. He left, in the fall of that year, and I believe soon became a pupil of Dr. Wood, of Boscawen, and there fitted for college, and entered, August, 1797. I remained at Exeter till July, 1798, then entered the Freshman class in Dartmouth College, where I found Daniel Webster. An intimacy increased between us from that time till we left college; and indeed till we both became settled in business, and so much engaged in our several vocations that we seemed to have no time or opportunity to continue our former correspondence; although, in our occasional business communications, we would regret its interruption and make new resolutions.

Daniel Webster's habits in college were good. He had the highest sense of honor and integrity. He was sure to understand the subject of his recitation; sometimes, I used to think, in a more extended and comprehensive sense than his teachers. He never liked to be confined to small technicalities or views; but seemed to possess an intuitive knowledge of whatever subject he was considering. He did not find it necessary, as was the case with most of us, to sit down to hard work three or four hours to make himself master of his lesson, but seemed to comprehend it in a larger view, and would sometimes procure other books on the same subject, for further examination, and employ hours in close *thought*, either in his room or in his walk, which would enlarge his views, and might at the same time, with some, give him the character of not being a close student.

He was a favorite with the class generally; interesting and instructive in conversation; social and very kind in his feelings; not intimate with many. His compositions and college themes, orations in the society, and occasional written exercises, all showed the marks of great genius and great familiarity with history and politics, for one of his years. He did not speak on Commencement day, but gave a very fine oration before the "United Fraternity." He gave, a short time before, an excellent eulogy on his classmate, Simonds, of whom he speaks in a letter to me dated at Salisbury, June 14, 1801, as follows: "Dear Hervey,—My first business is to inquire about Simonds. Oh, that I could be assured that he is recovering! but perhaps this is a happiness never to be allowed us. Let our prayers ascend together for his well being, whether with us or in another world. If there be any possible way of communication, pray let me hear how he is." And in another letter, in October, 1801, in answer to some remark I made on the subject, in a letter to him, Mr. Webster says:—

"If the funeral oration be thought decent, I am content; equal to the subject it is not. The death of Simonds was a theme on which the first writers ought to be proud to point their pens. *Hei mihi! Qualis erat!*"

The above is an instance of the kind feelings and high estimation which Mr. Webster was always accustomed to exercise towards those whom he considered true and worthy friends. I have some fifty letters from him, all good, and some superior, according to circumstances. I will close this long letter, by copying the last letter received by me from Mr. Webster, in answer to a request that he would, if consistent and convenient, favor me with his influence to procure some place for me, by which I could obtain a comfortable support for myself and family. It is as follows:—

Washington, February 5, 1849.

MY DEAR OLD CLASSMATE, ROOM-MATE, AND FRIEND,—It gives me very true pleasure to hear from you, and to learn that you are well. Years have not abated my affectionate regard. We have been boys together, and men together, and now, are growing old together; but you always occupy the same place in my remembrance and good wishes. You are still James

Hervey Bingham, with your old bass viol, with "*Laus Deo*" painted upon it; I hope you have it yet; and I am the same Daniel Webster, whom you have known, at Exeter, at Lempster, at Charlestown, at Salisbury, at Alstead, at Portsmouth, Claremont, Boston, and Washington. And now, my dear friend, after this retrospective glimpse, let me say, that I know nothing of those who are coming into power; that I expect to possess no particular influence or association with them; but that, if any occasion arises in which I can be useful to you, you can command my most attentive services.

Will you please give my love to a lady, whom I had once the honor of knowing as Miss Charlotte Kent.

DANIEL WEBSTER.

Such was the letter. *I* consider it the most elegant and comprehensive document that was ever embraced in the same small space. By the "attentive services," promised in that letter, I hold my place here, and *hope* the influence may continue through the next administration, if I should live to need the benefits of it.

Very respectfully, your obedient friend and servant,

JAMES H. BINGHAM.

REV. S. OSGOOD TO PROF. SANBORN.

Springfield, December 5, 1852.

DEAR SIR,—I received your letter of the 1st instant, enclosing one of mine to my old friend, Daniel Webster. I deeply regret that I have not preserved any of his letters to me, except two that I received from him after he became Secretary of State. Mr. Webster was an early and dear friend of mine, and continued his friendship to the last. A few months before his decease, he sent me one of his speeches, superscribed, "For my old, long tried, and highly valued friend, Rev. Dr. Osgood." I have no doubt that he felt all that he expressed; for he had uniformly treated me with respect and affection; he always called on me when he stopped in this place, and often invited me to visit him at his home. He came to Fryeburg in 1802, and took charge of the academy, boarding in my father's family. As I was so near his age and had nearly closed my preparation to enter college, at an advanced standing, we soon contracted an intimate friendship, which was mutually preserved amidst all the changes of our lives. You ask: "Was he grave or gay; serious or trifling?" I answer: he was always dignified in his deportment. He was usually serious, but often facetious and pleasant. He was an agreeable companion, and eminently social with all who shared his friendship. He was greatly beloved by all who knew him. His habits were strictly abstemious, and he neither took wine nor strong drink. He was punctual in his attendance upon public worship, and ever opened his school with prayer. I never heard him use a profane word, and never saw him lose his temper. He was at that time in straitened circumstances, and paid his board by copying deeds for my father, who was register for the county. He spent all the time he could save from labor and necessary recreation in study and in meditation in the fields. He was very fond of this kind of relaxation; and many were the rambles which we took together. While at Fryeburg, he delivered an oration on the Fourth of July, which was greatly admired by the Federal party and much disliked by the Democratic; but it had great merit and was a finished production. I frequently saw him after I was settled in the ministry. I spent some hours with him, at his own house, in Portsmouth, soon after his marriage with Miss Fletcher. At that time, his religious sentiments corresponded with my own. In Dorchester, he attended Dr. Codman's church, and was punctually present at two services. When he passed a Sabbath in Springfield, he seldom went to any other church than ours. Mr. Howard informed me that he once called on Mr. Webster, while here, to conduct him to the sanctuary. When they left the hotel, Mr. Howard said: "Now I will go wherever you desire to go." Mr. Webster said: "I think I will go and hear my old pupil." He never spent but one Sabbath here after that. It was our Communion, and he partook with us. I have thus hastily answered all your inquiries.

With much respect,

SAMUEL OSGOOD.

MR. PETTENGILL TO PROF. SANBORN.

Salisbury, January 14, 1853.

DEAR SIR,—From boyhood to manhood, and from manhood to the termination of their lives, I knew the brothers, Ezekiel and Daniel Webster well; and I regret that I am not able to recollect more incidents of their early days. Few of the contemporaries of Ezekiel and myself, and few, indeed, of our classmates remain to tell the story of the life of my departed friend, or record his virtues. Most of our classmates have entered the portals of the unseen world, and have left only some ten or twelve, out of thirty-four, treading the vestibule. I understand from the tenor of your letter, that a somewhat minute account of your father-in-law is desired, as also his standing in college and his character as a citizen and a man. My relation must necessarily be minute and circumstantial, if I aim to inform or interest you; and some particulars, I well know, may be considered trifling and unessential to general readers, and especially to those who were strangers to my esteemed friend.

Of his father, Hon. Ebenezer Webster, I have a perfect recollection, as to form and features. His stature was nearly six feet. He was compact, robust, and well-proportioned, and, late in life, inclined to corpulency. His complexion was dark; a broad and projecting forehead; eyes large, black, and piercing, overshadowed by heavy brows. With respect to intellect, he was a perfect example of a strong-minded, unlettered man; of sound common sense, correct judgment, and tenacious memory; all of which desirable mental qualities were for him, to some extent, a substitute for education. He was a resolute, determined character, and never easily turned from his purpose, when once convinced that it was right. He was among the early settlers of Salisbury, at a time when that portion of the country was almost a wilderness; and the place where his sturdy arm first felled the forest, was purchased, some two or three years since, by his son, Hon. Daniel Webster. It is situated on the North Road, so called, about three miles from Franklin village, and about the same distance from the East meeting-house, in Salisbury. The location was not a very eligible one for Judge Webster. The land was of an inferior quality. It must be recollected, however, that when he first became a settler in Salisbury, it was a day of small things. He was poor, and made a pitch, as they called it, where land was cheapest. On this spot, beside a small brook, the father of the Websters first erected his log house, the foundations of which are still visible; and in this place his sons first saw the light. On this same brook, in the course of three or four years, he erected a small gristmill for the accommodation of himself and his neighbors. A venerable lady, living near me, now eighty-seven years of age, has recently informed me, that, when twelve or fourteen years old, she was often sent to this mill, on horseback, with a grist, as was the custom of those days, when carriages were unknown. While her grist was grinding, it was her custom to visit the family; and she has a perfect recollection of Ezekiel and Daniel, then small boys. She also informed me that "the Captain," as he was styled, a few years later erected a framed house, at that day called "a saw-mill house," from its resemblance to a saw-mill, being low, long, and narrow. In this house he and his family lived many years, till he sold and removed to the banks of the Merrimac, now Franklin, to the house which he occupied at the time of his decease. It is now called "the Webster Place." Judge Webster was much in town business; for many years in succession he was chosen moderator in the town meetings, and one of the Selectmen. He was also frequently called to represent the town of Salisbury in the Legislature. He was an officer in the revolutionary war, and commanded a company at the battle of Bennington. A sergeant of his company informed me that he was among the first to scale the Tory breastwork, as it was called; and that, when he came out of the battle, he was so covered with dust and powder that he could scarcely be recognized. I have been informed that the Captain often repeated, with much pleasure and exultation, the laconic address of General Stark, previous to the engagement. With the mother of Ezekiel, I was partially acquainted. She, like her husband, was of a dark complexion, with strongly marked features, indicative of a strong mind and sound sense. So we see, that, from both parents, the sons inherited that strength of intellect which, in after life, rendered them so conspicuous. The well, dug by the Judge, in the early days of his pilgrimage, near the log-cabin, still remains; and both of his distinguished sons, whenever they visited the place of their birth, which was often, made it a point to drink from "the old oaken bucket," in remembrance of the days of their childhood. Of Daniel Webster, I need not speak. The world has long since made up its judgment respecting the talents, character, and virtues of this eminent statesman; and any additional remarks from an obscure individual would be lost, like a ripple upon the bosom of old ocean. In accordance with your request, I will proceed to speak of Ezekiel Webster, as I knew him in youth and mature age. For more than twenty years, we were inhabitants of the same town, and very frequently together. At the age of twenty, and from that time to the day of his sudden death, we were intimate friends. His form and features are still present to my mind's eye; and could I command the chisel of a Praxiteles, I could transmit him to posterity, as I saw him in the prime of life and the maturity of manhood. His height was about that of his father, nearly six feet. He was an improved edition of his father, in form and features, and had such a form as a statuary, without any disparagement to his art, might select for a model. His complexion was some shades lighter than that of his father or brother. The form of his head and face was essentially Grecian; his forehead broad and elevated; his eyes large, dark, and brilliant, and the whole contour and expression of his countenance such as to inspire confidence in his friends, and command respect from his enemies, if he had any. Many years before that sad and sudden stroke, which deprived the community of his talents and usefulness, his hair, which was abundant, became white as snow, which gave him a venerable appearance, some years in advance of his age. All who saw him in the maturity of his manhood, were impressed with his dignified personal appearance and the striking expression of his countenance. His boyhood and youth, till the age of about twenty, were spent with his father, in agricultural pursuits; and in manual labor, he is said to have excelled most of his competitors. He enjoyed in early life only the advantages of the common schools of his native town. In his twentieth year, through the influence of his brother, then a member of Dartmouth College, with slender means,—for his father was not affluent,—he began to prepare for college. At the academy in Salisbury, then a new institution, and something of a novelty in that part of the country, Ezekiel

Webster commenced his preparatory studies. The writer was a member of the same school and engaged in the same pursuits; and what he now says is from personal knowledge. Mr. Webster had previously attained to a competent knowledge of English grammar and arithmetic. He commenced, at Salisbury, with the Latin grammar; all the necessary parts of which he dispatched in the same time employed by ordinary students in learning the declensions of substantives. His mind was vigorous, his memory tenacious, and his industry incessant. He therefore mastered Æsop's fables in Latin, and the history of Eutropius, preparatory classics at that day, with great ease and expedition. When he commenced Virgil, he was classed with one whom, in a few days, he left far in the rear, to plod along as best he might. No doubt Webster's progress in the language appeared to his tardy companion like a dream. I think that he attended only two terms at this school, during which time he read the Æneid, besides the preparatory books above named, and a part of the four Evangelists in Greek. He often read three or four hundred lines of Virgil at a lesson. He finished his preparatory studies with Dr. Wood, of Boscawen. While in college, he ranked with the first in his class, in all the different branches at that time taught at Dartmouth; and was particularly noted for his industry, sobriety, and regular deportment. During his residence at college, he taught schools in the winter vacations. One of his schools was in Salisbury, in the district where I now live. He had charge of a numerous and disorderly multitude; and from his known character for firmness and resolution, I have no doubt that he trained, governed, and instructed them well. For the last half of his senior year, he was engaged much of the time in teaching a select school in Boston; impelled to do so, as I learned, from want of funds. When he came on for examination, it was expected by some that he would be found in arrears; but it was soon ascertained that he had lost no ground and was able to compete with the best of them. During his entire college course, he sustained the reputation of a regular, industrious, and well-grounded scholar, and a young gentleman of good habits and exemplary morals; and what was of equal value, and told much in his favor, he acquired the respect and love of his class. He commenced the practice of the law in Boscawen, in 1807, in the office that had previously been occupied by his brother, Daniel. On the Fourth of July of that year, at the request of the principal inhabitants of his native town of Salisbury, he delivered an oration, which, for sound sense, correct reasoning, beauty of style, and purity of diction, has been excelled by few of the numerous productions which that occasion has called forth. Whoever has read that address must regret that so few of the products of his pen have been given to the world. Indeed, whatever proceeded from his tongue or his pen bore the marks of a sound and discriminating mind. He soon attained to an extensive practice in his profession; and his standing at the bar, in the counties of Hillsborough and Grafton, was among the first; not so particularly as an advocate, at the outset, as for the soundness and safety of his counsel. He was well grounded in the principles of the common law, which enabled him as it were by intuition to seize upon the strong points of his case. This knowledge he used to the best advantage, and often to the discomfiture of his opponents. For some years before his decease, he rose to eminence as an advocate in the county of Merrimac, where I doubt if he had a superior. I have reason to know that his brother Daniel often consulted him, not only on difficult points of law, but upon the most common interests of life. In the Legislature of New Hampshire, in which he often sat, his candor, moderation, and good sense, obtained for him the same respect and influence which he had in society, wherever he was known. In private life, he was an example of moral rectitude; sober, studious, industrious, and contemplative. In the relations of son, brother, father, and husband, his example is worthy of all praise and imitation. He was fond of agriculture and horticulture. His beautiful grounds, garden, and buildings, on Boscawen Plain, were a proof of his refined taste and laudable industry. He took a lively interest in agriculture, and his townsmen are much indebted to him for improvements in various branches of husbandry. Learning and religion also received his warm and constant support.

Very respectfully yours,

THOMAS H. PETTENGILL.

MR. ABBOTT TO PROF. SANBORN.

Nashua, February 5, 1853.

My dear Sir,—Your favor, asking for my early recollections of Mr. Webster, was duly received, and has remained much too long unanswered. I have sought in vain to find a file of papers, which I am sure I laid by many years ago, but have failed in finding. They could never have been destroyed by me, nor wittingly by any of my household. I do not yet despair of putting my hand on them, at some lucky moment, when I am not seeking for them.

My acquaintance with Mr. Webster commenced immediately after his graduation, at Dartmouth College, which was in August, 1801. The office of Mr. Thompson, with whom I was then reading law, was situated nearly opposite his father's house. As there were but few companions for us in that place, we at once formed a friendship, which has never been interrupted. In his earlier days, he always made my house his home, when he was travelling in this direction. Mr. Webster remained at home, as I think, till about the 1st of November following, when he took his departure for his school in Fryeburg, on horseback, with his wardrobe and library in his saddle-bags. I accompanied him across the river, where we shook hands, mutually agreeing to correspond.

Mr. Thompson had an extensive library, not only of law but of history. I think Mr. Webster occupied himself at that time more with the latter than the former, but he was always busy at something. He was fond of hunting and fishing, he was "an excellent shot" then; and what time we could conveniently spare from the office, we used to employ in ranging the neighboring woods for partridges, quails, squirrels, &c.; and the pond, where he afterwards kept his boat, we occasionally visited with great success. He seemed to be acquainted with everybody in that region, and always had a pleasant word for each.

I recollect an incident which showed his scrupulous integrity. Mr. Thompson was postmaster, in Salisbury, while I was in his office. In his absence, I had the entire charge of it. One morning I found a letter on the desk, addressed to his brother Ezekiel, at Hanover, marked as a double one. When I took it up to mail it, knowing the superscription to be Daniel's, I said to him, if you had not marked it double, I never should have suspected that it was so. "I thought as much," said he, "but I remembered to have read somewhere, that it is better *to be* honest, than to *appear* so." At this time, two pieces of paper, however small, constituted a double letter, with double postage, which to Hanover was twenty cents, which he paid. The letter contained only a twenty dollar bill, which he was sending to his brother. This was done when money was very scarce with him.

I have no recollection of ever meeting Mr. Webster at any boarding-house or public room on the Sabbath. The family were all strict observers of the Lord's day. He almost invariably attended church, which was four miles distant, though he generally rode on horseback. In the whole course of our acquaintance, of more than half a century, I have never heard him use a profane word. He wrote for Mr. Hough's paper, at Concord. His signature I do not now recollect. I believe the Newsboy's Address for January 1, 1802, in poetry, of course, was written by him. Ezekiel was at Hanover, or out of college teaching school, while I was at Salisbury. I recollect seeing him but once, and then for a short time only.

The father was a right down plain, honest farmer of the "old school." Independent and frank in his own opinions, he was willing others should enjoy theirs, if they differed from him. His bright and active years were passed before I knew him; but he was always industrious about the useful but less arduous duties of the farm.

If I recover my lost letters, I shall be able to give you some more facts at a future time.

Very truly your friend,

DANIEL ABBOTT.

MR. HOTCHKISS TO PROF. SANBORN.

Shreveport, Caddo Parish, Louisiana, February 25, 1853.

DEAR SIR,—In answer to the inquiries contained in your letter of November 22, respecting the college life of my classmate, Daniel Webster, I will now give you such facts as I can recall. I joined the Freshman class at the beginning of the second term. As I entered my class for the first time, being a stranger to all present, I scanned with deep interest the personal appearance and attainments of every member. I also observed the manner in which each one performed his part in the recitation. All did well. I thought Webster acquitted himself admirably, and, indeed, a little better than the rest. I can truly say that all his exercises, through his whole collegiate course, improved in excellence as time advanced. He was always punctual in all the recitations, exercises, and studies of the class. Daniel Webster never required as much time to make himself familiar with the subjects of his studies as many others, who also performed well their parts. His range of study was more general than that of his classmates. The ease with which he acquired knowledge afforded him much time for promiscuous reading. His leisure hours were not lost; they were occupied in the way of literary improvement. He took time for exercise and recreation, and joined in the sports and amusements common to students at that time. Their pastimes consisted in the game of ball and other athletic exercises.

Webster was never an idle student, as some persons falsely and erroneously believe. I have often been questioned on that subject, and have always taken upon myself the pleasing task of promptly denying the charge and correcting the mistake. In the pursuit of useful knowledge no person could be more assiduous than Daniel Webster. No blame could justly be brought against his moral character; no person could impute to him a mean or unworthy act. In his intercourse with society, he was kind, affable, and courteous. He was an agreeable companion, and was highly esteemed by his college acquaintances. There were, perhaps, as many good scholars in our class as could be found in any other class of the same number. Webster was considered the best. Often, in our private circles, the subject of his superior scholarship and fine talents was discussed. From my first acquaintance with him I had predicted for him a brilliant future, and I have seen that prediction signally verified.

Respectfully yours,

E. HOTCHKISS.

MR. SHATTUCK TO PROF. SANBORN.

Lancaster, Mass., December 27, 1855.

Dear Sir,—Yours of December 21 is before me. You ask for reminiscences of the college life of the late Hon. Daniel Webster. So far as I am aided by an octogenarian memory, I would say, that Mr. Webster's habits of study while in college were good. His mode of recitation was prompt and off-hand; ever standing side by side with the best specimens of scholarship in his class, and in some particulars, especially in composition and oratory, ahead of them all. His deportment was easy and gentlemanly; his dress decent, suited to the occasion; nothing superfluous or deficient. I never knew, or heard, or thought of any thing objectionable in his moral character. He was sometimes humorous, always companionable and pleasant. He possessed a very clear and comprehensive mind, and on graver subjects was bold and lion-like in language. I have heard of some anecdotes of Mr. Webster's college life which seem to have no foundation in truth. If the events reported ever occurred, I was not cognizant of the facts.

Respectfully yours,

N. Shattuck.

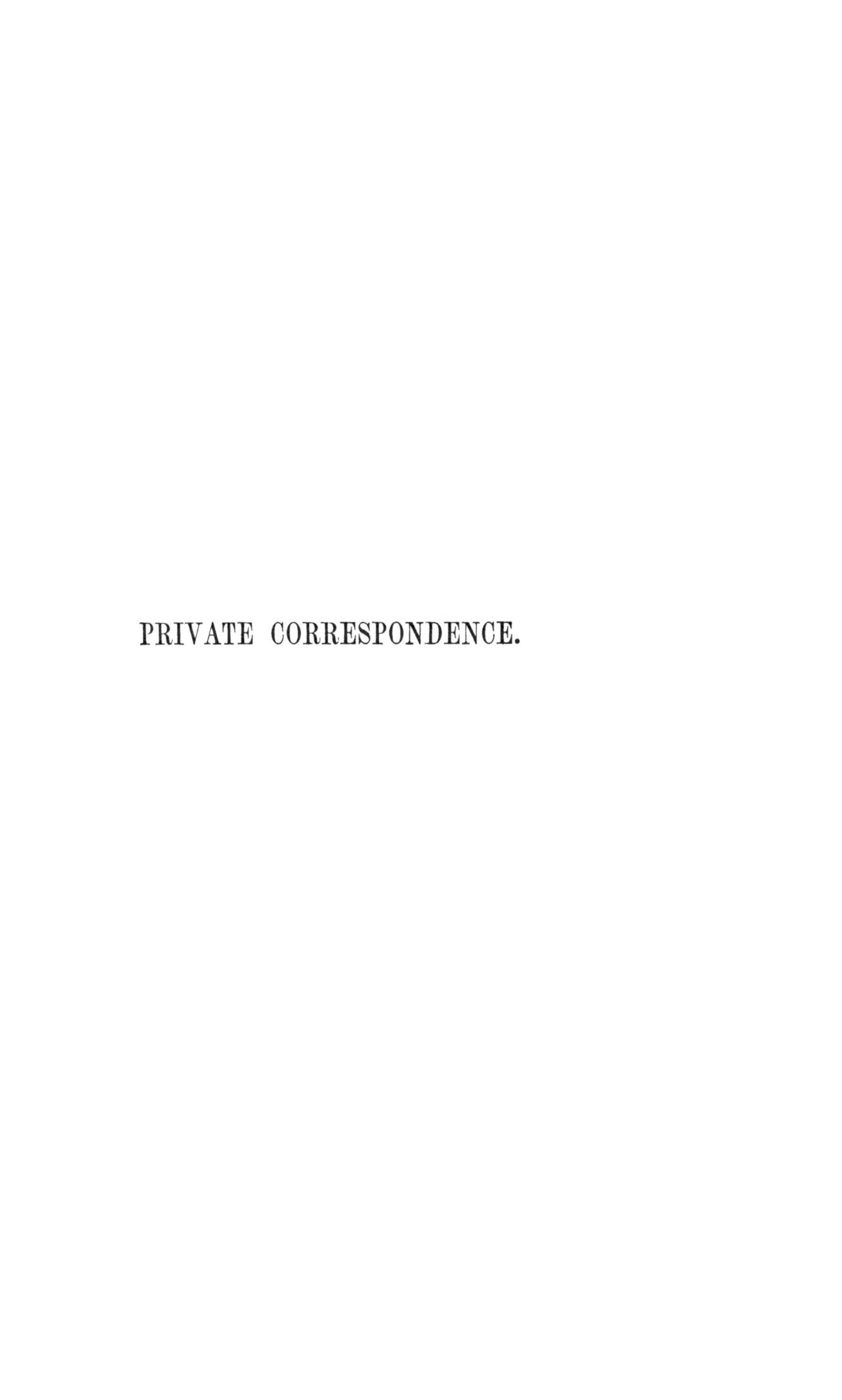

PRIVATE CORRESPONDENCE.

PRIVATE CORRESPONDENCE.

DANIEL WEBSTER TO GEORGE HERBERT.

Dartmouth College, December 20, 1798.

Yes, George, I go, I leave the friend I love,
Long since 'twas written in the books above;
But what, Good God! I leave thee, do I say?
The thought distracts my soul and fills me with dismay.
But Heaven decreed it, let me not repine;
I go; but, George, my heart is knit with thine.
In vain old Time shall all his forces prove,
To tear my heart from the dear friend I love;
Should you be distant far as Afric's sand,
By Fancy pictured you'd be near at hand.
This shall console my thoughts, till time shall end,
Though George be absent, George is still my friend.
But other friends I leave: it wounds my heart,
To leave a Gilman, Conkey, and a Clark;
But Hope through the sad thought my soul shall bear:
Bereft of hope I'd sink in dark despair.
When Phœbus a few courses shall have run,
And e'er old Aries shall receive the sun,
I shall return, nor more shall fear the day,
That from my friends shall take poor me away;
O then roll on, ye lagging wheels of time,
Roll on the hour; till then, dear George, I'm thine.

D. W.

Let love and friendship reign,
Let virtue join the train
And all their sweets retain,
Till Phœbus' blaze expire;

Till God, who rules on high,
Shall rend the tottering sky,
All nature gasping die
And Earth be wrapt in fire.

Dartmouth College.

D. W. TO G. H.

SALVE!

February 25, 1799.

BUT quit old Pegasus and soar on high,
In Fancy's air balloon traverse the sky,
Where hills of hail and heaps of snow are seen,
Kept in reserve, Heaven's awful magazine.
Then bend your course aloft beyond the sun,
Where other globes in other orbits run;
Where other Comets glide along their spneres,
And other planets measure other years;
Where other men inhabit realms afar,
To whom our sun is but a twinkling star.
Then further soar along the Milky Way,
Where our old sun ne'er cast a glimmering ray.
When thus, dear George, you see with wondering eye
Systems on systems roll along the sky,
Then, friend, consider that there is a God
Who rules this vast machine, and governs with a nod.

MELA.
Dartmouth College.

DANIEL WEBSTER TO GEORGE HERBERT.[1]

(EXTRACT.).

Dartmouth College, January 7, 1801.

I FIND, brother George, that if I would allure an answer to my letters, I must exalt my subject from those trifles which effemi-

[1] Mr. Herbert had now graduated and removed to Stockbridge, Mass.

nate our sex, to those affairs which mark the man of information and business. I shall likewise, perhaps, find it necessary to round my periods with more attention, and endeavor to grace my sentences with the flourishes of rhetoric. For the sake of continuing a correspondence, I would willingly attempt any thing within the compass of my capacity, but the frog must not strive to swell to the size of the ox.

Two things I can't say I like; Jefferson's election to the Presidency, and Hamilton's letter. Of the two, I prefer the former. There is some consistency in the Jacobins raising Thomas to the Executive Chair; it is in conformity to their avowed principles. But Hamilton's letter is void of congruity.

Let us just notice one absurdity, which you have undoubtedly observed. Hamilton proposes to prove that there are certain essential defects in the character of Adams, I forget the particular expressions, which unfit him for the office of Chief Magistrate; he labors hard to substantiate this point, and thinks he has done it. What is his conclusion? He does not wish to withhold a vote from Mr. Adams. Now mark the consistency. He thinks there are a hundred men in the United States better calculated for the Presidency than Mr. Adams, for there certainly are that number who do not possess these essential defects; yet he wishes, or professes to wish, every vote given to Mr. Adams. Is this consentaneous to all that independence which he sets out with? Is it agreeable to that rigid republicanism which glowed in the breasts of Aristides and Cato?

We are every day expecting the electioneering for governor to commence in this State with warmth. I never yet drove my quill in such a case, perhaps never shall. I may laugh a little! Langdon, it is expected, will be the anti-Federal candidate. Gilman, the Federal; if he declines, Peabody, of Exeter.

Hem! Hem! I am clearing my throat. George P., the son of Professor W., observed the other day, (as it was spoken in confidence, I will allow you to make more of it than of general report): "I am told," said he, "that Herbert is somewhat unwell, and I believe there is a weed growing round our house, which would cure him. Mary is also somewhat sick, and I am told there is an herb now growing in the western part of Massachusetts, which would help her." These observations were made in Mary's hearing, who replied: "Since you have discovered a weed which you suppose would be beneficial to Mr. Herbert, you are in duty bound to communicate your discovery to him." I pledge myself, Herbert, for the truth of this; but shall tell you no more of the good or bad things said of you here, till I know more distinctly your intention. If you are seriously and honorably inclined, I can tell you enough to give you perfect confidence of success; if you only wish to amuse yourself, and sport with the girl, I beg you not to make me your instrument. This however I know you cannot intend. I know the nobleness of your soul and the purity of your heart. Command my service in any way, not inconsistent with the character of a Christian and a gentleman, and I will serve you to the *ne plus ultra* of my talents.

Since you have not answered my other letter, I fear I have offended; I hope not; for surely you will not accuse me of vanity, if I tell you that you have not a friend in existence who means better than DANL. WEBSTER.

FROM MRS. HERBERT, TO REV. C. D. HERBERT.

(Inclosing the preceding letters.)

Ellsworth, March 6, 1856.

MY DEAR SON,—I am very sorry to disappoint any expectation which Mr. Fletcher Webster may have been led to entertain, that I would be able to furnish him with any considerable memorials of his late father. Indeed, I have very little in my possession; only one letter now remaining of his correspondence with your father, which is dated the last year of his college life. But, as this is rather interesting and indicative of the future man, I will enclose it to you, and you can transmit or not, to Mr. F. W., as you shall think fit. I find also two little fragments of poetry, written when he was very young. They seem quite characteristic of the writer, and are creditable both to his head and heart. And I also find quite an interesting document, entitled "Constitution of the Federal Club," with several signatures appended, among which is that of Daniel Webster. These were doubtless intimate friends and choice spirits, of that early period of life; and probably not one of them now survives.

Messrs. Bracket and Clarke were subsequently settled in the

legal profession in New York city. The former died about 1830; the latter, ten or eleven years later. Mr. Clarke had long since united with the Society of Friends, some said in order to advance his professional interests. Your father said, "No, it was in accordance with the natural dictates of his heart; he was born a Quaker!"

Tristram Gilman was a Maine lad, the son of a clergyman, the Rev. Mr. Gilman of North Yarmouth. He died early. Mr. Coffin, familiarly called by his college friends, "little Natty Coffin," from his diminutive person, was also of Maine, and your father's predecessor in this place. On finishing the term of study in Mr. Sedgwick's office, your father, on the suggestion and recommendation of Judge Parker, hastened on to Ellsworth, quite ignorant that the young lawyer lately established here, but now about leaving, was none other than his quondam friend, Natty Coffin! Their mutual recognition and surprise were very amusing.

Mr. Pierce, after graduating from Dartmouth, was some time principal of New Ipswich Academy. I know nothing of him in after life, or of Conkey or Cram.

I have heard your father speak often and much of Daniel Webster, for whom he had the truest esteem and friendship; but it is so long since, that particulars are much obliterated from my mind. I would gladly recall them, if it were possible.

As your brother George went on to St. Augustine the last year of his college life, about 1834, he was detained a few days in New York, and took the opportunity to pay his respects to Mr. Clarke, who treated him very kindly, and recognized him as his father's son. The presence of the young collegian seemed to open afresh the genial heart of the good old man to reminiscences of his own college life, and he gave many pleasant anecdotes relating to those happy times. I should think that a more than common attachment existed among the members of his class, in general, and that many of them were bound together by the closest ties of friendship. Mr. Clarke related that some of these friends, or brothers, as they called each other, had rooms adjoining; and, in order to facilitate their social enjoyments, they made an opening in the intervening partition, which was by some ingenious device carefully secured from the general observation, but admitted of free ingress and egress to the occupants of the two apartments; and it would seem that, like the early Christians, they had all things common. The first to rise in the morning, dressed himself in the best which the united apartments afforded; and so of the rest successively, but woe to the latest riser, whose equipments might have been furnished at Rag Fair!

Mr. Clarke was himself at one time the fortunate possessor of a new beaver hat; not one of the light, cheap, silky, effeminate fabrications of later times, but a real eight or ten dollar beaver, well made and weighty. It was the envy of all the college.

The new beaver was one day missing. He sought it everywhere, in vain. In his researches, he happened on an old felt hat battered and broken, which he was fain to wear, rather than none. Things continued thus for several weeks, when "friend Dan" returned from a distant town, where he had spent the vacation in school-teaching, and with him came the beaver, which he had tacitly borrowed for the occasion! They shook hands, re-exchanged hats, and were better friends than ever.

These are pleasant anecdotes, such as old men love to recall of their innocent boyhood; but I have heard and could tell of far better, relating to those times, more significant of good, if I could but distinctly remember them. Young Webster seems to have been greatly beloved by his early friends, who prognosticated his future greatness, though they could not, perhaps, have anticipated that he would so early have become famous.

I never saw Mr. Webster, excepting in the winter of 1808, when, with your father, I spent several weeks in Boston. Mr. and Mrs. Webster, from Portsmouth, were at the same time visitors in that city. They were guests in the family of Mr. Perkins, a young M. D. recently from Hanover, and one of the fraternity of attached friends. To his house your father and myself had frequent invitations, and nothing could exceed the high enjoyment evinced by Herbert and Webster in the renewed intercourse.

The appearance of Mr. Webster at this time, still youthful, yet mature, his fine person and dignified demeanor, though in the social private circle most gentle and endearing, is altogether indescribable. Mrs. Webster was very sweet and lovely. Her smile was perfectly charming and long to be remembered. Some few years after, I asked Mr. Allen, (Frederick H.) then a young man and recently returned from Washington, where he had accompanied his father, if he saw Mrs. Webster. "O yes, indeed," he said, he "met with her at the great levee." The lady friend who "patronized him," after having presented him to several ladies, said to him, "and now I am about to introduce you to Mrs. Webster, whom you will find shining among these dazzling luminaries with all the sweet and gentle radiance of the Evening Star!"

But I must stop. Please make my best excuses to Mr. Fletcher Webster, and forward to him such of the manuscripts as you think best. They look very worn out and shabby, and in self-justification, I must say, so did they when I first saw them, nearly half a century ago!

MR. WEBSTER TO MR. BINGHAM.

Salisbury, February 5, 1800.

THE political events of Europe, my friend Hervey, are so novel and unexpected, revolution succeeds revolution in such rapid succession, that it is sufficient to overpower the understanding and confound the calculations of the most sage politician. These events are attended with such important circumstances, involve so many and so various interests, that schemes either of aggrandizement or of defence are agitated and devised in every cabinet of Europe. Nor is it to be expected, at this eventful crisis, that the decisions of our Executive are to be uninfluenced by considerations of transatlantic occurrences. Were we, like China, divested of every commercial engagement, we might, like that empire, remain unmoved, while convulsed Europe tottered to its base. To suppose that the liberty of United America, depends on the balance of power on the Eastern continent, is an idea exploded by every whig of '76, and which ought to be deemed absurd and preposterous. But our connections with foreign nations are such, that to preserve unaffected our commercial interests, while revolutions are making such monstrous strides in Europe, is beyond the reach of human sagacity. Adams, however, has hitherto conducted us in tolerable safety through the dangers which have beset us, and on him, under the guidance of an overruling Providence, we must rely, as the only rock of our political salvation. I, who am a mere novice in the science of politics, have done calculating. I have heretofore applied logical, metaphysical, mathematical, and philosophical theorems, but have found them all insufficient to solve one political problem.

Who thought, six months ago, that Bonaparte, who was then represented as lying with his slaughtered army on the plains of Egypt, to taint the air, and gorge the monsters of the Nile, would at this time have returned to France, have destroyed the Directory and Legislative Councils, have established a triumvirate, and have placed himself at its head—which is saying, have virtually made himself sovereign of France? Who could have predicted that the Duke of York, who so late was marching victoriously through Holland, should ere this time have entered into a convention, by which he was to give up all his booty and prisoners, and evacuate the country? Or, whoever supposed that Paul, emperor of Russia, who so lately was raising one hundred and eighty thousand men, to reinforce his armies, should now order Suwarrow, with his veteran Cossacks, to quit the field and return home? The occurrences hitherto would have warranted the most extravagant expectations; but these events must have been, I think, unprepared for. What unknown cause has wrought these changes? I cannot determine. I am weary of conjecture. But, when baffled in attempting to scan the horizon of European politics, could I turn my eyes home and be presented with such a prospect as was afforded five years ago, I should lift my heart to Heaven in a transport of devotion, and exclaim, "Let France or England be arbiter of Europe, but be mine the privileges of an American citizen." But, Hervey, our prospect darkens; clouds hang around us. Not that I fear the menaces of France; not that I should fear all the powers of Europe leagued together for our destruction. No, Bingham, intestine feuds alone I fear. The French faction, though quelled, is not eradicated. The southern States in commotion; a Democrat the head of the Executive in Virginia; a whole county in arms against the government of McKean, in Pennsylvania; Washington, the great political cement dead, and Adams almost worn down with years, and the weight of cares. These considerations, operating on a mind naturally timorous, excite unpleasant emotions. In my melancholy moments, I presage the most dire calamities. I already see, in my imagination, the time when the banner of civil war shall be unfurled; when Discord's hydra form shall set up her hideous yell, and from her hundred mouths shall howl destruction through our empire; and when American blood shall be made to flow in rivers, by American swords! But propitious Heaven prevent such dreadful calamities! Internally secure, we have nothing to fear. Let Europe pour her embattled millions around us, let her thronged cohorts cover our shores, from St. Lawrence to St. Marie's, yet, United Columbia shall stand unmoved; the manes of her deceased Washington, shall guard the liberties of his country, and direct the sword of freedom in the day of battle. Heaven grant that the bonds of our federal union may be strengthened; that Gallic emissaries and Gallic principles may be spurned from our land; that traitors may be abashed, and that the stars and stripes of United Columbia may wave triumphant! So much for politics.

I have received your letter, as you must know by my delaying to visit you. I shall visit you next Saturday, other things being equal. You wonder I did not write, and are about to conclude that my friendship for you had decreased, but, James, form no rash conclusions. I did write soon after your departure; I wrote very soon; I wrote then. I prepared a letter too long, and too nonsensical to be read with patience, and determined to send it by Mr. Wilson, but did not see him. I then despatched the *animal* by another conveyance, but after a few days travelling it returned. However, after a little refreshment, the *gentleman* moved again, and I conclude by this time is arrived at Sanbornton; where I presume you will deal with his honor according to the fitness of things, that is to say, read till you are tired, then burn him. By last mail I had a letter from Fuller—all well. N. and B. were to go last week. S. F—er, and Mary, *la bonne*, have gone. Thus you see the circle is broken; well, Hervey, let us then apply ourselves more closely to study. I have to impart to you from Mr. Fuller, the love of all the ——. My school increases fast enough. Instead of twenty, I have fifty, and shall have more; five English grammarians, I mean students in English, and two Latin scholars. I had a letter not long since from J. Nelson, and hope to see him on Saturday at Sanbornton. Much speculation is made here on the scribblers for the Dartmouth Gazette. Old Icarus is handled without ceremony. I shall tell you hereafter some pretty things about it. Our family would reciprocate their respects.[1]

I am, Sir, with much respect, yours in the indissoluble bonds of fraternal love. D. Webster.

MR. WEBSTER TO MR. BINGHAM.

Salisbury, February 11, 1800.

Brother Bingham,—I now sit down in poor spirits to write a poor letter, to—a poor fellow, shall I say? No, say rather, to the friend of my heart, the partner of my joys, griefs, and affections, the only participator of my most secret thoughts. I arrived here yesterday, seasonably for school, and having undergone the fatigues of the day, I retired to rest at nine o'clock, and surrendered myself to the dominion of Morpheus. At ten, I was awaked, and informed that Captain McClure, and Senior Curtis were below. I soon disengaged myself from the "slumbering god," and hastened to extend them the friendly right hand, accompanied with a hearty how do you do! They left Hanover almost two weeks since; and have taken a tour to the southeast. By them I was favored with two letters from our friends at college, which, although dated some time ago, gave me much pleasure. Clark writes that he has taken the school there at twenty-four dollars per month. Doctor Marsh offered himself for fifteen, but was not received. "This," Clark observes, "feeds my vanity, but not my purse." In the course of his letter he observes, "blow ye Northern blasts with tenfold fury; beat back the pestilential breeze of matrimony, or my *Icarus* is fallen forever!" What does he hint at here? How should he know that I was just about to (try to) be married? My amour, you very well know, had not commenced the last time I wrote to him. He says he is well and happy; that he has heard from many of our friends who are in health. This information carries joy to the hearts of J. H. B. and D. W. While you rejoice with me in the health and happiness of our brother students, I presume from the goodness of your heart, that you will join me in commiserating him

[1] A portion of the above appeared in the Dartmouth Gazette.

who stands next to yourself on the catalogue of my friends. I mean Bracket; he has lost a sister; he is afflicted, and we will mourn. We have seen him in those happy hours, when every heart palpitated with joy, and every eye sparkled with benevolence; and we should be equally happy to meet him now and mingle souls in mournful sympathy. Though not personally acquainted with the deceased lady, it is enough to entitle her to a share in our remembrance that she was the sister of J. W. B. For his sake, then, we will shed the friendly tear and embalm her memory in our hearts. After the people were gone to bed, I wrote an answer to Clark, and presumed to offer him your best respects; this I conceived I had a right to do, since, between you and me, *cor corde mutatur.* I also wrote to H. W. F., and endeavored, with as much delicacy as I was able, to return the ——— *puellarum pulcherrimarum* so politely bestowed on J. H. B. and D. W.

Capt. McClure, in his journey, saw Freeborn, and D. Osgood, and J. Dutch, &c. who are well. . . . . In the letter which you did me the honor to send me, you have the following sentence, "*cave, nequis videat*, &c.;" though it be very handsome Latin, and I can find no fault with it as a critic, yet, my dear Hervey, I must confess it surprises me much. Do you suspect my integrity? Do you imagine that I would do any thing which should endanger your reputation? I certainly suspect no such things from you, and therefore never think to insert such an idea. If a letter from a friend chance to be written inaccurately, as is often the case when written *calamo currente*, which, by the way, could not be said of yours, it behooves the receiver to consider it accordingly. Upon the whole, that sentence, though its like is frequently seen in letters, argues a suspicion of my sincerity, which, were I assured it really existed, would prove an eternal alloy to my felicity. But I am willing to impute it to custom, to compliment, or, as you say, to any thing else rather than to suspicion.

It is now nine o'clock; before I began this letter I read a chapter in Mallet du Pan's History of The Destruction of the Helvetic Union. I read till I saw Switzerland ravaged and depopulated, her sons barbarously butchered, and blood flowing in torrents from the side of the Alps! All this I saw done by the intrigue of perfidious France. The scene was too affecting; I closed the book and exclaimed, "Havoc and spoil and ruin are thy gains; destruction is thy sport; blood, groans, and desolation are thy triumphs, thou magnanimous republic!!! Switzerland, which has been a republic for almost five hundred years, is now no more. The descendants of the immortal Tell, who rescued his country from Austrian tyranny, have nothing now left, as the historian observes, but rocks, ruins, and demagogues." "Ah, curst ambition, what hast thou done!" Nor is it enough that Switzerland, Venice, Genoa, and every other republic in Europe has fallen a prey to the despots of Paris; one quarter of the world cannot satiate their ambition. The worshipper of the Alcoran must be molested, the wandering Arab attacked, and slaughter carried to the forests of Africa. Their empire must be bounded only by the limit of their ambition; their ambition is coextensive with the universe. I expect that Blanchard will soon be despatched with his aërial squadron to attack the moon; to revolutionize the Lunarians by the same means that Talleyrand used to disturb the peace of his Satanic Majesty. . . . . No more politics.

"——Sylvarumque potens Diana." *A Fable.*

Bright Phœbus long all rival suns outshone,
And rode triumphant on his splendid throne;
When first he waked the blushes of the dawn,
And spread his beauties o'er the flowery lawn,
The yielding stars quick hastened from the sky,
Nor moon dare longer with his glories vie;
He reigned supreme, and decked in roseate light
Beamed his full splendors on the astonished sight.
At length, on earth, behold a damsel rise,
Whose growing beauties charmed the wondering skies!
As forth she walked to breathe the balmy air,
And view the beauties of the gay parterre,
Her radiant glories drowned the blaze of day,
And through all nature shot a brighter ray.
Old Phœbus saw—and blushed—now forced to own,
That with superior worth the damsel shone.
Graced with his name, he bade her ever shine,
And in his rival owned a form divine!

I am, Sir, with much respect, yours in the indissoluble bonds of fraternal love, DAN. WEBSTER.

DANIEL WEBSTER TO EZEKIEL WEBSTER.

Hanover, April 25, 1800.

EZEKIEL,—I promised to write to you once more this week; to-morrow is the last day; well I will write now, but what shall I write? I know not. I have written so frequently this term, that I have exhausted my stock. In the last letter I had from you, you were telling something about "that fountain of science." What fountain do you mean? My brain? That is a fountain which was always dry; a droll fountain truly. Do you mean the whole institution? Perhaps, indeed, there may be some degree of science in college; and I should be very willing to borrow or buy a little of a fellow-student for the sake of amusing you.

Therefore, since we are wretchedly poor, you will be good enough to take the will for the deed, and believe that I would do as much to entertain and instruct you as any man living. That "instruct" is a very presumptuous word; erase it, and write in its room some one not quite so assuming.

By this time you have passed over "*Arma, virumque cano,* &c." I presume you scold a little, but don't be frightened.

You tell me that you have difficulties to encounter, which I know nothing of. What do you mean, Ezekiel? Do you mean to flatter? That don't become you; or do you think you are inferior to me in natural abilities? If so, be assured you greatly mistake. Therefore, for the future, say in your letters to me, "I am superior to you in natural endowments; I will know more in one year, than you do now, and more in six than you ever will." I should not resent this language. I should be very well pleased in hearing it; but be assured, as mighty as you are, your great puissance shall never insure you a victory without a contest.

Adams, my very good room-mate, has just come on. I feel at home now, since my wife has returned. You will ask why he did not call on you; he came by way of Walpole. He will probably go home by way of Salisbury, in August, and I presume he will tarry with us a few days.

There is now before me a newspaper, in which votes stand thus: Gilman, 7,302; Walker, 4,638. These, when added together, make as great a number, nearly, as was given in for governor last year. If, then, this statement be true, which we have no reason to doubt, Walker cannot be elected. In Massachusetts, I think it uncertain whether the *Strong*-man, or the *weak* envoy will be chosen to fill the chair of the supreme executive. I hope, however, that the best man will command the suffrages of his fellow-citizens. But an election of much greater importance than either of the above will demand our attention next September. The question will then be, whether John Adams or Thomas Jefferson shall be President of the United States.

This is the fifth letter I have written to you since I saw you; the last letter I received from you was dated the 8th of April, when it seems you had had none from me; by this time, however, I conclude you have received a number.

I wish you to inform me how many students are now at the academy; whether any will enter college soon; where you board, what you study, &c., &c.

As I have now finished the sheet, you will permit me to take my leave, while I subscribe myself ever yours,

DANIEL WEBSTER.

P. S. Respects to all.

MR. WEBSTER TO MR. BINGHAM.

Beechnut Hall, Hanover, December 28, 1800.

DEAR JAMES,—Long are the faces of Hanoverians. Jefferson's Presidency which now seems certain, sets not very well on our stomachs. All the tonics of our political faculty cannot make it digest readily. Burr, too, nettles us more than any vegetable burr in our fields. However, what cannot be cured must be endured. So, friends Jefferson and Burr, we leave you for more pleasing subjects.

Hervey, do you remember the *oculum?* Yes, I know you do, and will while you live, I shall, be sure. You know how poets sing of the dove that has lost its mate, or you know how Ossian's maid of Cromla weeps, when the green grass waves o'er the tomb of her lover; now make proper deductions for the *licentia poetica*, and you will learn my feelings since your departure.

You must know that I have made great advances in music since you left us. I have not indeed obtained any knowledge in the cords or discords of strings or voices, but have attended to the music of the soul, the harmony of the passions, and the vibrations of the intellectual cords. I have not been vexed nor discomposed; very gay, nor very melancholy; very learned, nor —pardon me—very ignorant, since I saw you. I am fully persuaded that our happiness is much at our regulation, and that the "Know thyself" of the Greek philosopher, meant no more than rightly to attune and soften our appetites and passions till they should symphonize like the harp of David. Mr. Stewart has shown us some fine ideas on it. He is an author whom I admire more than any writer I have perused.

Dear Bingham, it is now half-past ten in the evening. I am alone, save a certain fellow by the name of *Nap*, who, by his unceasing clack, one would think would never be able to indulge sounder sleep than a *nap*. Fanny, whom I consider our sister, has just retired, and the hour is arrived when you and I were used to pile up our books and converse with a fondness I always approve, though sometimes think almost childish. If I had any thing which the world ought not to know, what a happy moment this for telling it to you! But nothing occurs which you have not heard; you know every impression on my heart as perfectly as the letters of the alphabet. I need not go to the world to bring senseless stories to your ear; you must already be surfeited with Hanover reports, and it will not gratify you to learn your friend is implicated in them. I saw S. a moment this evening. If the vices, which sometimes tarnish her sex, were hanging round her heart, they certainly did not appear in her countenance. As I rose to leave the room, a Miss, who sat next her, made a very saucy remark. The voice of S. only replied, "Why!" but the gem which sparkled in her eye completed the sentence. As for myself I was silent, but I turned my eyes towards the censorious animal, and if I looked as I felt, I fancy she repented what she had said. I am not consequential enough to furnish a reproof, "*a negligendo*," but if an inexplicable line of conduct will confound them, I will see two very severe observing Misses entangled in perplexities.

Perhaps I have been imprudent, but nobody shall be unhappy for my imprudence, but myself; for the fulfilment of this promise I pledge my honor. If I ought to, I will. Nobody knows whether I wish to.

I had yesterday a letter from my father. He says I may, if I please, visit Boston this winter. I shall not hesitate to accept his invitation.

Wednesday evening, 8 o'clock.

To-morrow, Hervey, is the first day of the year, and of the century. In conformity to custom and the feelings of my own heart, I wish you a happy new year. We are just now entering upon a century, which none of us will probably live to see closed. There is something solemn in the idea, that a period of time is now commencing which will carry us all to Shakespeare's bourn whence no traveller returns. The "narrow house" is our final mansion, and "there he lies," is an observation which ere long will be applicable to us all. May we so conduct, that the "narrow house" shall be to us a palace of joy, and that the good man may say, concerning us, "there he lies," with his hand on his breast, and a tear in his eye!

I am, dear Hervey, your

Dan'l Webster.

P. S. Fanny sends her compliments. I dare not inform the other ladies that I was writing to you, lest they should give me so many compliments for you, that I could write nothing else. Do not fail to write me immediately. I shall be hereabout three weeks longer.

MR. WEBSTER TO MR. BINGHAM.

Hanover, January 17, 1801.

Brother Bingham,—On the eve of departure from Hanover, I devote a moment to him whose residence here renders Hanover agreeable. Next Monday, health permitting, I set out for Salisbury, not blessed, as the last year, with the company of my Hervey. No event worthy of remembrance has transpired since you left us, except the ill health of brother Shattuck, who has been unwell a number of days, but is recovering. I have had a letter from C. Gilbert, dated at Brookfield. "After a tour of two or three hundred miles," he writes, "friend Upham and myself arrived here." Bliss is pedagoguizing in York State, the other honorable senator I have not heard from.

Fanny and Dan. took a ride to Lebanon the other day, and I felt the magic of friendship increased by conversation. She would be remembered to you. Mr. Bing. is so, without variation. I have an invitation to accompany a gentleman to Boston, perhaps I told you, which I think of accepting. Carey writes to Ripley that he shall leave his school in Salem in April. Salem! Enchanting name! Who would have thought that from the ashes of witches, hung a century ago, should have sprung such an arch coquette as should delight in sporting with the simplicity of

DAN'L WEBSTER.

Do write me immediately; send to Hanover or Windsor, and then by mail to Salisbury. A letter from Hervey always carries joy to the bosom of Daniel.

Good-bye; may you be blessed of the Lord.

DAN'L.

MR. WEBSTER TO MR. FULLER.

Salisbury, January 26, 1801.

WHY, brother Fuller, what should induce you to present to me such a request, at this time? Surely, if you knew my situation you would not think me able to write a letter all in rhyme. I have been, for many days, shut up in my room, and am just now creeping from the clutches of a fever. The Muses, you know, are not often seen hovering round the bed of an invalid; like other females, they wish only to familiarize

———"with swains of limbs robust,
"And vigor unabating."

Thus, friend Habijah, I have a very good reason for apologizing and soliciting a release from the task. But I am very seriously impressed with a sense of your situation; accustomed from infancy to the communion of the Parnassides, and encouraged and cherished in all those habits which attach you to their society, a discontinuance of their intercourse at so unexpected a period must very sensibly diminish your enjoyment. Influenced by these feelings, dear Chevalier, I am induced to address the prayer of a valetudinarian on your behalf to the throne of their highnesses, the Parnassides.

Ye Muses! Say, for what black crime unknown,
Ye stay your influence from your darling son!
What direful causes, as old Maro sings,
Of all his troubles are the fruitful springs?
What nymph, offended at his labored grace,
Eludes his arms, and shuns his chaste embrace?
What star malignant o'er his birthday hung,
And froze the streams, just rolling from his tongue?
Or what drear comet spreads infectious fires,
And seals the lips, that poetry inspires?
Has some proud nymph, of our terrestrial kind,
Shot poisoned arrows thro' his sickening mind?
Has Mary, vastly knowing of her charms,
Set on the dogs, and warned him from her arms?
A sad mishap! But such as oft takes place,
None hold possession long in Mary's grace.
Is this the cause why all his lines, that rose
To flowery rhyme, now sink to lazy prose?
Is this the cause why now he hangs his head,
Nods in his school, and sleepless turns in bed?
If this the cause, the Muses I acquit,
And you, Friend Fuller, you shall have a bit
Of my advice. The Muses are not blamed,
If, by some earthly goddess more inflamed,
You leave their glorious service, and engage,
With nymphs terrestrial, Venus's wars to wage.
Aonian maids despise to share your heart;
Give us the whole, they cry, or not a part.
But if, O Muses, if some other cause,
Has lost your son protection from your laws,
For him I intercede. If e'er my prayers
Arose as welcome offerings to your ears,
If e'er I eulogized your powers divine,
Or sketched your glories in the sounding line,

If e'er you bore me on your fleety wings
To where your chorus tune their lyric strings,
If e'er I knew you on Parnassus's height,
Bedecked with pearls and strewed with living light,
Hear my request, who now before you bend,
Hear my request; for once forgive my friend!
If he has told too much of lies, or truth,
Forgive it, as the foible of his youth.
Whate'er his crime, forgive, forgive this once,
Nor call him more a blockhead nor a dunce.
Now, mighty Muses, to your favor take him,
Nor thus, with unrelenting heart, forsake him!

I have labored thro' my petition. It is undoubtedly a very fine sample of poetry; I shall not and have not read it over. As my ill health prevented my visiting at Commencement, I sent your letter by a safe hand. I was to set out for Boston this day, had I been in health. J. Wheelock called on me yesterday, and made one of the family to church. I did not perceive that the severity of the weather had lessened the longitude of his nose.

I have had but one ride since I arrived here, which was to Boscawen. Saw Miss ——, &c. Miss O., I am told, is very sick; possibly she now is departing into a world of spirits, pure and lovely as her own. There can be no danger in avowing a passion after its object has ceased to exist. If ever I had a wish; but what am I saying? I leave the subject; were I writing a system of Philosophy I should digress into the vale of feelings; but I am abrupt and impertinent. Pardon me for the ideas I have suggested.

I am, dear Weld, your affectionate,

DAN'L WEBSTER.

Respects to Mr. Davis and lady, your friends *et cetera.* Good night; sleep sound.

MR. WEBSTER TO MR. BINGHAM.

Salisbury, June 14, 1801. T.'s Office.

DEAR HERVEY,—My first business is to inquire about Simonds; O, that I could be assured he were recovering; but perhaps that is a happiness never to be allowed us. Let our prayers ascend together for his well-being, whether with us or in another world. If there be any possible method of communication, pray let me hear how he is.

I have next to tell you that I am in no inconsiderable consternation. About ten minutes ago friend Gilbert and I were taking a walk a few rods down street, when we perceived a chaise, containing a gentleman and lady, the latter of whom we concluded looked very well, while at a distance; judge my surprise, when I saw, as the carriage passed me, that its fair inhabitant was no other than SALLY! The chaise drove so fast I only had time to bow and blush, and receive a smile and a look as the carriage passed on.

I hoped she would stop at the tavern, but no. On inquiring of my father, I found the gentleman to be a young major, by the name of Hale.

So Sally you see is gone; yes, gone! gone! I was going to Concord to-morrow, but . . .

Good-bye, Jemmy! I am your
DAN'L WEBSTER.

Love to Fanny. Tell no one where I am. Don't know when I shall return.

MR. WEBSTER TO MR. BINGHAM.

Salisbury, September 10, 1801.

DEAR HERVEY,—I can find no other method of writing to my Hervey, than by the circuitous journey which our friend Hutchinson proposes to take. He is now here, on his way to N. Ipswich, and on his return home will lodge this at Charleston. I am now settled down in the office, where I expect to obtain a smattering of law knowledge. With me is Mr. Abbott, whom

I mentioned to you at Commencement. If any one could fill the place vacated by your absence, it is he.

Company, other than what occasionally falls into the office, we have none. This you might conclude from the situation of the place. My present business is the perusal of Vattel on National Law. I expect next to review Burlamaqui and Montesquieu, and to read Hume, before I commence an inquiry into the principles of municipal and common law.

Thus am I. Now, pray, how are you? What law-shop, what divinity-closet, or what medical chamber confines you? I presume, however, you are not yet engaged in either, but I apprehend you are thinking about something.

Mr. Green, the attorney at Concord, communicated a wish to me, that I would give his compliments to some respectable young gentleman, and inform him that he expects soon to be in want of a clerk, and that any gentleman of character and promise, who may feel disposed to read in his office, shall be entitled to his tuition *gratis*. Mr. Green is a respectable law character, and his reputation as a private gentleman, no one, as I know, impeaches. Board at Concord is easily to be obtained on reasonable terms.

Now I would not advise, but suggest a few considerations. It is not to be doubted that you can obtain more information in four years, with the deduction of three months from every year, than by three years' continued application. That is, if in those said three months you are able to read law, when not in school. At Concord, you could undoubtedly obtain employment three months in each year, and the amount for your wages for this time would pay your board the other nine months.

Concord is a pleasant village. Mr. McFarland, Mr. Flag, and others, would unite with you in harmony of sound and harmony of sentiment. The town library affords a field of miscellaneous reading, and, another source of improvement, the ladies of Concord are very learned.

If it be an observation of weight, that in the event of your living there we should meet often, I submit it.

Duty to Mr. Green obliged me to mention his proposals, in the first instance, to the best man I knew, and my own feelings urge me to address the request to you with particular earnestness.

I have not heard from Hanover since I left. I hope the best things for them all, philosophy, divinity, &c.

Give my regards to your good father, Captain Minor, Doctor Merrill, and all friends, and believe me ever to be yours,

DAN'L WEBSTER.

MR. WEBSTER TO MR. BINGHAM.

Salisbury, September 22, 1801.

BROTHER HERVEY,—I yesterday opened the packet which contained your letter, with a mixture of hope and fear, anxiety and indifference. As it came by way of Hanover, I suspected it might be a communication from that place, replete with groans and despondency, which, however I pity, I cannot relieve. But when I perceived it bore the marks of your penmanship, I confess in honesty, that I felt more exultation of spirit than has been my allotment since I saw you last.

I have been fixing on a time to visit you ever since Commencement, but the uncertainty of finding you has kept me from attempting it.

I am sure you must read with pleasure and advantage in Mr. West's office, if you should conclude upon it, as I hope you will, if you do not see fit to come down nearer us.

I have precipitated myself into an office, with how much prudence I do not now allow myself to reflect. I am not like you, harassed with dreams, nor troubled with any waverings of inclination; but am rather sunken in indifference and apathy. I have read some since Commencement, learned a little, forgotten a good deal, and should be glad to forget much more. As to Coke and Blackstone, whom you mention as my probable intimates, "I tender them the homage of my high respects," and leave the "tenure of their position undisturbed." With the assistance of my first minister, Monsieur Gallatin, formerly called Leo, I have dismissed from the office of this life, a few federal partridges, pigeons, and squirrels, and have drawn from the abundance of Merrimac a few anti-federal fishes, no loaves, such as sword-back, perch, and flat-headed demi-semi-crotchet-quavers, *alias* scaly flat-sides. I'll mend pen.

Thus, you see, I follow the fashion of the great.

There is a disciple of Hume, the skeptic, in the other corner of the office, who doubts whether the sun be anything or nothing. I shall leave Abbott to convert him from his errors, and go on to tell you that I have seen Dr. Gerrish, who had much to interrogate about you, and joined his request to mine that you would come to Concord if agreeable to your interest.

Sanbornton folks are as usual. Andrew does business as fast as ever, and every week calls at the office. I must have some dinner.

I expect to meet many disappointments in the prosecution of the law. I find I have calculated too largely on the profession.

For this reason I have engaged a new auxiliary to support me under mortification; it is tobacco. I have heard much of philosophical fortitude, but never knew what it was, unless it be a sullen unfeelingness, a cold temper, or inhuman heart. But tobacco inspires courage of another kind, deliberate, yet immovable; affectionate and feeling, yet despising danger. Since I have used this great catholicon, I suspect that Cato and John Rogers were not unacquainted with the virtues of the goodly leaf; else whence derived they their firmness? Oh! tobacco, how many hearts hast thou saved from the destructions of coquetry! How many throats of bankrupts hast thou preserved from their own penknives!

Come, then, tobacco, new-found friend,
Come, and thy suppliant attend
  In each dull, lonely hour;
And though misfortunes lie around,
Thicker than hailstones on the ground,
  I'll rest upon thy power.
Then, while the coxcomb pert and proud,
The politician learned and loud,
  Keep one eternal clack,
I'll tread where silent nature smiles,
Where solitude our woes beguiles,
  And chew thee, dear tobac.

If you will write me immediately, dear Hervey, and inform me where I shall find you, I will set out in the course of a few weeks. I would not ride forty miles to see anybody living but yourself; but since 'tis you, I will do it gladly. I have a thousand things to talk about beside my tobacco. College still has its impressions. My thoughts will look back to Hanover now and then, but as they cannot contemplate you there, they turn back dissatisfied. Ezekiel sets out next week for the place of his residence. I shall send the Carey letters by him to Hanover, where he will put them in the mail.

Lemuel is reading divinity at Boscawen with Mr. Wood, and is the only one of our class I have seen since the valedictory day. You will see the propriety of apologizing as much as possible for the sterility of Commencement. Tell people it is because they discouraged genius.

I hope to squeeze your hand soon; till when I have no other enjoyment than books afford, together with the society of my second Hervey, Abbott, and Mr. Thompson, who, when he relaxes from business, which he prosecutes with unwearied attention, is entertaining and instructive.

Good-bye, Jemmy; you may guess, but I cannot tell, how much happiness is wished you by

D. Webster.

P. S. Look, I really have written this illegibly and inaccurately. Pray let no one see it, for though it is shameful to be under the necessity of such a request, I am unwilling to be exposed. Present me to your parents and friends with respect.

MR. WEBSTER TO MR. COFFIN.

Salisbury, October 3, 1801.

Dear Sir,—You will have the goodness to pardon me for not sending you a catalogue by Mr. Whitmore; he left so abruptly, that it was out of my power. I now enclose you two, and wish you much entertainment in the perusal.

I fell into a law office, pretty much by casualty, after Commencement, where I am at present. Considering how long I must read, prospects are not very flattering, but perhaps I may find room hereafter in some wilderness, where the violet has not resigned her tenement, to make writs without disturbance of rivals, if there should be nobody to purchase.

Our Commencement was not so long in exercises as is usual. I hope, however, the audience accepted what was performed well. Lyman, it is said, gave a good Philosophic. The Valedictory was thought decent. The Forensic and Dialogue were not so argumentative and amusing; the other performances were in unknown tongues.

Our class are much inclined to the law, but I believe we have all mistaken our talents. We have those that might be good divines, and perhaps eminent physicians. But, in honesty, it is not my opinion that any individual has brilliancy, and at the same time penetration and judgment enough, for a great law character.

Present me, if you will, to Mrs. and Mr. Mellen; to friends Charles, Noyes, &c., and assure yourself of the esteem of

DANIEL WEBSTER.

P. S. Please give me an account of the business I left at your office.

MR. WEBSTER TO MR. BINGHAM.

Salisbury, October 26, 1801.

O BINGHAM, and Bingham forever! There is a kind of magic in your pen; I know not how it is, but if you write in a language perfectly unknown, you afford me more pleasure than a well-penned and intelligible letter from a common friend. Of all folks in the world I should last think of flattering you; but, in honesty, I knew not how closely our feelings were interwoven; had no idea how hard it would be to live apart, when the hope of living together again no longer existed. However it may be thought rebellion against nature, I must confess, if I were this day to embark for Europe, my regret at leaving any other person would not be greater than at leaving you. You may judge therefore, whether your letters are not acceptable.

I rejoice most heartily to learn that you are settled so agreeably. Charlestown must be a pleasant place. Though your cousin Solon be absent, yet you will, no doubt, find friends. I agree with you, that Mr. Hale is one of the best "*fraters.*" So far as I know him, I highly respect him.

Report speaks extremely well of Mr. West; representing him as the oracle of the law, in Cheshire County. The only objection I ever heard against him, is his unwillingness to enter into public employment, at a period when the perverse nature of the times renders his talents and character necessary. You must, I think, make proficiency with him; if I judge from your progress hitherto, you will take your leave of me soon. You have actually read almost as much law as I, though you have been at it not half so long. I was reading Shakespeare, when I received your letter, but soon laid him by, and took up Blackstone.

Mr. Thompson has gone to Boston, Mr. Abbott to Salem, and I am in consequence alone, and shall be probably for some weeks. I have made some few writs, and am now about to bring an action of trespass for breaking a violin. The owner of the violin was at a husking, where "His jarring concord, and his discord dulcet" were making the girls skip over the husks as nimbly as Virgil's Camilla over the tops of the corn, till an old surly creature caught his fiddle and broke it against the wall. For the sake of having plump witnesses, the plaintiff will summon all the girls to attend the trial at Concord.

If the Funeral Oration be thought decent, I am contented; equal to the subject it is not. The death of Simonds was a theme on which the first writers ought to be proud to point their pens. "*Hei mihi! Qualis erat!*" I know not how many times I have been asked, whether you were not to read law in this quarter. A lady observed, she should be very well pleased to have Mr. B. in the office. Surely she would not be more pleased than I. My old friend Harper is expected here soon, to finish his reading. A rich acquisition to the gallantry of our office. The scarcity of company here renders it impossible to spend time pleasantly abroad; for entertainment, I betake myself to Mr. T.'s *belles-lettres* library, which affords a pretty variety of reading. How Mr. Harper will relish our amusements is not to be told; I wish he may be pleased.

Friend Lemy is at Mr. Wood's, reading the best of all professions. He certainly has gained cent. per cent. the last year. Campbell went to Concord after Commencement, and rode round with Miss Abbott; he 's gone! Cupid has bored his heart through like a sieve. Doctor Gridley is really doing well; he thinks you neglect him in not writing to him.

"Powerful," indeed, is our representation to Congress. Goodrich, Granger, Edwards, step ye aside! I have not heard a word from F. Hunt; nor from Herbert. Am alarmed at intelligence from Clarke; he is said to be declining visibly! Brackett, I believe, is in good health . . .

Afternoon.—The most unpleasant information I have yet to communicate. The "state of things" renders it highly doubtful whether I stay in this office two weeks! I certainly shall not under present circumstances. My father sets out on a journey next week, the issue of which will determine me. It mortifies me, beyond expression, to relinquish my study at this period; but I cannot, cannot help it! Necessity is unrelenting and imperious. If I should leave this place, I look to the Province of Maine for residence; or perhaps Salem. Am I to run Carey's race? O! O! Dear Hervey, how changeable is fortune! Seven weeks ago I was fixed, and you wavering; now you are settled, and I probably on the point of removing. I never was half so much dispirited as now. Though I make myself easy as I can, yet I am really very unpleasantly circumstanced. Well, I owe submission to the awards of Providence. I will submit. I must see you before I go, if I should go, for probably I shall not meet you again very soon.

I look with great anxiety to the termination of next week. May it be successful!! Good-bye, James, may mercy take care of you. Accept all the tenderness I have.

D. WEBSTER.

Mr. Thompson is made Trustee of Dartmouth College.

Doctor Gerrish is anxious to see you. Of nobody he talks so much when I see him. I tell him you will no doubt visit Sanbornton in the winter, and we calculate on having a good interview. But I am resolved to see you before winter, else, perhaps, I shall see you not at all. Lovejoy is happy as a churchman with his new little wife. All the rest of Sanbornton is just as you left it. Doctor G. lives in his own house; has taken in a family.

I thank you for your receipt for greasing boots. Have this

afternoon to ride to the South road, and in truth my boots admit not only water, but peas and gravel-stones. I wish I had better ones. As for my new "friend tobacco," he is like most of that name; has made me twice sick and is now dismissed.

Heigho! A man wants a remedy against his neighbor, whose lips were found damage feasant on his, the plaintiff's, wife's cheek! What is to be done? But you have not read the law about kissing. I will write for advice and direction to Barrister Fuller.

N. B. Let no one know that I think of quitting these realms.

Write often, my best friend, for these conveniences of correspondence may not last long. As you once told me, "write soon, write very soon, write now!"

MR. WEBSTER TO MR. BINGHAM.

Salisbury, December 8, 1801.

My best Friend,—Some few days since I received your letter dated October 30. What accident retarded it so long I know not, but I was almost afraid that you had forgotten to write me. Perhaps it was detained at Hanover, though I could wish it to hurry through that place as fast as possible. When I wrote you last, I had little expectation of writing you again from this place. Having found myself at home after Commencement, I found on consideration, that it would be impossible for my father, under existing circumstances, to continue Ezekiel at college. Drained of all his little income by the expenses of my education thus far, and broken down in his exertions by some ever lamented family occurrences, I saw he could not afford Ezekiel means to live abroad with ease and independence, and I knew too well the evils of penury to wish him to stay half beggared at college. I thought it therefore my duty to suffer some delay in my profession, for the sake of serving my elder brother, and was making a little interest in some places to the eastward, for an employment. My father, however, determined, if possible, to hire a few hundreds, till future days, being very averse to my leaving him. He accordingly rode to Exeter, told his Excellency*

* Governor Gilman.

of the state of affairs, and the good Governor helped him to what he wanted, on reasonable terms. This was much more favorable than I expected, and I have now hopes of continuing here for the present. Scarcely five miles absent from this place have I been since Commencement. I defer all short visits, till I can put them together, and make them reach Charlestown. You say I must be there in May; but I say I must see you before that time. I will not consent to your propositions, if they put our meeting so far forward. Ezekiel tells me you have been at Hanover. Well, what did you see and hear? I think I can answer myself. You saw Nabby and heard Wisdom sing. Did the girls all smile on you? Did Weld rejoice to see you? Did Shattuck reach out slowly an honest hand? Did Merrill call to see you, and did good Sir * * *, with a hypocritical smile, and a bishop's bow, say, "How do you, Mr. Bingham?" and falsely add, "I'm glad to see you?" All this, I make no doubt, took place. Hammond picked a bone with me at Thanksgiving; there is an honesty about him I always loved, though it is sometimes quite unaccommodating to squeamish stomachs. He tells me that the U. F. are full in all their cases, times, and modes, while the Socials *gaudent vocativo*, which, you know, is almost always wanting. I fear Hammond is in a labyrinth of entanglements. Mary, *la bonne*, I suspect, sends her heart after him wherever he goes. If there were to be a new edition of human nature, I think it would be found expedient to give the girls stronger ribs and a thicker pericardium. I say a plague to the girls, if they cant keep their little beaters at home.

The only news I hear, is the marriage of our classmate Taylor! Can you believe it, it staggers my conceptions absolutely. Methinks I can this moment see the good man, in his usual altitude, addressing his mate, and with clerical gestures breathing out the pathos of the English Iliad, thro' "hems" and "hahs."

"Andromache—my—soul's—far—better—pa-part!!"

The day of his marriage he thinks, no doubt, the first of his happiness; the language of Milton will aptly apply,

"All Heaven
And happy constellations on that hour
Shed their selectest influence!"

Freeborn called and spent four or five days with me lately; he is now at Hanover with Dr. Smith. Noyes is keeping school, school, school. Bliss is reading divinity with Mr. Wood.

Since Gideon became Postmaster-General, Mr. Thompson is uncertain about his continuance in the deputy post-office. He is acquainted with Gideon, and thinks it a good time to see whether democratic rage is stronger than every other principle. But I think Gideon will oust him, for there are several gentlemen this way, who are heirs in expectancy and reversion, and they will make every endeavor to get it for themselves, as they suppose, poor souls, that an office which affords eight or ten dollars per annum, will make them rich!

I have read Robertson, Vattel, and three volumes of Blackstone, and a little miscellaneous stuff of no account. I hope to go on more rapidly now, for I feel more at ease than I have done heretofore. My old and good friend, Harper, is with us. I presume he will give us an oration on the 28th instant, on Free Masonry. No doubt he will be eloquent and impressive, and though anti-masonic Robison were now groaning in Tartarus, the flashes of Harper's genius would enlighten his black atmosphere, and dart truth and conviction into the recesses of Pluto's kingdom!!

Mr. Abbott is my only inmate; he is good and friendly, and I shall sincerely lament the hour that takes him from the office. I wish you knew him; you would surely respect him.

Do write me every time you think you can afford it. I wish to write often, very often, for your letters to me I prize at the value of a "cow and calf."

Depend on it, I will see you the first visit I make, and depend, too, that I ever shall esteem you,

"My true and honorable friend,
As dear to me as are the ruddy drops
That visit my sad heart."

DANIEL WEBSTER.

Postscript. I see no ladies; they are scarce articles with us. The *Damas* are all at Charlestown. Do give my love to some of them, for you know my heart always overflows with affection for the sex. Where do you board? Will you write me next mail?

Do you hear from C.? Tell me about him if so. Give my best respects to your honored father, Captain Minor, &c.

Good-bye, Good Boy. D. W.

"Ireland's Hogarth" I know would delight me. Painting and statuary are arts of which I have very imperfect conceptions. Poetry I have read and music have heard, but the speaking canvas and the breathing marble are not familiar to me. If I can, I will tarry with you long enough to peruse it. Have you read Cowper's piece on Conversation? You will find it in his first volume of poems, and I promise you pay for reading it. It snowed some last night, I rejoice to see it. How innocent Madam Nature looks with such a zone about her! Is it not prettier than the red ribbons of our Misses? Red is a bloody color; I like it not.

MR. WEBSTER TO MR. FULLER.

Since, friend Habijah, you are thus distrest,
Since Love's fierce tortures thus inflame your breast,
Since * * * 's charms forever haunt your dreams,
And her fair form before you always seems,
A little poetry, perhaps, might roll
Love's boiling torrent from your troubled soul.
I too, with Muses straying thro' the grove,
May soothe my pains, though not the pains of love.
For those blest fields, where Love's gay Graces reign,
I once have tried, and tried, alas! in vain.
No longer on those verdant banks I tread,
No longer wander o'er the flowery mead;

Those fragrant lawns of Love, which you explore,
I once, perhaps, have known, but know no more.

Come then, together let us beat the field,
Where Arts and Science their best laurels yield,
Together let us climb the ethereal height,
Where Freedom's flambeaux shed a living light!
To sing Columbia, then, shall be our care,
Her arts, her arms, her heroes, and her fair.
Columbia, hail! Thy glories fire my song,
Thy worth deserves, to thee the bays belong!
See Science glow within thy peaceful realm,
See her bright blaze old ignorance o'erwhelm!
See yon proud dome now register her name!
See Dartmouth blazon the bright rolls of fame!
Columbia's arms, too, soon shall awe the world,
And kings and tyrants from their thrones be hurled,
Her every hero shall a Eugene prove,
And bow to no one, but the thundering Jove.
Her fair now rival Argos's nymphs divine,
Though all her daughters, not like * * * shine,
For when she gently rolls that sparkling eye,
When her soft bosom heaves the tender sigh,
Not Venus' self to Paris did appear
Half so divine, so lovely, or so fair!!

D. WEBSTER.

MR. WEBSTER TO MR. BINGHAM.

Fryeburg, February 25, 1802.

MY GOOD HERVEY,—The date of this will inform you where I am. Yes, James, I am at Fryeburg. I came here six weeks ago, and took charge of the Academy. My engagements are for two quarters, and the probability is I shall then leave here. It is quite an object with me to put myself into some urbanic place, the time I am out of study. Nothing here is unpleasant;

there is a pretty little society. The people treat me with kindness, and I have the fortune to find myself in a very good family. I see little female company, but that is an item with which I can conveniently enough dispense. Your old acquaintance, Mrs. Dana, lives next door, I am frequently there; they live in a neat, handsome, sociable style. Nabby is somewhat expected here soon; Mr. and Mrs. Dana are now gone to Hanover, and will wish her to return with them. O, Bingham! But a schoolmaster must not sigh. Having said so much about myself, I will next talk of you. You are not noted, that I know of, for paying your *devoirs* to that uncertain gossip called Fame; yet the creature, through some unaccountable fancy, seems disposed to treat you with caresses. Mr. Hutchins from Concord was here lately, and told me the proprietors of their public school had determined to write you a pressing invitation to accept the instruction of it. I gave him no encouragement, for I thought you in better business, but told him you were the man, if they could obtain you. If you should go, you will find every attention. H. is attempting to instruct there in music, and has rendered himself absolutely ridiculous. His Jacobinism has increased his infamy, for having written a frothy, silly, senseless, ungrammatical, misspelt letter to some of his democratical friends, it, perchance, got into the columns of the Courier, and was fine sport for our brother-students who live in that quarter.

Billings is keeping school at Sanbornton; he boards with Lovejoy. I was there on my way hither, and pressed Phœbe's hand, and inquired if she thought Mr. Billings a clever man; she said he was not clever like Mr. Bingham. I told her there were different ways of being clever; she smiled significantly, and was silent.

I have heard nothing from Hanover, since Zeke left it. He had just arrived at Salisbury when I set out for Fryeburg. * * * * wrote me that she was going to Connecticut. I wish her every blessing, but cannot tell what may arise hereafter. I don't know but my happiness must be sacrificed to hers. She said you had a letter for me, and intimated strongly that she wished me to see it. You may, if you please, put it into the mail, and direct to me at Fryeburg.

Solon, I fear, is shut out of business. The judiciary bill is knocked on the head. Smith will probably return to the bar. "This is a land of Liberty, and the Constitution." Huzza!

Do write me the very next mail, and add one more to that long chain of obligations, which bind to your bosom your everlasting friend,

D. Webster.

MR. WEBSTER TO MR. FULLER.

Fryeburg, February 26, 1802.

Once more to prattle on her darling theme,
Once more to wake the soft mellifluous stream,
That brings us all our blessings as it flows,
Whose currents Friendship's golden ore disclose,
The Muse essays her little skill;
And tho' her lightsome lay,
No master's hand display,
Tho' loose her lyre and wild her song,
Though Seraph fire tip not her tongue,
The friend—Oh! such a friend—will hear her still.
O Memory! thou Protean friend, or foe,
Parent of half our joy, and half our woe!
Thou dost the rapture which I feel impart,
And thou the griefs that press around my heart;
Thine is a motley train;
Despondence there is seen,
And Sorrow, palefaced queen;
And Gladness there, with merry face,
That ne'er did wear a sad grimace,
And buxom Pleasure sporting o'er the plain.

* * * * * * * * *

* * * * * * * * *

Next moment, lo! Appears
Some plenteous cause of tears;
Some pleasure fled, for pleasure flies,
Or Symonds, sped beyond the skies,
And memory cancels all the good she grants—

But if I poetize further upon *Memory*, I shall not have room to tell you half what I wish. So sweet Miss Muse, we will dismiss you.

Friend Shattuck may have told you that I am here. 'Tis true, Habijah, contrary to all my expectations I am here. I cannot now address you as a brother-student in law, I am neither more nor less than a schoolmaster, and as such you will not, perhaps, feel yourself much flattered to hear from me. You will naturally enough inquire what circumstances have induced me to relinquish the law. I will answer all your questions when I see you next. Till then be satisfied with this, that I thought it best. Six weeks I have been on this ground; in about five or six months, it is not improbable I shall leave it. Which way my next motion will be, it is not to be told or known.

* * * * * * * * * *

I have been writing some poetry. I shall not inform you what I have written, but, from the accompanying inimitable apostrophe to memory, you will judge of the quality of all I have written.

You will possibly wish to ask how many Misses there are here. I do not precisely know. I forgot to bring a stick, to cut a notch, like the Indian, for every one I see; but I have heard no complaint of scarcity. There is one who is amiable, and who has this moment passed by this table. 'Tis her opinion, it seems, that "Mr. Webster is a very bashful man." He will never give her reason to think otherwise. But these things are all vanity. I was last at Concord in September or October. I can tell nothing about your friends there. Our visit in June is blown over, but you must go without me; you will have a better visit.

If it will not be burdensome, pray write me a word, I mean a good many words, by Esquire Dana. I want to hear a good deal about old Han. Pray be particular and long in your account of that place. Whatever you can make acceptable to your family, whether love, respects, or compliments, pray give them from me. Brother Shattuck is entitled to a high place in my memory, and tell him he possesses it. I cannot tell when I may see you, but if I live and have health, I shall expect to dart an eye upon the I. C. School as soon as next Commencement, surely and without fail. D. WEBSTER.

How are your parents, your sisters, your friends. In short, how is every thing? And, above all, are you the Newsboy's message-maker? Who is Bum? Do answer all these things, and oblige THE SCHOOLMASTER.

Mr. Dana is the only neighbor I call on with great pleasure and little ceremony. I have exalted ideas of his lady. I can say with Shakespeare, that she is one "who paragons description and wild fame."

Mr. Dana is quite good and civil... Have you heard from Bing. Gil. Nye, or any other of our friends? Clark, Bracket, and Her.?

MR. WEBSTER TO MR. FULLER.

Salisbury, May 3, 1802.

FRIEND FULLER,—If you had not offered an excuse, still as it is, your long silence had been forgiven you. That fancy that roams in "orbs beyond Herschel," hardly stoops to the humbler sphere of friendship and correspondence; and while we are pleased with its flights, we must excuse any neglect it occasions. Really, it pleases me to see you on the Muses' wing again, and I must be allowed to say that Telephus's Ode to Washington hath in it some true relish of the Parnassian waters. I hope you will find Maine more suited to poetry than I did; although I rattled in as many as twenty rhymes while in that Province. These, you know, are a pretty large number for me. To be serious, if you find it convenient, I would earnestly advise you to cultivate any propensity to poetry which you may possess. I do the same by myself, not from any wish to show my productions to the world, but for amusement, and to keep alive some taste for the *belles-lettres.* The law is certainly, as seems to me, rather hard study, and to mollify it with some literary amusements I should think profitable.

Hanoverians, you perceive, ever searching for novelty, have started the project of a Literary Tablet. How do you think it will succeed? My own expectations are not, I confess, very sanguine. The repeated failures of such attempts forebode disaster to the Tablet. However, I wish it well. Do you calculate on becoming a writer for it? Say, honestly. If such a thing should commence, suppose we take some little pains to start up some of our classmates now scattered over the world's wide wilderness, to hold a friendly chit-chat together in the columns of the paper? Will it do, or are we all too great dunces to write a paragraph? I have another whim in my head which may prevent me, otherwise I would be willing, in conjunction with my friends, to make one serious effort to render the Tablet respectable.

Your "excellent society of ladies" is almost enviable. If the "Beauties of the West" will not compare with them, I am sure you will never be able to resist. Ere this, I could warrant, you are gone, gone hook and line, and love betide you! It is true, as you say, that there is prospect of all the Hanover *Ribs* being sold before you and I can become purchasers. How do you think it would do to forestall the market, and, for the sake of security, to bespeak a Rib in season? Hah, hah, hah.

I am now in expectation of making a visit to old Hanover at Commencement, if I can learn that any choice friends will be there. Do you expect to attend? I hope you will. Pray let me know soon if you shall be at Commencement, as my determination is not to go unless I can understand that my friends will be there.

* * * * * * * * * *

Yours, dear Fuller, very sincerely,

DANIEL WEBSTER.

MR. WEBSTER TO MR. BINGHAM.

Fryeburg, May 18, 1802.

"DEARLY BELOVED,—Suffer me to bespeak your attention for about six hours, to the volume I am about to write to you. Having just rambled to the adjacent intervals, which on account of the late rains are all overflowed, and exhibiting almost a "shoreless ocean," I set myself down by the parlor fire to improve a moderate degree of health and spirits, in addressing almost the earliest friend I have on earth. I have a good many things to talk about, and am not disposed to curtail the conversation. Since I wrote you before, I have been within forty miles of you; but stay, I am too far forward. About three weeks ago we had our semi-annual exhibition. The performances of the school were such, I believe, as gave satisfaction to the Trustees. In truth, I was not much ashamed of their appearance. The Trustees were pleased to pass a vote of thanks, as also to present their preceptor a small extraordinary gratuity. Following exhibition was a vacation of 2½ weeks. Forgive me for writing in figures. I shall be glad if I can find paper for all I have to say to you, without stating my ideas by Algebra. This vacation I had devoted to the reading of Sallust, but on the day of Exhibition I had a letter informing me that 'Zeke' was very sick at college. I had heard also that a young man at Salisbury, who was just about marrying my oldest sister, was on the verge of death, and had expressed very particular and urgent reasons for seeing me once more. Under these circumstances I immediately set out for New Hampshire. I wênt directly to Hanover, where I found my brother on the recovery, though much out of sorts. There also I saw Fanny and kissed her, nobody else. She was in decent health when I first saw her, but was taken with the cramp the night I arrived. I said but little to her. I also saw Sophia; the palpitation at her heart will not, I fear, suffer her to be a great while company for us mortals. She has frequently, you know, been charged with having palpitations of that organ, but I think she has one attached to her now that may produce greater evils than any preceding one. I had not opportunity to chat with her save in company. Mary Woodward I shook by the hand, and was treated by her with more respect than that family have ever before shown me. Tenney was there; he had a hard time with the measles, though some thought the measles had the hardest time. I met with Merrill; we have agreed to correspond. He mentioned with much satisfaction some letters he had received from you. I said "Yes, Sir" to Shattuck, winked at Fuller, and shook hands with Freeborn, and drank an Indian health with Hammond, Cooke, &c. Nabby was at Woodstock. I saw her not, yet I think I looked that way to see about the weather. Being so near, I wished beyond expression to ride to that place where my Hervey lives; but the vacation was so short I could at most have tarried but one night, which would have been tantalizing to my feelings. I therefore adjourned it till September, when I expect to leave this place, and when, if it please Providence to preserve me, I shall spend a week with you, certainly, certainly.

When I reached Salisbury, I found that the young man whom I mentioned in the first page of this document, had been dead several days. To the last he appeared oppressed with something he would reveal to no one living but myself, and that opportunity never occurred. What this was, I cannot conjecture; it might be something important, and it might be a whim of a sick man's fancy. If he had done me any injury for which he wished forgiveness, God knows I heartily forgive him. Peace to him!

I saw our classmate, Noyes, in Concord; a brother pedagogue. The Hon. Sirs. Merrill, Noyes, and Webster I would have called, from their profession, Messrs. "Syncope," "Verbum Personale," and "Nominativo Gaudent;" these would be pompous and sonorous names, significant of the high honors we bear, being clothed, like Mr. Jefferson, "in the mantle of our country's confidence." By the way, if the mantle of public confidence be such a robe as I consider his Excellency wearing, it would be my preference to wander about like the prophets of old, in sheep-skins and goat-skins; but we shall talk more of politics in the next volume. I will go right on with my story,

> "And jog on steady by the road,"
> "Nor wander into episode."

I spent a few days at Salisbury, and thence took my departure again for this place. Had a pleasant journey, save the inconvenience which arose from bad roads and bad taverns. I came to one innkeeper's by name Knight. From his appearance I thought he could be no Knight of the 'Garter,' or of the Bath, but because I was much annoyed by a creature that stood in the corner, I put him down for a Knight of the Blue Dyepot.

I arrived here last night; but must fill this page by relating a little anecdote that happened yesterday. I accidentally fell in with one of my scholars, on his return to the academy. He was mounted on the ugliest horse I ever saw or heard of, except "Sancho Panza's" pacer. As I had two horses with me, I proposed to him to ride one of them, and tie his bag fast to his Bucephalus; he did accordingly, and turned her forward, where her odd appearance, indescribable gait, and frequent stumblings, afforded us constant amusement. At length we approached Saco River, a very wide, deep, and rapid stream, when this satire on the animal creation, as if to revenge herself on us for our sarcasms, plunged into the river, then very high by the freshet, and was wafted down the current like a bag of oats! I could scarcely sit on my horse for laughter. I am apt to laugh at the vexations of my friends. The fellow, who was of my own age, and my room-mate, half checked the current, by oaths as big as lobsters, and the old Rosinante, who was all the while much at her ease, floated up among the willows far below on the opposite shore.

END OF THE FIRST VOLUME.

P. S. I am now going in to see Mrs. Dana; when I return, I will go about the remainder of the work.

VOLUME II.

I will in this volume, my dear Hervey, give you some account of my circumstances, feelings, and prospects. The salary afforded me is three hundred and fifty dollars exclusive; board is one dollar and seventy-five cents; this is my academic engagement. Fortune, like other females, does not always frown. My landlord is Register; and as he is extensively in business I do the writing of his office; this is a little decent perquisite. If I will tarry, the Board will increase my salary, and do every thing for me in their power. A compensation annually of five or six hundred dollars, a house to live in, a piece of land to cultivate, and, *inter nos solos*, a clerkship of the Common Pleas, are now probably within the reach and possession of your friend, D. W.

What shall I do? Shall I say "Yes, Gentlemen," and sit down here to spend my days in a kind of comfortable privacy, or shall I relinquish these prospects, and enter into a profession where my feelings will be constantly harrowed by objects either of dishonesty or misfortune; where my living must be squeezed from penury, (for rich folks seldom go to law,) and my moral principle continually be at hazard? I agree with you that the law is well calculated to draw forth the powers of the mind, but what are its effects on the heart; are they equally propitious? Does it inspire benevolence and awake tenderness; or does it, by a frequent repetition of wretched objects, blunt sensibility and stifle the still, small voice of mercy?

The talent with which Heaven has intrusted me is small, very small, yet I feel responsible for the use of it, and am not willing to pervert it to purposes reproachful or unjust, nor to hide it, like the slothful servant, in a napkin.

Now, I will enumerate the inducements that draw me towards the law. First and principally, it is my father's wish. He does not dictate, it is true, but how much short of dictation is the mere wish of a parent, whose labors of life are wasted on favors to his children? Even the delicacy with which this wish is expressed, gives it more effect than it would have in the form of a command. Secondly, my friends generally wish it. They are urgent and pressing. My father even offers me—I will some time tell you what—and Mr. Thompson offers my tuition gratis, and to relinquish his stand to me.

On the whole, I imagine I shall make one more trial in the ensuing autumn. If I prosecute the profession, I pray God to fortify me against its temptations. To the winds I dismiss those light hopes of eminence which ambition inspired and vanity fostered. To be "honest, to be capable, to be faithful" to my client and my conscience, I earnestly hope will be my first endeavor. I believe you, my worthy boy, when you tell me what are your intentions. I have long known and long loved the honesty of your heart. But let us not rely too much on ourselves; let us look to some less fallible guide, to direct us among the temptations that surround us.

Good-night; to-morrow I will finish this. How pleasant would be this eve, if I could chat it away with J. H. B.

Wednesday Morning. In politics, my friend, we coincide in sentiment. With you I believe that the present administration cannot long be popular. Our Constitution has left, it is true, a wide field for the exertions of democratic intrigue, while it has strongly fortified against executive encroachments; this is the general nature and construction of governments perfectly free. They are much better secured against tyranny than against licentiousness. Yet it has been said with as much truth as eloquence, that "the thunderbolt of despotism is not more fatal to public liberty, than the earthquake of popular commotion." It would be a phenomenon in history, it would be like a comet which appears but once in a hundred centuries, if there should be found a government advancing to despotism by regular and progressive encroachment. The path to despotism leads through the mire and dirt of uncontrolled democracy. When this government falls, it will owe its destruction to some administration that sets out in its career with much adulation to the sovereign people, much profession of economy and reform, and it will then proceed to prostrate the fairest institutions of government by the pretext of saving expense, but really for the sake of destroying constitutional checks.

The late Congress have done wonders; they, however, have greater wonders to perform, if they can convince the people of America universally that they have done right. The business of destruction has progressed charmingly, and its effects have been felt. Bayard, Morris, and Tracy have produced a change in the public sentiment which will continue. The nation, I hope in Heaven, will awake to some view of her situation. Boston and New York have determined to return to their first love; the commercial interest will follow them, and we shall have an "opening to better times." This Commonwealth, you see, continues strong in the service and in the faith. Federal characters have bestirred themselves; if I may be allowed a play upon words, they have turned out strong, to keep in Strong.[1]

Every advice I have from you gives me pleasure; pleasure it is indeed to hear that you are rapidly progressing in knowledge and reputation, almost the only things worth living for. I learnt at Hanover that your situation was very pleasant at Charlestown; that your virtues had secured you friends and admirers, and that your industry was proverbial. I find you are leaving the friends of your youth in the background; but remember, Jemmy, we will not suffer you to run away with all the reputation without a contest.

I shall occasionally address you a volume through the summer, and am happy in the opportunity which this affords me of expressing my eternal attachment, to my dearest J. H. B.

DAN'L WEBSTER, *Ped.*

[1] An allusion to Caleb Strong, Governor of Massachusetts, to which Maine at that time belonged. He was the candidate of the Federal party.

MR. WEBSTER TO MR. PORTER.

Fryeburg, June 4, 1802.

HEALTH to my friends! began my earliest song,
Health to my friends! my latest shall prolong,
Nor health alone—be four more blessings thine,
Cash and the Fair one, Friendship and the Nine.
Are these too little? Dost thou pant for fame?
Give him ye Powers the bubble of a name!
Ask all of Heaven an honest man should dare,
And Heaven will grant it, if it hear my prayer.
'Tis true, let Locke deny it to the last,
Man has three beings, Present, Future, Past,
We are, we were, we shall be; this contains
The field of all our pleasures and our pains.
Enjoyment makes the present hour its own,
And Hope looks forward into worlds unknown;
While backward turn'd, our thoughts incessant stray
And mid the fairy forms of memory play.
Say, does the present ill afflict thee more,
Than that impending o'er a future hour?
Or does this moment's blessing more delight,
Than hope's gay vision fluttering in thy sight?
Call now the events of former years to view,
And live in fancy all thy life anew.
Do not the things that many years ago,
Gave woe or joy, now give thee joy or woe?
In this review, as former times pass by,
Dost thou not laugh again, or weep or sigh?
Dost thou not change, as changing scenes advance,
Mourn with a friend, or frolic at the dance?
Think when thy worth attracted SIMONDS first,
And with new sorrow give him to the dust?
With present time thus Hope and Memory join,
This to bear back, and that to extend the line,
And all must own, except some learned dunce,
That every man lives three times and at once.
I'll state a case; but Vanity, the elf,
Obliges me to state it of myself.

In latitude some more than forty-three,
And longitude, say seventy-first degree,
Where Saco rolls, (a name so rough and fierce
It frights the Muse to bring it into verse,)
Tied to my school, like cuckold to his wife,
Whom God knows he'd be rid of, runs my life.
Six hours to yonder little dome a day,
The rest to books, to friendship, and my tea;
And now and then, as varying fancies choose,
To trifle with young Mary, or the Muse.
This life, tho' pleasant of its kind, is yet
Much too inactive, I'm resolved to quit.
Now Spring comes on, her milder sceptre wields,
And fairly fights stern Winter from our fields.
Yon grassy glade with gaudiest tulip dressed,
Where the Muse wanders "willing to be pressed,"
Where "Doves" gay frolicking on ulmar "boughs"
Force one to instant rhyme, of "Loves" and "Vows,"
Would be delightful, were that thing called mind
Pleased with the present and to fate resigned;
But on the soul if wild ambition seize,
Farewell, as Horace sings, I think, to peace!
Our college life, whate'er the proud may say,
To our existence is the month of May.
O then I knew not, or I felt not, care;
Thoughts, free as nature, and as light as air.
Yet even then, ingratitude how base!
We thought we lived in quite a piteous case,
E'en then we deemed our fates were much to blame,
And called Miss Fortune many a saucy name,
Though life's gay stream ran dimpling all along,
Smooth as the numbers of a tuneful song.
There we had friends enough, and books a score,
Appointments some and disappointments more;
Could court the Muse and as you know dispense,
For pretty little rhymes, with all our sense.
Could sit down sociable as mother Bunch,
And "dip in sentiment," or "dip in punch"—
May Heaven forgive the man who with all these
Cannot find cause enough to be at ease!

God gave me pride—I thank him; if he choose,
To give me what shall make that pride of use,
Chance and the talent, I'll adore his Will;
If he deny them, I'll adore it still.
Now Hope leans forward on Life's slender line,
Shows me a doctor, lawyer, or divine,
Ardent springs forward to the distant goal,
But indecision clogs the eager soul.
Heaven bless my friend, and when he marks his way,
And takes his bearings o'er life's troubled sea,
In that important moment may he find
Choice and his friends and duty all combined!
And Heaven grant me, whatever luck betide,
Be fame or fortune given or denied,
Some cordial friend to meet my warm desire,
Honest as John and good as Nehemiah.

D. WEBSTER.

MR. WEBSTER TO MR. PORTER.

DEAR JOHN, Since writing the within I had the pleasure of yours by Mr. Hall. You are truly very good to remember an old friend in absence, and the date of this will inform you that I was not behind you. I rejoice to hear that F. is in a way to recover; she seems to be a peculiar mark for the arrows of affliction. 'Tis true, as you say, that misfortunes fall on the most worthy, and that they fall in crowds: "Woes cluster, rare are solitary woes." There is no doubt design in all this, whether we perceive it or not. The reason you assign I think not a wild one. Mr. Bingham's death gave me a momentary surprise. I would mingle with the family on this occasion whatever their feeling is, or should be.

Federalism, it seems, revives. 'Tis a good cause, and it must prevail. It unites in its support more than two thirds of the talent, the character, and the property of the nation. This is too much for any administration to contend with. I congratulate you on choosing Merrill: he certainly should have received my vote had I been on the ground.

My best love to Nehemiah, I shall write next opportunity; read the enclosed and deliver. Adieu. D. W.

MR. WEBSTER TO MR. MERRILL.

Fryeburg, June 7, 1802.

My dear Friend,—I have frequently taken up my pen to write to you since I arrived here, and have as often laid it down again without executing my purpose. The truth is, I was willing to write you something a little better than my correspondents generally have the fortune to receive. But, after all, I am commencing in my old way, resolved not to delay till chance might inspire me with an idea worth your reading, lest you should suppose me backward in entering into a correspondence, which I contemplate with pleasure.

You must therefore console yourself with reflecting that correspondence is a kind of commerce, where the greatest gain per cent. uniformly attaches to the greatest capital, and that there is as much to be learned in writing a good letter, as in reading one. Besides, you will remember that I am in Pequawket, a most savage name, and you will therefore suppose a most savage country. Whenever, therefore, I am dull and blundering you must not charge the fault upon me, but upon Pequawket; thus I shall shift much responsibility from my own shoulders. I will, if you please, devote this to giving you some little account of my situation, business, amusements, and so forth; and beg of you a description of yours. Whatever relates to my school you can guess in the general, and particulars cannot be interesting. This village is new but growing, already much crowded with merchants, doctors, and lawyers. There are here a good number of men of information and conversable manners, whom I visit without ceremony, and chat with as I should with you and Bingham. Among these are Mr. Dana, whom you know, and Mr. McGaw, who boards and lodges with me.

Fame has told me, though she is said to be a notorious liar, that you are a finished gallant; it will be natural therefore for you to inquire about the number and beauty of our Misses.

In point of beauty, I do not feel competent to decide. I cannot calculate the precise value of a dimple, nor estimate the charms of an eyebrow, yet I see nothing repulsive in the appearance of Maine Misses. When Mr. McGaw told me he would introduce me to the Pequawket constellation, it sounded so oddly, that I could not tell whether he was going to show me *Virgo*, or *Ursa major*. Yet I had charity to put it down for the former, and have found no reason to alter my decision. Being a pedagogue and having many of the ladies in school, I cannot set out in a bold progress of gallantry, though I now and then make one of them my best bows and say a few things *piano*, as the musicians have it.

When I go into the study of a friend, I look about and inquire for the books he is reading; to save you that trouble, I will tell you my reading at present. I think it may be advantageous to communicate mutually an account of our studies, and reciprocate any new ideas that are worth it. I am now upon Williams's Vermont, which I never read before. 'Tis my object to investigate some facts relating to the political history of the United States.

I have been perusing, as an amusement, the "Pursuits of Literature," the book which has excited so much curiosity among the learned, and called down so much condemnation of democracy. I am not certain you ever read it, because I do not recollect having seen it at Hanover. I think it well worth a reading. The scantiness of the Poem itself, and the abundance of Notes, bring to my memory Sheridan's elegant metaphor of "a neat rivulet of text meandering thro' a meadow of margin."...

Report has just reached me that the marshal of N. H. is removed. I confess I did not much expect it, but these are Jefferson's doings, and they are marvellous in our eyes.

Adieu, my good friend. D. WEBSTER.

P. S. I congratulate the people of Hanover on the election of their anniversary orator; and wish him better success than some of his predecessors.

Wednesday Morning, June 9. Since I wrote the within, which I had intended for the mail, Messrs. Hall and Whitmore have called on me. I am quite sure you did not know of the opportunity of sending me by them. They tell me that Politics stand 120 to 14; good, good. The sun is everywhere rising. The waning orb of democracy must soon be eclipsed. The penumbra begins to come on already.

Pray put a line in next mail, for one who is much your friend.

D. W.

MR. WEBSTER TO MR. FULLER.

Fryeburg, June 11, 1802.

My dear Boy,—I hope you will not be vexed at me, when I tell you that I was a little vexed at you for not transmitting a word by Mr. Hall. I could not invent for you the least excuse, and was resolved to be silent in my turn. Last night, however, after tea, I lighted my cigar and took a turn among the meadows. Nature was all smiling, and by a kind of sympathy she drew me in to laugh with her, and my resentments all went off in fume; so this morning, about the time when you are hearing the prayer-bell with great composure, I am devoting a moment to my own, and I hope, to a friend's amusement. Were I a devotee to Cupid, I should improve this morning in penning something which I have heard called a love-letter. A romantic imagination might find, as I think, ample scope among meadows and dales, and "moss-crowned banks," and "purling rills," and "songsters of the grove," and "morning breezes," and other apparatus of love-poetry. How unfortunate, that I neither am, nor can feign myself to be, in love with some Dulcinea of such beauty as "paragon's description," such charms as force mankind to "worship where they dare not love," of such dignity and command in her aspect, and such unaffected modesty and reserve, that even "her shadow dare not follow her, when she goes to dress!" All these pretty sayings, picked up at the expense of so much time, must all be useless for lack of some one to address them to. Alas! Alas!

* * * * * * * * * *

Did you reveal any thing I told you of ****? If so, I am almost sorry, but forgive you.

Pray put a line in next mail for your old, your cordial friend,

D. Webster.

P. S. Distribute my love to whomever will receive it.

MR. WEBSTER TO MR. BINGHAM.

Fryeburg, July 22, 1802.

Lovely Boy,—When one has nothing to say you would think he might as well be silent. But you know there are folks whose words are in inverse proportion to the ideas they convey. If I could write you one concise, elegant letter, which met my ideas of perfection, I would be mute for a season with great willingness; but I find myself obliged to send one written messenger to apologize for a former, and in this way am never like to be out of business. Some ten weeks ago, as I should think, I did myself the honor to address to you a huge folio, the longest I ever wrote, which is saying a good deal; and the dullest too, I fear, which is saying much more. I am suspicious you did not receive it, as it went by private hand, and as you never have answered it; to have answered it methodically, would be like a comment on the Law of Nations, yet you would certainly have notified me of the receipt of it. Your last letter, which I have received, was dated early in April. One, two, three, almost four months since! a vast while truly. Yet it proves that you are agreeably employed; for if you are at all like me, when "grief sits heavy at the heart," friends will occupy the next place.

Friday, 23. Since writing the above that "urbanic and extended figure," A. Alden has called, and spent a day with us. He possesses, I find, a "mind not to be changed by time nor place," and bating some extravagant eccentricities, would be an amusing fellow. He tells me that Mrs. Bingham is about removing to Oxford, since the death of her husbandman. I lately received a letter with this indifferent and insensible postscript, "Mr. Bingham is dead." It instantly struck me that . . . and I was chilled to petrifaction; God be praised, I could otherwise account for the postscript!

Augustus informs me, that the 5th of July was kept with rejoicing, and that friend Merrill delivered an oration well calculated to "magnify the federal cause and make it honorable." I have engaged him, "the said Merrill," in a correspondence, for I think him a worthy fellow, and almost the only S. F., who possesses any liberality of mind; though those pious folks would be very angry at me for saying so. By the way, Daniel Abbott writes me that he has been at Charlestown; that he saw and instantly knew you; that he shall no longer distrust physiognomy, and that you parted under agreement of correspondence. I rejoice if my name has been the means of introducing two of the best men in the world to each other. I would indeed give my pipe and its contents to see you together this lovely morning, before school, and that is more than I would do to see half the people in the world together. The hours devoted to the effusions of the heart are to me the most dear. In participation of sentiment and feeling, emotions of a tender and pleasing kind are excited; and the rhetoric of the eye and the hand puts me in rhapsodies sooner than that of Cicero or Chatham. "One may as well not be, as be" and be alone in the midst of society, devoted to himself, and excluded by suspicious jealousies from the bosom of others.

With much pleasure I observe the name of your worthy father on the list of Federal representatives this year. The Jacobins in the middle of the State had calculated with confidence, as I found when I was there, upon having a legislature after their own image. They were drunk with joy at the prospect; but the gentlemen may now "put a little water to their wine."

As to our friends, I can tell you but little. I correspond with few, and others I know nothing of. Brackett writes me that he is well situated at Rhinebeck, on Hudson River. He humorously informs me how he has been caught in the lure of an Albany heiress, like a pheasant in a snare. We ought, I think, to wish him, rather than her, a safe delivery. Clark informs me that he is still at Flushing, easy and contented, "living on the fat of the land." From Hanover I hear as often as the old gentleman Zek. sees fit to write to me, and now and then, though very seldom, I have a line from somebody else. And now, having modestly enough spent the bulk of three pages in talking about myself, I will reserve this space for a postscript, to acknowledge as I hope the receipt of one from you by the mail which is expected soon.

Good-bye, give your father the best respects of

DANIEL WEBSTER.

P. S. Well, the mail comes, but no wished-for letter. Yet Hervey will think of me soon and let me know it.

I have seen a letter from Portsmouth, which informs me that J. Wentworth, the democratic lawyer and ode-maker, has had a most severe flagellation from Jere. Mason, Esq., for personal abuse, and another from the editor of The Oracle.

MR. WEBSTER TO MR. FULLER.

I CANNOT read; to think is as bad; I will therefore write, though it be

Sunday, August 29, 1802.

DEAR CHEVALIER,—A handkerchief hoops my head, the bed supports my legs, and the table my arms. In this attitude of contemplation, perhaps you will rather think it an attitude of sleep, I have consumed three full minutes in thinking of some decent excuse for so long neglecting to write you. I despise to say, like a lazy collegian, "Unwell, Sir," nor can I say in truth, "Didn't hear the bell," since your last letters gave me quite an audible call. On the whole, I perceive none in which I shall get off with honor, unless I undertake an encomium on taciturnity, and say, that although men arrogantly boast of the privilege of speech, it is indeed a much greater privilege to be silent. But I think I will not retail the pretty sayings I have on this subject; they are better reserved "to decorate the morality of a Newspaper Essay." Your letter shall be drawn from my files, and answered methodically. *Imprimis*—you referred me to Alden for domestic news. I turned to that authority, and found a few pages fertile of the subject; among the rest that St. John paid you an agreeable visit, that you had a pleasant dance, &c. Now dancing is a good, and, as I suppose, an innocent amusement, but we never need go to halls and assembly rooms to enjoy it. The world is nothing but a contra-dance, and every one, *volens*, *nolens*, has a part in it. Some are sinking, others rising, others balancing, some gradually ascending towards the top, others flamingly leading down. Some cast off from Fame and Fortune, and some again in a comfortable *allemande* with both. If you should ask me what station I allot myself in this dance of life, I should be staggered to tell you, though I believe, by some confounded ill-luck, I have slipped a foot, and am fairly on the knee here in Pequawket. In your last letter but one, you insinuate that you can hardly write, because a certain Miss. had just passed your office. I know not who the said Miss. was, but will bet my tobacco-box that I can guess within three. It was either Mis-Fortune, or Mis-Information, or Mis-Conduct, and which of the three you must inform me. I fear you will be so uncharitable as to say the latter.

I was in Concord nearly a fortnight. A man is known by the company he keeps. I shall almost suspect the purity of your principles. "I hope," say you of the D.'s daughter, "that she has no affectation." I hope so too, but then we may sometimes hope what we do not believe. You add, "I believe her a good girl." If I were really her admirer, such a cold sentence should cost you a duel; there is no 'excellent,' 'transcendant,' 'transparent' in it.

* * * * * * * * * *

Good-bye. I cannot say when I shall see you.

D. Webster.

P. S. You will naturally inquire how I prosper in the article of cash; finely! finely! I came here in January with a horse, and watch, &c., and a few "rascally counters" in my pocket. Was soon obliged to sell my horse and live on the proceeds. Still straitened for cash I sold my watch, and made a shift to get home, where my friends supplied me with another horse and another watch. My horse is sold again, and my watch goes I expect this week; thus you see how I lay up cash. If Cook or somebody else does not soon come to relieve me, I shall be so rich that I shall be worth just nothing at all.

DANIEL WEBSTER TO EZEKIEL WEBSTER.

Salisbury, November 4, 1802.

Now, Zeke, you will not read half a sentence, no, not one syllable, before you have thoroughly searched this sheet for scrip; but, my word for it, you will find no scrip here. We held a sanhedrim this morning on the subject of cash, could not hit upon any way to get you any; just before we went away to hang ourselves through disappointment, it came into our heads that next week might do. The truth is, father had an execution against Hubbard, of N. Chester, for about one hundred dollars; the money was collecting and just ready to drop into the hands of the creditors, when Hubbard suddenly died. This, you see, stays the execution till the long process of administering is completed.

I have now by me two cents in lawful federal currency; next week I will send them, if they be all; they will buy a pipe; with a pipe you can smoke; smoking inspires wisdom; wisdom is allied to fortitude; from fortitude it is but one step to stoicism; and stoicism never pants for this world's goods; so perhaps my two cents, by this process, may put you quite at ease about cash. Write me this minute, if you can; tell me all your necessities; no, not all, a part only, and any thing else you can think of to amuse me.

You may tell Nelson that I forwarded his letters to Gilmanton, next day after my return, and attended to his other business.

The Hon. Mr. Marston has a young son, which, in token of past acquaintance, his wife thinks of naming for you.

We are all here just in the old way, always behind and lacking; boys digging potatoes with frozen fingers, and girls washing without wood. I shall not stir from the office again this winter, that I know of; nor then, unless I go for you. Pray attend to the little request about paragraphs, &c.

I shall depend on you. Soon you will know if —— or not.

Good-bye; be a good child, " mind your books and strive to learn."

D. WEBSTER.

EZEKIEL WEBSTER TO DANIEL WEBSTER.

Saturday, November 6, 1802.

A WRITER of no inconsiderable note, and one whom you hold in very high esteem, has remarked in some of his lucubrations, that a student's reading and conversation ought to be intimately connected with the subject of his studies.

Impressed with the justness and propriety of this remark, I

shall give you a few of my thoughts on Horace. Should they discover more pedantry than learning, more ostentation than judgment, I must beg you to pardon weaknesses which you never felt. I shall not assume the lofty eminence of a critic and bid Horace pass in review before me; but shall only exercise the privilege, which every person in the pit may rightly claim, of judging the performance of the actors. It may be called ungenerous to judge Horace by our own ideas of excellence; but remember it is not Horace I judge, but his works. If he had vices, let them be buried in silence; I will never call them up. In my opinion, his writings ought to be as severely criticized, as though they were written but yesterday. No lapse of time will justify the licentiousness of his Muse. But it must be acknowledged, that in his works beauties lie scattered with defects, on every page, and mingle in every line. We admire his sententious brevity, the effusions of his fancy, and the keenness of his wit. We are often disgusted at his praises of Bacchus, of Venus, or himself.

I have given you the above *morceau* of criticism on purpose that it might excite your risibility; for I believe you have not frequent occasions to laugh, while you are reading Blackstone, or employed in the good work of filling blanks . . .

These cold frosty mornings very sensibly inform me, that I want a warm great-coat. I wish, Daniel, it might be convenient to send me on cloth for one, otherwise I shall be necessitated to purchase one here. I do not care what color or what kind of cloth it is; any thing that will keep the frost out. Some kind of a shaggy cloth, I think would be cheapest. Deacon Pettengill has written offering me fourteen dollars a month. I believe I shall take it.

Money, Daniel, money. As I was walking down to the office after a letter, I happened to find one cent, which is the only money I have had since the second day after I came on. It is a fact, Dan, that I was called on for a dollar, where I owed it, and borrowed it, and have borrowed it four times since, to pay those I borrowed of.

Yours without money,

E. Webster.

P. S. Remember me to father, and mother, and all.

MR. DAVIS TO MR. WEBSTER.

Hanover, N. H., November 26, 1802.

HOLD! Hold! Friend Webster. Don't buffet me. Don't be too hasty; stay a moment. I tremble to ask you a civil question. Your seemingly awful denunciation awaits me. But I can endure a little chastisement. I'll e'en venture to out with my inquiry.

Will you—don't be out of humor, brother Daniel, for I am blazing with rage myself at the imposition of last year's Brum—I say, brother Webster, will you write the Newsboy's Message for January, 1803? Say yes. I can take no denial. You are acquainted with foreign political and local affairs, of which you have a correct view at a single glance. You need not ponder much on past occurrences. The transactions of the year, the month, and the day, it may be well to note. The President's message will come forth before a succeeding message is offered to our patrons.

Perhaps by this time you are a little twistified: "Stand off, Davis, for my whole artillery of execrations shall be levelled upon you for this unreasonable attack," says a ruffled mind. "I would have thee begone. Seek in the inner temple of Dartmouth." How am I treated! I have sought but can find none to my liking. I want no fungus Federal address, like unto last year's. I want a genuinely Federal Address, and you are the very person to write it. And this solicitation, Sir, is not from me alone; some of our most respectable characters join in this request. Please to give me a definitive answer immediately. I shall want the address or message the Saturday prior to the first day of January, 1803. I have lately received a letter from brother Brackett, which informs me that friend Clark was dangerously sick. You will perceive that W. has taken a companion in his literary peregrinations. It is conjectured that *Icarus* has flocked with the wild geese and gone South for a warmer climate. It is however expected he will return early in the spring. For news I refer you to Junior Ezekiel. Esquire Everett is candidate for councillor in this county; Mr. Gilbert declines—sorry.

M. DAVIS.

NOTE. The poetic address for the Dartmouth Gazette, January 1, 1803, was written by Mr. Webster, in compliance with the request contained in the above letter, and under the signature of 'Icarus' Mr. Webster wrote various poetical and prose articles for the same paper.

MR. WEBSTER TO MR. FULLER.

Salisbury, December 21, 1802.

Good Fuller,—If your clemency was exhaustible, I should expect the bitterness of censure. I deserve it, I own, and will explain to you how. Your kind letter was received in its proper time, and my eye run over its contents with pleasure. Immediately I prepared an answer, but by unaccountable negligence and forgetfulness, it was never put into the mail, and yesterday, in tumbling over some old paper, I found said letter snug as could be in the desk! Pretty soon after my arrival from the Eastward I went to Hanover, sanguine in the expectation of seeing you, among others of my friends. I had heard some talks of your intended departure, but I considered them as *vox et preterea nihil.* Alas! I found it true, you were really, to my great astonishment, gone! I hope and find by your letter, that you have mended your situation by the change. Hanover without you, was to me insipid. Yet I was there again about a month ago, and a ray of pleasantness shot across it, for Bingham was with me. We galloped over the plain one day. I was so busy all day doing nothing, that I did not find time even to eat my dinner, much less to chat with gypsies; for to tell you the truth now, I am hungry twice where I am lovesick once. Mary W. I saw an instant, but had not the happiness to see Excellence itself embodied in the shape of the other Mary. Some malignant spirit prevented me this pleasure by breathing forgetfulness on my nerves. I forgot to call.

It is not long since I was at Concord; we had fine times, singing and dancing, and skipping. There were a thousand inquiries about you. Really, Weld, you must not let the girls break their hearts for you. I asked Miss * * * if she wished to see Mr Fuller very much. She said that—that—that—that—, the Lord knows what she did say. I could not tell. There was a No, and a Yes, and a blush, and a smile, and a blush, and so you may make what you can of them. Give my love to Ripley; I cannot help entertaining a wayward affection for him though he be a democrat. He ought to write me, and I shall very soon tell him so. Pray write me immediately, write me now, tell me you forgive my carelessness, and then I will cheerfully write you again. Yours, D. Webster.

P. S. M. * * * *, Esq., is to be postmaster immediately. You say what a fine thing 'tis to be a Jacobin; I say what a dreadful thing it is to be a Jack-ass.

MR. WEBSTER TO MR. BINGHAM.

Salisbury, December 21, 1802.

Good Hervey,—Lovers, I have heard it said, are apt to write with trembling hand. If that circumstance alone be sufficient to constitute one, I am as valiant a lover as ever made a vow. My hand does indeed tremble, and my brain dances with twice as much giddiness as ever. But what would be imputed to love, if you were a lady, may now very fairly be ascribed to the measles. This ugly disorder attacked me about a fortnight since, and has formed a great syncope in my health and happiness. I am now convalescent, as the faculty say, and am today just able to scrawl you this; if it be very dull, pray do not blame me, but the measles; if you will agree to this, I shall shift much responsibility from my own shoulders.

The information you communicated, I will not call it an opinion, was fully anticipated. On reading the statute carefully, I found it expressly excepted specialties from its operation; and I find in Blackstone, second volume, on the nature and different kinds of deeds, that a bond under seal and sign-manual, is a specialty. So in that quarter I have "no loop to hang my hopes upon." Here give me leave to pronounce a wise opinion, viz: That the best way to study law is in relation to particular points. I had read the statute of limitations, I do not know how many times, nor how many times more I might have read it among others, without discovering that it did not affect a sealed instrument, unless I had looked in reference to that particular inquiry. It is very much so, I believe, with history. We read page after page, and retaining a slender thread of events, everything else glides from the mind about as fast as the eye traces the lines of the book. Yet, when we examine a particular occurrence, or search after a single date, the impression is permanent, and we have added one idea to the stock of real knowledge.

If you are entertained with politics, I will tell you for your amusement, that Mr. Thompson is about to be turned out, as the phrase is, from the post-office at this place, to give room to Moses Eastman, Esq. The latter gentleman has already received his appointment.

Make my compliments acceptable, pray do, to your good cousins E. and P. I remember with joy and gratitude the kindness and hospitality with which I was treated in the family.

There is not half room enough left to enumerate all the good wishes my heart feels for you. It will save me a deal of trouble in this way, if you will only wish at once for everything you honestly can, and I will cheerfully "second the motion."

Yours, D. Webster.

P. S. This has been delayed so long you will answer it. I mean you will write another, for there is nothing in this requiring an answer; you will write me a line, I say, soon, yes, immediately, 'twill be better than "puke or pill" to cure me of the measles.

MR. WEBSTER TO MR. MERRILL.

Salisbury, January 4, 1803.

Dear Merrill,—I think it quite time, don't you? that I write you a letter. I thought so yesterday morning, when I was within five miles of you, am entirely persuaded of it to-night, when I am not within forty. A letter—well, a letter should be amusing. Ah me! A dreadful task that for my brain! So then, I must follow the custom, and put down this sentence "Alas! what shall I say," when indeed I have nothing to say, and also this pathetic exclamation, "I can no more," when I really can no more.

Mistaken I am, Tommy, if it do not require some taste as well as literature to form a letter, without any particular subject which shall gratify a correct scholar. This night I have counted over my own qualifications for this business of letter-writing, and find them not a little deficient. There are some great embarrassments in the way. Hear one now. The critics tell us that a letter, to be interesting, should be a "transcript unaffected of the heart." So, then, one has nothing to do, but to sit down and transcribe his heart to his correspondent. This copy will be, it seems, a charming, entertaining epistle. But lack a-day, me! what can a poor scribbler do, if he happen not to have his heart about him? If now my heart is rambling up and down the Connecticut, or, if fixed to some spot there, how in the world can I copy it? But as respects you and the folks that way, it is no matter if you have the original among you, surely you can well enough do without the copy. Thus you see, I shall cleverly be excused from writing you an "entertaining letter." On the opposite page I said something about being within five miles of you. True, I kept Sabbath at Lebanon, with E. Porter. I almost determined to go to Hanover and take a peep at my friends, but as my tarry could not have exceeded a few hours, I thought it would be mere tantalizing with my feelings. This time I did not "a-wooing go," but you may expect very soon to see me on a pilgrimage, not however to Mecca, nor Medina.

> To the shrines of dead saints let the pilgrim repair,
> And bend o'er their ashes in praise and in prayer,
> I love living goodness, nor ever shall find,
> A brighter example than glows in her mind,—

whose mind? you will say; ah, ah, Mr. Tommy, that is an inquiry to puzzle you, and even I had as lief take a problem in Euclid to solve as that question. The Lord knows whose mind, but 'tis hers. That strain of poetry you will confess to be such as might fall from the lip of a true inamorato, and if you will only point out somebody to be antecedent for that pronoun "her," I will give you a pipe of tobacco.

This law-reading, Thomas, has no tendency to add the embellishments of literature to a student's acquisitions. Our books are written in a hard, didactic style, interspersed on every page with the mangled pieces of murdered Latin, and as perfectly barren of all elegance as a girl's cheek is of beard; you see I can't keep entirely off the girl's cheeks. The morality of the profession is, too, a matter of doubt, or rather it is a matter of no doubt at all. Mr. Bennett says that a lawyer, who preserves his integrity unspotted, deserves a place in the calendar of saints. If this calendar were entirely made up of lawyers, I fancy it would be a short, a very short list, not so long, if you take the whole world over, as a catalogue of Freshmen, and yet this is the profession to which I am devoting myself! O blindness! stupidity! infatuation! nonsense! folly! and

D. WEBSTER.

P. S. I will, on second thought, take off the edge of the above invective against my profession by reminding you that there have been a Papinian and a Hale, as eminent for piety as for talents, and our late Chief Justice Ellsworth demands a mention in company with these ornaments to their profession.

I regret that my sheet is full, but you must write me, and then I shall feel authorized to fill another. Pray do not delay.

Mr. Granger has removed Mr. Thompson from the post-office here and appointed Moses Eastman, Esquire. Now just between you and me, not to let the world hear, it is a dreadful thing in these times to be a Jack-ass. They were never in greater demand—Mum!

MR. WEBSTER TO MR. COOK.

Salisbury, January 14, 1803.

WELL, brother Cook, is it not time that you and I should interchange a word by letter? Indeed, I thought it quite time some while ago, and bore on my mind a fresh impression of the promise you made me to write, but as yet no letters have arrived. But perhaps it is owing to miscarriage in mail. Lackaday! Since these Jacobin postmasters have crept into office, one cannot for the soul of him, get a letter that never was written.

But I will pardon you; your entire devotion to business would render you pardonable, if you should neglect to write even to your sweetheart. Don't you suppose now that I must be a little envious of the lustre of your pedagogical fame? A priest's word may surely be relied on, but your philosophy would hate to hear a compliment.

It has been twice in the way of business for me to be at Hanover since I saw you. Everybody I saw, and some of the ladies particularly, inquired about Mr. Cook; but here again I shall wound your philosophy. Our college friends were in fine mood, triumphant over their enemies. Bingham, that good soul, whose spirit is harmonious as his music, galloped on to the plain with me, and we spent a day among the folks. One of your female acquaintances is gone, fairly gone, I understand, into the land of love and courtship. I do not now tell you who it is, nor who is become proprietor in the premises, for certain reasons. The authorities were in November very much probably as you left them in August. I could not see any diminution in the length of noses, nor in the volubility of lip-licking tongues. Professor Woodward has been entirely out of health, as Zeke tells me, all the fall, and Doctor Smith has sold his house with an intention to fix his residence in Windsor.

I am not informed what profession you are determined to study, but if it be law, permit me to tell you a little what you must expect. My experience in the study is indeed short, but I have learnt a little about it. First then, you must bid adieu to all hopes of meeting with a single author who pretends to elegance of style or sweetness of observation. The language of the law is dry, hard, and stubborn as an old maid. Murdered Latin bleeds through every page, and if Tully and Virgil could rise from their graves, they would soon be at fisticuffs with Coke, Hale, and Blackstone, for massacring their language. As to the practice, I believe it a settled matter, that the business of an office is conducted with the very refuse and remnant of mankind. However, I will not too far abuse my own profession. It is sometimes lucrative, and if one can keep up an acquaintance with general literature in the mean time, the law may help to invigorate and unfold the powers of the mind.

By this time you are quite tired of this conversation. Well, my friend, then go away and relieve your worry by chatting with the fair ones, after which, if you please, sacrifice a moment to the unrewarded trouble of writing a line to

Your very humble servant,

D. Webster.

MR. WEBSTER TO MR. BINGHAM.

Salisbury, February 22, 1803.

My good Hervey,—Yours of January 29, was received in due season. I thank you for the expressions of friendship it contained, and for the assurance that a part of your time is devoted to me. At this period of our acquaintance I need not tell you what pleasure I receive from your letters, nor with what exultation my heart glows under the impression that our early congenial attachments will never be sundered. It may look a little like vanity, flattery, and puerility, but I think I may say that you will continue to occupy the parlor of my affections, till Madam comes! Madam, you know, must have the parlor, but even then you shall not be cast off into the kitchen. Depend on it, if Madam treats you, or anybody else who is an older proprietor than herself, with prankish airs, we will soon away with her into Lob's pound.

You solicit my sentiments upon politics. Really, I don't know if I have any political sentiments. Kaimes tells us that sentiment is something which savors of passion or affection. Now I profess not to have the least affection for the men in power, for the means by which they obtained it, nor for the use they put it to, so I can't say whether I have any political sentiments at all. It is very strange, Bingham, and very true, that men do as often as otherwise choose the most ignorant of mankind to instruct, and the most wicked to govern. I feel a good deal of interest, perhaps more than I ought, in the termination of the ensuing election. Can you help, can I help, can anybody of sense help despising mankind, and despising himself for belonging to mankind, if in every instance vice and folly laugh virtue and wisdom out of countenance? With us it is seriously fearful that the Senate of our Legislature will be Jacobinical. Districts No. 1, 2, 4, 5, and 7, 8, 9, are some of them undoubtedly democratic, and the rest awfully suspicious. In this district (No. 8,) we send a man, and nobody can tell why we send him, unless it be that he is absolutely the greatest dunce in the district. From all these evils may the Lord deliver us!

Permit me to mingle a sentiment of sorrow with yours for the death of your aunt, that worthy woman of whom I have often heard you speak, before I had the happiness to see her. You will long feel her loss; you will feel an absence about your heart, where there has once been the purest esteem and affection. Friends, like all things, may leave us.

> "Year following year steals something every day,
> At last they steal us from ourselves away."

You mention not having heard from Hanover for some time; I have heard from that place every now and then through the winter. Once, since I saw you, I was in sight of the old town; I looked that way and past on. At Lebanon I met with Timothy Heifer; in two minutes I knew more about the "gestion" of Hanover's affairs by half than if I had been reading friend Davis's Gazette. Experience Porter spent some days with me lately. He has become quite gallant, and told me all about the girls, and it all amounted to nothing at all.

Yesterday I was at Sanbornton, and had the pleasure of hurting myself by being tumbled out of the sleigh into the snow with Mrs. Lovejoy. I told them all I was sure you would come and see them in June, and they all rejoiced. Pray do not let them, nor me, be disappointed.

When I parted with you, you mentioned, I think, that C—— was at New York, but was expected to come to Lempster to take a school. Is he now there? If so, jog him by the elbow, when you see him, and tell him to call to mind D. W.

Ask your cousin Enos if he recollects any thing about a lad that made you a visit, or rather visitation, last fall. If he answers affirmatively, give him my compliments. He appears to be one of those frank souls that I am fond of. To be sure you must pass an hour now and then very agreeably with your cousin P. Does not your generous spirit sometimes feel willing to share that happiness with your friends? Lackaday me! Some of your friends have no pleasure like that, yet they are happy enough. D. WEBSTER.

N. B. I do not much approve the literary taste of your Charlestown ladies!

P. S. My office-mates, John Doe and Richard Roe, send love to you.

MR. BINGHAM TO MR. WEBSTER.

Charlestown, N. H., April 8, 1803.

My dear Friend,—Here I am, with the whole office to myself, except that part occupied by the honorable gentlemen of the shelf. Mr. West and Mr. Briggs are now attending our Common Pleas Court at Keene. Mr. Sumner likewise. Rice is also there, waiting his destiny. From this you will naturally conclude, that Mr. Foster and myself are the only "law characters" in the place: hem! hem! and I think quite enough, without they are better.

It is in vain, Daniel, to aspire to eminence in law, or any other profession in this country. Our fortunes are not adequate. The main point, to which our ambition is to be directed, is the attainment of a necessary support. Were the sons of America perfectly independent; had they wealth enough to carry them through life, without toiling and sweating, to gain a subsistence for themselves and families; then we might see men of eminence and deep learning amongst us; then would a Locke, a Newton, a Shakespeare, and a Milton grace our land, and immortalize our fame in the literary world. Nothing then would those who had a mind to devote themselves to study have to impede their progress; nothing to engage their attention, but a steady uniform course of literature. It cannot be supposed that the natural genius of Europeans is, in any degree, superior to that of Americans. Our clime is as favorable as theirs; our constitutions equally sound and rugged. It must, I think, be attributed to education; and this education must be the result of fortune and independence. But what signify a few years at our infant universities, and that too perhaps half taken up, in devising means to procure our maintenance there the other half? And admitting that one pass his four years at college, and is not troubled with these evils. If he enter the profession of law, for instance, it is impossible to keep from his mind the thoughts of his future dependence, knowing that his time henceforward must be spent in the practice of the science, if he should be so lucky as to obtain any, and not in investigating and exploring the science itself; and if he have no practice, why he has nothing to do, but to change his employment or starve.

Sad alternative! Well, well, Dan, we have to live this life but once, and it ought to be our object, in whatever employment we may be engaged, so to conduct as to acquit our consciences, and promote the happiness of our fellow-travellers in the journey of life.

I am now perusing Bohun's Institutio Legalis. It is pretty tough, and I believe very good. Mr. Sprague used to say, "To take up that, is like taking a bull by the horns," and you know I am not very stout, therefore I cannot manage it very well.

I hear Mr. Campbell is chosen Register of Deeds for the county; he now lives at Acworth, will probably move to Walpole. I saw Dr. Smith a few moments the other day, who tells me he has moved to Cornish, and Freeborn is there with him. He is one of those souls in whom goodness abounds. I give myself the pleasure to hope that I shall see him soon. I have not heard one word from my father since you left me; so that I can tell you nothing about going to Concord in June. If he is willing and will help me off as I wish, I shall most assuredly visit you. L—— was extremely disappointed at not seeing Mr. Webster, and the only consolation appeared to be, "that you would call when you come again." Enos is well, and often speaks with pleasure of a certain Mr. Webster, "who made me a visit last fall," and sends his compliments to him. —— told me a few days since, that when I wrote I might give her love to you, if I thought you would accept it. She is a good girl if I am not mistaken.

P. S. Give my love to your office-mates and others.

Ever yours.

JAMES H. BINGHAM.

EZEKIEL WEBSTER TO DANIEL WEBSTER.[1]

May 15, 1803.

DANIEL,—It did cut truly and it was the unkindest cut of all. I hope we shall not have many more "slices from that loaf." I have hastily examined my own resources, and find them inade-

[1] This letter refers to a request from Mr. Davis to Ezekiel Webster to edit the Dartmouth Gazette anonymously.

quate to the management of such a work. Indeed, I never thought them competent. I have now no idea of undertaking the business, I could not afford to do it under two or three dollars a number, and Mr. Davis would be unwilling to give, perhaps, as many cents. It would be impossible that the editor should remain perfectly unknown, and he would be sure to have all the odium thrown upon him if it failed, and would receive no praise if it succeeded. Do not have an idea that I ever had vanity enough to think myself able to conduct such a work. Ascribe it to the want of money, which, at that moment, would have induced me to undertake any thing. Mr. Cook and Sam. Osgood were on the plain not long since. All well at Fryeburg, when they left the place. Sam. has an idea of entering Junior at Commencement. I do not know but I should accompany Sawyer to Salisbury, if our studies were not so very important, studies no less important and interesting than Euclid and Homer. I shall expect to see you here some time this month. I may want to see you by that time. Next Wednesday is Sophomore quarter day. Brown has the Latin; Lyman the Greek, and Whiting the English oration.

Good-bye, E. WEBSTER.

MR. WEBSTER TO MR. BINGHAM.

Salisbury, May 18, 1803.

DEAR HERVEY,—Yours of April 8 was received at the very moment when I wished for it. This is the fortune which attends all your letters. At present, I suppose, Charlestown does not experience such a paucity of "law characters" as at the date of yours. It is a little presumptuous to expect you will find time to read this in the middle of a court week; but I know you to be pretty industrious, and to find time for many things.

The late term in this county was very interesting, as they say, for I had not the pleasure to attend. There were more indictments than have been known for a long time; a sure proof how rapidly we advance in perfectibility. Hillsborough, you know, is the most democratic county!

Russell, the pure printer at Concord, has found it convenient to abscond. He happened very unfortunately to be engaged in counterfeiting money in Connecticut some years ago, and the vindictive tyranny of that Tory State hath pursued him to this very hour. His Godwin-taught friends, say, it is abominable to punish a citizen for mere misfortunes. Aye!

What you have said of the obstacles in the way to eminence in this country, hath much truth to support it. But what then? Must we sit down contented in the lowly valley of inferiority? This is a cold, poor, comfortless place. If the hill of difficulties be so high we cannot climb over it, yet perhaps we can make a shift to creep round it. At all events it is worth the trial. I do not soon expect to see in America, a Locke, a Newton, a Pope, or a Sir Joshua. But Mansfields and Kenyons, I believe, we shall rear in the next age; and the reason of the difference is that eminence will be sought with more ardor in the lucrative professions, than in the abstract sciences and the fine arts.

Lemy Bliss was this way the other day, and has passed into Vermont in character of a preacher. Success to him!

At present I peruse Hume and Woodeson. Next week I expect with all deference and modesty to introduce myself to that prince of the laws, Sir Edward Coke. If any difficulty arises between him and me, as no doubt there will, my master T. is ready to appear in character of umpire.

The first day of June, about nine o'clock in the morning, I shall see you, I am sure I shall, at Stickney's in Concord. Till then, and forever after, good-bye.

Yours in truth,

D. Webster.

P. S. The compliment you communicated, strongly fastens on the memory of the heart. Proffer a great share of my love in return.

Mention me to your cousin Enos, whenever you have not something better to say to him. D. W.

EZEKIEL WEBSTER TO DANIEL WEBSTER.

Hanover, May 21, 1803.

DANIEL,—I acknowledged, in my letter by Mr. Sawyer, the receipt of the cash you sent me, and for which, if you think proper, you will give my thanks to Mr. T. T.

Though that sum relieved me from many embarrassments, yet I assure you my finances are not in the most prosperous condition. My note to Pomroy was upwards of forty dollars, besides many other bills of minor amount. You hinted to me in your last, that I should have some money soon. The very suggestion seemed to dispel the gloom that was thickening around me. It seemed like a momentary flash that suddenly bursts through a night of clouds, or as Young says:

"So looked, in chaos, the first beam of light."

You informed me that you were to meet in council at Concord. Whenever you meet, let money be the object of your consultation. Mr. Davis no doubt will wish you to write for his paper, The Tablet, should he commence its publication. But whatever celebrity a newspaper essayist may gain, unless accompanied by something more substantial, it will never feed or clothe him, it will never buy him a pair of boots or purchase a nightcap. I shall send your boots by mail. Since I began to write this letter, I have heard something which so agitates me, I can neither think nor write. I may let you know what it is next Saturday.

Good-bye and may God bless us.

E. WEBSTER.

EZEKIEL WEBSTER TO DANIEL WEBSTER.

Dartmouth College, May 28, 1803.

DEAR DANIEL,—In my last letter I informed you, that a little affair had taken place which so discomposed me, that I had neither the control of my thoughts nor the command of my pen. The little affair was nothing less than the discovery of a plot, which had for its object the destruction of the Fraternity, and not merely the Fraternity, but the conspirators aimed at the abolition of every society in college. With the secrecy of Jesuits, they drew up a paper to that effect and used all their influence to procure signers. And they were but too successful. A solitary few only,

> " Apparent rari nantes in gurgite vasto,"

remained unshaken; but one in the Freshman class, one in the Sophomore class, and three in mine. Many of our best members, however, were absent. By a little exertion, we procured more than one fourth, a number sufficient to prevent the alteration of any article in the constitution. The conspirators, driven to despair by this measure, and conscious of possessing a large majority, made an effort to expel those members who were opposed to them, and then they could alter the constitution, or destroy it at their pleasure. Seaver was designated as the first victim of their cursed policy. But the attempt failed, and we are yet members. I am sorry to tell you that every fellow from Salisbury, but myself, enlisted under the banner of the conspirators. The Social Friends witnessed like troubles with ourselves; but they began at their last meeting a glorious work, and may they perfect it. They expelled two, and others will have to walk soon. It is but right that the person who raises a storm should perish in its ravages.

This conspiracy, I believe, is unparalleled. It does not resemble that of Brutus, for Cæsar was a tyrant, and Brutus an " honorable man." It is not like Catiline's, for Catiline himself was a saint compared with some of the fellows who plotted this scheme. If it has its parallel, it is in the conspiracy of the Pazzi against the celebrated Lorenzo the Magnificent.

At the next meeting is our election. They will carry every thing before them. Well, let them, for the triumphing of the wicked is short. You have probably received your boots. If they do not suit, you have the liberty of returning them. I wish you a good and happy election.

E. WEBSTER.

MR. WEBSTER TO MR. FULLER.

Salisbury, July 2, 1803.

Esquire Weld,—Your last kind letter was not answered by the next post, as you requested, and for a very good reason. I was about going to "the college," and delayed writing, that I might give you some account of things there. Well, now you are all alive to hear the news, as in due order you shall. I arrived there just as St. John was receiving the compliment of a sermon from brother Barber, and an address from brother Wm. Woodward. This over, your humble servant had the honor of dining with General B.'s daughter S——. O! how deliciously the dinner tasted! Then, after strolling up to college and down to brother Davis's, your servant aforesaid, walked down towards the bridge to the house of Deacon Fuller, if you recollect where it stands. There he found Mr. Preceptor Merrill in the wickedness of a game of backgammon. A cup of tea, however, induced him to forbear reproaching them for gambling, and he almost wished he could play himself.

About nine he wandered "unfriended and alone" into the ball-room. What a congregation of beauty! Whose heart but must flutter a little at so many pretty faces? Ah! here was all one's safety; attention was so much divided, that it could not fasten anywhere, and though he "trod among a thousand perils," came off unhurt. About eleven I tumbled into bed, at Dewey's, with our old friend Campbell, but the witches were so much in his head I could not sleep. By the way, Campbell told me he is going to Portland in August. Saturday I wasted in troubling brother Davis and a few other good folks, and Monday went off for Woodstock. I saw some of the nice Vermont folks, and Monday returned to Hanover. Tuesday afternoon visited with a thousand good people at Deacon Fuller's; really Weld, bad as you are, I should have been glad to see you there, merely because it would have been more like old times. On retiring, the possessor of my arm was so preposterous as to say, "Weld is truly very sprightly and amiable!" With all the rhetoric I had, I could not beat her out of this foolish idea, and I believe in my soul she will carry it to her grave with her. Alas, alas, the perversity of female minds! As you are now purchasing probably in the District of Maine, and will not settle your possessions in this State, I wish to bargain with you at Commencement for a quitclaim of all right and title, in possession or expectancy, to the premises hereafter laid, as I have thought of pitching that way. Among sixty Misses in the ball-room I could not discover the paragon, till she was pointed to me. Her features had strayed out of my mind in the roll of two years, though your memory, I fancy, is something more tenacious.

Nabby R. is gone, gone, gone. " Happy the man."

I will not fail to scold Bingham, as you request, when I write to him next.

You know what will oblige me; writing immediately to your brother student, brother college-mate, brother class-mate, brother Frater, brother Adelphian, and friend,

DAN'L WEBSTER.

N. B. The narrative part of this epistle is equal to the travels of Robert Wren.

MR. WEBSTER TO MR. MERRILL.

Salisbury, July 30, 1803.

FRIEND MERRILL,—What kind of punishment you will inflict on me for taxing you with this at the present time I cannot say. I only know that you are a man of clemency, and shall not think myself hardly dealt with, if you do nothing more than retaliate.

In truth, I am solicitous to draw from you a letter, and send this very much for that purpose, although you will think it doing evil, that good may come, and therefore contrary to sound morality. When I saw you last you talked of writing me soon, and I have been "punctual as lover to the moment sworn" in my semi-weekly attendance at the post-office, ever since.

Peter Pindar singeth that "man's thoughts are ever busy, all alive," and I believe he singeth truly. My own thoughts, I am sure, are the most industrious members of my commonwealth, and they travel all around the circuit of the spheres in the little space of time in which I am snuffing my candle. In this journey they will sometimes stop at Hanover, as the end of their road, merely, I suppose, because you and Zeke live there. I dare not suspect any other reason, for sending a flight of the mind that way, because he that suspects is in a fair way to be convinced. You know what the scripture saith of him that doubteth, and, more to my present purpose, you know what the poet saith,

> "And you're undone, the fatal shaft has sped,
> If once you doubt whether you love or no," . . .

These reasons determine me to be convinced that it is only on account of my male friends, that I ever think of Hanover. I can perfectly see you at this moment, with an aspect half smiling, and half satirical, as you have read above and are now saying,—

"Ah, brother Dan! brother Dan! Mary has caught thee, and holds thee fast as the folks did the spirit in "Lob's pound." Ha, ha! Tommy, I wish I could see you, and convince you how much you are mistaken. But I believe you must live in your prejudice until Commencement, and when brother Herbert takes her by the foretop and saith, "Thou art mine," you will see how gladly and cheerfully I will part with what I never owned. I rejoice at a little bit of news I hear from college, in which I think I can trace the marks of your own finger. Zeke tells me that H. H. are letters component of P. B. K. Good!

I saw our classmate Noyes this week. His orbit of pedagogical fame is very bright. I think they will never consent to part with him at Concord.

Good-bye. As to love and compliments I send no particular directions, you know I trust all to your disposal.

D. Webster.

P. S. Pardon this valetudinary epistle; excessive heats you know dissipate ideas as well as strength.

MR. WEBSTER TO MR. BINGHAM.

Salisbury, September 3, 1803.

It is something uncertain, brother Jemmy, whether I am indebted to you in the sum of one letter, or you to me; but I am resolved to place it beyond all doubt. The last I had from your Honor gave me a good account of the Federalism of your own town, Lempster. It is to be hoped, notwithstanding the efforts of the redoubtable Mr. Haines, that Lempster will not worship idols, as the fashion of many is, at this day, of Jacobinism and iniquity, which two words are so closely allied in signification, that the latter always follows the former, just as in grammar, "the accusative case follows the transitive verb." Friend Flavel is yet, in some respects, as appears by the toast he gave, much too honest for a democrat.

I expected somewhat to hear from you from Commencement, as I was informed from the sweetest lips on all these plains, as I verily believe, although entirely upon credit, that your fair and good cousin Mary was to be there, in company with her friend Miss Laura Hubbard, and of such a party I concluded your philosophy would not restrain you from being one; if it should, thought I, 'tis a very bad philosophy; worse, much worse, in my opinion, than that new species against which our Federal clergymen so loudly and justly declaim. But, if Zeke is to be believed, you did not show yourself at college. You were perhaps more happy at home; or perhaps you thought as I did, that a dozen dollars would slide out of the pocket in a Commencement jaunt much easier than they would slide in again after you got home. This was the exact reason why I was not there, for there were some people there whom I much wished to see. I flatter myself that none of my friends ever thought me greatly absorbed in the sin of avarice, yet I assure you, Jem, that in these days of poverty I look on a round dollar, if it be my own, with a great deal of complacency. These rascal dollars are so necessary to the comfort of life, that next to a fine wife they are most essential, and their acquisition an object of prime importance. Oh, Bingham, how blessed it would be to retire with a decent, clever bag of Rixes to a pleasant country town, and follow one's own inclination without being shackled by the duties of a profession! But this is a dream, and it vanishes soon.

Zeke says that Bracket gave a poem to the P. B. K. which was really dulce, full of the "grit," as Corey used to say. It will be printed. I am glad that the New York climate has not corrupted his heart, and turned his head. Say, James, when I am to see you here. It seems to me I have some strong claims on you for a visit, and shall begin to complain gently if you do not perform it soon, very soon; you know how your promise stands.

Accompanying this is one to good old Corey, send it to him when you have an opportunity. Give my compliments, if you please, to Mr. Briggs, and my love to Harry, if he is in town; same sort of currency to our friend Hall; and last of all, but not least of all, present me, in whatever manner will be most acceptable, to your and my friends Polly and Enos.

I am, Sir, your most dutiful, most obliged, most obsequious, most loving, most unworthy, ever grateful, ever affectionate, and ever during friend, and humble servant, client, tenant, and bondman.

D. Webster.

MR. WEBSTER TO MR. BINGHAM.

October 6, 1803.

Hervey,—One Joseph W. Brackett probably handed you an urbanic letter from me, written at Hanover, in which I promised to send you soon an epistle, "three feet long," in answer to several questions you ask respecting my wanderings to and fro. Here then you shall have the three feet.

And first, my father has an important suit at law pending before the Supreme Court of Vermont. This has frequently called me into that realm, in the course of the past summer. Mr. Marsh of Woodstock is of counsel to us, wherefore I have made him several visits, in arranging the necessary preliminaries to trial. This circumstance, I fancy, originated the suggestion that I contemplated reading in his office. In reality, I have no such idea in my head at present. Heretofore I have been inclined to think of Vermont as a place of practice, and as preparatory therefor have thought it possible that I might read a year in that State; but I never carried my views so far as to fix on an office, and at this time have no views at all of that kind.

Secondly. You have heard that I contemplated finishing my studies in Massachusetts. There is more foundation for this than the other. It is true I have laid many plans to enable myself to be some time in Boston, before I go into practice, but I did not know that I had mentioned the circumstance abroad, because it is all uncertain. I believe that some acquaintance in the capital of New England, would be very useful to us, who expect to plant ourselves down as country lawyers. But I cannot control my fortune; I must follow wherever circumstances lead. My going to Boston is therefore much more a matter of hope, than of probability; unless something like a miracle puts the means in my hands, I shall not budge from here very soon. Depend on it, however, James, that I shall some time avail myself of more advantages than this smoky village affords. But when or where you and I know equally well. If my circumstances were like yours, I would by all means pass a six months in Boston. The acquaintances you would be likely to form there, might help you to much business in the course of life. You can pass that time there just as well as not, and I therefore advise to it, as far as I ought to advise to any thing. But "some men are born with a silver spoon in their mouths, and others with a wooden ladle!" Would not you thank me to mend my pen?

If you can tell what it is to read Coke in black letter on a day too warm for a fire and too cold to be without one, it will save me any description of myself. When tired of old Coke, I look at Smollett's continuation of Hume's history. The whole of my reading, however, does not amount to much. I can hardly be called a student at law. The law question that now puzzles us in this quarter, is whether Bonaparte, when he shall have gone to John Bull's palace, and taken hold of the ring of the door in the name of seizin of the whole Island, will be such a king against whom it will be treason, in an Englishman, to fight? But they may settle this among them; you and I will not give our opinion without a fee!

I shall be alone here for three weeks. Why will you not just take your horse and gallop down here? Do come, pray do. 'Twill take but just a day from your father's. I will tell you when you must come. On the 15th instant. I shall be at Warner, which is not more than twenty-five miles from Lempster; come then and find me there—will you not be there? Say "aye," do. I shall look for you.

I am, as I have been time whereof the memory of man runneth not to the contrary, your friend, D. WEBSTER.

MR. WEBSTER TO MR. FULLER.

Salisbury, October 6, 1803.

Dear Fuller,—The burden of my letters has been so much an account of some jaunt, that I have made to Connecticut River, that you will ere long suspect me of having particular business to transact in that quarter. However, I think I may say that I have lately performed the last tour that way, that is to be done for some time. Last week I was two days on "the plains," and passed them very pleasantly. I was at your friend's; passed an evening in a large circle at the Printer's, where was the Paragon, and M. W., and Sophia, &c. "And there were many more, too many for me to name." As I did not expect to behold their faces very soon again, I felt much like enjoying their enrapturing conversation a few evenings more, but it was not very convenient. There I found J. W. Brackett, on his way to New York. Jo. means to figure in the world, and I say fortune speed him. He is a clever fellow, and if you and I had a little of his dash, it would be better for us. The world is governed more by appearance than reality, and therefore it is fully as necessary to seem to know something, as to know it in reality. A perfect character in these respects is he who has a good deal of outside with a good deal within, but if one must be dispensed with, it is deserving some consideration which is most important, the appearance of knowledge, or the reality of it.

There were some fellows at college with us, who were quite as much in the "nine holes" respecting cash as you and I. These fellows are doing finely, and if we will but aspire, we may do finely also. Brackett left college as poor as Phi Beta; he has read his profession under fine advantages, and is now able to figure with horse and chaise. Clark has become a quaker, associated himself with a rich house in New York, and gone to India with good prospects. How well you are doing I cannot tell, but I am just as I was, neither poorer nor richer; more studious or less so; but having a little more ambition to court the muse of law, and no desire to court anybody else—hardly.

You are pleased to say that it would be agreeable to see me

on the Kennebec in the course of the year. That is not likely, unless I go that way to tarry. The next time I set off, I bid farewell to this spot. Pray write me what your circumstances, advantages, hopes, and prospects are, whether there be any little nook left unoccupied where one might get a living, &c., and, where do you intend to plant yourself?

In answer to all this, write soon, and oblige your friend,

D. Webster.

EZEKIEL WEBSTER TO DANIEL WEBSTER.

Hanover, October 18, 1803.

Dear Daniel,—Having no news to communicate, I must have recourse to such thoughts as my studies suggest, to fill up my sheet.

Horace very justly observes that it is pleasant, sometimes, to relax the mind and dissipate attention; and he might have added with equal propriety, that it is also useful and requisite; for relaxation from study is as necessary to the mind as rest from labor to the body. The strongest intellect cannot bear constant exertion without impairing its faculties. The bow which is always kept in tension loses its elasticity. Nor can the bird of Jove, though the boldest and strongest in flight, always keep upon the wing. Since the mind is not capable of uninterrupted exercise, it becomes a matter of great importance to discover what will best recreate and strengthen its debilitated powers. Here the physicians of the mind, no less than those of the body, have differed in their prescriptions. One advises us to frequent company; another exhorts us to retire into solitude. Cicero tells us that he used to withdraw from the fatigue and bustle of the forum, into his closet, and there relax and refresh his wearied mind by reading the poetry of Ennius and Archias. Their writings must have afforded infinite pleasure to a person of a taste so exquisite as was Cicero. He was philosopher enough to know that whatever pleases the mind enlivens it; whatever delights, invigorates. Perhaps the poetry of no nation ever abounded more in ingenious fiction and agreeable narratives than the Latin; and consequently, none was ever better adapted to relieve and renovate the jaded intellect. Unhappily, English poetry affords no such amusement. Although it contains every thing that is brilliant in imagery, splendid in sentiment, or elegant in diction, yet it wants that gay fancy, that innocent humor, which can

——— "light up a smile on the aspect of woe."

Departing from its original intention, which was to please, it assumes the austerity of the moralist and indulges in the subtle refinements of the metaphysician. The student who resorts to poetry, fondly hoping to find something that shall recreate, soon discovers that he is reading, in verse, the metaphysics of Locke, or the philosophy of Newton. Whether poetry has suffered by the change, I presume not to say, but will venture to affirm that it is less suited to repair the intellect when weakened by intense application to scientific or abstruse subjects. Here, when poetry fails us, we find the advantage of novels, a species of writing in which fancy lives, wit sparkles, and sentiment animates. The censure cast upon novels has been as extravagant as undeserving. The commission of almost every crime has been ascribed to the perusal of a novel or romance. Amid such a variety, that there should be some poor ones, is not questioned; that they frequently produce bad effects, is not disputed. If it be an objection to novels that they may be perverted from their original purpose, the same may be made to every kind of writing and to every branch of science. It may be urged against natural philosophy and metaphysics. Where did Hume and Berkeley learn to live upon ideas but from the study of metaphysics? Where did Herbert, Bolingbroke, and Shaftesbury imbibe their deistical principles but from the study of natural philosophy? These are consequences infinitely more injurious to society than that the tear of sensibility should start over a tale of fictitious woe, or that compassion should be awakened for sorrows that were never felt; yet no one has ever made this a serious objection to the study of metaphysics or natural philosophy. The great benefit of novels is, that they agreeably entertain, during a vacant hour, and vacant hours men must have; that they are better adapted than any other kind of writing to restore the powers of the mind, when exhausted; to regale it, when saddened; to enliven it, when languid; to strengthen and invigorate it, when weakened. If they are not essential to an education, they are not entirely useless. If they are not the corner-stone of our intellectual structure, they are the minor decorations of the work, which give grace and beauty to the whole. They instruct as well as please. Milton was particularly fond of novels and works of fiction; and by them he sublimated that imagination which so astonishes throughout his writings. They are often the convenient medium of imparting moral lessons. Men are peculiarly fond of instruction conveyed by fable; and when the story of a well-written novel is plain, its language chaste, and its sentiments pure, a work of fiction possessing these qualities and portraying human character with accuracy will ever find readers and ever captivate their souls while men remain true to their nature. Here I must suspend my remarks for the present. Write soon.

Yours, as ever,

E. WEBSTER.

MR. WEBSTER TO MR. MERRILL.

Salisbury, November 11, 1803.

WHETHER you see fit to knight me for a fool or a philosopher is not very material. The characters, I believe, suit me about alike. But true it is, I am so much of one or of the other, that I was quite able to understand the whole of your letter from beginning to end, notwithstanding the modest things you are pleased to say about its want of connection. Without a compliment, friend Merrill, you have really the art of writing a very interesting letter; either by the choice of your subject, or by the management of it, or both, you contrive to engage all my attention. Your last was received on a Sunday's noon. It a little injured the effect of a good sermon; but that is a trifle. You have confirmed what I have long strongly suspected, and I shall have reasons for thanking you for telling me the truth, as it came to your knowledge, "without partiality and without hypocrisy." So then, Merrill, it is so. It is so absolutely; I have no doubt of it, and every dictate of prudence and propriety enjoins me to be silent, and let it be so. But I have heard that Lucan, of old time, could not tell how to determine the cause, when the deities espoused one side and Cato the other; and although all the dictates of prudence and propriety be arrayed in argument, if —— be opposed to them, how can I but hesitate? But I do not hesitate, the thing is as good as at an end. It is known only to you and me; when we meet we will drink a toast to the power of forgetfulness. You shall agree to forget all the weakness and vanity which this unreserved intimacy has disclosed; and on my part I will promise to forget—to forget—forget every thing. The summer is now over; its fervors no longer inflame the fancy. Winter is at hand; he is a sober moralist, and will doubtless lesson me into moderation, and into hopes not above my desert. Philosophy and tobacco, too, beside winter, are fine emollients. What I can expel by reflection, and what will go off *in fumo*, at the end of my cigar, will leave me little of disappointment and nothing of uneasiness. It is now probable that your friend D. W. will much sooner be saying, "May it please your honors," and "Gentlemen of the Jury," than "celestial maid," and "angelic creature." But although I shall be sufficiently satisfied with myself, if I can at any time attract a little attention when it is not otherwise directed, and never aspire to be able to turn the current into one channel when it is strongly impelled in another, yet I still believe that all ——'s love in this case will be lost. My opinion of F. is just what it has been, and it is confirmed by hearing that he has been violently in love, since he left college, with a lady in Massachusetts, whom he knew, at the time, to be engaged. FINIS.

Enviable was my fortune last week in having Bingham with me three days. Seven years' intimacy has made him dear to me; he is like a good old penknife, the longer you have it the better it proves, and wears brighter till it wears out. I believe he will do better in life than many who figured beyond him in the university, because he has a "spirit of detail;" he is minute and particular; he adjusts trifles, and these trifles compose most of the business and the happiness of life. Great events happen seldom and affect few; trifles every moment happen to everybody, and though one occurrence of them adds little to the happiness or misery of life, yet the sum total of their continual repetition is highly consequential.

Accuracy and diligence are much more necessary to a lawyer, than great comprehension of mind, or brilliancy of talent. His business is to refine, define, and split hairs, to look into authorities, and compare cases. A man can never gallop over the fields of law on Pegasus, nor fly across them on the wing of oratory. If he would stand on *terra firma* he must descend; if he would be a great lawyer, he must first consent to be only a great drudge. Bingham and I passed a unanimous vote that you ought to be here with us. What a fine *triumviri* we should have made; too fine to meet often in these regions. This is modest.

Compliments to whomever they will pass, and assurances of friendship and esteem to yourself sendeth

Your friend, D. WEBSTER.

I hope you have destroyed the letter to J. D. Esquire. Whenever you feel uncommonly lazy and insipid sit down and see if you can write a letter as foolish and as full of I's and Me's as this.

MR. WEBSTER TO MR. MERRILL.

Salisbury, December, 1803.

WHAT a fine time to write to Merrill by Capt. Woodward, if Merrill had only answered my last! Oh, the rogue, of how much happiness has he deprived himself by delay! For although my letter should be a very poor one, it would be received in a manner to make it acceptable. Capt. W. would say: "Mr. Merrill, there is at our house a letter for you, will you call?" So after tea Merrill would jog up to Professor W.'s, and being there he would pleasantly pass an hour in company with the Queen of hearts, that peerless Virgo, with whom, if one might unite himself, and thereby become Gemini, he would be the most enviable of all the constellations.

For his sake then I will away with ceremony, stumble head and shoulders into his presence, and salute him.

DEAR MERRILL,—I have more than one, or two, that is to say I have three reasons for writing you now, although my last has not been answered. The first is, to give you the pleasure in the above eloquent soliloquy mentioned; the second, because I do not wish our correspondence to assume an air of formality, but that an unexpected epistle may arrive now and then fresh and warm from the heart; the third, that, having a little bit of leisure, I know not how to employ myself better.

Virgil says; you know I always loved Virgil; I never laid him aside for Pope or Peter Pindar, for poetry or politics; I never neglected him to talk about the Muses and Parnassus, and Helicon, and the Pierian Spring, to write learned essays for debating clubs or squibs for the newspapers; and without irony, I never put him by, thank Providence, for Martin's Philosophy or Watt's Logic; Virgil says, in the character of Æneas, the brave boy who bore his father from his burning capital, just as an affectionate rat will lug off a decrepit parent from a building in flames; Virgil says: "*Pulchrum inter arma moriri.*" Yes, Virgil, thou speakest sapiently; it sure is "a pleasant thing to die in arms," and, reverently be it spoken, it is a pleasant thing to live so too.

There, Thomas, this is the essence and quintessence of my thoughts upon matrimony; and much as you read eulogies upon that subject, I will bet five pence you never before heard this passage of Virgil made use of for that purpose. I am a surprising creature at invention!!!

John Porter, in his official capacity, has notified me of the wishes of the P. B. to write them a poem. If six of the nine Muses were to stand at my elbow and promise that, according to their best skill and discretion, they would inspire every line, word, and syllable, semicolon, and comma, I should not choose to undertake to write a poem. I left making rhymes when I left college; and as to poetry, I do not know that I ever made any. So you must put your heads together and make another, and I hope a better choice. If Mr. Everett, of Amherst, could be prevailed upon to undertake it, he would do great credit to the society and the university. I do wrong to tell you that I have made no rhymes since I was graduated. Two great occasions have called forth each a wondrous piece of verse; one, I shall some time show you, to make you laugh; the other, I have put down to make you cry; for, if an author may judge his own works, it is by far the most sublime and pathetic I ever wrote. But I must disclose the occasion of such a daring effort. On the afternoon preceding the evening of a ball, a lady of my acquaintance trod upon some sharp tool and cut her foot. On this, my Muse, who had slept some years, broke out, "like an Irish rebellion," when nobody expected it, and produced the following, which in point of sentiment and language, I know you will think equal to any thing in Homer!! Here it is, read it.

Rust seize the axe, the hoe, or spade,
Which in your foot this gash has made!
Which cut thro' kid and silk and skin,
To spill the blood that was within;
By which you're forced to creep and crawl,
Nor frisk and frolic at the ball!

But Clara, Clara! were thy heart
As tender as thy pedal part;
From thy sweet lips did love but flow,
Swift as blood gushes from thy toe,
So many beaus would not complain
That all their bows and vows are vain!

There, Merrill, is not this Homerican? Adieu!

D. Webster.

I have not space here to put down all I hear of the popularity of a certain friend of mine, nor how he becomes a tutor without ceasing to be a gentleman, a sight I would give more to behold than to see the transit of Venus.

MR. WEBSTER TO MR. BINGHAM.

Salisbury, December 23, 1803.

Dear Hervey, — I cannot say that your last arrived as soon as I looked for it; for I am always looking for your letters; but I had it as soon as I had a right to expect it. Frequent letters are not, perhaps, absolutely essential to friendship; but they are the best and most natural consequence of it. You and I should certainly be always friends, if we never wrote another syllable to each other; but we should be friends to little purpose, if we never mutually contributed any thing to soften care and cheer the heart. Your letters have become a settled portion of my happiness; the force of habit is added to the force of esteem, and if you should intermit writing for a long time, there would be a kind of vacuum in my pleasures that I could not handily fill with any thing else.

I verily believe you had a jaunt in getting home, and was really alarmed for you, when you gave the description of your dangers among the rocks and hills of Warner and Boscawen; but I recollected that you were snug by the office fire, and, though the rocks might tumble, you were safe. Your patience, I trust, was as long as the road, and Enos's colt I believe to be a match for all the hills between this and "No. 4." As to the "amusement and information which you found at Salisbury," you speak very complaisantly. You learned, perhaps, a little in the shooting way, and you heard an elegant strain of music, on a fine morning, from the top of a tree, and played some backgammon with Phebe; these are, I believe, all the items of your "instruction and amusement," and they do not form a very long list. But whatever pleasure you received, you certainly conferred much. The squirrels chipper now undisturbed, and I shall suffer none to trespass on our ground till you come again.

I have had a letter from Fuller, and one from Freeborn. The former can't help saying a little about the girls, and after praising them very judiciously, concludes by saying he sees them very seldom. You and I make no such pretensions to philosophy. If I could be more among good girls than I can, I should certainly avail myself of the opportunity. I consider such company the school of refinement, and quite necessary to prevent those roughnesses of temper and manners that a clouted student and a man absorbed in business are certain to contract. It is not he who spends most hours over his books that is the most successful student. It is impossible to keep the mind on the stretch forever; it will sometimes relax; and though we may keep our eyes on our books, it will steal away to easier contemplations, and we may run over pages without receiving an idea. I know this is the case with myself, and believe it is with others. The true science of life is to mingle amusement and business, so as to make the most of time. "Every man," says Johnson, "must sometimes trifle; and the only question is, whether he shall do it alone or in company;" whether he shall waste his hours in solitary visions and drowsy contemplations, or, mingling in society, partake of that cheerfulness and joy that give new energy to the mind, and promise to reward exertion with new success.) Here is the end of my sermon. Freeborn has gone to the South, I know not how far.

Zeke is at Sanbornton. He comes home once in a while, sits down before the kitchen fire, begins to poke and rattle the andirons; I know what is coming, and am mute. At length he puts his feet into the oven's mouth, places his right eyebrow up on his forehead, and begins a very pathetic lecture on the evils of poverty. It is like church service; he does all the talking, and I only say, "Amen, amen."

Your little sister's death, I hope you consider as you ought. I have no great opinion of the goodness of that heart, on which such things make no impression. Innocent little thing! thou hast been a stranger to guilt, and therefore art such to grief. Sweet be thy rest! 'tis the repose of innocence. Respected be thy memory! for thou wert the sister of my friend.

Give my love to "our folks," and believe me, dear Bingham,

Yours, affectionately,

D. Webster.

A FRAGMENT.[1]

Hail, Poesy! thou nymph of every grace!
In form unrivalled, of angelic face!
Far brighter beauties on thy brow appear,
Than Thomson found to deck the rolling year;
More dulcet nectar gathers on thy lip,
Than Virgil's Gods of old were wont to sip.
Who can resist thine all-subduing charms?
Heaven in thy smiles, Elysium in thine arms!
But hold, Encomium, while the bard shall trace
The nymph's descent from some illustrious race,
To what great sire her lineage shall he follow?
Say, who begat her, Denham, Wash, or Waller?

1 The original of this, in Mr. Webster's handwriting, is believed by Thomas Porter, Esq., who furnished it, and who was graduated in 1803, to have been written while Mr. Webster was in college.

Whom does she call her father, Smith or Broom,
Yalden or Dryden, King or Sprat, or whom?
A dubious case! Old Johnson, critic sage,
Says she was born in many a different age,
That Chaucer first produced her to the light,
Next solemn Milton, ere he lost his sight,
From ravished Genius gave the damsel birth,
Who grew from him, like giants from the earth:
Decrepit Pope, for one poor weak embrace,
Is called the sire of that immortal race,
Whose poetry now thunders round the ball,
And tells how heroes or how sparrows fall,
Princes or parrots meet some dire mischance,
Ladies lose hearts or garters at a dance.

MR. WEBSTER TO MR. DAVIS.

Boston, January 18, 1804.

My Friend, — You have been too long a citizen of this world to expect permanency in any of its enjoyments. Untried, as you may be, in the school of affliction, and few and light as have been your misfortunes, compared with those of others, you must yet have seen, what every one sooner or later is compelled to see, that he who would raise a column of durable happiness, must not lay its foundation in the earth. Of all calamities, the loss of friends impresses us most solemnly, because it is irretrievable. Ruined fortunes may be repaired; reputation, unjustly ravished, may be restored; enfeebled health may be renovated. But what shall repair the ruins of the grave? What shall restore the breathless object of former affection? What shall renovate the slumberer beneath the clods of the valley? At this moment I know you are lamenting the loss of an excellent woman whom you loved as a parent, and whom all justly loved for the surpassing benevolence of her heart, and the sterling goodness of her character.

During my residence at Hanover, I had more than one opportunity of witnessing the unwearied kindness and attention of Mrs. Fuller to the sick and the necessitous. I have seen the aspect of disease brighten at her approach, and sorrow and anguish banished by her kind and tender solicitude. I have seen her house and her heart open to receive friendless strangers, and to soothe and comfort the sick and the forlorn.

Yet, however useful, human life must end. Though crowded with virtues, its date is momentary; though all be done that can be done, how little is the amount! It is the tenure by which we hold all our friends, that when He calls, whose right to them is greater than ours, we must give them up. It is the part of wisdom to think, often and seriously, on the title to the good things we enjoy; and first and chiefly, to be anxious of placing our happiness where vicissitudes cannot change, nor accident destroy it. Low, and cold, and silent as your parent now is, must you, and I, and all our friends be. Happy, then, if we shall deserve to have shed on our graves the tears that bedew hers. I know nothing so mortifying to the vanity of the heart as the reflection, that we must one day depart, without having our absence felt beyond the circle of a small acquaintance. Yes, it is a truth, more solemn than the language it is conveyed in, that when

> ——— "You and I are gone,
> This busy world will still jog on;
> Will sing, and dance, and be as hearty
> As if we still were of the party."

Well and wisely is it ordained that men shall see their own presumptuous folly in the fate of others. Good or great characters decease, are lamented, and in a few brief moments forgotten.

Who, then, shall be mad enough to think himself of consequence?

> "Rebuking Heaven ne'er called with louder voice,
> On swelling mortals to be proud no more."

Adieu, my good friend,
D. WEBSTER.

MR. WEBSTER TO MR. DAVIS.

Salisbury, February 5, 1804.

DEAR SIR, — A part of a cold Sunday shall be employed in writing to you. Prevented by the weather from manifesting my devotion at church, I will manifest my friendship.

It was the hope of indemnification that induced me to write to you, and as long as that hope continues, I shall be punctual. There is nothing which gives me more pleasure than a sociable family letter, filled up with those thoughts which swim on the surface of the mind. Such letters savor of conversation, and are a tolerably good substitute for it. But I did not intend here to give a lecture on letter-writing.

I went to Concord a few days since, just to see Sophia and get my cheats, &c., &c.; and so I was really cheated. She had taken the liberty to go home. Well, tell her not to hurry in making my *flamadiddles.* I shall not want them till Commencement. I have chatted with my brother about the matters and things which you mentioned to me. If he goes on again, he will probably accommodate you with any attentions in his power to bestow. But it is uncertain whether he ever summers among you again. This is told you in confidence. I pray you not to mention it to any person. If it be of any importance to you to know, I will inform you shortly of his going, or not going again to Hanover, with certainty.

Cold fingers, you know, make short letters.

Adieu.

D. WEBSTER.

P. S. No progress in electioneering as yet. I believe they at Portsmouth begin to stir. Those folks, you know, "are very busy, all alive." The Federalists, as their manner is, sit still and sigh at the depravity of the times. But sighs, and tears, and broken hearts are not worth a biscuit; they cannot get a vote. Colonel K. will probably be candidate for senator in this district against Esquire Bradley. The prospect is that a good democrat will be chosen. In Concord, J. Green, Esq., is mentioned as Kent's successor as representative.

I believe I mentioned to you that I have had a notion of

making a communication to Miss Hough on the subject of L.'s property in the office at Concord. I should have done it before now were it not for the fear of saying something which might possibly injure the feelings of Mrs. K. and her friends. If it were practicable to go clear of that, I believe it would do good to have the thing known. I expect you will write me by the bearer, whether such a thing would not, in your opinion, be advisable. Pray let me hear from you and of the health of Mrs. Davis, as I understand she left Concord unwell. If you follow my example in making a short letter, pray follow it also in adding a long postcript.

MR. WEBSTER TO MR. BINGHAM.

Salisbury, March 16, 1804.

Good old Companion,—I have a thousand things which are secrets, and as many which are no secrets, to say to you in this letter. I hardly know where to begin, for there is such a struggle in my brain as to what shall be said first, that likely enough I may run over two pages before I say any thing.

Yours of 22d February, was received March 12. "Hope deferred maketh the heart sick." I pray you never to delay writing so long again for any event; for even one so important as the commencement of your labors as a lawyer, hardly atones for so long waiting.

By this time you have decided where you intend to advertise writ making; let me know about it directly.

Several gentlemen of the profession have mentioned to me two or three towns, in Cheshire county, where an industrious young man might probably make a moderate living. Washington, Westmoreland, and Chesterfield have been named. As to the first, if you settle at Lempster, as I suppose you will, it will be too near to you; so let that go. The other two I wish you to write me about as particularly as you can. I know I am in great season, as I have a year longer to read, but there are some other reasons, which induce me to wish to know generally what part of the country I shall inhabit. It is more than probable that I shall be leaving this place in April or May. If I could think it likely that I should hereafter find a resting-place at some town in Cheshire, I should be fond of reading in that quarter a while. Now, you know, if I could have my wish, I should be as fond of being in Mr. West's office as anywhere. Silence! Don't whisper a word; don't ever think aloud; but ponder these matters a little at the bottom of your heart, and write me. Inquire if any charitable clever fellow at Charlestown would keep me, and get his pay when he could. Utter not a word for the soul of you; but let me hear from you forthwith.

So, by the help of a little good testimony, you came off victorious in your first attempt. Well, that is a good omen; go on as you have begun, always, unless when your client's cause is an unjust one.

I was lately in Concord, where I heard of our friend Mary. I shall not put down here all the civil things that were said of her, because, you know, I should make a bad figure in reciting compliments. My brother Zeke has made his bow, by letter, to President Wheelock, and gone to Boston. He has there taken a school, which I engaged for him in January, for you must know I have been at Boston since I last wrote you, and has the prospect of making something a little decent. Merrill was this way at the close of the last term. He is quite a beau for a tutor.

Whitaker has opened his office in Providence. Fuller wrote me about two months ago; he will probably settle in Augusta.

As the last dull paragraph to a very dull letter I will tell you, that I have been out of health for some weeks, that writing is very uneasy to me, and that this is, I believe, the only letter of friendship, which I have undertaken to write these two months.

Sick or well, however, I am not the less your friend,

D. W.

Write me forthwith.

MR. WEBSTER TO MR. MERRILL.

Salisbury, March 16, 1804.

YES, Merrill, a comparative estimate of the pleasures of ambition and of friendship will set the latter in an enviable view. Fame, if obtained at all, costs much. The pursuer after this ever flying goddess must climb over cliff and hill, "o'er many a frozen, many a fiery alp." Men are inclined to throw every thing in his way, and he must therefore prepare to counteract everything. Men's passions may be split, like the earth, into zones, and in every region the ardent follower of fame will find obstacles. First, there is that cold, arctic indifference that will not take the trouble to admire or applaud anybody, or any thing; next, there is temperate reserve, prudence, discretion, or whatever you call it, that dares not praise, lest the object of its praise, by some possibility, be unworthy; and last, and worst of all, come the torrid heats of resentment, rivalry, emulation, and opposition. But suppose your candidate for the caresses of Madam Fame survive all this; suppose he pursue unremittingly the object of his love through "antres vast and deserts idle," through every difficulty, and over every obstacle, till at last he overtakes her ladyship, and is permitted to kiss the hem of her garment on Mount Immortality, what will the dear-bought damsel boot him? If he take her to his bosom, she has no flesh and blood to warm it; if he search her pocket, he finds nothing but poverty; if he taste of her lip, there is no more nectar in it than there are sunbeams in a cucumber; every rascal who has been bold and fearless enough, Nimrod, Catiline, Cromwell, and Tom Paine, all those have had a smack at her before him; they have all, "more or less," become famous, and will be remembered much longer than better men.

Yet, Merrill, you and I have some ambition; so has, or so ought to have, every one. So much ambition as shall prompt to laudable exertion and industry; so much as is well consistent with the duties and the honest pleasures of life; as induces a wish to make ourselves respected by our friends and not entirely despised by our enemies; and on the score of property, so much ambition as instigates to the acquirement of a decent, competent estate, enabling us to treat our friends as they deserve, and to live free from embarrassment; this degree of ambition is rational and necessary.

Mr. Noyes handed me your letter written at Newburyport, which was cordially received, as any thing of the kind from you always will be. You must have seen Miss Thompson at Newburyport, because she mentions you in some of her letters to her friends here. She is one of our sort of girls exactly. You must have been pleased with Miss T.'s countenance, and, take my word for it, the whole volume, as far as I have perused it, is equally fair as the title-page.

When you have an opportunity, if you please, you may mention my esteem as a friend to M. W. and N. R. Write me when you have leisure, which I hope you will find directly.

Yours in all sincerity,

D. Webster.

N. B. My brother has taken up his residence in Boston. He bids me mention his respects to you as a private gentleman and as an officer of college.

I was within half a dozen miles of you about 20th of January, but did not know it till afterward.

If you write Tenney, give him my compliments.

MR. WEBSTER TO MR. BINGHAM.

P. S. The top of a letter is a new place for a postscript; excuse it, for its design is to beg you to give my love to your and my friends P. and E.

Salisbury, April 3, 1804.

Good Hervey,—I am really much obliged by your ready attention to my requests; as also by your saying, that as Mr. West leaves the matter with you, I "may venture to jog on." Captain Enos is precisely the man for me; if ever I eat bread at "No. 4," it will be at his table. The distance from the office is not too great in dry weather, and in wet times one has nothing to do in Charlestown, but just to step "the other side of the street."

I am now going, James, to give you a full survey of the "whole ground," as it respects my prospects, hopes, and wishes. The great object of a lawyer is business; but this is not, or ought not to be, his sole object. Pleasant society, an agreeable acquaintance, and a degree of respectability, not merely as a lawyer, but as a man, are other objects of importance. You and I commenced the study, you know, with a resolution which we did not say much about, of being honest and conscientious practitioners. Some part of this resolution is, I hope, still hanging about me, and for this reason I choose to settle in a place where the practice of the bar is fair and honorable. The Cheshire bar, as far as I have learned, is entitled to a preference in these respects over that of any county in the State. You know my partiality for Connecticut River folks generally. Their information and habits are far better, in my opinion, than those of the people in the eastern part of the State. These reasons compel me to say with you, "it is a goodly land," and to make it my wish to settle therein.

E contrà. Many of my friends are desirous that I should make an attempt to live in Portsmouth. Mr. Thompson, my good master, knows every thing about the comparative advantages of different places, everywhere in New Hampshire, except Cheshire county. He has frequently suggested to me, that Portsmouth would be a good place for a young man, and the other evening when I hinted my inclination for Cheshire, he said he had a high esteem for the people that way, but added that he still wished me to consider Portsmouth. He says there are many gentlemen of character there, who would patronize a young lawyer, and thinks that even Mr. Attorney-General would be fond of the thing.

Mr. T. will have business, on which I shall be at Portsmouth as soon as the roads are passable, and out of respect to his opinion, I shall make no certain arrangements for my future reading till that time. At present, I do not feel that Portsmouth is the place for me.

In the way of study, my present pursuit is some little knowledge of pleading. I am reading what Bacon has collected on that subject, and yesterday, you will hardly believe me, I travelled through a case in Saunders of eight Latin pages. Saunders inserts all the pleas, and abridges the arguments of counsel; he is therefore, I take it, very useful to those who, like myself, are a good deal ignorant of the forms of pleading. I mean to lay my hands heavily upon him, and in one month I hope to be able to give some account of him. The winter has passed away more pleasantly than any I ever before passed at Salisbury, as far, I mean, as my health, which has not been the best, would suffer it to be pleasant. Mr. T.'s sisters have been in this realm, and being very excellent folks, added much to what was before very small society in Salisbury. Miss Poor is in town, yet it would please her vastly if you would just call and play a game at backgammon with her again. She says I unreasonably monopolized your company last fall, at the expense of the folks in the house. I told you how all that matter was and would be; I don't see how I can live any longer without having a friend near me, I mean a male friend, just such a friend as one J. H. B. Yes, James, I must come; we will yoke together again; your little bed is just wide enough; we will practise at the same bar, and be as friendly a pair of single fellows as ever cracked a nut. We perhaps shall never be rich; no matter, we can supply our own personal necessities. By the time we are thirty, we will put on the dress of old bachelors, a mourning suit, and having sown all our wild oats, with a round hat and a hickory staff we will march on to the end of life, whistling as merry as robins, and I hope as innocent. Good-bye to this nonsense, and, by way of contrast, good-bye to you. D. W.

EZEKIEL WEBSTER TO DANIEL WEBSTER.

Boston, April 4, 1804.

DEAR DANIEL,—I most readily concur in the opinion that the present scene of your life as well as my own, is marked with "dark traces and heavy shades." The map of human life is checkered with misfortunes and disappointments. A continual sunshine of prosperity does not accompany man in his transit from the cradle to the grave. Penumbral shadows of doubt, perplexity, and anxious care mark the pathway of the most fortunate through the course of life; and often the moment of greatest obscuration is the very period when he is about to enter upon a new profession. Yet, at solemn and distant intervals, a ray breaks through this gloom and opens to the imagination a vista of better times. Let this ray cheer and console us. It is a sweet delusion. I am glad that you feel no "depression of spirits." I cannot see any reason for an indulgence of melancholy, though there appears abundant cause. Fortune is a mistress not to be melted into pity by the plaintive lamentations of her stricken votary. Persevering enterprise alone withstands her frowns. Agreeably to your injunction, I have thought and meditated upon your letter, for three days, and for no inconsiderable portion of three nights, and I now give you the result as freely as I earnestly wish your welfare. I am directly opposed to your going to New York; and for several reasons. First, the expensiveness of a journey to that city, and of a residence in it, is with me a material objection. Secondly, the embarrassments to which you will be liable, without friends to assist or patronage to support you. Thirdly, I fear the climate would be injurious to your constitution. I have now told you what I would not have you do, and I also tell you what I wish you to do. I would have you decamp immediately with all your baggage, from Salisbury, and march directly to this place. This is the opinion I have maturely formed for which a thousand reasons might be urged. They are too numerous to be mentioned, nor is it perhaps necessary, for I say to you imperatively, "come." It is the easiest thing in the world for a fellow of any enterprise or ability to support himself here, very handsomely, without descending to any business incompatible with the situation of a gentleman. Here, too, is the focus of information. Any person, however stupid and inefficient, cannot but learn something. With a head ever so impenetrable, some ideas will penetrate it. I will state to you a single circumstance which, I think, will remove all doubt about paying your way. I have now eight scholars, in Latin and Greek, whom I shall be obliged to dismiss if I cannot have an assistant, and I dare not, at present, hire one. The tuition of these eight scholars will pay for your board. They recite twice in a day, and it will take you about three fourths of an hour to hear them, each time. Here, then, you can support yourself by the labor of one hour and a half each day. If you will spend that time in my school daily, I will board you at as genteel a boarding-house as you can wish or the place affords. Consult father, the family, and your friends, and start for Boston the next day after the receipt of this letter. Another such an opportunity may never occur. Come, and if you don't find every thing to your liking, I will carry you back to Salisbury, with a chaise and six, and pay you for your time. I must say again, consult father; if he approves, take the patriarchal blessing and come.

I am as usual, &c.,

E. WEBSTER.

N. B. Be careful to remember those books. If you do not come, write immediately.

Remember me most affectionately to the family.

E. W

MR. WEBSTER TO MR. MERRILL.

Salisbury, May 1, 1804.

DEAR MERRILL,—There is no business so pressing, and no amusement so entertaining, from which the heart will not sometimes stray away to repose itself in the contemplation of old and undiminished friendship. I sometimes sit down to my books, transport myself to the court-house in London, and listen to wise judges and ingenious lawyers. But ere I am aware, thought wings itself to Hanover, to Charlestown, or the residence of some other friend, and I awake from the pleasant little vision, scarcely knowing where I left off in the lawyer's argument, or his Lordship's charge. A little business, which I shall mention anon, affords me a pretty fair excuse for writing you at this time. I am glad it is so. I am happy in the opportunity of spending, I mean of enjoying, a half hour with Merrill. What is this world worth without the enjoyment of friendship, and the cultivation of the social feelings of the heart? For a life consumed in money-seeking, fame-seeking, and noise-making, I would not give more than eighteen pence, which is seventeen pence halfpenny, one farthing more than it is worth.

O, Thomas, Thomas! I wish I could see you. Since I last pressed your hand, my life has abounded in some incidents which I could magnify into matters of mighty little consequence. Poh! poh! What trumpery! How microscopical is self-love! It makes us think that trifles, light as air, affect our friends because they affect us, or, to speak metaphorically, it swells a little piece of salt not bigger than a chestnut, into an immense mountain forty-five miles long. My heart is now so full of matters and things impatient to be whispered into the ear of a trusty friend, that I think I could pour them into yours till it ran over. But perhaps if we were to meet this hour, I should not be able to make out one sentence of any consequence. I have often been caught so, and have been so much mortified, that all my boasted sources of conversation could hardly be formed into a paragraph long enough for the use of two commas and a semicolon.

I desire most earnestly to hear from you, to hear directly from your heart and your heart's concerns. Pray how do you feel in and about the heart? And how does it feel about the heart of ——? Well, pardon me; I am apt to put impertinent inquiries; but they allow you an opportunity of exercising your virtue in forgiving; a good trade, and which you will never find opportunity to leave off, so long as your acquaintance with me continues. Pray tell me all that may be told.

Now, business. We are informed that a new statute of the corporation of the college has ordained that a student forfeits his connection with college, by an absence of so long a time; how long a time, and what is the whole account of the business?

These inquiries, as you will guess, are on account of my brother. I wish to know whether it is probable he can be graduated with his class. I believe he wrote the President and asked him that question, but I do not learn that he ever has received an answer. If the President forgets to give himself the trouble to answer him, he will expect me to get him the information some other way. You can if you will, and you will if you can, tell me all I want to know about the college laws in this respect. I should be sorry to have the old fellow trudge all the way from Boston to Commencement for nought.

I look forward to Cambridge Commencement as the time when I shall see you; perhaps it may come before, and whenever it does come, it will be welcome.

I can think of nobody at Hanover to whom my compliments would be worth six pence. So Merrill must keep the whole; they will do him little good, but they will cost him nothing.

Very sincerely yours,

D. Webster.

DANIEL WEBSTER TO EZEKIEL WEBSTER.

Salisbury, May 5, 1804.

Dear Ezekiel,—Salisbury, you perceive, as yet heads my letters; and how much longer it may, I can hardly tell. I know it is much better for me to be absent, and I am zealously laboring to put myself into a new situation. If I recollect, I informed you my intention was to depart, as soon as it is possible for me to get a little cash, to enable me to rig out; for when I leave this vale, emphatically a "vale of tears," I am determined to be under no obligations to anybody in the neighborhood, except those of gratitude and friendship. I never heard what particular substance Archimedes wished his desired fulcrum to be, resting on which, he was going to move the world; but if his design had been to move every thing in it, he would have wished it cash; of all things of a perishable nature, it is worth the most. It ever did, does now, and ever will, constitute the real, unavoidable aristocracy that exists and must exist in society. I had an expectation of putting into execution a plan that would have made me able to see you immediately. It was well laid, and I begged of father to attend to it last week, at court, but he forgot it.

I shall continue to scrape round me and let you hear how I speed. John Smith has left college; he never sent me any word about your matters, and believes I have not heard from Hanover since I saw you. I have been thinking that if it can be well dispensed with, you would choose not to attend Commencement. You have never written me any word about your finances at present; but if you could get forty or fifty dollars in the course of this month, you had better transmit it to me, and send me on to Hanover with it, to intercede with his excellency about giving a degree without your presence; and to secure the trifles you have there, and to pay the aforesaid forty or fifty dollars to your creditors. Father has sent 0000 to Mr. Lang, and I don't believe he will; I don't honestly see how he can. Let me hear from you what you think in respect to this idea. I should abominate to look over your shoulder, in Boston, and see you break a seal and read: "Dear Sir, the little trifle you owe me," &c.

You see, I suppose, the accounts of our governor election as readily as I do. If all the votes be returned, Gilman will creep in, on the force of about one hundred and fifty majority. Pray write, forthwith.

Give my love to our friends. D. WEBSTER.

EZEKIEL WEBSTER TO DANIEL WEBSTER.

Boston, May 10, 1804.

DANIEL, — I received yours of the 5th instant, and agreeably to your request shall give you an account of my finances. The report will not be very elaborate; nor shall I be able to grace the cadence of many sentences with "money in the treasury." You know the conditions on which I took the school. The tuition of those attending the then present quarter was to be given to the Doctor; and, as luck would have it, not his sagacity, I found that almost all the quarters had expired, and were then commencing anew, when I undertook to teach the school. I would not mention this as any thing against the Doctor; for he certainly treated me with great politeness. It is mentioned only as it proves that I could not receive much money until I had kept two quarters. One for him and the other for myself must be out before I could have any demands for money. This, however, is not the case with all. A few will expire in July. Until then I have no way to make or receive a cent but by admission. This is not a very abundant source of supply. The sum is only two dollars, and this never to be received but once for any one scholar. Once admitted, and the scholar may stay in my school forever and for aye, without paying again his entrance money. I brought a few dollars from home with me, you know; but, as soon as I got into town, I found it necessary to new-habit myself; and, following your advice, I was determined to contract no debts while my money continued. Thus, dear Daniel, the end of the whole matter is that I am able to send you neither forty dollars, nor twenty dollars at present. However, I think it will not be a long time before I can say I owe no man any thing but "love and gratitude." I should be as unwilling as yourself to have you read over my shoulder, "Pay that thou owest." Saving debts of some few dollars, I owe no man any thing at Hanover but Mr. Lang and the authority. These debts are large enough to make them respectable. If these are demanded, they will be demanded in an honorable manner. They will not sell them to a friend, nor will they "tuck you by the arm" at every corner you may chance to meet them. In this situation, I thought and do still, it was best for you to come into town. The prospect may brighten, it cannot darken. I told you, in my last, a few dollars would be a pretty thing to bring; because, as I have written above, my bills will not become due till July. Pray, write often until you come, and let me know every thing local. Contradictory reports reach us concerning the New Hampshire election. Give me some account of it, in every letter, until you come. Old South continues laboring in the "good cause," sometimes under one signature and sometimes under another. Like Goldsmith's redoubtable gander, he is determined to defend the "wash-pond" of democracy as long as he has a "quill to brandish or a tongue to hiss." If John Smith has left college permanently, I must write to some friend to see to my affairs there, if neither you nor myself should go thither.

I am, &c.

EZEK. WEBSTER.

MR. WEBSTER TO MR. MERRILL.

Salisbury, May 28, 1804.

AND if it were a pleasant evening, thought I, as I read yours of the 16th — if it were a pleasant moonlight evening, I should be willing to meet Merrill half-way, for sake of an hour's chat, even though that half-way might happen "in a marsh, or on a lake," or anywhere except in Ben. Thompson's tavern. I suppose I never shall have a heartier desire to see a male friend than I have to see your tutorship; but this, like some other more important wishes of the same heart, is not likely to be gratified. The first leisure, since the receipt of yours, is employed in answering it; for when you are wrong, I wish to have you right as soon as may be. My former letter was probably written hastily. I am not now fully possessed of the contents of it, but it is probable I said a good many things which I did not mean, and left unsaid a good many things which I might have said, and which it rested with your sagacity to discover. From what I wrote, you conclude that I am "about to be caught in the toils of wedlock." Ay, an ambiguity! Pray, do you mean the snares or the labors of wedlock? But you are wrong; there is no such thing, nor any thing very much like it. This said wed-lock is a very dangerous sort of a lock. Once fastened, it is fastened forever. It is a lock that one can't unlock; you can't break it, you can't pick it. Therefore I say again that this is a very dangerous one. In that idle reverie of the imagination that is called a "brown study," I have sometimes fancied myself a king, governing by wise maxims; a priest, making good sermons; a doctor, a lawyer, and a thousand other things; but in the most wayward frolic of fancy, I never dreamed myself to be a husband. A husband!! My pen flies and hurries from that word with an unusual degree of speed, and I am not sure that I could prevail on myself even to write it again.

But this is all nonsense. I will try to be serious, for you appear to be so. Seriously then, Merrill, I am making no progress towards matrimony. In point of time, I am twenty-three years nearer to it than when I was born; but, in point of probability, I cannot say that I am any. You ask me to mention names, and say you would trust as much as that to a mail carrier. Really, Thomas, I love your zealous cordiality. Your earnestness to know the truth of your conjectures, I regard as a proof of friendship, and of the interest you take in my welfare. You have a right to know all, and, *tempore proprio*, you shall know all. I can say that there is no name which I could write, that is, or ever probably will be, in any way connected with mine. All I have said does not prove that I carry about in my bosom a stony heart, unpenetrated and impenetrable; much less are you to understand from it that disappointment is about driving me from this world "by cold submersion, razor, rope, or lead." You are great in arithmetic. I will give you a problem; but, on a second thought, it belongs rather to algebra than arithmetic. As known quantities, take partiality and esteem, on one side, to an indefinite degree, which Judge Woodward says is much the same as an infinite degree. On the other side, take charity and condescension, but take with them also something like an *alter amator et connexio precedens.* Now, Mr. Algebraist, what is the result? Ah! it will be *minus!*

All these matters and things must rest here till I see you. There is no knowing what may be. Perhaps you and I shall cast lots for the privilege of making bows to M——y. Be not alarmed, for if it fall to my fortune, I will sell you my right, verily believing that before I see her again, her "Little Beater" (Bingham's name for heart) will be in the safe-keeping of my friend M.

You have very much bound me, by your attention to my brother's matters. When I write him next, I will mention the subject of an oration. He has some reluctance to public exhibition, and perhaps will hardly be willing to prepare, under the idea that the occasion might happen. If not absolutely the last, this is near to being the last letter which I shall write you from Salisbury. I am now pretty well determined to go to Boston, about the first of July. I am now ready for my departure, and only wait to give myself the pleasure of a ride to the upper part of Maine, to accompany thither Miss Poor, who has been a while in Mr. Thompson's family, and whom you have heard mentioned. In this route I shall see Mr. Dana's folks. If they are as inquisitive as ever, they have probably learned something of their cousin's state of mind. If they say any thing interesting to you, like as not I shall tell you of it; though, by the way, I suppose you know much more than they do. I shall hardly see Hanover at Commencement. Good old village, adieu! You ask me to tell you what to do. I would if I could; but am scarcely able to direct myself. My wish is that you should be, in a great degree, what I can sincerely say I think you in a very respectable one, learned, deeply learned in biblical erudition. At this time more than any other, we need ministers who can furnish us with weapons to defend our faith.

Pray, write me in season, so that I may receive your letter before I set out on my journey, about 15th of June. Tell me whether you shall, and be sure to say you will, be at Cambridge Commencement. Tell me every thing about everybody, and what everybody says about every thing.

Who is more heartily yours than

D. W.?

DANIEL WEBSTER TO EZEKIEL WEBSTER.

Salisbury, June 10, 1804.

Dear Ezekiel,—Yesterday evening I returned from election, in about as good spirits as you would naturally suppose, after being witness to the triumph of democracy. J. T. Gilman is elected Governor by a majority of one hundred and thirty-two votes, if I recollect right. The Senate is seven Democrats and five Federalists. Nicholas Gilman is President. John Langdon is Speaker of the House, by a majority of twelve. Nat. Gilman was yesterday elected Treasurer, by three votes majority; but on examination it was found that there were several more votes received than there were voters in the house! What an everlasting disgrace to New Hampshire that there are such scoundrels in her government. This is about as clever as a Boscawen town meeting. To-day, at ten o'clock, they were to proceed to a new choice for Treasurer. I have not heard the result. Bradley and Bingham bring me the only word I have heard from you, since Mr. Greenleaf's return from Boston. The former tells me he understands you intend putting your name in some office, forthwith, after Commencement. That is right. Make a good choice of an office; he mentioned old Judge Sullivan's; I should think that might do very well.

Feeling some anxiety about your "sheep-skin," I wrote to Merrill, and begged him to put his finger on the President's pulse, and tell me how it beat. He writes in return that if you attend Commencement there is no doubt you will have your degree. He said that it would be well for you to prepare an English oration for Commencement. I promised to mention the thing to you. If you should have one of the very first stamp I should like it.

I talk of going for Mr. T. to East Andover, to accompany Miss Poor to her friends. As soon as this is over I intend going to Boston.

For cash I have made out. Perhaps in three weeks you may see me in Short street. Our cousin Nat. is getting better. Aunt Esther is about rushing into wedlock; next week she sets out into life. Zeke, I don't believe but that Providence will do well for us yet. We shall live, and live comfortably. I have this week come within an ace of being appointed clerk of the Court of Common Pleas for Hillsborough county. Well, you will say, you are no better off than if you had not come within an ace. Perhaps I am;—say nothing, but think a good deal, and do not distrust the gods.

I shall write you before I go to East Andover, if I go at all; if I do not go I intend seeing you directly.

Keep the contents of this page a close secret; write me immediately, and believe me,

Yours affectionately,

D. Webster.

EZEKIEL WEBSTER TO DANIEL WEBSTER.

Boston, June 17, 1804.

Good Daniel,—I was not very well the day our friend Bingham left town, or I should have written by him. I had not written immediately before, for I thought if you were about coming into town, you would make it in your way to be here about election time in this State, and concluded it might be probable that while my letter was finding its way to Salisbury, you might be moving towards Boston. Your last, however, lets me know that you are still in Squam, but will be in "Short street" in about three weeks. A very delightful place! We shall be glad to see you. Come as soon as convenient. Mr. Thompson sends you upon business to East Andover? Be faithful to your employer, and do not lay your action so as to be nonsuited; for you must remember that nothing but the death of the party will enable you to bring a new suit. I think, Daniel, you made a very good supper upon a "white raven," when you were going to have so cleverly the clerkship of Hillsborough county. It would, though, be a very pretty thing and I advise you to use all honest means to procure it. It will answer very well for the present. In that office you may make a little money, become acquainted with the forms of legal business, and be prepared to enter your profession with many advantages with which you could not at present. You know, however, much better about this than myself. Ask me about a school and I am equal to you. Democracy has triumphed in

New Hampshire. It is nothing more than I expected, and what I told you. In my opinion there is not a nook or corner in the United States that will not be revolutionized. The contagion of democracy will pervade every place and corrupt every generous and manly sentiment. It cannot be successfully resisted. The pestilence will spread in a favorable state of the atmosphere, notwithstanding all the medical exertions of the most skilful physicians.

I am glad Nat. is getting better, and that aunt Esther is about to be married.

Remember me to all the family, and tell them all to write me by you. Good health, a pleasant journey, and a quick arrival at this place.

I am, &c. E. WEBSTER.

MR. WEBSTER TO MR. BINGHAM.

Salisbury, June 18, 1804.

JEM,—By this time you are seated fair and easy at your office table, and ready to receive communications from your friends. "Communications!" What have I to communicate? Alas, alas, my noddle affords an argument against the old maxim of the Schools, that nature abhors a vacuum. I believe I told you every thing in the short space of time we chum'd together at Polly's house, and among other things I told you I would write you in a week. It is for the sake of fulfilling this promise, and not because I have any thing, black, white, or gray to write to you, that I now lay aside my garden hoe, and take up an instrument which I handle much more bunglingly, a pen. To-morrow morning, if the wind blows precisely from a N. N. W. point; if the sun puts on a cool garment, and does not sweat himself to death, as he has done a week past, with his fearnought; if the great sieve of the skies does not drop down its waters too copiously; if every thing is fair and handsome, cool, and comfortable, why then I shall set out for East Andover to gallant Miss Poor to her friends.

Our honorable court are going on finely. They have passed a set of resolves approbatory of the present administration; they have agreed to the amendments to the Constitution, by a majority of seven. They intend, as we hear, to district the State for the choice of Representatives to Congress. The electors, they say, shall be chosen by the people on a general ticket; and the people are to be told to be sure to vote for the democratic ticket. Mr. T. told me that Mr. West was to be candidate for a seat in the Senate, about to be vacated by the expiration of Judge Olcott's time. And this is all the political news, which has yet transpired from the Honorable General Court of New Hampshire.

A few days since I received a letter from Freeborn; he is in Edgefield District, South Carolina. He writes that he has a good stand for the distribution of medicine, but says the ribs that way are rather ugly. He passed some time at Washington, Norfolk, and Charleston, and seems to write in his usual flow of spirit.

I shall see Cook; shall I give your Honor's love to him? Ay, I will even venture it; give mine to Harry. There was something which I intended to have said to him in a P. S., but just at this time I can't recall it.

On a review of this letter, I find that if my character for letter-writing were not already established, this would fix it completely.

Good-bye. You will never have another such an interesting letter as this. Two prodigies come not in one age.

D. WEBSTER.

DANIEL WEBSTER TO EZEKIEL WEBSTER.

Salisbury, June 18, 1804.

DEAR EZEKIEL,—Day after to-morrow, if the wind blows from the right point, I start for East Andover; on this tour I expect to be absent about twelve days; and soon after my return here, I expect to be in Boston. The season is now so far advanced, I intend to make my calculation, so as to be merely seasonably in town, to learn the arrangements of your school and be able to manage it, till you go after your degree. Now I want you to be particular. Some time ago you mentioned to me a few Latin and Greek scholars; since then you keep glued lips on the subject of your school. I desire to know whether you can employ me; how many hours per day; in what doing, and for what reward? All these questions you must certainly answer; and have your answers here by the time I return. Tell me into whose office I had better go; whether letters of introduction and from whom would be useful; in short, tell me every thing; and as an inducement I will now tell you all I know about our New Hampshire politics.

The propositions in amendment of the Constitution passed by a majority of seven. It is probable Nicholas Gilman or Jonathan Steele will be elected Senator to Congress, in the place of Judge Olcott, whose time expires next March. Mr. West will be the Federal candidate. I know not if this election is to be made this session. It is said the representatives to Congress will be chosen by districts. I know not who are candidates on either side. The electors, they say, are to be chosen by the people on a general ticket. The Democratic candidates are thought to be Goddard, Langdon, Allen, Tarlton, Obed, Hall, &c. The Federalists meet to-night to agree on their list. The probability is, it will contain the names of Jere. Smith, Tim. Farrar, Ben. West, perhaps T. W. Thompson, Arthur Livermore, Wm. Hale, Oliver Peabody. This is my conjecture, perhaps I am incorrect. The court have had the grace to add five hundred dollars to Chief Justice Smith's salary; this, it is thought, will keep him on the bench.

Apropos, they have passed a set of resolves complimentary to the present administration!

In the neighborhood, we have nothing new. Everybody is well except Uncle Will, and he has just told me to say to you he is better. Aunt Jones is married to old Uncle Adams. Hymen came down one evening and did himself the honor to unite the glowing lips of youth and beauty.

Mr. Davis was this way at election time; he brought nothing from Hanover, worthy to be told.

Adieu. Pray do not fail to write me, so that I may find your letter here when I return. Give my love to Doctor and Mrs. Perkins.

DANIEL WEBSTER.

DIARY.

[The following fragment of a Diary, kept by Mr. Webster while a student at law, being all that has been preserved, is inserted here, in the order of time, and is interesting as containing sketches of some of the eminent men then at the Massachusetts bar.]

July 17*th*, 1804. Arrived in Boston.

19*th*. Paid Elijah Chamberlain thirty-nine dollars and forty-eight cents, for my friend D. Abbott, Esq.

20*th*. Waited on Mr. Gore; and, by the kindness of my friend Bradley, prevailed upon him to receive me into his office. Paid two dollars to Dr. Perkins's boy for Repertory. Paid Mr. Bradley three dollars for tickets.

24*th*. Entered the office of the Honorable C. Gore, as a student at law. Bought *annu. pro mea* ——

28*th*. Took up at Mr. Chamberlain's three dollars twelve and a half cents.

29*th*. Wrote Sarah.

30*th*. Paid seventy-five cents for thread gloves.

August 1*st*. *Scripsi meæ* ——

2*d*. Dr. P., debtor, fifty-four cents, paid. Wrote Freeborn Adams, a few days ago.

5*th*. Dr. P., debtor, twenty-five cents.

7*th*. Pay to J. Bradley, for J. McGaw, Esq., two dollars and fifty-six cents; handed it to S. Bradley. Bought, yesterday, Pursuits of Literature, for one dollar and sixty cents. Wrote Mr. Hough for Courier, 4th instant; also, wrote Bingham, same day. Paid twenty-five cents, for Dr. Perkins, to Bradley, in way of tickets.

10th. Finished reading Ward's Law of Nations, two vols., and began Vattel.

18th. Went from Dr. P.'s to McC.'s to board. Sent by E. twenty dollars to Mr. Abbott. Paid one dollar and fifty cents for door keys; one dollar and eighty cents for locks and keys.

31st. Attended the trial of Blood, for passing counterfeit bills; heard Otis, in his defence; very fluent, rapid, and ingenious; Davis, on the part of the government, shrewd and dextrous, but using language incorrect and often inelegant.

September 1st. Handed Dr. P. thirteen dollars.

4th. Finished reading Evans's Essays on the "Account for money had and received," and bills of exchange. Wrote to J. McGaw, Esq., yesterday.

14th. Paid S. A. Bradley five dollars for some small notes, *et cetera.* Wrote Mr. Bigelow. Finished Evans on Insurance, some time ago; read Boswell's Hebrides.

17th. Professional life affords fewer prospects of making great estates, but more certainty of earning a comfortable living. Mercantile business is precarious though often exceedingly lucrative; professional, seldom very lucrative; but generally, certain; therefore, I rejoice that I am in the way of a profession. Oh, Instability! To-day, I have heard of mercantile failures. I philippize against that employment now; to-morrow, perhaps, I shall hear of great and heavy gains, and shall then eulogize it.

22d. Returned from Worcester; heard A. Walcott say that the Democrats had lost ground in Connecticut, at this fall election; that the constitution plan was rather unpopular; and, as he thought, premature.

24th. Socrates said, if you marry, you will repent; if you neglect it, you will repent. Read Viner's Title of Pleadings yesterday, and to-day. It is not so copious nor so instructive as what Bacon says, under the same title. Wrote Mr. Peirce, some days ago.

26th. Read one hundred pages in Abbott on Shipping; derived much instruction from it. "If a captain in his voyage hypothecates his ship to different loaners, and to a greater amount than the value of the ship, the last loaner shall be entitled to priority of payment; because it is that loan which preserved the ship."

October 1st. Finished Abbott on Shipping; a valuable treatise: "If C. D., by a proper deed, authorize A. B. to execute a bond or other deed for him, A. B. may do this either by writing C. B. by A. B., his attorney, or by writing A. B. for C. D., provided he delivers the instrument as the deed of C. D," page 300. I prefer the former mode.

4th. Read the first volume of Moore's Travels.

5th. Finished Vattel, for the third time in my life. "If goods are found remaining in the hands of an insolvent factor, they may be claimed by the consignor; because a delivery to a factor does not of itself alter the property." Abbott on Shipping, page 233. By the civil law, and by the laws of Russia and France, if a man become bankrupt, the seller of any goods to him, if he could identify the goods unsold, in the hands of the bankrupt, might claim them, and should not be compelled to divide them with other creditors. This is very different from the law of England, by which goods become, by actual or constructive possession, the absolute property of another and equally liable to all creditors' claims.

9th. Looked through the "Elements of Common Law," by F. Bacon, Lord Verulam. If there be any ambiguity apparent in a deed, it shall not be allowed to clear it by averment of matter of fact; this is *ambiguitas patens*, namely, the uncertainty appears by inspecting the deed; this is to be cleared by construction, not by averment. But if there appear no uncertainty in the deed or will, but yet certain facts exist which create an uncertainty, then it is proper to aver; as if A., by will, give an estate to his son; here is no *ambiguitas patens;* but, if it be afterwards known that A. have two sons, then it may be allowed to aver that he intended his eldest son.

11th. Read Viner. Title, Obligation. "If three bind themselves and each of them, it seems that two of them cannot be sued. If a bond be written jointly and severally, though the delivery be at several times and places, it is yet both joint and several. If a man covenants with ten and each of them to make sea banks in D., and does not, whereby the lands of two are injured, those two may have their actions." Bond to two, for two thousand pounds, to pay one hundred to one and one hundred to the other; if one obligee die, *quære*, if the other shall have the two thousand pounds; I think not; but there is authority of contrary opinion. See Dyer, p. 350, and Bacon *in loco.*

If condition for an obligation be insensible and contradictory, it shall be rejected, and the obligation shall stand. If A. promise to pay ten, without saying to whom he promises, it shall be intended that the promise is made to the person to whom the payment is to be made. This ought to be alleged in the writ, otherwise it will not appear that the plaintiff is entitled.—Littleton. If a man bind his heirs to pay a sum and does not bind himself, it is void; for no man can charge his heir but as part of himself. If three are bound and one is impleaded and the plaintiff recovers, and after impleads another, the first recovery is no bar; for, judgment is not satisfaction; contrary, if plaintiff take execution, by his recovery, a co-obligor must plead satisfaction. If two are jointly bound, and one die, you can only sue the survivor, and not the executor of the deceased also; otherwise, if they are bound jointly and severally. After assignment of a bond, the money is the assignees'; and payment to the obligee, after notice of the assignment, is not good.

> " My heart still hovering round about you,
> I thought I could not live without you;
> Now we have been two months asunder,
> How I lived with you is the wonder."

Empedocles—Behemoth—scarlet die.

16*th*. Bought hat for seven dollars.

18*th*. Read Bacon's Title, Obligation. If two are bound jointly, and one dies, the survivor shall be alone chargeable; and the executor of the deceased shall not be bound. In this case, the declaration *v.* survivor should state the death of the co-obligor. Dyer, 19, 310. If two are jointly and severally bound in an obligation, and the obligee releases one, both are discharged; and, *à fortiori*, if it be a joint bond. Coke, Litt. 232. One surety may compel another to contribute. If the condition of an obligation consist of two parts in the disjunctive, both possible at the time of making, and after, one becomes impossible, by the act of God, the obligor is not bound to perform the other. Ray, 373. The alternative is for the benefit of the obligor. A bond with condition to kill J. S., is void; but a feoffment, on such condition is good, for the law will, in each case, remove the temptation to do evil. C. Litt. 206. If I contract to deliver forty yards of cloth, and cut it in pieces, and then deliver it, 'tis a breach. If a man be bound to pay money, at a day, and he pay it before 'tis due, 'tis a good payment, and such payment may be given in evidence, under *solvit ad diem.* Coke L. 212. A bond, dated May 12, payable on the 13th of May following, is payable on the 13th of May next year. In cases where notice and request are necessary, yet the obligor is disabled by his own act from performing his bond, it is forfeited without notice. In debt on a bond, for the performance of several things, it is not enough for the defendant to plead that the condition is not broken; he ought to show how it is performed. This sort of general pleading was never admitted. In debt on obligation the defendants cannot plead *nil debet;* he must plead *non est factum,* or a release, &c. N. B. *Scripsi,* 4 Man.; C. W.; Judge Wood; New Hamp. Mem. Con.

November 28*th.* Returned from Albany.

30*th.* Wrote my father, Mr. Thompson, and T. A. Merrill.

December 6*th.* I have to-day paid Mr. Chamberlain thirty-four dollars; fourteen in specie, at the shop; twenty in bills, at the house. Lent him one hundred and ten dollars; received it. Wrote to Mr. Caldwell, and requested him to serve the summons, Gore *v.* Brazer. Wrote to Dinsmore, Esq., Keene, and enclosed Lowe's receipt.

January 2*d.* Mr. Gore told me that when he was in practice in this town, formerly, he made from one thousand five hundred to two thousand guineas, the year. Judge Tudor, Messrs. Morton, Hitchborn, Lowell, and Edwards, were the chief men then in practice. He was invited to be Comptroller of the Treasury, but declined. Mr. Davis was then appointed. When Mr. Gore went to Europe, he recommended Mr. Dexter to be his successor. Mr. Dexter declined, and General Washington appointed Mr. Davis.

19*th.* Finished reading Gifford's Juvenal.

March 5*th.* This day, in one of the rooms of the state house, in presence of Isaac P. Davis, and Samuel A. Bradley, and Jem Dix, Jr., I examined the letters to Callender from Jefferson. Mr. Dix told me he had often seen the signature of Mr. J., and on being asked whether he doubted that Mr. J. really signed the letters in question, he said, "he did not." I preserve this precious confession against a time of need.

SOME CHARACTERS AT THE BOSTON BAR, 1804.

THEOPHILUS PARSONS, Esq. is now about fifty-five years old; of rather large stature and inclining a little to corpulency. His hair is brown and his complexion not light. His face is not marked by any striking feature, if we except his eyes. His forehead is low and his eyebrows prominent. He wears a blue coat and breeches; worsted hose, a brown wig, with a cocked hat. He has a penetrating eye of an indescribable color. When, couched under a jutting eyebrow, it directs its beams into the face of a witness, he feels as if it looked into the inmost recesses of his soul. When Parsons intends to make a learned observation, his eyebrow sinks; when a smart one, for he is, and wishes to be thought, a wit, it rises. The characteristic endowments of his mind are strength and shrewdness. Strength, which enables him to support his cause; shrewdness, by which he is always ready to retort the sallies of his adversary. His manner is steady, forcible, and perfectly perspicuous. He does not address the jury as a mechanical body to be put in motion by mechanical means. He appeals to them as men, and as having minds capable of receiving the ideas in his own. Of course, he never harangues. He is never stinted to say just so much on a point, and no more. He knows by the juror's countenance, when he is convinced; and therefore never disgusts him by arguing that of which he is already sensible and which he knows it impossible more fully to impress. A mind thus strong, direct, prompt, and vigorous is cultivated by habits of the most intense application. A great scholar in every thing, in his profession he is peculiarly great. He is not content with shining on occasions; he will shine everywhere. As no cause is too great, none is too small for him. He knows the great benefit of understanding small circumstances. 'Tis not enough for him that he has learned the leading points in a cause; he will know every thing. His argument is, therefore, always consistent with itself; and its course so luminous that you are ready to wonder why any one should hesitate to follow him. Facts which are uncertain, he with so much art connects with others well proved, that you cannot get rid of the former, without disregarding the latter. He has no fondness for public life, and is satisfied with standing where he is, at the head of his profession.

J. S. is a man of some understanding and a great deal of ambition. He is the reverse of Parsons in many respects. He has less learning, less perspicuity, less force, less pertinency. He rolls on his cause with an immense labor, deals in much sour invective, and acts in that way, as if he supposed the court and jury against him. He has, however, much industry, and is said to be a man of excellent private character. I should think him near sixty.

Samuel Dexter, Esq., is about forty years old; a man of large size and noble appearance. His complexion is dark and his eyes dark, large, and prominent. In point of character, Dexter undoubtedly stands next to Parsons, at the Boston bar; and in the neighboring counties and States, I suppose he stands above him. He has a strong, generalizing, and capacious mind. He sees his subject in one view, and in that view single and alone he presents it to the contemplation of his hearer. Unable to follow Parsons, in minute technical distinctions, Parsons is unable to follow him in the occasional vaultings and boundings of his mind. Unlike Parsons too, he cannot be great on little occasions. Unlike him, Parsons cannot reject every little consideration on great occasions. Parsons begins with common maxims, and his course to the particular subject and the particular conclusion brightens and shines more and more clearly to its end. Dexter begins with the particular position which he intends to support. Darkness surrounds him. No one knows the path by which he arrived at his conclusion. Around him, however, is a circle of light, when he opens his mouth. Like a conflagration seen at a distance, the evening mists may intervene between it and the eye of the observer, though the blaze ascend to the sky and cannot but be seen. Mr. Dexter is not a great student. Early attention has stored his mind with an immense fund of general principles, and he trusts his own powers in the application. He is generally opposed in causes to Parsons, and their contest is that of exalted minds. No fretting, no bickering, no personal asperity ever exists between them. Dexter is not rich. He lives upon his profession, which, as I was told, by a pupil of his, affords him an income of near five thousand dollars. He once received fourteen hundred dollars for arguing a cause for the Spanish consul.

MR. WEBSTER TO MR. BINGHAM.

Boston, August 4, 1804.

DEAR HERVEY,—Boston, this marvellous town, full as you know it is of every thing of every sort, has not altogether enough in it, nevertheless, to fill the whole capacity for happiness.

Neither business nor amusement hath charm enough to supersede the use of friendships, "ancient and honorable." I am in great want of a letter from you; and as the readiest way of getting it, I write this as a sort of dun, a creature handily manufactured by one of our profession.

I have been in Boston, according to Sir Isaac Bickerstaff, "the full term of twenty days," in which I have enjoyed good health, the use of a good office, and the company of some good friends, three as comfortable things as a body could wish for. I am in the office of the Hon. Christopher Gore, lately returned from London, where he has resided the eight last years, as a commissioner under the British treaty. I neither knew him, nor had letters to him when I came into town, nor was I acquainted with anybody that did know him. I was pleased with his reputed character, and knew that the chance was, that he would not have a great deal of small business to do in his office; such was the office I wished to enter. On the whole, I preferred it to any office in town, and had reason to suppose that it would not be disagreeable to him to take a clerk. What was to be done? How should I become known to him? I meditated on these questions a day or two, and, at last, luckily thought that I had a tongue in my head; and that, *Deo volente, et modestia non pugnante*, I could tell him my own name. I consulted with Bradley, and on the whole we concluded that being both strangers, we would go, and introduce each other. We succeeded admirably. Mr. Gore agreed to receive me, but not understanding Bradley very distinctly when he mentioned my name, I had been in the office a week or so before Mr. Gore knew the name of his clerk!!! This I call setting out in the world! Mr. Gore is a fine man; learned and communicative, and I could not possibly be better situated; but I most devoutly hope that I shall never have to set out again.

Jerome, the brother of the Emperor of the Gauls, is here;

every day you see him whisking along Cornhill, with the true French air, and his wife by his side. The lads say, that they intend to prevail on American Misses to receive company in future after the manner of Jerome's wife; that is, in bed. The gentlemen of Boston treat Monsieur with cold and distant respect. They feel, and every honest man feels, indignant at seeing this lordly grasshopper, this puppet in Prince's robes, dashing through the American cities, luxuriously rioting on the property of Dutch mechanics or Swiss peasants.

Will you do me a favor? Mr. Sumner is Coleman's agent to receive payments for the New York Herald. I began to take the paper some time in the fall of 1802; can't say exactly when. I have sent to the printer three dollars. Now I wish you to pay Mr. Sumner what there is due, and send me an account of it, and I will forward it to you again by the next mail. I would send it now, but cannot tell within a dollar or two what is due. If you will attend to this thing and write me forthwith, you will oblige me. I wish to have the paper stopped. Give my love to our friends, and believe me yours affectionately,

D. WEBSTER.

MR. WEBSTER TO MR. BINGHAM.

Boston, September 14, 1804.

DEAR HERVEY,—I should be glad if I could think of a great many wise and useful things to say to you now, just as you are preparing to clothe yourself in the character of a lawyer. Having however a subject nearer home, for all the admonitions with which my mind furnishes me, I shall leave you unadvised.

I wish you were here. Boston would please you as a place of professional study. I could, however, only wish you here under particular circumstances. You say the want of cash prevents you, and if it were not for that you would pass a six months here. I do not know whether I should advise it. You are now ready to open an office, open; you are ready to make writs, make them; you are ready to go about getting money, get it. This is my advice. If I had gone my time, I would not stop to study law anywhere; not because I think it a good calculation to hurry into life; but I am argued into the notion by that all-powerful argument, the necessity of being in business. Write me in less than two minutes after you receive this, and let me know where you are going to fix yourself. Having settled, for I suppose you intend to stay in Cheshire county, I wish you to give your opinion of the then best vacancy in Cheshire, together with the opinion of others whom you hear mention the subject. I mean to stay here, if I can, till my time is out, and in the interim I wish to inform myself, so as to be at no great loss for a stand. If I am not earning my bread and cheese, in exactly nine days after my admission, I shall certainly be a bankrupt. Fuller was lately here. He said much about Bingham, and appointed once or twice to write to you, but something prevented. He had with him a Miss, who is said to be his intended. She appears a very sensible, agreeable girl. Mary Smith is in town. I have made her my humblest bow. Last evening I was at Perkins's; some one knocked; the door was opened; when, with precisely the old swing, entered that "urbanic and extended figure," Augustus Alden. He is very well; resides at Augusta, a student at law. Adieu, good fellow, adieu,

D. Webster.

Give me information about my newspapers, that I may reimburse your expenditures on the subject. Zeke sends love.

MR. EBENEZER WEBSTER TO HIS SONS.

Salisbury, October 6, 1804.

Dear Sons,—I received a letter from you by Mr. Sawyer. I was very happy to hear that you were in good health. I have a sufficient reason for my not writing by the last mail. A week ago last Tuesday, I attended the funeral of Benjamin Page; came home and went to bed as well as usual. About twelve o'clock, I was taken with a violent pain in my side, which terminated in a pleurisy fever. I had a physician sent for as soon as possible. He took some blood from my arm, which gave me some relief; but I lay in this distressed situation until Thursday, before I could be moved, even to have my bed made. The fever has now abated, so that I am able to walk about a little.

Had I sent for you when I was first taken, I thought it impossible for me to live in such distress until a messenger could get half-way to Boston; if I had written by the mail, it might have given you anxious feelings for me; for these reasons I have omitted writing until now. I wish you to write by the next mail, by all means. Your mother's health is much better than when you left her, though very poor now. We have got our new cider made, and this day began to gather our corn; our potatoes are dug. I have great reason to be thankful that I am able to subscribe myself your living and affectionate father.

EBENEZER WEBSTER.

MR. THOMAS W. THOMPSON TO MR. WEBSTER.

Salisbury, October 17, 1804.

DEAR SIR,—I returned from Haverhill and Hanover last Sunday, after an absence of nearly three weeks. Upon my return I received yours of the 27th ultimo.

Unfortunately the rule of the bar is as you suspect, and the business entirely escaped my mind at September court. I was at the court but about an hour. I did not attend October court at all. I feel criminally negligent, and to quiet my own mind and make you some amends, I have written this day a circular letter to each gentleman of the bar in the county, propounding you for admission, and preparing their minds to dispense with the letter of the rule, considering it was established when the terms were three months only apart. An association of ministers meet this day at Mr. Worcester's, and your father has undertaken to disperse the letters by the mail and by those ministers. I flatter myself this propounding will answer your purpose. If not, I feel confident the court will admit you without the recommendation of the bar. No exertion shall be wanting on my part to procure you the recommendation of the bar.

The death of President Willard affected me very sensibly. I not only esteemed and respected him very highly, but I loved him. My two years' residence at Cambridge as a tutor, gave me an opportunity of knowing him perfectly. To strangers his address was rather of the repellant sort, to his friends he was amiable in the highest degree. My opinion is that the corporation cannot select a more suitable person to fill the vacancy occasioned by his death than Judge Davis. If Judge Davis had more dignity of person, his appearance would I think, be more presidential. This is a trifling exception. I can't help feeling a strong attachment to my Alma Mater, and this attachment, together with my general regard for the interests of literature and religion, creates a strong anxiety to have that chair filled by the very best man that can be had. The influence of a President of that university may be of incalculable importance. Why is not a Professor of Divinity chosen? I wish you to unravel this mystery. I suspect the corporation have different views upon the subject; some wish for a Calvinist, others for an Arminian. I conjecture that the difficulty of supplying that vacancy results more from something of that kind than from a lack of candidates of respectability, who would accept the appointment. I wish you to inform me.

I am much pleased with the communications signed Mass. and W.[1] and I can assure you they have excited a very interesting inquiry for the author. The former I recognized; the latter I had not seen till after the receipt of your letter. Go on. Catch every leisure moment. If pecuniary compensation should not follow, you will have a satisfaction of a higher nature.

It gave me no small pleasure to learn that you had found a seat in Mr. Gore's office, and I made an effort, the effect of which I have never learned, to interest Mr. Gore's feelings in your favor. Mr. Saml. Torrey is his brother-in-law, and my effort was directed through him.

I wish you could persuade Park or some other good soul to preserve a volume of the best eulogies on Hamilton. I am confident a subscription for that purpose would run well. The best I have seen are Nott's, Mason's, Otis's, and Ames's. Cheetham's ought not to be omitted.

If you propose to pass the winter in Boston, I should like to know it in order to give you some commissions of a troublesome kind. I shall wish you to write to me often, and you must pardon me if I insist upon paying the postage upon my own and your letters. At some distant period I shall not object to your paying your proportion.

1 The Editor has not been able to find these communications.

I hope you keep up your acquaintance with my friend, Captain Wm. Parsons. Say, how is this?

We have had as yet very few particulars of the destruction done by the late storm in your quarter. At that time I was at Hanover with my family, and was obliged to remain there three days before I dared set out for home, and then I was two days and a half travelling home. One person counted one hundred and sixty trees, which were blown across the turnpike between Clough's in Enfield and Thompson's in Andover. The snow in the woods was from one to two feet deep. When I came through on Saturday it was upon an average one foot deep, and so solid as to bear me for miles without leaving scarcely any impression of my foot. We were eight hours in the carriage, riding eighteen miles. At the Plain, the snow was about six inches deep after the storm, and very solid. The orchards and woods through the country have sustained immense damage.

I have for a long time endeavored to purchase, without success, Roscoe's Life of Lorenzo de Medicis. Will you purchase it for me and send it up by some of our traders? My wife has heard much of a novel called The Minstrel, and wishes you to purchase it for us. Please to let me know the prices, and I will transmit you the money by the return of the mail.

Should you have occasion to borrow money, please to let me know it, and if I have it on hand I will accommodate you with it as long as you please, at six per cent. annually.

Your friends here are in usual health, excepting Mrs. Hadduck, who is quite unwell yet.

My regards to Ezekiel.

I am, dear Sir, affectionately yours,

THOS. W. THOMPSON.

N. B. I wish you to procure me a copy of the act incorporating the Exchange Bank, or such parts of it as will be necessary to show the principles of that institution. If it is published with the public acts, perhaps you can procure a printed copy, and forward to me. Furnish me, if you please, with any information you may possess that will be useful in understanding the manner in which it is conducted.

Enclosed is a ten dollar bill, for which you will please give me credit towards the disbursements I have requested.

MR. WEBSTER TO MR. FULLER.

Boston, October 17, 1804.

Dear Fuller,—If it be as cold at Augusta as it is here, and if you were called up last night, as I was, to see a house burn down, you will wonder how I happen to take a notion to write to you this morning. The motive is, I have several things to say to you, which I had better say now while they are recent. Day before yesterday I had a letter from brother Davis; all finely at Hanover; pumpkin pie and professors plenty; wheat and poetry a good deal blasted; girls and gingerbread as sweet as ever. Last Sunday evening, to-day is Wednesday, I had the pleasure of a moment's chat with —— ——. She appears much out of health, and though she laughs as heartily as usual, I suspect the good girl is declining. She was here on a short visit, and has returned. I could not parry several questions she asked me concerning my friend ——, and concerning certain other things that concern him. I was obliged to tell all I knew, how could a body help it? One cannot get rid of a lady's question by evasion; she will immediately assail in another shape; she will know the truth and the whole truth. Even if I had the honor of being interrogated by a female with respect to any affair of my own, I should recite the facts and answer her questions in as simple and plain a style as John Bunyan's; for I hold it an established point, that when a woman has a right to know a thing, you cannot content her with any thing short of the whole matter.

* * * * * * * * * *

Once or twice I have had the honor of bowing to Miss Paine in the streets. Possibly, it may be well that I am not in a way to cultivate the acquaintance to which you introduced me. She might perhaps write her name upon my heart as fairly as I can write it upon paper. Yet that would not be a singular case, for there has been many a lover before me, who has had Pain in his heart.

Freeborn has written me a very pretty letter. He likes every thing in Carolina except the ribs; those he thinks poorly polished. Charles Gilbert has been in town since you were here. His health is very low, but he flatters himself that it is mending.

* * * * * * * * * *

I owe you one dollar and ten cents, and interest three years; this shall be as good as a note for it till it is paid.

Make my best respects and present my best wishes to Miss G. I am not the less interested in the welfare of a good woman, because her welfare is a part of the happiness of my friend Fuller.

Adieu, my dear Sir,—Adieu.

D. WEBSTER.

DANIEL WEBSTER TO EZEKIEL WEBSTER.

Worcester, Tuesday Evening, November 5, 1804.

DEAR ZEKE,—So far so well. Mr. Chamberlain thinks of setting out this week for Canaan, N. H.

The object of this is to request you to go to him and beg him not to say to anybody in or about Salisbury, that I am gone on this journey. I forgot it—You will find some cash with him, unless you have got it.

Adieu. If I go to Connecticut River, I will write you thence.

D. WEBSTER.

DANIEL WEBSTER TO EZEKIEL WEBSTER.

Springfield, November 9, 1804.

DEAR ZEKE,—I write to fulfil my promise, and not for the purpose of disburdening myself of the history of any events which have happened on the road. In travelling from Worcester to Albany, the direct path is through Northampton; yet one may go by way of Springfield, if he will. "For which reason we resolved to go by Springfield." Don't impeach the strength of this motive. It is not solely on a journey performed in a post-chaise that caprice chalks out the route. 'Tis the same on the journey of life.

We are below Northampton some twenty miles, and on the east side of the river; ten miles south of this is the north line of the land of "Steady Habits." Riding from Boston here, is just like riding through New Hampshire and Vermont. The same prospects, the same people, the same modes and manners of life. An uneven, mountainous surface extends from the neighborhood of Boston to within ten miles of this place. These ten miles are measured over a dead, flat plain, covered with pitch pines. In my course hitherto I have met with nothing novel or unusual to me, if I except a toasting-iron, which I saw at Brookfield. Ardent of knowledge and desirous of making the most of my travels, I seized my pencil, "warm and glowing" like the object, and sketched a likeness of this toaster on a leaf of my pocket-book.

This day is a very snowing one. We shall be embargoed if the weather does not change soon. It not only confines us to this town, but even to the house. I can see nothing. I recollect of hearing father speak often of the marvellous elm trees in Springfield. I intended to enclose two or three of the largest and handsomest of them in this letter, for your use; and ten minutes ago sallied out with great coat and umbrella, in order to examine them; but the storm drove me into the house again before I had gotten three rods from the door stone. I shall, however, keep the said trees in my mind, and visit them the moment it leaves snowing.

Here is before me the oddest picture I ever noticed. I know not what it is designed to represent; but I believe it must be Venus and some female attendants taming some Cupids. The old lady has one of her sons in a cage, out of which he is sticking his nose and lamenting like a thrush. She has another fast by one wing, while he flutters in the air like a wounded partridge; and, as we suppose, exclaiming most dolefully. One of the attendants has another little god between her knees, and while his lower extremities are thus confined, he is striving and fluttering like a bird, which endeavors to rise with a strap at its legs. Now, I suspect that on paper all these make but a poor show; but they look well on canvas; and if you will not believe me, you may come and see.

Thank the storm for this letter; for had the weather been fair I should this moment have been rolling on to the "high houses, with the gable ends towards the street."

D. WEBSTER.

MR. WEBSTER TO MR. MERRILL.

Boston, November 30, 1804.

My dear Friend,—Having been absent from town some weeks, yours of October 20, did not reach my hand till day before yesterday. All that I know about "evanescent subtenses" or "conterminous arches" might be collected on the pupil of a gnat's eye, without making him wink. This, however, I know, that my friendship for Merrill is a sentiment in no degree evanescent, an arch both ends of which rest in the foundation of my heart. I was sadly grieved that you did not write me sooner. My heart suggested a thousand excuses. "Merrill is busy; new employments fill up all his time; he is making his acquaintances, and has much visiting to do;" but I never suspected that you were ignorant of the place of my residence. W. Woodward, Esquire, made me your compliments just before I left Salisbury, and in your behalf asked me where a letter would find me. I told him Boston. As Dr. Perkins and my brother were at Commencement, I took it for granted you knew that I was in this marvellous town. So much for explanation. I am now here, believe me; you are at Middlebury; and let us take care to remind each other of these facts often. Now hear me talk a little about myself. I am in the office of Christopher Gore, Esq., who has lately returned from London, where he has resided for eight years, as an American commissioner, to settle commercial claims between the two nations. He is a lawyer of eminence, and a deep and various scholar. Since I left John Wheelock, I have found no man so indefatigable in research. He has great amenity of manners, is easy, accessible, and communicative, and, take him all in all, I could not wish a better preceptor. My acquaintance here does not extend very far. It were much easier for me to form connections than to support them. There are many young men of my own age with whom it would be easy to associate; but a young man who has a fortune to spend, is not a proper companion for another who has a fortune to make. There are, however, some families into which I have free ingress here. I resort sometimes to play backgammon with the girls, in order to keep off the glooms,

"With speech so sweet, so sweet a mien,
They excommunicate the spleen."

There are many fellows in this town from abroad, who like myself fall under the general class of adventurers. Some for knowledge, some for fame, and some for cash. A similarity of pursuits attaches these to each other; and, if I must say the truth, I think they are rather envied than despised by the natives of the peninsula. You would be astonished at the portion of the active business of the place, of every kind, that is done by men who moved here from the country. Yet, as far as my circumstances will admit, 'tis my endeavor to become acquainted with the aboriginal Bostonians. It is not the locality of the town, it is not a sight of Beacon Hill, or the Long Wharf, that renders Boston useful as a place of residence for a stranger; but the conversation, the acquaintance, the connection, the intimacy which one has with the Boston folks. An English lord, when he travels to view the continent, carries with him English companions, English servants, and English books. He will stop nowhere but at an English inn, and converse with nobody but his countrymen. How superlatively ridiculous this is! What use is there in going to France, if he must carry England with him? Now this is quite too much the case with young gentlemen who come here from the country to read professions. They associate together; they almost invariably fall into the same boarding-houses; and of the manners of Boston folks they catch none hardly of the spirit; of their habits they learn few beside the bad ones.

Dear Merrill, I reciprocate your wishes for a meeting most cordially. Why were not you at Cambridge Commencement? I explored every countenance I met, with the strictest scrutiny, to see if I could not make M.'s face out of it, but M.'s face was gone to Middlebury. Of the heart and the heart's concerns I can say nothing, for want of room to say enough. Merrill, if in your walks you should happen to meet with Wisdom and Folly, in whose hands should you look for the sceptre of this world? For my part, I deny *mente et lingua*, *pugnis et calcibus*, *unguibus et rostro*, the old Grecian definition of human nature. "*Animal, bipes, implumis, rationalis*;" so says Plato of Man. I contradict him; and to put the thing beyond doubt, I will write my verdict in poetry of the most sublime kind,—*favete Musæ*—*audi* Merrill!

What nonsense lurked within the pate, oh!
Of definition-making Plato,
Who sang in philosophic metre
" Man is a rational and biped creature?"
Many do think, and so do I,
Old codger, that you—told—a lie;
And yet, perhaps, you surly lout,
There is a hole where you'll creep out;
Males you call rational, but no man
E'er heard you say the same of woman!

Yet I do believe we are pretty much alike. I should rejoice to chat with you, and inquire and inform about all matters and things. Pray write me all you know about Hanover, and write me as soon as you receive this. A letter in four or five months is four or five times too seldom. Adieu.

D. Webster.

MISS SALLY WEBSTER TO DANIEL WEBSTER.

Salisbury, December 21, 1804.

Dear Brother,—With pleasure I can now inform you that your friends in this place are all in good health, except Mrs. Hadduck, who is very unwell, but we think her some better than when we wrote before. Before we received your letters by the mail, we heard that you were gone to New York, with a gentleman, at the moderate price of seven dollars a day for your company. It seems, Daniel, that your company is very agreeable in Boston, as well as in Salisbury. We should all be willing to give as much to see you in this town, if we had the change as handy as you have in Boston. I cannot think of any news to write to you about at present; the people here move on in the same old way as when you were here. Sometimes we have junkets, sometimes we have freewillers' meetings. I had almost forgotten to do my errand to you. A gentleman called here the other day, and asked me if my brother Daniel was then in Boston, and if I had heard from him lately; and he would have me by all means write to you and send his most profound respects, as his regard for you was very great. I asked him to sit down, but he could not tarry a moment longer than to do his errand. I have now done mine, and if you can ever find him out or tell me what his name is, I shall be very glad to know, as I never saw the man before, or any thing that looked like him. Before I have finished my nonsense, I must tell you that our neighbors, opposite the door, fought a duel the other day, one with the gridiron, the other with a candlestick. The female, however, came off victoriously, and he, with all speed, ran here for some lint and rum, to be applied immediately, for he was bleeding to death with a wound in his head, caused by the gridiron. I fear you will now say: "If Salisbury females fight with such weapons as gridirons, it is best for me to stay where I am," and by that means we shall not see you this winter. I hope Ezekiel will write soon if he is not too much engaged in his school. We have no school here now, but expect one soon. Moses will go all the time. Do write every opportunity, and consider that if my letters are not agreeable to you, yours are both pleasing and instructive to me. Mother sends her love to you both, and thanks you for your wishes to send her a present, but as she is in no present want of any thing you can get, she will not trouble you for any thing now. I must now end my letter by subscribing myself your friend and often obliged sister,

SALLY WEBSTER.

[Postscript dictated by Judge Webster to his daughter, and signed by him.]

DEAR SONS,—Governor Gilman has called on me for money. He has a large payment to make out soon, and wishes my assistance. If you can hire me forty or fifty pounds, at Boston, and send it on by the next mail, I will return it as soon as I can. Perhaps I cannot before March court. I can settle with Mr. Whitehouse without troubling you, but I cannot make out for the governor as I should be glad to, unless I can hire some money. Nathaniel Webster would like to take your horse and sleigh and meet you at Dunstable, or go on to Boston, if you think it best, and will write to us when you wish to leave Boston. We received a very acceptable present from you, which makes us very comfortable this cold weather. As to the place of your settlement you must determine for yourself. Esquire Bowers, Mr.

Greenleaf, and others, are very anxious to have you at the Centre road. Write by the next mail whether you can obtain the money or not.

EBN. WEBSTER.

MR. WEBSTER TO MR. BINGHAM.

Dear Boston, January 2, 1805.

DEAR SQUIRE,—A letter from you always gives me two happy half hours, one when it is received, and another when it is answered. Figure to yourself, then, a large room in the third story of a brick building, in the centre of Boston, a sea-coal fire, and a most enormous writing-table with half a cord of books on it. Then figure further to yourself your most obedient, with his back to the fire, and his face to the table, writing by candlelight, and you will precisely see a "happy fellow." There, now, is a famous dash at description! Now let me try my talents at narration. Well, then, on the fifth day of November, being election day, at just twenty-seven minutes and a half past twelve, I left Mrs. Whitwell's, Court street, Boston, and on the twenty-eighth day of the same month, at one o'clock, P. M., arrived at the same Mrs. Whitwell's, in the same Court street. You can easily determine, from the above account, where I went!! If, however, you should be puzzled, I will tell you; to Albany. Yes, James, I have even been to Albany. I cannot now tell you why, nor for what, but it was in a hackney coach, with a pair of nimble trotters, a smart coachman before, and a footman on horseback behind. There's style for you! More than all this, I had my friend at my elbow. Now why the deuce must I ruin this account by informing you that it was a male friend? Yet this regard to truth must be kept up, though it is a shackling thing. Well, to proceed: my expenses were all amply paid, and on my return, I put my hand in my pocket, and found one hundred and twenty dear delightfuls! Is not that good luck? And these dear delightfuls were, 'pon honor, all my own; yes, every dog of 'em. Now don't you think I would jump to go to Albany again? But to be serious. I really went to Albany, in November, with a gentleman of this town, for which I received the above reward; and I'm so proud to have a dollar of my own, I was determined to tell you of it. Of my journey and all that I saw and heard, I cannot give you a particular account now.

At Hartford, I saw Simeon Lyman. He is a merchant. I dared not go to see Fanny; though I would not for any thing have her know that I passed so near her. Do you ever hear from her? How is she? Does she mention my name in her letters to you? At Providence I saw Nye, who is a student at law; and Whitaker, who is a husband and a practitioner. On my journey, I met with F. Hunt, at a tavern. He is settled in Hampshire county, Mass., not far from the line of Connecticut.

Well, my dear friend, I rejoice that you are settled under circumstances so promising; you have passed the crisis; you lived through the hour of anxiety and uncertainty, and you see before you a respectable living. I rejoice; and while you prosper, I will rejoice. I expect to be admitted in March, at Amherst, or in April, here. 'Tis not true that I determined to open an office here. I have no thought of it. I thank you for the information you give me about Cheshire County. At present, I incline to think it not unlikely that I shall go to some of the places you mention. But before three months expire, somebody may pop into them all; there is no knowing. Do let me hear from you often, and believe me yours, firm and strong.

D. WEBSTER.

MR. WEBSTER TO MR. FULLER.

Boston, March 10, 1805.

Dear Fuller,—Whenever I see the face of Mr. Whitwell, I am reminded of my duty. For two months, he has been a standing monitor, notifying me every time I enter the State House, to write to Fuller. Not that he has ever spoken to me, or I to him, but that he always brings you to my mind; and being remembered, you call on me for an answer to your last. Since I saw you, I have flown to Albany; rested my wing for a while, and next perched at Hudson; oiled my feathers there, and proceeded to Hartford and Providence, and after cooing and chattering with Nye and Whitaker, fluttered into Boston. Shortly after, the ill health of my father summoned me to Salisbury. I went, had the pleasure of seeing him recover, took his blessing, and hied back again. In two weeks I again put myself in motion, and like Noah's dove, shall flutter, with faint and wearied wing, over the deluge of this world, seeking for rest. In some country town in New Hampshire I shall probably put off my character of a rover, and fix my feet for a season. Having been for the winter a wandering comet, in the spring I become a falling star, and shall drop from the firmament of Boston gayety and pleasure, to the level of a rustic village, of silence and of obscurity. From this village, however, wherever it is situated, the voice of friendship will issue; you will hear my accents and be invited to answer to them. In the meanwhile, wish me well, as the only service you can for the present render me.

The discussion you had with the "five ladies in Boston," on the question whether Mr. W. was a "plain man," must have been, I think, very edifying. It requires, certainly, a vast variety of knowledge to manage this question creditably. You must, for instance, know geometry; for how could you speak of the angles of his phiz, unless you understood decagons and rhomboides? And chemistry, and sculpture, and architecture, and gardening would all be necessary. If, however, you will admit the reasoning of Granger, the Parisian, I can easily prove that I am the handsomest man in New England. This is the process: Boston is the handsomest town in New England; Tremont is the handsomest street in Boston; Scollay's are the handsomest buildings in Tremont street; Christopher Gore's office is the handsomest room in Scollay's buildings; and I am (now) the handsomest man in Christopher Gore's office, *ergo*, I am the handsomest man in New England; Q. E. D. Now if this cause stands over for second argument, I shall entreat my counsel to make use of this reasoning. We had fine fun here of "Allen's motion;" the poor fellow now sits in his seat, still as a sitting hen; scathed and blistered by the thunderbolts that knocked him down, he has such a dread of making motions, that he seems afraid to move his limbs. —— is acquitted. So much for —— and ——; so much for —— and the devil. These four illustrious personages I consider the real agents in the whole business; though perhaps not in equal degrees, for I take it the last-mentioned gentleman has more modesty than to come in for an equal share. If the devil has any regard for truth, he must confess that, at the head of —— Club, either of the other gentlemen is much more of a devil than himself.

Make a low bow for me to Miss G., and assure her I esteem her for your sake and her own.

Yours truly,

D. Webster.

MR. WEBSTER TO MR. MERRILL.

Boston, March 10, 1805.

Dear Merrill,—You did not knock at our office door. "Come in," said I, the moment my ear informed me that any knuckle was in contact with the panel. "Come in," said I many times, when the knock existed only in my imagination. But Merrill came not. Well, "*pie fata decernunt*," I shall now never see the rogue in Boston. 'Tis no matter; I shall see him somewhere else. I write you this, to inform you that you need not write me until you hear from me again. I shall leave this town in twelve days, and that part of *terra firma* where I shall next perch is at present *terra incognita*. If, however, it should be within mail-shot of Otter Creek, I will salute you from my new residence immediately.

So Merrill has preached. I congratulate you on having entered your profession. The moment when we first make trial of our talents in that employment which we have chosen for life, is a most solemn one. What conflicts, what alternate triumphs between the rival powers of Hope and Fear! Feeling all these myself, I heartily rejoice that you have got over them and made a beginning. I only saw Professor Shurtleff in public, and had no opportunity of asking him how Merrill appeared in the desk. But I have no fears; 'tis not for friends to flatter; but I am sure you will do well. Now perhaps you would say something like this to me. Poor human nature! How entirely sure we are and easy about everybody's fortune but our own.

As it is a principal object in the correspondence of scholars to commune together on their studies and pursuits, I should now be very glad to rehearse to you a long list of corpulent volumes which I have read, and inform you of new regions of literature which I have explored. But alas, alas! if I except a few slender and lean professional books, the rest and residue of my reading would make a sorry account. I could hardly get beyond item the second. Gifford's Juvenal has amused me for some evenings. Gibbon's Life and posthumous works, Moore's Travels in France and Italy, *et pauca alia similia*, have rescued me from the condemnation of doing nothing. At present, I am earnest in the study of the French language, and can now translate about as much, for a task, as we could of Tully in our Freshman year.

Political altercation is very warm here, both within the legislature and without. Mr. Allen, a Democratic member of the House, made a motion to dismiss the State printers from their employment for publishing some gross reflections on Mr. Jefferson. The orator was proceeding with great zeal to represent the sin of this conduct in the printers, when one of the Federalists arose and knocked him down with an unexpected thunderbolt. He produced proofs and documents to establish all the charges made in the paper. But you have seen all this in the newspapers. You did not tell me any thing of our friend M——y W——d. Pray who is to lead her off? I hear nothing of those things here; inform me if you know. Dear damsel; I should like once more to survey her tenement of clay, and listen to the accents dictated by the inhabitant within. But when, or where, or whether at all, all is uncertain. Yes, every thing is uncertain except one thing, which is that I am your sincere friend. D. WEBSTER.

DANIEL WEBSTER TO EZEKIEL WEBSTER.

Boscawen, April 25, 1805.

DEAR BROTHER,—I had learned the loss of my money from Mr. Fifield's own mouth, whom I happened to see in Newburyport, before the reception of yours. I am far from feeling any uneasy sensations on that account. It was mere misfortune, nobody is to blame; the sum was eighty-five dollars.

I believe that in writing a hasty epistle to D. Abbott, and another to yourself, last Saturday, I sent yours to him and his to you. You were probably perplexed to understand what you received. Father's ill health and other circumstances induced me to take a stand here. My prospects of business are moderate at present.

It is utterly out of my power to repair the loss of eighty-five dollars. I hired that money of a friend in Salisbury, and cannot, as I know, hire a like sum. My hopes from T. W. T. all failed.

If Mr. Parker[1] can be persuaded to retain the books till next week, I will write you again, and inform you whether there exists a probability of my being able to take them. My trunk of clothes I will thank you to put into Bancroft's stage-coach, and send to D. A.'s office in Dunstable. He will forward it to me by a stage-coach, which runs from Dunstable to this place. Please to coil a rope or line round the trunk to prevent it from bursting; see it in the coach yourself; tell Bancroft I am an old customer, and he must be very careful about it.

I do not think there is any chance of my getting Mr. Parker's money. I will however try, and write you again by the mail, which arrives in Boston Saturday, next week. Folks at Salisbury are all well as usual. Father is getting abroad cleverly.

Adieu, D. W.

P. S. *Thursday Evening.* Since writing this letter, I have been to Hopkinton and have just returned. I cannot say that I have a prospect of forwarding the money for my books. In June I expect to be in Boston. If in your opinion it is best, you may pay Mr. Parker his outsets and break up the bargain; or if you can find any one who is fool enough to lend you the money till June, and you think you can make out a part of the money then, you may send me the books, and you shall own the proportion for which you pay. However, I have no expectation of this kind. I have seen Fletcher to-day. He is earnest to make a bargain with you; and on the whole, I incline to think you had better make up your mind to that purpose. My business is worth a little. I believe I earn my daily bread. With a premium, it might possibly be effected that Mr. Parker, with Mr. Thacher's security, would wait all June for his money; could you in that case make out a part of it? Try Parker, and if so, I will, being notified, write to Mr. Thacher on the subject.

Write to me every week for the present. B——, your eight dollar friend, is not heard of. The opinion prevalent is, that he was a spirit, come from the "vasty deep," for some unknown purpose. The academy has walked down to the south road.

[1] Samuel H. Parker, Esq., now living, in good health. He has stated to the Editor that he remembers the matter of the books very well.

Mr. Eastman has undertaken to keep a grammar school going in it ten years, on condition the neighbors will board for seven shillings and sixpence the week. Mr. Fifield's family felt pretty sensibly Jonathan's misfortune; but I believe are now reconciled to it.

Fol de dol, dol de dol, di dol;
I'll never make money my idol;
For away our dollars will fly all.
With my friend and my pitcher,
I'm twenty times richer,
Than if I made money my idol;
Fol de dol, dol de dol, di dol!

DANIEL WEBSTER TO EZEKIEL WEBSTER.

Boscawen, April 30, 1805.

DEAR ZEKE,—As yet I find it not in my power to procure any money for the purpose of paying for my books. I therefore am under the necessity of requesting you to make my peace with Mr. Parker. Give him something, if aught you have to give, to indemnify him for his trouble and expense, and ask him to put the books again on his shelves. In the course of the summer perhaps I might find a chance to procure the cash; but probably he would be unwilling to keep the books any longer in uncertainty. The books which I own, he will give to you, and you may, at some convenient time, send them to me. Considering your circumstances, I do not imagine it to be in your power to borrow the cash for a couple of months in Boston. If you should providentially light on a chance, and it should be necessary to procure a surety, be pleased to carry this letter to my friend, Mr. Thacher, and I think he will be friendly in the case, as I have in many instances found him so before.

My residence here is tolerably pleasant. I live with Mr. French. Some little business is done here, and I get a part. In time, perhaps, I shall gratify my moderate, rational wishes. Mr. Putney has failed. Mr. D—— is convalescent from his sickness of the purse, and expects to be in business again soon.

Mr. Lovejoy will shortly occupy the store in which Mr. Putney traded.

At Salisbury, the folks are in usual health. Father is much better than in the winter. N. Webster keeps school in his own district; his health is tolerable. Pray write me often; without books and with little business, I have much leisure to peruse and answer letters.

Make my love to my friends.

Yours, D. Webster.

P. S. Since sealing this, my books have arrived all safe. I owe Mr. Parker many thanks for his friendly conduct respecting them. I do not find a list or bill of prices of the books among them. I wish you would ask him for it, and enclose it to me. I shall take true care that the contract within be punctually fulfilled.

EZEKIEL WEBSTER TO DANIEL WEBSTER.

Boston, May 3, 1805.

Good Daniel,—In one of my late letters I requested some particular information respecting the probable conditions on which the clerk's office might be obtained, and likewise the probable emoluments of the office. I confess, Daniel, my acquaintance with the business of teaching a school does not increase my love of it. If ever I have built any castles in the air, I demolish them as readily as ever you saw me demolish a potato when we travelled over the Zahara of America. It would be the consummation of my wishes to get into some business which would be adequate to the support of a small family. I hope you will embrace the safe opportunity to write, particularly by Mr. Fifield, and give me your advice without any reserve. Colonel Sam. Thatcher has given me a pretty good offer to go into his office; it would be something more than pretty good, if I contemplated a settlement in that section of the country. I am glad you do not make money your idol. If I should ever worship it, 'twould be from the same motives from which the Indians worship the devil; to deprecate evils. As to the politics of this place, I can probably give you nothing new.

The election occurs next week. The legislature is to fill the office of Lieutenant-Governor. A majority of the members elect are undoubtedly Federalists. As Mr. French does not leave town till to-morrow, I shall send by Mr. Fifield the letter I prepared for him. I shall write too by Mr. Fifield to father. You have never told me how you came to dine on a white raven of ——'s cooking. He was the last man in the world who would have prescribed that dish for your stomach. Write me very often and believe me, Yours, E. Webster.

MR. WEBSTER TO MR. BINGHAM.

Boscawen, N. H., May 4, 1805.

Dear Bingham,—You must know that I have opened a shop in this village for the manufacture of justice writs. Other mechanics do pretty well here, and I am determined to try my luck among others. March 25. I left Boston, with a good deal of regret, I assure you. I was then bound for Portsmouth, but I found my father extremely ill and little fit to be left by all his sons, and therefore partly through duty, partly through necessity, and partly through choice, I concluded to make my stand here. Some little business is doing in the neighborhood, and of that little I hope to get a little part. This is all that I can at present say of my prospects. For one thing I ought to be thankful. If poverty brings me so near the wind that I cannot stay here, in duty to my stomach, I have only to take my hickory and walk. The disagreeable incumbrances of houses, lands, and property need not delay me a moment. Nor shall I be hindered by love, nor fastened to Boscawen by the power of beauty.

Our friend Lovejoy will open a store in this place next week, in which he will put Warren, his brother, and Thomas, son of Major Taylor. I shall be glad to have them here. One disaster has happened to me. With the assistance of my friends, I collected eighty-five dollars and sent to Boston for the payment of a bookseller, with whom I had contracted for a few volumes. But the cash was stolen from the pocket of the bearer, after he got into Boston, and I lose all. Books, therefore, I must go without for the present.

When I have more leisure, I will write you more at length The object of this is only to tell you that I am here, and pray you to write to me. How much did you pay Mr. Sumner for my New York paper?

Adieu, my old, good friend,

D. WEBSTER.

EZEKIEL WEBSTER TO DANIEL WEBSTER.

Boston, May 12, 1805.

DANIEL,—Your letter of April 30 came to hand last evening. Some person, in his great wisdom, erased Boston from the back of it, and wrote Boscawen, N. H., which officiousness probably prevented my receiving it before. You know the state of my finances and my wish to assist you. Whatever is possible for me to do, shall be done. I will confer with Mr. Parker on the business to-morrow, and let you know the result immediately. If you have no business or but very little, you ought at least to have books, so that you may become learned, if not rich. If I should not be able to send your books, you must turn author, and write your dissertation on the Constitution of New Hampshire. Before you assume this new character, I will say to you in the indignant language of Johnson:—

"Yet think what ills the scholar's life assail;
Pride, envy, want, a patron, and the jail."

With respect to the Fletcher business, I leave it to be managed very much according to your discretion. To me there seems a degree of meanness or of disgrace, in seeming to purchase an office. I hope I do not feel too squeamish or over-delicate on this point; and I am confident, likewise, that you would never agree to my taking it on terms inconsistent with the character of a gentleman. Have you ever mentioned it to the court, and what say they? Who, in point of law and equity, should lose the eighty-five dollars, you or Mr. Fifield? With me there is a doubt. Osgood thinks that himself should lose twenty; Fifield twenty; you twenty, and I twenty; or more accurately, that each of us should lose a quarter of the whole sum. I shall direct this letter to Salisbury; and if that be not the best place for you to receive your letters, inform me. Did you secure Mr. Gore's debt against Putnam? Have you received your trunk in safety? How do you like "Democracy unveiled?"

Give my respects to Mr. Wood's family, for I fancy you see them occasionally. Tell the family at home that I am well and want to see them very much.

Yours truly,

E. WEBSTER.

MR. WEBSTER TO MR. MERRILL.

Boscawen, N. H., May 14, 1805.

DEAR MERRILL,—When I wrote you last I was in Court street, Boston, and now I am in Court street, Boscawen. March 24. I left the lively capital of New England, not without regret. Whether a good or evil star led me to this little village, I know not. All that I can say about myself at present is, here I am. If you pass this way you will find me just as happy to see you as ever; and happy I should be at such an event at Iceland, or the Cape of Good Hope. Not a sentence which had Merrill's name in it has sounded in my ear this many a day; you, yourself, uttered the last. Not a soul from Hanover have my eyes beheld who could say anything about you. I presume, however, that if I give this a direction to Middlebury, it will hit you. Where will it find you? How employed? My heart feels a sort of vacuum when it cannot fancy the situation of my friends. While you resided at Dartmouth College, I could trace you in your morning vocations and in your evening walks. At sunset I could see you enter the chapel, could hear the bell, and follow you through every scene of business and amusement. How is it at Middlebury? You have there too, I suppose, vocations, and walks, and chapels, and bells. But I know nothing of them; tell me, therefore.

It was a part of our original plan of correspondence, I think, to inform each other of our studies. I have no great feats in that way to recount at present. In Boston, I was not altogether idle, but my reading was mostly appropriate to my profession. Gifford's Juvenal I looked at, and Gibbon's Life and posthumous works by Sheffield; Moore's Travels in Italy and France; Paley's Natural Theology, and a few others. Natural Theology is an ingenious little thing. Gifford's Juvenal is worth perusing on more accounts than one, though I believe that work is daubed with too much indiscriminate praise. Gifford was certainly a very accomplished scholar, was originally the tenant of an easy seat, with three legs, in vulgar dialect called a shoemaker's bench. But he ran away from his leather apron and his lapstone, and fled to Parnassus. Gibbon's Life is the history of a Deist. He was, as I think, a learned, proud, ingenious, foppish, vain, self-deceived man. If unbelief be a crime, how criminal is he who exercises talents and learning to infuse it into his own heart? Gibbon, from Protestant connections and family, deserted to the faith of the church of Rome, and thence to the faith of Tom Paine.

Our friends, dear Merrill, are every day disappearing. Alas, poor Gilbert! The herds of the valley graze the turf that lies upon thy bosom! But Merrill and Webster will preserve thy memory in the urn of their hearts.

Adieu, my good friend; write me forthwith, I pray you. If this letter is dull and insipid, impute it to dull weather, headache, east wind, or any thing else, so you hold me faultless.

Yours truly,

D. Webster.

DANIEL WEBSTER TO EZEKIEL WEBSTER.

Boscawen, May 16, 1805.

Dear Zeke,—This will be handed you by Mr. French; if you have any thing to send to me, he will bring it. I was at Salisbury yesterday. The family are well as usual. Father is desirous you should write to him and you must do so forthwith.

Adieu, D. Webster.

P. S. I greatly need a few small blank books, which Mr. Parker prepared for me.

MISS SALLY WEBSTER TO EZEKIEL WEBSTER.

Boscawen, May 25, 1805.

DEAR BROTHER,—What can be the reason of my not receiving any letters from you for so long a time? Are you so much confined in your school, that you have not time to write, or can it be that you are so much delighted with the people of Boston, as to forget your friends in the country? No; I cannot think that to be the case. I would rather impute your neglect in writing to hurry of business, want of conveyance, or any thing than want of friendship.

You will conclude by the date of this letter that I am at Boscawen. I left home one week since, and left your friends well. Father's health is much better than it was last winter, and I hope that, by proper care, he will yet be able to attend to business for years to come. Joseph expects to go up country this summer to buy him a farm, which I think will be the best thing he can do. Daniel is at the other end of the room, filling a blank; he looks very pleasant. I suppose he intends to get a dollar for it, towards the eighty he has lost. It has been remarked by some one that a bad beginning makes a good end; if that is the case, I think he will undoubtedly have a good end.

Uncle Webster's family are well, and some of them employed in the business of instructing youth, which I think must be very agreeable. Nath'l is keeping school at the Corner. Polly begins next week at Danbury. Ruth is expected to keep in some part of town. Betsey Quinby is to begin a school next week in N. Chester; L. T. somewhere else. So you see we have instructors as plenty as in Boston. I wish you to let me know when you expect to come home.

Miss R. Fifield expects to spend, I understand, some part of the summer in Boston with her brother, which I think will be a very pleasant thing for a young lady.

Do, Ezekiel, write me a letter by the next mail after you receive this, if you think it worth answering, and consider that letters from you are not only pleasing but instructive; be assured that no person would more gladly receive instruction than your sister,

SALLY WEBSTER.

EZEKIEL WEBSTER TO DANIEL WEBSTER.

Boston, May 19, 1805.

DEAR DANIEL,—Before Mr. French had given me your letter, I had forwarded your trunk, with the blank books you so much need for the entry of your fourteen actions. When Mr. Parker consented to send you the books, I called on Mr. Thacher, as you directed, and requested of him the favor of his signature, with mine, to a note of one hundred dollars, to Mr. Parker. He consented to do it with pleasure, and very politely went with me to Mr. Parker; but the latter did not wish it; so I gave him my note for the sum, on demand.

Mr. Thacher sent me a book directed to you. I fancy it is "Democracy naked." You may guess the design, if he has not mentioned it in his letter. I had the honor to dine with Mr. Emerson, and he made particular inquiry concerning you, and added that you write very handsomely. Mr. Fifield goes on Friday to Salisbury; I shall write to father by him, and likewise to yourself. Let me hear from you often, and know whenever you have swelled the number of your entries to fifteen. Every particular will be pleasing.

Just meeting-time; farewell. E. WEBSTER.

EZEKIEL WEBSTER TO DANIEL WEBSTER.

Boston, May 30, 1805.

THE letter sent by Miss Fuller, will fully compensate for the negligence alleged in your complaint against me. If you charge me again, I shall put in what I believe, in law, is called a rebutter. Yesterday was election. For clerk of the House, Tillinghast had 175 votes; C. P. Sumner had 146; T. Bigelow had, for Speaker, 169; P. Morton, 151. The last vote was the best test of the strength of the parties. The Federalists had a majority of eighteen. The whole number in the House, was 324. Otis was declared President of the Senate. This morning they fill the senatorial vacancy for the county of York. Had the votes been legally returned from the little town of Shapleigh,

Heath would have been chosen Lieutenant Governor. As these votes will probably be rejected, the choice will devolve on the Legislature. When Mr. Parker gave me the books, he said you had taken a bill of them, and was to leave it with me for him to sign, when I took the books. You probably have it among some of your papers. I called, however, for a new one this morning, and was unable to get it seasonably for this communication, on account of his absence. The business of Mr. Thacher has, before this time, explained itself; and the weather-bound letters have arrived. Do you find any business that ever calls you to Concord? Write soon. E. WEBSTER.

Sally will have a letter from me immediately. I am under an engagement this morning, which prevents my writing to her by Mr. Fuller. E. W.

DANIEL WEBSTER TO EZEKIEL WEBSTER.

Sunday, June, 1805.

DEAR ZEKE,—I got home alive last evening, although most killed by hot weather; have not seen our folks, but hear they are well. Pray send me a pair of gaiters like Fifield's. In going to church to-day, I felt that man is dust, and can think of nothing to guard against sand better than they do.

Adieu, which is a very affectionate term from the French *à dieu*, and is synonymous with, "I commend you to God."

Mr. French keeps at French's. D. W.

EZEKIEL WEBSTER TO DANIEL WEBSTER.

Boston, July 10, 1805.

GOOD DANIEL,—Your letter by Mr. French was given to me at half-past ten o'clock on the day on which Mr. French was to leave town at eleven. I roamed about town till twelve o'clock, to find the said gaiters, but could not hear of any; nor have I been able since to see any in the shops. I shall keep them in remembrance, and the first pair that is to be bought, shall be sent to you. We had two orations in this town. French, I am told, is a young tallow-chandler in this place. His oration, of course, must have been warm and fluent. I fancy his eloquence bordered a little on that species which the rhetoricians call the oily or smooth. Tell me what was done at Salisbury, and in what manner. The bell is now tolling for the funeral of Mrs. Rowe, the former owner of Rowe's pasture, adjoining my school-house. It is in contemplation to erect a market there, for the convenience of the people at the south part of the town. I am determined, I think unalterably, to leave my school in April. Look about you a little, and see where there is a good place for me in New Hampshire. It is probable that I shall leave town about the time in which I leave my school. Is Grace in Salisbury, and is B. attentive to her? Do you go to Commencement? I shall send you Dutton's oration, if I see the man who carries the letter. I did not hear it, nor have I read it. It was said not to be very extraordinary. Let me know if Chandler is in town for I want to write to him.

I am yours, in haste,

EZEKIEL WEBSTER.

DANIEL WEBSTER TO EZEKIEL WEBSTER.

Boscawen, July 28, 1805.

DEAR ZEKE,—If I have not written you for some weeks, it is not owing to pressure of business, want of remembrance, or any other describable cause. It is one of those omissions which occur in life without bringing with them any color of excuse, and for which we offer no apology, because we wrongly think them unimportant.

In the history of myself, I believe my last chapter left me just arrived from Boston. Shortly after, the 4th of July appeared, and I made my bow and my speech to the Salisburians. Both parties celebrated the day, and Mr. Pettingill entertained his Democratic friends with an oration on the Centre road. The Federalists dined at Rogers's; the Democrats, at Caleb Cushing's. Shortly after 4th July, I began to wane in health, and am now quite out of sorts; able, however, to keep about and perform all the business I can find.

I shall make about as many entries at the next courts as I expected to; perhaps a few more. I pick up, however, but very little cash, hardly laying my hand upon a dollar.

What shall we do with Parker? The folks at Salisbury enjoy about their usual health, and things there remain *in statu.* Fifield's father and mother were at South road, the 4th, and very well. James Brackett spent a day with me last week; he is gone to Londonderry, and perhaps to Boston. Chandler is not in town, and is not expected until Commencement.

This will be left in the post-office by Mr. Dix; you will probably find him at Wyman's, and he will bring any communications you may wish to make, as also my gaiters, &c.

Yours, D. WEBSTER.

N. B. Do you think that Dr. Perkins would loan us fifty dollars, for Parker, till September?

EZEKIEL WEBSTER TO DANIEL WEBSTER.

Boston, August 1, 1805.

GOOD DANIEL,—Mr. Dix very politely handed me your letter. Your ill health is a sufficient excuse for not writing. I should have written myself before this, but waited, expecting to reeeive a letter from you, by every mail.

You will be glad to hear that the health of the inhabitants of this town is as good as it has been for many years. There is no case of yellow fever, or any other epidemic. Its appearance in Providence and New Haven alarmed the people here very much, and called forth some pretty rigorous and necessary regulations from the board of health. Favorable official communications from those places, have induced the board to admit travellers from them, without subjecting them to the process of purification. I have sent you a pair of gaiters. There were none for sale; but Mr. F. was so kind as to part with his. Mr. Thacher wished me to mention to you, when I should write, that he had looked for something from you. I can hardly tell what shall be done for Mr. Parker. I will make an attempt; and if I can get thirty or forty dollars, I will pay them to him. You observe a smart quill war between P. and H. The latter appears most valorous when writing a paragraph in the Chronicle office. I am so languid and indolent this afternoon that I cannot fill the next page. Write soon. God bless you.

E. WEBSTER.

DANIEL WEBSTER TO EZEKIEL WEBSTER.

Boscawen, August 9, 1805.

DEAR ZEKE,—Mr. Fletcher having failed and shut up, it seems probable that something will now be done about the clerkship. Mr. F. is in your favor, and we shall endeavor to make matters work at September court.

The legislature have diminished the fees somewhat; but it is now worth one thousand dollars per annum. Write me by Mr. French, without fail, whether you wish it.

D. WEBSTER.

EZEKIEL WEBSTER TO DANIEL WEBSTER.

Boston, August 14, 1805.

DANIEL,—When I heard of Fletcher's failure, I concluded that there was, on that account, less probability of a vacancy in the clerkship. In answering your question, I hardly know what to say. I should wish it, if I considered that I might do better than in a profession. In that office, you know, a man stands on a mine which may be sprung at any moment. In a profession, he is on a little surer ground. When the storm beats he can buffet it. Men must be sick; and they will be dishonest; and the few upright will want lawyers to protect them from rogues, and physicians to heal their maladies. The fees of the clerk may be frittered down, till they bear no proportion to the labors to be performed. These are the considerations which suggest themselves to me, on thinking of the clerkship; I mean, in thinking of its dark side. On the other hand, a thousand dollars step up and demand for themselves much consideration. Another circumstance of considerable weight is, that it might be three or four years before I shall be able to do any thing, if ever, in the practice of the law. In the office, the emoluments will be immediately consequent upon the earning of them. In law, we let out, on interest, the study of Coke, &c. &c. What part of my time will the business of the office occupy, and where must the office be kept? The answers to these questions would have some influence upon my determination. The conclusion of the whole matter, in my own mind, is perplexing. You know the whole ground better than myself. If you and father think it best for me to seek it, I shall think so, and thank you for any assistance you may afford.

I am as ever, yours,

E. Webster.

EZEKIEL WEBSTER TO DANIEL WEBSTER.

September 15, 1805.

Daniel,—I take a little from this day, to write you. Perhaps you have heard alarming stories respecting the health of this place. It is indeed pretty sickly among children, but not more so than usual among grown people. No case of yellow fever has occurred. Private letters say it is very malignant in New York, and considerably so in Philadelphia. I have enjoyed always perfect health since I wrote you. I was one evening quite sick, took an emetic, and in the morning was well; never less languid and weak at this season of the year.

I have heard Mr. Nott preach this morning. I cannot say of him as my dear Cicero said of Archias, the expectation formed of him was great, and he surpassed it. He is, however, a man of abilities, and a scholar. The object of his discourse was to prove the resurrection of our Saviour. His subject did not admit of much embellishment. He managed it very ingeniously, and argued like a man who had not learned his logic from the syllogisms of Watts.

I saw, in the Chronicle, a puff for Mr. Langdon and the legislature, in granting aid to Dartmouth College. Will you give me a few facts respecting it? Did not Langdon oppose every petition offered while he was in the House? Did he not object to the judges of the Supreme Court being a committee to report the expediency of giving assistance? Did he not, when that committee had reported one thousand dollars, vote for Dr. L.'s motion to have it five hundred? What was the late grant? Had he any official business in it? Will you, if convenient, give me answers to these questions? Langdon's speech, and Colman's anecdotes of Bradley, do not seem to make the people in this place think him worthy of their late honors. I saw a few remarks, made in the Gazette, respecting them. Did Bradley ever have a college education? Will you tell me, too, how the thing happened? Did J. T. consent?

Should you go within ten or twenty miles of Hanover, it would be well to call there and have the few old books we have, put into a chest, which I believe is in Jarvis's room, and sent home.

I often see Mr. Thacher, and he as often inquires for you. He expects something from you, at least a letter.

If the letter I wrote you in Latin frightened you, only tell me and I never will write you another. Pray, pray send me a letter soon, and tell our folks you have had this from me.

In my next, I shall be able to let you know when I shall be at Salisbury.

I am yours, EZEK. WEBSTER.

EZEKIEL WEBSTER TO DANIEL WEBSTER.

Boston, October 17, 1805.

I DO assure you, Daniel, I was serious in stating to you the reasons for my not coming to Salisbury. I thought you in earnest in requesting it; and I was in hopes that the inconveniences I mentioned, would appear as formidable to you and the family, as they did to me. I have no reason to think I was hypochondriacal when I wrote that letter; that a sickly imagination swelled molehills into mountains; or that indolence cried, "Behold a lion in the way." I wanted to see the family and yourself, and I thought that you wished to see me.

I believe your situation to be distressing enough; but I do not know how I could help you, if I were present. As to arrangements to be made, I know of none but to pay the debts, and make the family as comfortable as we can.

A few days after I wrote you, Mr. Parker called at my school-house and told me that he wanted the remainder of my note of one hundred dollars. I borrowed thirty and gave him. He said he expected the rest to be paid this month, and wished you to settle your notes with him within the same time. I understand Mr. P. to mean, that he is obliged to make out some money at that time, and that he depends upon receiving all the money due from you and me. From this statement you can judge, as well as myself, what sum will answer for him. I can only say, God bless you; for I fear Mr. White will leave town before I can deliver this to him.

EZEKIEL WEBSTER.

DANIEL WEBSTER TO EZEKIEL WEBSTER.

Boscawen, November 15, 1805.

DEAR ZEKE,—I should be inexpressibly gratified if you would accompany Nat. into this quarter. But there will be so many folks in the chaise with him, I suppose it will be inconvenient. Besides, as there is nobody in Boston that can read or write except yourself, it will be next to impossible for you to leave your school.

Again, as there is no stage-coach running on any part of the road from Boston here, no chaises passing, and not a horse in the country, nobody knows how you will get back again.

With affection, but in despair of ever seeing you,

Yours, &c. D. W.

N. B. Forty dollars enclosed for Mr. Parker; I wish you to tell him, I hope to get his Carrigain money early next month.

MR. WEBSTER TO MR. BINGHAM.

Boscawen, December 7, 1805.

Dear Hervey,—You and I hear of each other as seldom as if we were in different kingdoms. This is not as it should be. We are not kings, nor emperors, nor presidents, and therefore have not such a pressure of state affairs on our hands, as to afford an excuse for neglect of private friendship. Nor is either of us, that I know of, in love up to desperation; and as to myself, I can say safely, that writ-making does not *in toto* absorb me. Wherefore it seems proper for us to point our pens again, and to scribble and figure away on paper, as in time of old.

I have been thinking you would visit the Legislature at Portsmouth, and come this way. I should press this point, if I was not going to Boston. About the 22d instant, I shall be, I expect at Portsmouth, and why may I not find you there? We will stroll round town a day or three together, then you shall come to Boscawen and see Counsellor Webster's office, &c., and the Counsellor and Barrister Bingham will have many learned conversations, &c., all tending to the benefit of society. Say will you come, most noble Barrister?

Enclosed are two shot, which I wish you to discharge by means of your Shrieve, and send the same to me by mail before Amherst Court. If you cannot go to Portsmouth, write me the very next mail.

Holloa! A client. Good-bye. Yours with undiminished love and tenderness,

D. W.

MR. WEBSTER TO MR. BINGHAM.

Boscawen, January 19, 1806.

Dear old Friend,—I now sit down to give you some account of myself; a thing which I have long neglected, and which, like other accounts, swells rapidly by being let alone. I have no expectation of redeeming by this letter the vacuity and nothingness of the last I wrote you, which, when nihilities shall all be collected and classed, will hold a conspicuous rank.

In truth, I have observed an oyster-like silence, which would be very laudable towards my enemies; *absque hoc*, that you are one of that number. I now mean to treat you with a course of epistles, thick at least, if not charming, and to make my winter evenings pleasant, at the expense perhaps of the pleasure and tranquillity of yours.

Since I last saw James H. Bingham, I have passed through a variety of scenes, if scenes they can be called which affect only an individual. It is now eight months since I opened an office in this town, during which time I have led a life which I know not how to describe better than by calling it a life of writs and summonses. Not that I have dealt greatly in those articles, but that I have done little else. My business has been just about so, so; its quantity less objectionable than its quality. I shall be able at the end of the year to pay my bills, and pay perhaps sixty pounds for my books. I practise in Hillsborough, Rockingham, and Grafton. Scattering business over so much surface is like spilling water on the ground. In point of profit I should do better, much better, if it were convenient to attend the courts in one county only. So much for business. Now as to fame. In this point I am rather waning. When I was in college, Bliss, and the Smiths, and Crowel used to come to me to correct their themes, and I thought myself a promising character; my creditors thought so also. At present, I believe I am in the rear of them all. Of the Smiths, one I hear is a minister, and one a major. Yes, Wm. Coit is a major. Bliss is stuck on to the side of the great hill, that lies between you and me, and certainly holds a more elevated station than I can boast. I make no poetry; five lines to D. Abbott are the Alpha and the Omega of my poetical labors for a year. In this particular, however, I mean to reform. How would it do, think ye, to write writs in verse? For instance, let one be *clausum in his verbis*, that is to say, being interpreted, wrapt up in these words:—

All good sheriffs in the land,
    We command,
That forthwith you arrest John Dyer,
    Esquire,
If in your precinct you can find him,
    And bind him, &c., &c., &c.

If the legislature will but put our writs into a poetical and musical form, it will certainly be the most harmonious thing they ever did, and you and I shall like them vastly better than we do now.

In the next place, as to politics. Here my lips are glued. I live in a family who think differently from me on political questions, and it is therefore decent to be silent. They are charitable enough, however, to tolerate my errors, and I, at length, feel no restraint arising from the propriety of being silent; though you know there is a great regeneration to be wrought before I shall feel democratically. Last year I wrote a political pamphlet in two days, which I have had the pleasure of seeing kicked about under many tables. But you are one of the very few who know the author of the Appeal to the Old Whigs. Keep the precious secret.

Now, having told you all about my business, my fame, and my politics, there is but one point more to be discussed before I shall have completed the account of myself; and that one point is love. On this head, which, like a good many other heads, is rather barren, I can at present say nothing only that I am not married, and seriously am inclined to think I never shall be. The example of my friends sometimes excites me, and certain narratives I hear of you, induce me to inquire why the deuce female flesh and blood was not made for me as well as others; but reasons, good or bad, suppress hope and stifle incipient resolution.

Thus far I have dilated on that dear, precious, ever present, and ever unexhausted subject, self. I thought proper to give you the above description, because our correspondence has been so long intermitted, that though you are acquainted with my "rise and progress," you might yet know nothing of my "present state."

Three weeks since, this day, I dined in Boston, at the table of Mr. Thacher, and in company with Mr. Buckminster. They inquired very particularly after you. Pray, James, why do you never visit Boston? You would certainly find it for your interest, as well as amusement, to extend your acquaintance there. If you feel what I feel, the burden of perpetual solitude and seclusion, you would sometimes run away eagerly to the busy haunts of men. Since I returned from Boston, I have attended the Common Pleas at Portsmouth. Your old and valued friend, Saltonstall, was there; he is growing to be quite unwieldy in size, but has good-nature in proportion. A large man, who is surly, is a frightful thing, and the species ought to take arms against him. Lawrence is settled in Epping; you probably remember him, which, *inter nos*, is not requiring of your memory to retain much.

Solon, your cousin, seems fast rising into business and reputation; he is an intelligent, gentlemanly man. I believe he studies, and have no doubt he will succeed to every rational expectation. Study is truly the grand requisite for a lawyer. Men may be born poets, and leap from their cradle painters; nature may have made them musicians, and called on them only to exercise, and not to acquire, ability. But law is artificial. It is a human science to be learnt, not inspired. Let there be a genius for whom nature has done so much as apparently to have left nothing for application, yet to make a lawyer, application must do as much as if nature had done nothing. The evil is, that an accursed thirst for money violates everything. We cannot study, because we must pettifog. We learn the low recourses of attorneyism, when we should learn the conceptions, the reasonings, and the opinions of Cicero and Murray. The love of fame is extinguished; every ardent wish for knowledge repressed; conscience put in jeopardy, and the best feelings of the heart indurated, by the mean, money-catching, abominable practices, which cover with disgrace a part of the modern practitioners of the law. The love of money is the ruling passion of this country. It has taken root deeply, and I fear will never be eradicated. While this holds everything in its gripe, America will produce few great characters. We have no patronage for genius; no reward for merit. The liberal professions are resorted to, not to acquire reputation and consequence, but to get rich. Money is the chief good; every eye is on it; every heart sighs for it. When the day will come when these things shall be ordered better, you and I cannot tell, but will hope that it will come some time. Our profession is good if practised in the spirit of it; it is damnable fraud and iniquity, when its true spirit is supplied by a spirit of mischief-making and money-catching.

I have looked to see you this way this winter. Shall you not come? Will it be easy for you, if you cannot come, to attend Amherst Court in March? Pray invent some way wherein I may have the pleasure of seeing my ancient and honorable friend. I never hear from Fanny. Alas! Poor girl, if you live, I pity your sufferings, and if your sufferings are over, my heart shall embalm your memory! If you know any thing about this interesting object of regard and compassion, pray impart the knowledge to me. Make my respectful compliments to your father when you see him; he has probably nearly forgotten me. Six winters ago, you and I were together in his house. What a considerable portion of human life is six years; and yet how short the retrospect!

Adieu, my dear friend. Yours affectionately,

D. W.

MR. WEBSTER TO MR. M'GAW.

Boscawen, January 12, 1807.

DEAR M'GAW,—You call yourself such hard names in your letter that I begin to think they are well applied. I was entirely unsuspicious before, but I know nothing against your credit as a witness, and if you affirm that you are a "lazy scoundrel," the point must be considered as proved. But I forgive you, fully, freely, frankly. A man that hath both a fame to regard, a purse to regard, and a wife to regard, must be excused from any particular attention to his friends. A wife, I take it, reverently be it spoken, is like a burning-glass, which concentrates every ray of affection that emanates from a husband's heart. We single dogs have attachments which are dispersed over society, our friendships are scattered all over the world, and we love at a thousand places at the same moment; but you husbands carry all your wares to the same market. You have one bank, in which you deposit all your tender sentiments, wherefore I hold you all pardonable for forgetting your friends. Now all this is very pretty; but while I thus philosophize, my heart is in my throat, and tells me at every syllable that I lie. It tells me that its attachment to any one object, however ardent, however near approaching to adoration, could never sever the ties that hold it to its friends, and that in the commerce of affection there can be no monopoly; it rebels against the doctrine of concentration aforesaid, and kicks the business of the burning-glass to the devil. However, these things are all mysteries to us, the uninitiated, and it is presumption to reason about them. You husbands, happy race, could, if you would, tell us all about it. But I have said I forgive you, and though you were ten times more guilty than you are, yet, I being your confessor, either with or without reason, your sins would all be absolved. In August last, I was at the old place of our friendship, Fryeburg. I have no other sorrow for your leaving that town, than that you are so much further from the spot of earth I live on. And even this sorrow is diminished by my ignorance of the place which may hereafter be burdened by me. At present, my mind is not entirely easy at the idea of being long here. But habit, you know, does great things. And while I think little of any removal, I say nothing. Parker and wife are as comfortable as fancy can feign. When I call of an evening, I find them as snug and close as "Will and Mary, on the coin." Brother Eastman lost his wife of a consumption in November; he is becoming a gay young spark again. Mr. Thompson left his family at Salisbury, South Road, while he passes his winter, for the last time at present, as they say at the theatre, at the city of Washington. New Hampshire is precisely what you saw it last, and if I were to write till my fingers ached, I doubt whether I could give you an item that you would give a fig to know. The little quotation which you copied into yours, fresh from the lips of somebody, who stood at your elbow while you wrote, I was very much pleased with. I protest I think it the most eloquent little saying I have met with. Will you be pleased to ascertain how much of my love it is lawful for me to send to your wife, and when you have settled the quantity to a scruple, I pray you give it to Phebe, with the lowest bow you can make.

I am, dear Sir, very sincerely your friend and obedient servant,

D. Webster.

P. S. If you should be at Merrimac, let me hear of it.

MR. WEBSTER TO MR. MERRILL.

Boscawen, March 8, 1807.

My dear Friend,—Yours of February 13, accompanied by your election sermon, were duly received. I pray you, accept my most hearty thanks for both. How happy, my good friend, am I when the tedium of business is relieved by a communication of this sort. And I am more abundantly grateful, if the communication is a little moral or serious, because I am happy to have my mind called back from the pursuit of ordinary affairs to a contemplation of serious things.

As to your sermon, I cannot say what I think of it without seeming to flatter you. When I took it up, I took my pen determined to mark such passages "as pleased me." I assure you I have blurred and blotted you pretty well. Page 10 contains some paragraphs of excellent ideas; pages 14, 15, 16, and 17, are favorites with me. The comparison between Rome and Ætna, page 21, is entirely new, and, I think, highly striking and just.

It is indeed alarming, that private character weighs nothing in the scale of qualification for public office: as if a man had two hearts; a deceitful, depraved, wicked one towards his neighbor; an honest, pure, godly one toward his country! I cannot indulge myself in reflections on the growth of this and a thousand other pernicious sentiments among us, without falling into the horrors. Indeed, I fear that our country is growing corrupt at a rate which distances the speed of every other. I do not say that the degree of positive corruption at present is so great, but the course towards total depravity is swift. Nevertheless, you say truly, "The Lord reigneth;" and while I write that sentence, I feel a consolation in my heart which I would not exchange for the sceptre of Bonaparte. You observe, "that however melancholy prospects may be in this country, they are far worse in Europe." I thought you were going to say, "they are bright in heaven." As to any human exertions being able to rectify the disordered affairs of this world, it is all out of the question. Empires are crushed in a day. All that is ancient, all that is venerable, all that is valued in Europe, is overwhelmed by the mighty torrent of French power. Yet so did Cyrus, and so may God do, by means of any instruments, and you and I will endeavor, with his assistance, to rely on his protection.

The times are such I am surprised at nothing. If, before I rise from my table, I should learn that Bonaparte is in London, it would not astonish me. I am persuaded that a great revolution is taking place, not only in Europe, but through the world. Society is deeply shaken everywhere. The minds of men are flying from all steadfast principles, like an arrow from the bow. Principles are called prejudices, and duty, scrupulosity. Where all this will end, you and I cannot tell. May we at all times have grace to say, with honest and sincere hearts, "Father in heaven, thy will be done."

I rejoice that you have so comfortable a cage. A bird you cannot but find easily. Your friend Webster has neither cage nor bird. However, he lives in hopes.

I have no very great objections to sending you a copy of my Phi Beta Kappa speech; a small one, however, is, that not being printed I should be obliged to write it off. You must not disappoint us next Commencement. A journey over the mountain will do you no injury. Pray do not fail. When I have better health than at present, for you must know I am quite out of health, I will, I think, write you a better letter.

In the mean time remind me of the promise.

Adieu, D. Webster.

MR. WEBSTER TO MR. FULLER.

Portsmouth, December 2, 1807.

Dear Sir,—I have received yours of the 27th November, and will regard its contents.

* * * * * * *

I agree with you that it is strange we have not interchanged letters oftener.

If you have an excuse, in the pressure of family matters, I am clearly without one. I have not feasted the appetite of my eyes on the Paragon this long time. Yet I can well believe all you say of her, for I know you observe such things nicely.

I like very much your notion of coming this way with Mrs.

Fuller. If the fates are propitious, I hope I shall be able to afford you a shelter, in a year or two. I have been a young dog long enough, and now think of joining myself, as soon as convenient, to that happy and honorable society of which you are one; the society of married men. Can I do better?

I think when I saw you last I was about removing to this place. As yet I have little opportunity of forming any opinion of my prospects; in short, I do not regard prospects!

I am made up in my opinion to stay, and therefore, what I should see to be before me, would not alter my resolution. I do not look out, therefore, lest I should not be pleased with the view.

In all sorts of weather, however, I am and always shall be,

Your obed't serv't,

D. Webster.

I like the alteration of your name.

MR. WEBSTER TO MR. BINGHAM.

Portsmouth, February 27, 1808.

Dear Bingham,—"Friendship, like love, is destroyed by long absence, though it may be increased by short intermissions." I this moment read this sentence in one of the numbers of The Idler, and as I read, the idea of my old friend Hervey rushed into my mind.

What a horrible thing it is, my dear friend, that I have neither heard from you nor written to you for twelve months. How is it that our lips have been sealed so long? I would not have believed such a thing could happen, though ten wise men had foretold it. But so it is. When busied about many things, the mind is easily persuaded to defer until to-morrow that which there is no pressing necessity of doing to-day.

Since I have seen you and written you, I have changed my residence from Boscawen to this place. Some brief narration of my life since June, 1806, seems necessary to bring up the view of the present, so that we may go on in the old way of correspondence; for if ever I neglect writing you so long a time again, I shall have lost my senses.

My business at Boscawen was tolerable, but not altogether to my mind. A little money might be made there, but no pleasure of a social sort enjoyed. My brother Ezekiel was admitted to the bar in September last, and to him I made an offer of my office. The truth is, our family affairs at Salisbury rendered it necessary for one of us to reside in that neighborhood, and not being very willing to take charge of the farm, I concluded to indorse over to my brother both farm and office, if he would take both together. Being thus left to seek a new place of abode, I came to this town, a measure which I had in some degree contemplated for a length of time. I found myself here the latter part of September. I knew few people here, and Mr. Adams was the only person who advised to the measure.

Hitherto, I have done as much business as I ought to expect. There are eight or nine of us who fill writs, in town. Of course my share cannot be large, even if I should take my equal dividend. On the whole, however, I am satisfied that I did right to come, and suppose shall meet as much success as I deserve. I have a pleasant room, in a good situation; have made some additions to my library, which is, nevertheless, yet very small; have some pleasant acquaintances in town, and time rolls along pretty agreeably; "*jam satis est.*" I will expatiate no further on that endearing subject, self. Now, my dear Bingham, a little account from you, to balance this, would be truly a precious morsel, and I trust I shall not long be without it. Mr. Stevens, your cousin, I see often, and the oftener I see the better I like him. He boards with me, when here, and we have become a good deal acquainted. He tells me many things of you which I am fond of hearing. Among the good people of Alstead, I know you must be esteemed, and I fancy with the bad you will not be unpopular.

Pray write me a long epistle, and in the mean time give my love to the amiable P——y.

I am, dear James, with undiminished affection, your friend,

D. WEBSTER.

DANIEL WEBSTER TO EZEKIEL WEBSTER.

(EXTRACT.)

Portsmouth, March 3, 1808.

DEAR E.—I am just now distressed for some Hillsborough blanks. I must have twenty. If you send a coach with them, let me have that number by next Wednesday. It would seem a small business to send a boy down upon, but it is of very considerable consequence to me to have them, and if they cannot come otherwise, despatch J. Gilman, not telling him or any body what the business is.

Money I have none; I shall certainly be hanged before three weeks, if I cannot get some. What can be done?

Sue every body. I send the copy of the Peterson note. Sue young Doctor, without fail. Mr. Ladd, the bearer, is entitled to receive two hundred and ten dollars of J. Wilcox. Have you heard any thing about it?

Yours always, D. WEBSTER.

P. S. I shall almost perish if I have not my twenty Hillsborough blanks by Wednesday night.

DANIEL WEBSTER TO EZEKIEL WEBSTER.

(EXTRACTS.)

Portsmouth, March 9, 1808.

DEAR SQUIRE,—I have just been favored by the sight of Sir James Atkinson, Bart., convoying a few blanks, for which I am much obliged to you. He brings but twenty-one, of which I shall take the greater part, and send you the lesser.

* * * * * * *

I have already got to the second item in my will; expecting to be hanged, as I said; but not quite so soon. I think I shall subsist until March. "Sue every body;" that's the word.

As to the Gunpowder, he is gone a journey; if I have no earlier chance to send him, shall ride to Amherst, but think I shall send him sooner.

Tell Nat. that I do not thank him for his love. It is like the priest's blessing; if it were worth any thing he would not bestow it. If it were as valuable as ten minutes' time, I should not receive it, because he will not use so many minutes in writing to me.

Yours,

D. Webster.

MR. WEBSTER TO MR. BINGHAM.

Hopkinton, May 5, 1808.

I avail myself of Mr. Adams's politeness to give you thanks for yours of April 17. I do not charge you with that species of flattery of which deceit makes any portion, but the partiality of your feelings leads you to some rather warm and unjust opinions. I have nothing to charge against fortune, on the score of professional success, and yet I have nothing to boast, beyond the ordinary success of young men. I am earning a small living, and have long been convinced that I never shall be rich.

Horace Hall, our friend, told me in March that some of your friends intended to nominate you for a county office, which he named. I imagine your happiness depends very little on any thing of that sort, although I believe the office to be gainful. I was once a candidate for a similar office. I was anxious to obtain it for some time. At length it was offered me; but I had then grown sick of the scheme, and would not accept it. On the whole, I should advise you, if you should be invited to accept that office, to follow your feelings. If it will enable you to live in a more pleasant place, if it is pleasant to Madam, if it is more lucrative than your practice, all these things are in favor of acceptance. On the other hand, the duties are probably more irksome than professional practice, perhaps not more laborious, but probably more tedious.

I am glad your list is so good. Your practice must be much above mediocrity, and I am sure that what you get you will hold.

I had forgotten that I owed Mr. Temple, and now enclose you three dollars for him.

Give my love to P. and assure her I should be extremely happy to see her, either in her present name or any other that she may choose to assume.

I am, dear Hervey, yours, sincerely,

D. Webster.

N. B. I forgot to tell you, that in June next, I contemplate to set my bachelor friends a laudable example.

Excuse a blunder; I write in court; the region of blunders.

NOTE. The last line refers to his having begun his letter on the second page of the sheet.

DANIEL WEBSTER TO EZEKIEL WEBSTER.

Portsmouth, March 2, 1810.

DEAR ESQUIRE.—

* * * * * * *

Mr. K. writes that there is reason to fear that Boscawen will not be quite so Federal as last year. This will never do. Your characters are committed. Make Boscawen "toe the mark" once more, as nobly as last year. I cannot think you will fail in this respect. As to the Representative let that go easy. If the G.'s and C.'s are disposed that you should go, go; if not, altogether and heartily, stay. It would be weakening rather than increasing your personal influence, to go, unless it were *nem. con.* I should like, well enough, to gratify the good old Captain once. The time is nearly expired when we promised the Captain to take up his name. If he wishes it, it shall be done. Please see him immediately on the subject. Enoch G. of Canterbury, is the man I intend to obtain in his room. It would be expensive for me to go up on purpose. Will you, or can you, effect it for me? Please inform me by next post. I must entreat your special attention to this.

We must make one extra effort, this time, to bear down all vice and immorality.

You may depend on hearing that we do our duty this way. For Reputation's sake do yours.

Yours, &c.,

D. WEBSTER.

DANIEL WEBSTER TO EZEKIEL WEBSTER.

February, 1811.

DEAR ESQUIRE,—I send you the jalap, the gum opium, and some lemons, instead of oranges, of which there are none in town. If I can find any balsam-tolu, I will send it; as yet, have found none.

Our court is yet in session; this is Monday, the third week. I have no leisure at all. Am glad to hear your prospects are so good. Unless we are very much deceived, we shall do well. I do not think we shall get half; but I do think we shall come within seventy-five. Indeed, it is not impossible we may get half.

I am exceedingly alarmed about Sally.[1] The moment the court rises, I shall set out to see her, and, if possible, carry my wife. I hope you will attend her daily. Do not fail to write to me by next conveyance. If Mr. Wood does not come, put your letter into mail; I shall get it Tuesday.

We are all bustle—adieu. May God, in his great mercy, preserve us and bless us, and our friends.

Yours,

D. WEBSTER.

EZEKIEL WEBSTER TO DANIEL WEBSTER.

Concord, Friday evening, 6 P. M. June 4, 1813.

DEAR DANIEL,—The great men of the realm met here Wednesday. For Speaker, T. W. Thompson, 106; C. Storer, 75; scattering, 2. H. Hutchinson, Clerk of the House; Oliver Peabody, President of the Senate; S. A. Kendal, Clerk. Chase and Taylor elected by the people. No choice of counsellors, in Grafton, (according to the report of the committee,) Colby and Merrill, the candidates. Mr. Gilman's plurality over P. 809. Some votes given for Mr. G. were not legally returned; had they been, the plurality would have been as above; it will now be less.

His Excellency has been escorted this afternoon, from Pem-

[1] A sister, Sarah Jane Webster, who not long afterwards died of a consumption.

broke, by a more respectable and numerous escort than Concord ever witnessed, under the direction of Marshalls W. Webster, and H. G. Cilley. At this moment the bells are ringing and cannon firing, in demonstration of the people's joy. Thirsty, wearied, and covered with dust, I am now writing. At a previous meeting, Tuesday evening, it was unanimously agreed to support Upham, for Speaker; he, however, declined. To-morrow morning, ten o'clock, we go into the choice of Senator. Mr. Goddard our first choice; if he declines, Jeremiah Mason will certainly be the man. You may depend on this. It will be so.

I have given you good news enough for one letter. Pray write me often and long.

Yours, in love,

E. WEBSTER.

MR. WEBSTER TO MR. BINGHAM.

Washington, June 4, 1813.

DEAR BINGHAM,—I have nothing in the world to say to you of any importance; but after struggling with my conscience for some time on the point, I cannot make that out to be a good apology for not writing. It is sometimes important to know that nothing important can be told. In our political capacity, we, that is, the House of Representatives, have done little or nothing. The time for us to be put on the stage and moved by the wires, has not yet come. I suppose the "show" is now in preparation, and at the proper time the farce of legislating will be exhibited. I do not mean to say that the "projects" will not be opposed, as far as may be, nor is it certain that all the Democrats will "hang together," on the great subject of taxes; but before any thing is attempted to be done here, it must be arranged elsewhere.

Thus far the weather has been comfortable, and so long as one keeps within doors, the heat is not oppressive. Much walking, however, is not practicable, especially as there are few trees in this city, to keep off the sun. We have the advantage of you, in a better room to sit in, in having less to do, and in the means of acquaintance with a greater variety of characters. You have over us the advantage of having a majority on your side, as I trust; the prospect of a short session; the hope of doing some good, and a little society, pleasantly mixed, instead of the unvarying masculinity of our circles here. A few ladies, indeed, are to be seen by going to the weekly rout at the palace; but they are there only as so many curiosities—*raræ aves*—fit for all the purposes of social life, save only the unimportant particulars of speaking and being spoken to. I understand that in the winter session, when there are more ladies in the city, the aforesaid evil is in some degree mitigated. I have been to the levee or drawing room, but once. It is a mere matter of form. You make your bow to Mrs. Madison, and to Mr. M., if he comes in your way, but he being there merely as a guest, is not officially entitled to your *congé*. Monsieur Serurier, Madame Bonaparte, the Russian Minister, heads of departments, and tails of departments, members of congress, &c., &c., here and there, interspersed with military and naval hat and coat, make up the group. You stay from five minutes to an hour, as you please; eat and drink what you can catch, without danger of surfeit, and if you can luckily find your hat and stick, then take French leave; and that's going to the "levee."

Yours, with great esteem,

D. W.

I hope you will be mindful of us while you are at Concord. Very little of the proceedings of our general court, you know, ordinarily get into the papers. We shall, of course, be much dependent on the communications of our friends. If any thing should occur here, seeming to be interesting or important, I shall remember you.

EZEKIEL WEBSTER TO DANIEL WEBSTER.

Saturday, June 5, 1813.

Dear Daniel,—I wrote you last evening, giving some account of our doings. We have not done much to-day, save choosing a Senator in Congress. I imagine I shall be able to write you on Monday evening, and inform you whether Dr. Goddard accepts or declines. In case of the latter, we shall proceed anew, in the choice, and shall elect Mr. Mason. Of this I am confident. It must be so.

The judiciary and the election bills are now before the committees. Mr. Gilman has been qualified to-day, and has made his speech.

I have been told the President's message has a pacific aspect in the apprehension of many Federalists, in this quarter. I think it very warlike. If he has given the basis on which the treaty is to be made, under the Russian mediation, there can be no hopes of a treaty being concluded. If I understand him the British are to surrender the right of search for British goods or British subjects. The war, then, will be likely to continue as long as even the Kentuckians will desire. I expect no peace till the people make it. It will be, whenever it does come, the people's peace. We must make peace by speaking through our representatives. They must give the public mind an impression and direction, and that in its turn will strengthen their hands and encourage their hearts. You are in congress at a time when men who love their country and have talents to promote her best interests, would like to be there. It is a time for men to act in.

I have received three letters from you, and hope to receive many more. I should like to see the Intelligencer, if it is perfectly convenient. We have heard of the capture of The Chesapeake, and we all lament it. It is a great loss.

Monday, June 7. We have chosen the old Secretary, Treasurer, and Asa Dearborn, Commissary-General. Dr. Goddard refuses to go to see you. To-morrow morning is assigned for making a choice of Senator.

I will send you his letter next mail.

Yours, &c., E. WEBSTER.

DANIEL WEBSTER TO EZEKIEL WEBSTER.

Washington, June 28, 1813.

DEAR EZEKIEL,—I have not written you for some time, principally for the reason that I have had nothing to say. My last accounts from Concord are to the 21st instant. You had then refused to postpone the judiciary bill. I hope, and have no doubt, you passed it. You have learned the fate of my resolutions.[1] We had a warm time of it, for four days, and then the other side declined further discussion. I had prepared myself for a little speech, but the necessity of speaking was prevented. I went with Rhea of Tennessee, to deliver the resolutions to the President. I found him in his bed, sick of a fever. I gave them to him, and he merely answered that they would be attended to. We have received no answer. The President remains sick, although he is thought to be getting better.

We shall probably get up some resolutions, directly attacking the war. If so, I suppose I shall shoot my little gun. We have some fine fellows on our side of the House.

The weather has been tolerable, except four or five days. I should not like to stay here after the first week in July. As soon as my vote on the taxes is recorded, I intend setting out. The taxes will probably be laid; but it is not certain.

Mr. Mason[2] has been here a week. He will certainly obtain great weight in the Senate.

Give us a letter often. Yours,

D. Webster.

The British are in great force down the bay. Hampton, near Norfolk, has fallen into their hands.

DANIEL WEBSTER TO EZEKIEL WEBSTER.

Washington, July 4, 1813.

Dear Ezekiel,—You have done a great work at Concord; may your reward be great. I have received the judiciary bill, &c. All is right. I have no objection to the candidates you mention for judicial offices. I do not hear whether L. came into this.

We are yet on the taxes; they will probably pass. It will take so long to adjust the details, and to bring the bills before

[1] Resolutions offered by Mr. Webster, calling upon the President for information with regard to the French Decrees, repealing the Berlin and Milan Decrees, &c. &c. June 10, 1813.

[2] Jeremiah Mason.

the House to be discussed on their general principles, that I very much doubt whether any full discussion of the war will be had this session. For myself, I am determined not to remain here more than ten days. The weather is already very hot; more so than ever I experienced.

The President has sent no answer yet. I must in decency stay till he does, if it comes in any season, in order to see if supplementary questions are necessary. He will be followed up on that subject. An inquiry into the failure on the frontier is talked of; I think there will not be any time this session.

We have several projects, and a good many good hands to give a lift. We are trying to organize our opposition, and bring all our forces to act in concert.

There is recently appointed a kind of committee, to superintend our concerns, viz: Pickering, Webster, Wm. Reed, Baylies, Porter, Pitkin, Grosvenor, Oakley, Stockton, Ridgely, Hanson, Sheffey, and Gaston.

It will take us this session to find one another out.

Yours, D. W.

DANIEL WEBSTER TO EZEKIEL WEBSTER.

Washington, December 29, 1813.

Dear Ezekiel,—I arrived here last evening, and here learned of the Portsmouth fire and the consumption of my house. I have only time to say, that the safety of my family compensates the loss of the property. Mr. Mason urges me that Mrs. Webster may remain at his house till spring; I think this will be best, except perhaps a short visit, if the travelling should be good, into your quarter. I have not time to say more, but thought you would be glad to hear that I am in possession of myself after the knowledge of such a loss.

I am yours,

D. Webster.

MR. WEBSTER TO MR. I. P. DAVIS.

Washington, January 6, 1814.

Dear Sir,—Our town has met with another conflagration. I heard not a syllable of it till I reached here. I found a letter from my wife, but so horrible was the general account which the people about me gave, that it put my firmness to a severe test to open it. When I found nothing lost but house and property, you may well imagine how much I felt relieved from distress.

You will be glad to learn that my houseless family have found a good shelter for the winter. Whether at Mr. Mason's, or with my friends in the country, I do not yet know. They were offered an asylum at either place. I had at first almost made up a resolution to return immediately. Mrs. Webster had anticipated such a resolution, and in her first letter advised against it. On the whole, considering how critical the times are here, I shall, I believe, stay through the winter.

The great news from Europe comes seasonably; at least to me. It enables one to forget in some degree his own misfortunes. We have all been in danger of worse evils than burnings, and exposed to a foe more merciless than all the elements. I trust Providence has delivered us.

Bonaparte's disasters produce a visible effect here. The administration seems to be appalled. It seems at present to be suspending its war measures, and taking time to consider, and perhaps also to ascertain whether the voice of the party is still for war. There are evident symptoms of schism in the Cabinet, and in the party in Congress. Some construe the despatches to be pacific, others say they will bear no such construction. That is, those who are still for war, say there is nothing in the despatches; those who begin to grow sick of it, affect to see new evidence of a pacific disposition on the part of England, in these despatches, and in the speech of the Prince Regent. One of the leading Democratic Senators detained me half an hour to hear his comment on the word "Reciprocity" in the Prince Regent's speech. He thinks it a word full of peace, and hangs all his hopes on "Reciprocity." Monroe will have it, that the despatches are pacific; whence it is inferred that his "thoughts are turned on peace." In truth, his thoughts are turned principally on the next election. Armstrong can see nothing in the despatches which looks like sentiments of returning justice in the minds of the British ministry. He is still for trying the tug of war.

Monroe and Armstrong cannot go on long together. I have no doubt Armstrong will fall. *Vide* Democratic Press. If any thing prevents, it will be the influence of Clay, Grundy, and the other lights of the West, who are supposed to be for more war, and for Armstrong. Excuse a long letter; which when begun, was meant only for an envelop. Make my respects to Mrs. Davis and believe me with esteem,

Yours, &c., D. WEBSTER.

DANIEL WEBSTER TO EZEKIEL WEBSTER.

Washington, January 30, 1814.

DEAR EZEKIEL,—I enclose you a few creatures, called speeches. One of them you will find I have corrected, in some of its printer's errors, with my pen; please do the same to the rest, before they go out of your hands. I shall send a few to your townsmen, you will learn who by looking at the post-office, for I have not my list by me now, and so cannot say exactly for whom I shall send to you. Of those that come to your hands, give them in my name to those you think proper, Federalists or Democrats.[1]

The speech is not exactly what it ought to be. I had not time. I had no intention of speaking till nine o'clock in the morning, and delivered the thing about two. I could make it better, but I dare say you think it would be easier to make a new one, than to mend it. It was well enough received at the time, and our side of the House said they would have it in this form. So much for speeches.

What do you do with such a house full of women and children? Especially, how do you make out to keep the house quiet, with those two black-eyed, brown-headed, chattering, romping

[1] Speech on the "Encouragement of Enlistments," January 14, 1814.

cousins in it, and more especially with that one, which, though youngest, is yet biggest; but though biggest, I fear not best? As to him who sleeps in his borrowed cradle, and bears the loss of his own with so much moderation of temper, I trust he is born to be a philosopher. To all these, together with their mothers, you must give my love, for I have not time to-day to write more than this letter.

To whatever projects for carrying on the war government may adopt, they will find obstacles. There will yet be much discussion in both houses. Some excellent speeches have been made in the Senate, especially one on the non-importation bill, by Mr. Gore. As to the prospect of peace, my opinion is this: If the administration can get an army, they will still contend for Canada. If the high bounty will not obtain men, they will certainly try conscription. If Bonaparte rises, they will rise; if he is kept down and they can get no army, they will have peace, if they can get it. Write me often. Do you yet talk about the election? Who are candidates? &c. &c.

Yours as ever, D. W.

P. S. To Mrs. Grace Webster,—I am sorry the Rev. Ephraim has got our little white house, but we will find another. I hope you will do a good deal of visiting this winter, because it seems to be a leisure time. You must especially go and visit Mr. Wood and Mr. Price, and Deacon Gerrish, &c.; also all the Squire's neighbors, as well as the Salisbury "quality."

DANIEL WEBSTER TO EZEKIEL WEBSTER.

Washington, Friday, February 5, 1814.

Dear Ezekiel,—I received yours of the 23d yesterday, and Grace's of same date. You may depend upon our discussing public subjects here, at least freely and with spirit; of the ability, the public must judge. They are determined not to take up my resolutions this session; of this I am certain. But on the loan bill we hope to get a blow at them. That bill must go to a committee of the whole, by the rules; and the previous question cannot be called in committee of the whole. Gaston and Grosvenor are prepared to give great speeches on that subject. I do not think myself of trying again, unless my friends at the North should be of opinion that I can do better.

Mr. Gore's speech, a very good one, I shall be able to send you in the course of a few days. On the Maryland Memorial, a very animated debate happened in both Houses. Mr. King came out for the first time. You never heard such a speaker. In strength, and dignity, and fire; in ease, in natural effect, and gesture as well as in matter, he is unequalled. He did not make a set speech, and did not expect to speak at all, but the administration hands objected to printing the memorial. He made a few remarks on that point; somehow Giles got into the debate on the wrong side; I do not know how it happened, but one thing led to another till Mr. King came out in plump terms on the right of remonstrance and of resistance; he said it was a mere question of prudence, how far any State would bear the present state of things, &c., &c.

Are you safe in your election? Pray be in season in your measures. Who is councillor for Hillsborough? how does the New Hampshire sheriff manage? &c., &c.

Yours, D. WEBSTER.

MR. WEBSTER TO MR. C. B. HADDOCK.

Washington, February 7, 1814.

MY DEAR NEPHEW,—Although I have seen so little of you since you were a child, I yet take a great interest in your welfare as well on your own account as from an affectionate remembrance of your dear mother. Learning from your uncle Ezekiel, that you are passing the winter at Salisbury, I take the opportunity of writing to you, and of desiring you in turn to write to me.

You are now, I think, in your Sophomore year. I recollect that year was an interesting one to me from the studies that belonged to it. I suppose the course of studies is since that time a good deal altered; but it was then Geography, Logic, Mathematics, &c. As we had before been confined altogether to Latin and Greek, these other pursuits, in addition to their real importance, possessed the charm of novelty. Geography, especially, is an entertaining study; and its usefulness is as great as its pleasure. It is an indispensable preliminary to history, the ancient Epic poetry, and almost every other literary pursuit. I would advise you never to read the history of any country, till you have studied its geography. If it be ancient history, you must have before you maps of the country, with its ancient names and divisions. If it be modern history, you must have maps with modern names and divisions. You should learn to use the globes easily, and should use them frequently and freely. If you form at first incorrect ideas of the situations of the continents, the great seas, &c., you will find it very difficult to correct them afterwards.

The favorable accounts, my dear nephew, which I hear of your progress in your studies, make me hope that I can be in some degree useful to you by my advice. If I can, it will give me great pleasure. I wish you to write to me often and on any subject you please. I shall remember to write to you as frequently as my leisure will permit. I hope you will see your grandmother and aunt, and let them know you have heard from me. Make my respects to your father and mother, and remember me to William and Moses. When you have opportunity, I hope you will visit your little cousins at Boscawen.

Adieu, my dear nephew,

D. WEBSTER.

DANIEL WEBSTER TO EZEKIEL WEBSTER.

Washington, March 7, 1814.

DEAR EZEKIEL,—There has been hardly any thing transpiring here this month out of which one could find materials for a letter.

A bankruptcy bill is reported; probably it will not be acted upon this session. A bill making great alterations in the judiciary will most likely take the same fate, and indeed I am doubtful whether the important subject of the new tariff will not be postponed. If these things should all take place, we may adjourn next month; I think we shall.

The spring is coming forward here. The ground is settled

and dry; the birds are appearing, and the grass is green. But spring does not rush forward here, as it does in New Hampshire after it has commenced. It lingers and gets along by imperceptible degrees.

Almost all that I know about your election, I gather from the papers. They look well; especially Portsmouth and Keene. But before you receive this, the matter will be settled; so I will not trouble you on that subject. I imagine you will not be in a condition to like to talk about it; at least I fear so.

I have no faith in C——; I believe he will shrink and give in, and be paid for his compliance by the seals of state.

Mr. King will stand candidate for New York. There will be a severe contest in that State.

I think the nomination of General Brooks a wise measure.

Give my love to mother and your family, and let me hear from you. D. W.

DANIEL WEBSTER TO EZEKIEL WEBSTER.

Washington, March 28, 1814.

Dear Ezekiel,—I send you to-day Sheffey's speech. You will at least like its length and substance. We are yet to have one or two more in pamphlet form, which I will endeavor to obtain and send. In relation to the offer made by England to renew Jay's treaty, I intend to see and collect, and carry home, what evidence there is on the point. The news brought by The Rambler, has just arrived here; we have not had time to consider it. It is vast and momentous.

Most of the subjects intended to be acted upon this session are through. One of great importance has lately been started, viz: another bank project. The loan will fail, unless they can help it on by a bank. The National Intelligencer says it is necessary; and seems to intimate that that consideration ought to supersede constitutional scruples. Of course, I cannot desert my post here, while so important a project is in agitation. If this should go by, I may, and think I shall, be at your Hopkinton court. I have written the Chief Justice to send Judge E. to Haverhill. In the Supreme Court I showed myself once, twice, or thrice. In one case I charged a New Yorker three hundred dollars, and in two other cases, a hundred dollars each. So much for prize causes, &c.

There is no man in the court that strikes me like Marshall. He is a plain man, looking very much like Colonel Adams, and about three inches taller. I have never seen a man of whose intellect I had a higher opinion.

The court adjourned about two weeks ago. The Yazoo bill is through, passed by eight majority. It excited a great deal of feeling. All the Federalists supported the bill, and some of the Democrats. Georgians, and some Virginians and Carolinians, opposed it with great heat. Oakley made the principal speech of the Federalists in its support. Our feeling was to get the Democratic support of it. Clark of Kentucky, a pretty clever fellow, made a handsome speech in support of it.

Mason is going to be a great man. He ranks in the Senate, I think, next to King and Gore. He has made some very excellent speeches.

I give you joy of the election. We had here a great deal of distress about it, and could not have stood a defeat. You gave an enormous vote, nearly forty thousand. I do not hear who rides for Boscawen, but I suppose some of the old school. Your vote in Boscawen was a glorious one, but nothing gave me more pleasure than the regeneration of Salisbury. I hope that town may be kept right hereafter.

I have sent Gaston's speech to Captain Benj. Pettengill, who I hear is one of us; if not, it will do him no hurt. I think I shall send a speech or something to Caleb Knight. These speeches are a little too much like treatises.

Yours as ever, D. W.

Give my love to all your numerous family. I have to-day had a letter enclosing other letters, enclosing locks of hair, &c.

DANIEL WEBSTER TO EZEKIEL WEBSTER.

Washington, May 29, 1814.

CONGRESS adjourned yesterday, after half an hour's session. Two elections will be contested; Bayley's and Hungerford's, by Barret and Taliaferro. Messrs. King and Gore took their seats yesterday. There will be a new Senator from Delaware, Wells or Vandyke.

There is no present prospect, as I think, of peace, although the Madison men appear to be very confident of such a result from the Russian embassy. There will be difficulty about the taxes, inasmuch as the war party will be divided in respect to the objects of taxation. The whiskey tax will not be high. The domestic dram-drinking interest is astonishingly powerful.

I am going to-day with Col. Pickering, Mr. Stockton, and a few others, to dine with Judge Washington, at Mount Vernon. House adjourned yesterday to Monday.

Yours, D. W.

DANIEL WEBSTER TO EZEKIEL WEBSTER.

(EXTRACT.)

Washington, October 30, 1814.

DEAR EZEKIEL,—

* * * * * * *

We have as yet done little. The taxes are before us. I have marked out my course respecting them, and shall vote for nothing but the whiskey tax. This I am anxious to have laid. It will stop distillation in New England; a practice which is drawing upon our sources of life, and rendering us far more dependent than we otherwise should be upon others for bread. A few of our best Federalists feel an inclination to vote for the taxes, owing to circumstances, and the particular state of public opinion in their districts.

The terms offered by England, struck our folks differently at first from what they do on reflection. For my part, I expected no better; so feeble has the government shown itself, and so little able to carry on the war successfully.

We have a plan for a conscription. I think I have sent you its outlines. The bill is drawn principally on Mr. Monroe's first plan. Of course we shall oppose such usurpation all we can.

I should like to hear from you, respecting what is the present tone of public sentiment among you? What do Federalists think we ought to do here?

Yours, D. W.

DANIEL WEBSTER TO EZEKIEL WEBSTER.

Washington, November 8, 1814.

Dear Sir,—We are now taking up the conscription; we shall, I think, let Mr. Troup fill up the blanks, &c. before we state our objections to it. I doubt whether it will pass; but what else can government do? Voluntary enlistments will not answer. They must put themselves upon some measure of force, to get men. This they suppose will answer; but I suppose no such measure can be executed.

We have had a good deal of debate upon a certain volunteer bill; its object was to get up a sort of mongrel corps, in which members of congress could serve; half-way between regulars and militia. It contained, also, a provision for exempting these corps, after serving a time, from all further militia duty, either to the general government or the State. We finally laid the bill aside for the present. There is great distrust, jealousy, and division among the majority; but I know not whether any good will come of their schisms.

We have not heard any thing from New England, though we want to know how the tone of public feeling among you is.

The taxes will be upon you directly. The bank is uncertain. If they make a proper bank, some Federalists will vote for it; it is uncertain whether they will do this or not.

Give my love to mother and your family. I am in very good health. Yours,

D. W.

DANIEL WEBSTER TO EZEKIEL WEBSTER.

Washington, November 21, [1814.]

DEAR EZEKIEL,—At present we are engaged about a bank. The project brought in by the new secretary of the treasury was calculated only for the benefit of the holders of the stock, created since the war. The assessments on the shares were to be paid in, in such stock, principally at par; it being now much depreciated, this was giving its proprietors a great boon. After some days' discussion, this plan was abolished, and a new one is now before us; this is, that every share shall be paid for by the subscribers, as follows, namely, one tenth in gold or silver, and nine tenths in treasury notes; whole capital to be fifty millions. If this plan succeeds, the capital of the bank, when all paid in, will consist of forty-five millions treasury notes, and five millions specie; these treasury notes the government is to issue in payment of its debts, and it is expected that they will be received, and even bought up, by those who wish to become stockholders in the bank. After getting into the bank in this way, they are to be turned into government stock, bearing an interest of six per cent, and payable at the pleasure of government, so that the capital will then be forty-five millions stock, and five millions specie.

In the present plan, all Presidential interference in choosing directors, &c., and all obligation to lend the government money is struck out. Federalists have generally voted for the amendment in preference to the first plan, but they are pretty indifferent about any bank.

Mr. Mason's speech is published; it was well received, and is a solid argument.

We cannot learn whether the conscription will be brought up on Monroe's plan, in this House. Indeed, the party are all in a swamp, and I should not be surprised at any thing's taking place. Yours,

D. W.

DANIEL WEBSTER TO EZEKIEL WEBSTER.

Washington, December 22, [1814.]

Dear Ezekiel,—We have done nothing here lately, except with reference to taxes. They have all passed this House, except the land tax of six millions, last year three, which will be read the third time to-day. Giles's militia draft bill, which was altered in this House, so as to reduce the term from two years to one. The Senate have voted to disagree to the amendment. A conference will ensue, and the Senate will in the end probably recede from their disagreeing vote. This bill, as you will see, cannot be carried into effect if the state governments do not lend their aid to it. On a motion to strike out the first section of this bill, and on a motion to postpone indefinitely, the usual manner of moving to reject a measure, we made speeches; Stockton, Grosvenor, Shepherd, Ward, Miller, &c. Miller's and Stockton's are in the press; I shall send you sundry copies of each. Mine I have written out, but upon the most wise reflection, I have laid it up in the drawer; it will not, in my opinion, answer the expectation of those who heard it, and therefore I shall not publish it at present. Perhaps, during the session, we shall have conscription up in a worse form, though I believe the party are a good deal frighted at it.

We are expecting every day to hear from New Orleans. It seems certain that the English have sent an expedition thither; on its result, perhaps, the question of peace may depend.

Give my love and duty to our mother, and my love to your family. I intend coming home in February.

As to governor, let the people have their choice. Strengthen the state governments as much as possible; especially see if something cannot be done for the council.

Yours, D. W.

DANIEL WEBSTER TO EZEKIEL WEBSTER.

Washington, January 9, 1815.

Dear Ezekiel,—As conscription has gone by for the present at least, I thought that you might like to see the several documents. I send you Monroe's letter, Giles's bill, and the bill reported by our military committee.

The bank bill has passed our House in a form very much amended; it will now be harmless, as we think. We had a hard task to prevent its passing in its worst shape.

We hear that the British are near New Orleans; as that place is likely to become the theatre of interesting operations, I shall try to send you a map, &c.

I hear you talk of Mr. West for governor. If he will accept, and will be acceptable, it will do well; he would make an excellent governor. I think Cheshire would give him a great vote.

The taxes have mostly passed. The government put off the necessary work so long that they have been obliged to lay more than I think the people can pay; I have no belief they can be collected.

Mr. King is getting a good deal of popularity for having moved the postponement of Giles's bill; it was accidental and unpremeditated, and there was no debate. After we passed the bill with amendments, it was bandied about several days from house to house, on account of the disagreeing votes relative to the amendments. Being one day before the Senate, and it being known that public sentiment had terrified the vehement senators, Mr. King made the motion, some members happened to be out, it was immediately put and carried.

Mr. Gore has recently made a very great speech. I understand it is to be published, and shall send it to you. I know not whether occasion will offer for general discussion in our House soon, but expect it before we go. We shall take up the investigating report one of these days, and talk over the Bladensburg business.

Give my love to mother, and your family.

Yours, D. W.

DANIEL WEBSTER TO EZEKIEL WEBSTER.

Washington, January 22, 1815.

DEAR EZEKIEL,—

* * * * * * *

We have nothing from New Orleans later than the evening of 23d, the night after the first battle.

We had yesterday a letter from Secretary Dallas, giving a bad account of the treasury; five millions more of new taxes must be collected within this year, in order to get money enough out of all our ways and means to pay the interest of the debt, still leaving the whole expense of the year, forty millions at least, to be provided for by loans!

The administration is completely foiled in it's bank scheme. It has been a hard battle, and the defeat is complete. We were obliged to make a bank or let Dallas's plan go. A hundred of the narrowest chances alone saved us from a complete paper money system, in such a form as was calculated and intended to transfer the odium of depreciation from the government to the bank. It will be the subject of a week's talk when I see you. The present bank can probably do nothing; certainly very little during the war. When peace comes, it will be likely to do good.

There is no great business at present before us; what new projects will be got up I cannot say. I expect some great explosion yet before the session closes, on account of the state of the treasury.

I have sent you Stockton's and Ward's speeches; also my little talk about the bank.[1] My conscription speech must rest till another day. If a good occasion presents, I will shoot one little gun more, as Nat. says, this session. But I intend to go home, so as to be at February court.

Yours, D. WEBSTER.

1 Speech on the incorporation of a Bank of the United States, January 2, 1815. See Everett's edition of the Works of Daniel Webster, page 35.

DANIEL WEBSTER TO EZEKIEL WEBSTER.

Washington, January 30, 1815.

Dear Ezekiel,—I send you the Intelligencer containing our latest advices from New Orleans.

The President has negatived the bank bill. So all our labor is lost. I hope this will satisfy our friends, that it was not a bank likely to favor the administration. What is to be done next nobody can tell.

One or two more taxes are expected to be passed, one on income; I think the others recommended by the secretary will not go.

My intention is to depart hence in about eight or ten days, so as to be home at court, at which time and place you must come and see me.

I shall not probably find an occasion to say something which I should like to say; but I hope and think that Mr. Mason will discuss some subjects of interest, in a manner to awaken the attention of the people a little.

We are getting printed a little abstract of reports, bills, &c. tending to show the design of government on conscription, &c. I shall send a number of them to you for circulation. Give my love to our mother, your wife and children.

Yours, D. W.

MR. WEBSTER TO MR. D———

Portsmouth, August 25, 1815.

Dear Sir,—On my return from Exeter to-day, I found your letter from Hanover. On the subject of the dispute between the President and the trustees, I am as little informed as any reading individual in society; and I have not the least inclination to espouse either side, except in proceedings in which my services may be professional. It was intimated to me last spring, that the President might possibly institute process against the trustees for the recovery of money due him from them; that proceedings might also be commenced in the courts of law, to determine whether there had been a perversion of the Phillips fund; and that in case these events should happen, the President would be glad to engage my assistance as counsel. At Concord, the President suggested, in general terms, that he might wish to obtain my professional assistance on some future occasion, which I readily promised him. After Dr. Haven had left this place for Hanover, I received the President's letter, desiring me to be at Hanover at a time which had then already elapsed. I answered it by mail, not quite so soon as I should have done, if I had not expected some private conveyance; and, if I had not known that an answer by any conveyance would have been wholly immaterial at that time. If I had received it earlier, I could not have attended, because the court engaged me at home; and I ought to add here, that if I had had no other engagements at the time, and had also been seasonably notified, I should have exercised my own discretion about undertaking to act a part before the committee at Hanover. I regard that as no professional call, and should consider myself as in some degree taking side personally and individually for one of the parties, by appearing as an advocate on such an occasion. This I should not desire to do, until I know more of the merits of the case. As to the letter you enclose, and the mention made in it of myself, I can only say that I have no particular recollection of any conversation in which, more than on any other occasion when I talked of the subject, I expressed what is ascribed to me. Undoubtedly, however, the substance of what I should say on that subject, at any time, would be, that the trustees should make a reply; and that whatever they allege, they should fully prove by affidavits or otherwise. If, by "putting down a certain man," is meant a refutation of the charges contained in his publications, I certainly have felt, in common with every body else, as I suppose, a very strong desire that the trustees, for many of whom I have the highest respect, should be able to refute, in the fullest manner, charges which, if proved or admitted, would be so disreputable to their characters. My "desire" on the subject is just what I had imagined every one else felt, who wished to see a controversy cleared up and to learn the truth.

As to what you are pleased to say about my extricating myself from this affair, or of its being otherwise unpleasant to me;

as also what you observe of a suspicion entertained by some that Mr. Thompson had employed me to feel of Mr. Haven on the subject; give me leave to say that I should know better how to answer these remarks, if I were not writing to one for whom I have the highest and warmest esteem, and of whose sense of delicacy and propriety very few, certainly, at any time, have had occasion to complain. Towards those who harbor such a suspicion, I entertain no sentiment but contempt. On the merits of this dispute I perceive you are decided and warm. This is natural to the generosity of your nature, and the sincerity and warmth of your friendship. You speak in terms of pretty strong decision of individuals whom I regard as among the most valuable and honorable men in the community; but on this account I neither bring accusation nor insinuation against you. No suspicion of the purity of your motives, or the uprightness of your conduct, has come near my mind. I am not quite so fully convinced as you are, that the President is altogether right and the trustees altogether wrong. When I have your fulness of conviction, perhaps I may have some portion of your zeal. Whenever I have said any thing to either side, it has been to impress the necessity of moderation and candor, as they will do me the justice, I trust, to acknowledge.

If the friends of the President have any thing in any degree derogatory to the character of Judge Farrar, it will certainly have its weight; but it is not likely that the great body of the Federalists in the State will take much on trust from Democratic newspapers; they will look to the result of the inquiry by the committee. You may be well assured that in our nomination of governor, we have regarded nothing but the political interests of the State. I can but flatter myself that if you were better acquainted with circumstances, you would think less unfavorably of the conduct of your Federal friends. I am quite sure your patriotism and your candor will lead you to a thorough inquiry before you pronounce your disapprobation. In the mean time, give me leave to hope that Vermont, in which, I trust, this controversy has not been much felt, will set us so good an example next month, as will make us quite ashamed of apathy or disunion.

I am, dear Sir, with sincere and great regard,

Yours, &c. DANIEL WEBSTER.

MR. WEBSTER TO MR. W. SULLIVAN.

Washington, January 2, 1816.

☞ Do not read this while you have any thing else to do.

DEAR SIR,—I am glad to find you so well employed as in chasing whales, though they be dead whales. Having seen you last in your own chamber, I was glad to learn that you have got into court, and are fit to engage in such arduous enterprises as whaling.

Your account reminded me of some very ingenious and laughable remarks of Lord Erskine, in a *crim. con.* case, some twenty years ago. They are in one of the volumes of the Annual Register. Mr. Erskine was for the defendant; his defence was that the plaintiff had abandoned his wife, and put her to separate maintenance, and having thus voluntarily relinquished the comfort and society of his wife, he could not pretend that the defendant, by his interposition, had deprived him of these enjoyments. He then went on to say that the law of England in respect to wives, was just like the law of the Greenland fishery in respect to whales; whoever struck the whale, had a right to him, so long as he held on by the line. However the fish might plunge, or flounce, or curvet, though he should go to the bottom, or run away to the temperate or the torrid zone, while the striker held on by his line, the animal, however untamed or untamable, remained his property, and woe betide the wrongdoer that should interfere; but the moment he lets go his line, the animal, in the eye of the law, was *feræ naturæ*, and became the rightful property of the first taker. So, in the case of wives; while the husband holds on by his matrimonial string, however far the wife strays, to whatever great distances she may run out from the path of duty, or however crooked and eccentric her course, the law still regards her in *custodia viri*, and will allow no interference of third persons; but if the husband will choose to let this little cord drop out of his hand, in an instant all is over! The wife then runs "unclaimed of any man," and like the wounded whale, becomes the property of the next striker.

We are doing nothing now but to quarrel with one of our laws of the last session, called the horse law, its object being to pay the Kentucky men for all the horses which died in that country during the war. So far very well; but there was a section put in to pay for all houses and buildings burned by the enemy, on account of having been a military depôt. This played the very d——. All the Niagara frontier, the city of Washington, &c., wherever the enemy destroyed any thing, was proved to have been a military depôt; one tavern, twenty-seven thousand dollars, because some officers or soldiers lodged in the house a day or two before the burning; one great rope-walk, because a rope had been sent there to mend from the navy yard, &c. &c. Some say the fault is in the law, some say it is in the commissioner who executed the law, others say there is no error in either, and others insist that there are errors in both. I agree with the last, as the most probable proposition.

The bankrupt bill will be tried next week. It will be hard pressed by Hopkinson, but I cannot foresee its fate.

We then have the compensation to repeal, which I trust will not take us long. I fear a bare repeal of the law of last session will take place; then the judiciary projects must be disposed of. Then comes from the Senate the conscription law, as you justly call it. What inducement has one to resist this or any thing else? Two years ago, with infinite pains and labor, we defeated Mr. Monroe's conscription; nobody thanked us for it. Last winter our friends in the Senate got this militia bill thrown out; nobody knew or cared any thing about it. For two or three years Massachusetts has been paying from ten to twenty-five per cent. more duties on importations than Pennsylvania or Maryland. At the close of the last session, we tried to do something for her relief; but her Federal legislature takes no notice of the abominable injustice done her, or the plain violation of the constitution and laws, which has taken place to her great injury. All are silent and quiet. But when her Federal members who come here to be kicked, and stoned, and abused in her behalf, think proper to raise their compensation, so that it will defray their expenses, she denounces them, man by man, without an exception. No respect for talents, services, character, or feelings, restrains her from joining with the lowest democracy in its loudest cry.

Having thus written you a very long and dull letter, and come near to finishing with a fit of the spleen, I will conclude by sending to your household our sincerest gratulations, at the opening of the new year, and our wishes that all its days may be pleasant to you. I must add also, which you will be very sorry to hear, that the illness of our little daughter at Cambridge, has very much alarmed us, and we are in expectation that Mrs. Webster will be compelled to return. If so, she will be accompanied by her brother, to whom I have written to come here for that purpose, unless I should make such disposition of my business at the court as to permit me to return with her, which I do not expect. Yours truly,

D. WEBSTER.

DANIEL WEBSTER TO EZEKIEL WEBSTER.

Washington, March 26, 1816.

DEAR EZEKIEL,—I have settled my purpose to remove from New Hampshire in the course of the summer. I have thought of Boston, New York, and Albany. On the whole I shall, probably, go to Boston; although I am not without some inducements to go into the State of New York. Our New England prosperity and importance are passing away. This is fact. The events of the times, the policy of England, the consequences of our war, and the Ghent Treaty, have bereft us of our commerce, the great source of our wealth. If any great scenes are to be acted in this country within the next twenty years, New York is the place in which those scenes are to be viewed. More of this hereafter.

We are now coming to the end of the session. The bank is before the Senate, and in my opinion, will be a law in a week. Dallas is to quit the treasury, to be president of it.

The tariff is the only other important article before us. In three weeks I intend to be off. As to circuit, I decline Hillsborough and Cheshire, but perhaps shall be obliged to go to Grafton.

I am very sorry to hear of mother's continued ill health. The weather has now turned warm, and I hope she will experience the benefit of it. Here it has been very cold for three or four weeks; but spring seems now coming in earnest.

Give my love to mother and your family.

Ever yours, D. W.

DANIEL WEBSTER TO EZEKIEL WEBSTER.

Washington, April 11, 1816.

Dear Ezekiel,—I received yours yesterday, and I learned with great sorrow the illness of our mother and Mary. I have hardly a hope that the former can now be living. If she should be, on the receipt of this, tell her I pray for her everlasting peace and happiness, and would give her a son's blessing for all her parental goodness. May God bless her, living or dying!

If she does not survive, let her rest beside her husband and our father.

I hope Mary is not dangerously ill. You must write to me, addressed to New York, where I expect to be on my way home about the 28th or 30th instant. Congress will probably rise about the 22d or a few days later.

We have got through most of the important public business of the session.

Give my love to your wife and children, and may Heaven preserve you all.

Most affectionately yours,
D. Webster.

MR. E. WEBSTER TO MR. HADDOCK.

April 29, 1816.

Dear Charles,—Your grandmother continued to decline from the time you saw her, till one o'clock on Friday last. She was very sensible of the event of her sickness; and to that event she looked forward with perfect composure and resignation. She was buried yesterday at Salisbury, by the side of her mother and her husband. She spoke of you with great affection, and wished you all happiness in this world and the world to come. May God have us all in his holy keeping.

Yours affectionately,
E. Webster.

[In the early part of 1816, Mr. Randolph and Mr. Webster had some misunderstanding in the House of Representatives, which led to a challenge on the part of Mr. Randolph. The matter was, however, by the interposition of friends, amicably adjusted, and the following correspondence will show how entirely to the satisfaction of both parties.

It would seem that Mr. Webster kept no copy of his reply to Mr. Randolph's message, but after all was settled, wrote to him to request one, which Mr. Randolph forwarded to him.]

MR. RANDOLPH TO MR. WEBSTER.

Davis's, nine miles from Washington, on the Baltimore Road,
April 30, 1816.

Sir,—Your polite and friendly note was put into my hands this morning, under circumstances that did not permit me to write. I now regret very much that I did not leave Georgetown with you this morning. I have just dined where you breakfasted this morning with a most pleasant party. That reflection seems to add to the uncomfortable feel of solitariness that now assails me. Below you have the "Copy" of the paper, which you desired me to forward to you. Accept my acknowledgments for the terms in which that request is made, and believe me with very high respect and regard,

Your obedient servant,
John Randolph, of Roanoke.

MR. WEBSTER TO MR. RANDOLPH.

Sir,—For having declined to comply with your demand yesterday in the House, for an explanation of words of a general nature, used in debate, you now "demand of me that satisfaction which your insulted feelings require," and refer me to your friend, Mr. ——, I presume, as he is the bearer of your note, for such arrangements as are usual.

This demand for explanation, you, in my judgment, as a matter of right, were not entitled to make on me; nor were the temper and style of your own reply to my objection to the sugar tax of a character to induce me to accord it as a matter of courtesy.

Neither can I, under the circumstances of the case, recognize in you a right to call me to the field to answer what you may please to consider an insult to your feelings.

It is unnecessary for me to state other and obvious considerations growing out of this case. It is enough that I do not feel myself bound at all times and under any circumstances, to accept from any man, who shall choose to risk his own life, an invitation of this sort; although I shall be always prepared to repel in a suitable manner the aggression of any man who may presume upon such a refusal.

Your obedient servant,

DANIEL WEBSTER.

MR. WEBSTER TO REV. F. BROWN.

Portsmouth, June 4, 1816.

MY DEAR SIR,—I received yours last evening. You do not feel a stronger wish than I do, that nothing may take place at this session detrimental to the college, and I am willing to do any thing in my power to soften the irritated feelings of democracy towards it. I am under engagements to go to Boston to-morrow, and shall be in that town four or five days. From Boston I can go direct to Concord, if it should be thought useful. Mr. Mason will go up, I believe, the first of next week. I have some hope that the legislature will do nothing; partly, because I hope they will be satisfied in some measure with the report, and partly from the hopeless state of Dr. W.'s health. It is a favorite idea with some to create a new college. Would it not be well if this idea could be encouraged, and to let the ill humors work off in that direction? Suppose a proposition should be made for a committee to report at next session, upon the expediency of making a new college at Concord, and what donations, &c., could be obtained for such an object.

" Resolved, that a joint committee of both Houses be appointed to take into consideration the expediency of establishing a Seminary of Learning, in some part of this State, to be called the University of New Hampshire, and to ascertain what endowment for such institution could be obtained from private donation, and also what grants of land or money could be properly and conveniently made to the same by the State; and also to prepare a draft of a charter for such seminary; and to report at the next session of the Legislature."

Perhaps if something of this sort should be brought forward by somebody who has been favorably inclined to Dr. W., but who would wish to prevent violent measures, it might do good.

Mr. Tilton of Exeter, I should think, might do it to advantage. Think of this; Mr. Cutts, the bearer of this, is an intelligent friend of mine, and capable of being useful at Concord. I recommend it to you to cultivate his acquaintance, while there. He is intimate with Mr. Tilton, and indeed with most other leading men in the legislature. Any thing that shall postpone the subject, will give time to the present feelings to cool and evaporate.

I am, dear Sir, yours with esteem,

D. WEBSTER.

N. B. The resolution might say the charter should be drawn on the following principles:—

1. A board of trustees, to be inserted in the bill by the legislature, to fill up their own vacancies.

2. A board of overseers, viz: governor, senators, counsellors, and speaker of House of Representatives for time being.

3. An unlimited right of conscience, in officers, and students; no test, creed, or confession to be required of either, nor any preference, direct or indirect, of one religion over another. If any thing of this sort be done, it ought to be done early.

MR. WEBSTER TO MR. HADDOCK.

Portsmouth, June 26, 1816.

MY DEAR NEPHEW,—Nothing could have given me more pleasure than your letter, which I have received to-day. I was yesterday in conversation about you with Dr. Mussey, and begged him to make a communication to you, respecting your future course. Your letter gives me an occasion to write to you and to give you my advice.

I entirely agree in thinking that you ought to look around a little time, after leaving college, before you apply yourself to professional studies. A little leisure time and a little travel, will contribute to the improvement both of body and mind

Although I have no reason to doubt that you have made the most of your advantages, yet the manner and system of education in this State are necessarily much confined. A view of the world, a little broader and more extensive than you have yet had opportunity to take, is much to be desired. As to the project of employment in the line of instruction, I have no doubt it can be accomplished, if it should be finally your wish. Situations of that sort are readily enough found, I believe, by worthy young men, in the southern States and cities. I shall probably go to the South in the fall, and if you should incline to go with me, I dare say you would light on a situation to suit you. After your examination, I wish you to come and see me. You have often talked of this, but it has never been done. This summer will give you leisure. If you wish to prepare your Commencement exercises, you shall have a room for your studies. Perhaps I may go to Commencement. However that may be, I hope you will come and see me. Please let me know whether I may not expect you. I have it in contemplation to remove to Boston this summer or fall, though I do not, as yet, say much about it. If your inclination should lead you in that case to spend a few months there, in the fall or winter in pursuit of general literature, we would try to make your abode with us agreeable to you. Let me expect to hear from you.

I am, dear Charles, yours affectionately,

D. Webster.

MR. WEBSTER TO MR. JUSTICE STORY.

Portsmouth, July 30, 1816.

Dear Sir,—In the change which has taken place in the judiciary of this State, I feel a strong desire that a friend of mine should have a proper place in the new establishment. In this wish, I am influenced, I trust, not more by sentiments of personal respect than by a regard to the public interest. I refer to Mr. Adams. He has been for many years clerk of the Supreme Court; and during the period in which you honored us with an occasional attendance at our bar, you were sufficiently acquainted with the manner in which he discharged the duties of his office. I think him the best clerk I ever saw. If others do not agree to all this, they will hardly be able to mention many whom they think better. By the new law, the Supreme Court is to have a clerk in each county. Probably some gentlemen intended, by this, to effect a junction of the officers of County Common Pleas Clerk, and County Supreme Court Clerk. But this can only be done by consent of the two courts, for each has by the Constitution the appointment of its clerk.

What would be agreeable to Mr. Adams, and I think useful to the county, is that he should be clerk of both courts for this county. I imagine the justices of the Supreme Court will at once appoint him their clerk for this county. But this office would be very small of itself. It seems necessary to add to it the clerkship of the Common Pleas. I have no doubt Chief Justice Richardson will use his influence with the Court of Common Pleas for Mr. Adams's appointment. That court consists of Dan. M. Durell, Esq., Chief Justice, and Levi Bartlett, Esq., Associate. There is one vacancy.

I have thought, Sir, that it would be useful on this occasion, for these judges to know, that gentlemen of other States, who have been in our courts, have a favorable opinion of the official conduct of Mr. Adams, and I have ventured to think, that with others you have entertained that opinion, and that the expression of it by you would have its weight. New judges perhaps are not likely to appreciate the force of Lord Bacon's remarks upon the usefulness of a skilful and experienced clerk: and not having seen, some of them, many courts, they may not at once know the difference between good clerks and indifferent ones.

Your professional and judicial life has already been long enough to enable you to estimate these things justly.

Having said so much, may I now beg of you to write on this subject to your friend Chief Justice Richardson? This would give weight to his representation to the justices of the Court of Common Pleas, and if you should also address Chief Justice Durell on the subject, if you know him sufficiently, it would probably be extremely useful. I suppose the appointment will be made soon.

Pardon me for giving you trouble, and accept the assurances of my respect.

Your humble servant, DAN'L WEBSTER.

N. B. The health of the present incumbent renders some change necessary soon in the clerkship of the Court of Common Pleas.

DANIEL WEBSTER TO EZEKIEL WEBSTER.

Boston, January 19, 1817.

Dear Ezekiel,—Grace's illness has brought me home. We arrived four days ago. She has been declining almost ever since we left her, the middle of November, and was so low on our arrival, that we entertained very faint hopes of her recovery. Her case is consumption, and seems a good deal like dear little Mary's. Since our return, her symptoms have been a little more favorable, and might almost encourage a slight hope of ultimate recovery. Dr. Warren thinks, at least, that for a week she is no worse. She seems a little less languid, and has coughed less to-day than any day for a fortnight. My engagements in the court at Washington are such that, if possible, I must return. If Grace should grow no worse, I intend going about Thursday or Friday. We found little trouble in opening our house and collecting our family. Both Hannah and Phila are here. Eliza Buckminster is coming to stay with us awhile. We came home very quickly from Philadelphia, in four days. Mrs. W. stood the journey wonderfully well, and took no cold. I have not been out so much as to my office.

If your courts do not prevent, I wish you would run down and see the family.

We desire our love to all your family most affectionately, and to Mr. Kelly.

Most affectionately yours,

D. W.

DANIEL WEBSTER TO EZEKIEL WEBSTER.

Boston, Sunday, 1817.

Dear Ezekiel,—Our dear little daughter has followed yours. She died on Thursday evening at eleven o'clock, and was interred yesterday. Her death, though I thought it inevitable, was rather sudden when it happened. Her disease, the consumption, had not apparently attained its last stages. She had suffered very little. The day of her death, she was pretty bright in the forenoon, though weak. In the afternoon, she grew languid and drowsy. She, however, desired her friends to read and talk with her until a few minutes before eleven, when her countenance suddenly altered, and in five or six minutes she expired.

Mrs. Webster, though in great affliction, is in tolerable health. Our little boy is very well. To-morrow morning I set out on my return to Washington.

Eliza Buckminster is with us, and Anne Paige also arrived last evening. We desire our most affectionate regards to Alice and the children.

Ever yours, D. W.

MR. WEBSTER TO MR. HADDOCK.

Boston, June 21, 1817.

My dear Nephew,—I wish I was competent to give you useful advice on the subject of your letter. In general, it is a safe rule when a profession is chosen, to pursue it without distraction by other objects and engagements; but there may be cases fit to be exceptions. I have not much belief in the edifying nature of a tutor's employment. Many tutors have been good scholars, it is true; and so they probably would have been, had they not been tutors. To teach others the Latin classics, naturally renders one critical in the classics, as far as he goes in his instructions, but would not after all, give him much Latin. If you were to walk every day from Andover to Reading, and from Reading back to Andover, you would know the road very well from Andover to Reading; but this daily itineration over the same ground, would never bring you to Boston. The Latin should be learned for the sake of the good things which are in Latin. It is folly to learn a language and then make no use of it. What you should do, is not to go back again to prosody and syntax, but to read the whole of Cicero and Livy, and Quintilian, and the other great writers. This, I imagine, would be better done at Andover, where I presume are scholars, "ripe and good ones," than in the company of the Freshman class at Hanover.

There is also, generally, an advantage to be derived from varying a little the place and means of instruction. An entire education at Hanover, I should think, would be too confined. There are, however, considerations of another sort which we are often obliged to regard. How far the pay of a tutor may be convenient to you, I cannot say. You will perceive, on the whole, that I rather agree in the resolution you formed, while at Hanover. I dare say President Brown will find a very good tutor in your place; and as you are designed for a profession, I think he should leave you to pursue it. But I would not have you trust much to my opinion; for, after all, progress in knowledge depends less frequently on the opportunities enjoyed than on the use made of them.

I am, my dear nephew, your affectionate

D. Webster.

MR. WEBSTER TO MR. MASON.

Boston, September 4, 1817.

Dear Sir,—We are happy to hear that Mrs. Mason arrived safe, and hope that Jane's illness was not of long continuance. We think it would have been wise in you to have been here at the time of Commencement. It was, I thought, a pleasant occasion. I went to Waltham, and passed a few hours at Mr. Gore's, while Mr. King was there. Mr. King expressed great regret at your leaving him. He thinks you underrate the good which might have been done, but at the same time does not doubt that you will find it more agreeable to be at home.

Mr. Gore was pleased to have given you a mark of the esteem in which the learned hold you. As he is so much confined, it would be a very good thing for you to come and see him, if you should find it convenient, in the course of the autumn.

Judge Smith has written to me, that I must take some part in the argument of this college question. I have not thought of the subject, nor made the least preparation; I am sure I can do no good, and must, therefore, beg that you and he will follow up in your own manner, the blows which have already been so well struck. I am willing to be considered as belonging to the cause and to talk about it, and consult about it, but should do no good by undertaking an argument. If it is not too troublesome, please let Mr. Fales give me a naked list of the authorities cited by you, and I will look at them before court. I do this that I may be able to understand you and Judge Smith.

I hope you will do the needful about our lodgings at Exeter. I should not like to be too much crowded at Mr. Gardner's.

Yours, with great regard,

D. Webster.

MR. WEBSTER TO MR. MASON.

Boston, November 27, 1817.

Dear Sir,—President Brown has written to me respecting the college cause in its further progress. I have engaged to keep hold of it if I go to Washington this winter. He seems desirous of a final decision this winter. To this end it is necessary that the record should be forwarded as soon as possible. If you can have it sent to me, I will send it along. Mr. Brown does not know the necessary steps in order to the getting up and getting along the writ of error, and relies on you and Judge Smith. Causes, as you know, are entered at the supreme court, upon the arrival of the record. I should like to know something of the court's opinion; I wish you or Mr. Farrar could get a copy for me. If I go to Washington, and have this cause on my shoulders, I must have your brief, which I should get of course without difficulty, and Judge Smith's.

I must also have somebody to help me at Washington. I can think of nobody better for such a question than Hopkinson.

We have no news here. The court has commenced its session, and the chief justice intends to get through next month. Not a word is said about our congress election, since it is over.

Mr. Gore seemed to be very well, for him, a fortnight ago, and I believe continues so.

Will you inform me whether a copy of Judge Richardson's opinion can be had, and whether you can devise a mode in which I can get Judge Smith's minutes if I should go to Washington?

With many salutations for Mrs. Mason and the children,

I am yours,

D. Webster.

MR. WEBSTER TO CHIEF JUSTICE SMITH.

Boston, December 8, 1817.

Dear Sir,—I received yours of the 4th, yesterday. In relation to the special verdict, my impression has been that we should insert every thing to show, as far as we can, that the State did not found and endow the college. I should wish it rather to appear what they had not done, than what they had; but probably the one can only be shown, by showing the other. Therefore I think the jury had better find certain acts, grants, &c. and find that they are all the grants and acts made by the State. For the like reason, I should think it well to find the original grants, gifts, or endowments upon which the college set out. Perhaps these are well enough recited in the charter.

I should like to have all the late obnoxious acts found by the verdict. As to the assignment of errors, you will see the provision of the twenty-fifth section of the judiciary act. It will probably be better to assign the error relied on, namely, that the said statutes, of the said State of New Hampshire, are repugnant to the constitution of the United States and void. I do not know whether the general assignment would not be sufficient, but should prefer a special assignment also.

It is our misfortune that our cause goes to Washington on a single point. I wish we had it in such shape as to raise all the other objections, as well as the repugnancy of these acts to the constitution of the United States. I have been thinking whether it would not be advisable to bring a suit, if we can get such parties as will give jurisdiction in the circuit court of New Hampshire. I have thought of this the more, from hearing of sundry sayings of a great personage. Suppose the corporation of Dartmouth College should lease to some man of Vermont (e. g. C. Marsh) one of their New Hampshire farms, and that the lessee should bring ejectment for it. Or suppose the trustees of Dartmouth College should bring ejectment in Vermont in the circuit court for some of the Wheelock lands. In either of these modes the whole question might get before the court at Washington.

I suggest this only for consideration. Perhaps the known pendency of such a suit might induce Judge Smith, who fully intends to make the court's opinion in this case, to consider all the questions in the present cause.

If I argue this cause at Washington, every one knows I can only be the reciter of the argument made by you at Exeter. You are, therefore, principally interested, as to the matter of reputation, in the figure I make at Washington. Nothing will be expected of me but decent delivery of your matter. This seems perfectly well understood this way, and I have been often complimented by gentlemen saying that, if the cause goes to Washington, they shall have a chance of hearing something of Judge Smith's argument.

I have some notion of coming to Exeter for a day or two, to practise and rehearse before I go to Washington. To be serious, however, you and Mason must help me arrange the argument. The best mode will be, to have it written out, or all collected in notes, so that I can write it out.

For this purpose, I will see you or him, or both, before I go to Washington. As we know pretty well what will be the argument on the other side, at least you do, who have heard Chief Justice Richardson's opinion, we ought, in the opening argument, to cover the whole case.

I here subjoin a printed form of writ of error, and the copy of a citation, which I find in the district clerk's office.

Yours always,

D. WEBSTER.

MR. WEBSTER TO CHIEF JUSTICE SMITH.

Boston, January 9, 1818.

DEAR SIR, — I was not a little disappointed at your sudden departure from this town. Being under an obligation to go to Cambridge on Thursday, and expecting to meet you at Mr. Prescott's on Friday, it was quite unexpected to hear that you had left us. I wished to have said something on the college case confidentially. I shall now say it to Mr. Mason, whom I must see before I go, and he will communicate with you. My hopes of ultimate success are at present somewhat stronger than they ever have been. I must beg the favor of all your notes. I have not assurance enough, although not entirely destitute, to think of arguing this cause on my own strength. To argue it as you did would be more than I shall ever be able to do. I wish to present the cause fully and fairly to the court, and your notes will enable me so to do. If anybody is coming over, pray let me have them soon, and all of them. If you have no opportunity to send them direct, please forward them enclosed, to Mr. Mason. I am writing to him to-day, and will ask him to take care of the packet and to send it to me directly.

I am, dear Sir, with unabated regard, yours,

D. Webster.

MR. WEBSTER TO MR. MASON.

Boston, January 9, 1818.

Dear Sir, — Mrs. Webster's situation will compel me to be at home some days to come. I know not how many. I must, at all events, see you before I go south, and if I cannot go down you must come up. I have something to say to you on the college cause, as well as many things to talk over on other topics. I must leave here about February 1. If by the 20th instant I can leave home, I shall go down and stay a day with you; if not, you must come up.

Judge Smith has been here. I heard of him at the theatre, the assembly room, &c., and I saw him a little at my own house, but had not half the necessary conversation with him. I have written to him to-day for his notes, and desired him to send them to me or to you to be sent to me. Be good enough to send yours, as I wish to be preparing a little.

I have seen very little of Judge Otis. If, when I see him, he has any thing to say of Washington, I will let you know what it is.

Mrs. Webster is very well, and desires her love to your family.

I am, dear Sir, as ever yours,
D. Webster.

P. S. I understand President Brown will be here next week. I shall send him home by Portsmouth. I hear nothing bad about the college case.

MR. WEBSTER TO MR. MASON.

Boston, January, 1818.

Dear Sir,—I must either accept your proposition to meet you at Newburyport, or persuade you to come here. Our court yet holds on; and since I last wrote you, I have been requested to take charge, at Washington, of a cause of much earlier standing on the docket than any in which I had previously a concern. The consequence is, that I must depart somewhat sooner than I intended, and that I shall be pressed much for time while I stay. If I go to Portsmouth, there are persons who will expect to see me there; and indeed if I only allow the time necessary to go and return, staying a day with you, it will be more than I know how to spare. I must try to get off for Washington this day week. If you cannot come here, I will meet you at Newburyport, say on Sunday morning, if I hear from you to that effect. I hope, however, you will find it convenient to come here. You will have motive enough, in the natural desire of seeing Mary. If you will come up on Saturday, my house shall be closed upon us, we being in it, until your departure, on Monday morning, if such is your wish. On any other occasion, or at any other time, I would go a hundred miles to see you. I profess to be a sort of attendant on your course, in your orbit. But at present, if you can vary a little to accommodate the secondary planet, it would be a great favor. In addition to events in the house, I have been engaged for a fortnight, forenoon and afternoon, in indispensable drudgery.

Under these circumstances, I shall wait to hear from you by

Saturday morning's mail. I shall contrive to get to Newburyport by Sunday morning, if you so write. But I should esteem it a very particular obligation, which I would not request on slight reasons, if you could any way make it convenient to come here.

Mrs. Webster is getting along very well. The daughter is in good health, and seems to take the world easy.

With unabated regard yours,

D. WEBSTER.

P. S. I saw Judge Story as he went on. He said he had had a correspondence with you about "things;" but company being present, did not say what things. As usual, he told our lawyers here, that Mr. Mason was decidedly the first lawyer in New England.

MR. WEBSTER TO MR. MASON.

Washington, February 22, 1818.

MY DEAR SIR, — I have hardly found enough to write about to make a letter, since I have been here. I wrote Judge Bell some time since, and nothing new has occurred in his case since, which you will please to inform him. I have hopes it will go over, but it is yet a little uncertain. The docket is not quite so formidable as was expected. The college case is not yet argued; we expect it on this week. Wirt and Holmes are for defendant. Wirt is a man of a good deal of ability; he is rather more of a lawyer than I expected.

I have been once or twice in the house. Those New Hampshire members to whom I had ever been known came to see me, except the judge; I have seen nothing of him.

The bankruptcy bill, I fear, will hardly pass, though it will come near it. The western gentlemen say the circuit courts must be established this session. On the whole, I think there is a fair chance for the adoption of the measure.

The judge volunteered to tell me what correspondence had taken place, and he seems to be fixed in his purpose in that particular. You have a very ardent friend in Colonel Williams.

I dined with him not long since. He took occasion to speak of you in such a manner that I had a pretty full conversation with him. He is a very good fellow. I only wish to say on this subject as much as shall let you know that at present all things wear a very favorable appearance.

Mrs. Bagot inquires for Mrs. Mason, and Madame De Neuville asks for my brother-in-law, Mr. Mason; I informed her that my brother-in-law was very well. The ministers are hospitable as usual. I have been once at Mrs. Monroe's; it was very full. I have dined with the President. His style of life exceeds that of his predecessors. Washington is in all things pretty much what it was last year. I hope to get away from here early next month; but I shall stay a week or two if necessary, to observe the course of things. Give my love to Mrs. Mason; ask her to write often to Mrs. Webster.

Yours,

D. Webster.

MR. WEBSTER TO MR. SULLIVAN.

Washington, February 27, 1818.

My dear Sir,—The Divina Pastora has not yet come on, but I have no doubt it will, at this term. I have attended to the case, and am as ready for it as I shall be. The prosecution against Palmer *et al.* adjourned here from Boston, presents many questions much connected with The Pastora. I expected that would be argued first, but it seems at present it will not. I must, therefore, begin on the affairs of The Pastora.

The bankrupt bill is lost; it might have been carried if all New England had been in favor of it. I did not hear the debates, but report speaks well of the efforts of some of the Massachusetts members,—particularly Mills and Whitman. I have hardly been half an hour in either House of Congress since I came here, a proof, I hope you will think, that I have no wish to get back there. Mr. and Mrs. Otis live within three doors, but I see little of them. Mr. Ashmun, I believe, has gone home. There are in the city a great number of Bostonians, more than I ever saw before at once. Brother John has arrived, and, going to work on Congress pretty much as he does on the New Hampshire legislature, has got a bill through the committee of the Senate about patents. Col. Perkins is expected to-day, I believe. Brother Amory and I are all the brethren of the Boston bar here, —I forgot Mr. Blake. Ogden, and a Mr. Baldwin from New York; Hopkinson, Sergeant, and C. J. Ingersoll, Philadelphia; Harper, Winder, Baltimore; Wickham, Leigh, and Nicholas, from Virginia; Berrien, from Georgia, and the gentlemen of this District. Gaston was expected, but has not come. Court meets at eleven, hears long speeches till four, and adjourns. I have dined abroad every day since I came but one; and the principal reason is, that the only boarding-house where I could get a seat at table, is one in which one would seldom wish to dine at home. I have a room and a bed at a friend's house, Dr. Hunter's, and get my coffee in the morning with his family. So, on the whole, I am better off than most of my neighbors. I am filling up this sheet without saying what I had in view, principally, in writing to-day—here it is.

There is a prospect that the bill establishing circuit courts may pass at this term, making one judge on each circuit. —— and ——, as well as Mr. ——, will probably seek to be made judges.

There is some chance, I think, of having a word to say on that subject ourselves. Therefore I am very desirous that Governor Brooks, Chief Justice Parker, General Sullivan, Mr. Prescott, and other such men, should not commit themselves to any candidate hastily, on the supposition that there is nothing but a choice of evils. You know Governor Brooks better than I do. Is there not danger of his lending his influence to some person, out of his disposition to oblige, before he knows the whole ground?

What induces me to write this, is that if such an office should be created, certain republican gentlemen here, would make an effort to get the appointment for Mr. Mason of New Hampshire. Judge Story, I believe, would exert himself to that end. Mr. Mason has left a high law character here, and several of the Democratic Senators, from the East and the West, would like to show him their respect, by recommending his appointment to such a place. Some of the Democratic gentlemen from New Hampshire would also urge his appointment. Now, if Governor Brooks and the Suffolk bar think they can do no better, would it not be well for them to hold themselves free to support Mr. Mason in case, &c.? This, of course, is pretty confidential. You may mention it, if you see fit, to Mr. Prescott, or a few other friends, but I would not have it spoken of aloud. As soon as the least chance of passing the bill appears, the candidates will spring up. No time should be lost to put Governor Brooks on his guard, if done at all.

I do not write to my wife to-day; will you let her know of my welfare, and will you make a bow to Mrs. Sullivan, and shake hands with her, on my account?

Yours, dear General,

D. Webster.

MR. WEBSTER TO REV. MR. BROWN.

Washington, March 13, 1818.

Dear Sir,—The argument in the cause of the college was finished yesterday. It occupied nearly three days. Mr. Holmes ventured to ask the court whether it was probable a decision would be made at this term.

The chief justice in answer, said, that the court would pay to the subject the consideration due to an act of the legislature of a State, and a decision of a State court, and that it was hardly probable a judgment would be pronounced at this term. You can draw any inference from this which you think warranted. If the court saw no difficulty in coming to the conclusion that the decision in New Hampshire was right, it is not probable that, knowing the state of the college, they would put off the final decision for a twelve months. Mr. Wirt said all that the case admitted. He was replied to in a manner very gratifying and satisfactory to me by Mr. Hopkinson.

Mr. Hopkinson understood every part of the cause, and in his argument did it great justice. No new view was suggested on the other side. I am informed that the bar here are decidedly with us in opinion.

On the whole we have reason to keep up our courage. I am particularly glad that an ejectment is brought. It is just what should be done. You will see the necessity of not giving too much publicity to any thing written by me on this subject. You may say, however, to your friends, and give the students to understand, as far as useful, that the cause looks well here. I think it does look so at present, although I am not perhaps the best judge. The inference, too, to be drawn from the court's postponing the decision, is a very fair one to be used in the extent stated above, by you.

As to the opinions of the bar, you would do well not to state that on my authority, although I believe what I have said to be strictly true. If any thing further occurs relative to the case, I shall write you again.

Yours truly,

D. Webster.

MR. WEBSTER TO MR. MASON.

Washington, March 13, 1818.

My dear Sir,—The argument in the college case terminated yesterday, having occupied nearly three days. On being inquired of by defendant's counsel whether the court would probably give a decision at this term, the chief justice answered "that the court would not treat lightly an act of the legislature of a State and the decision of a State court, and that the court would not probably render any judgment at this term." The cause was opened on our side by me. Mr. Holmes followed. His propositions, as near as I recollect were, 1. No jurisdiction, because both parties in same State. 2. Charter of 1769 not a contract; trustees, public officers, like judges, and sheriffs, &c.; college a part of government, &c. 3. All corporations abolished by Revolution. 4. If charter a contract, not impaired, a great kindness to old trustees to send them new assistants, &c. Upon the whole, he gave us three hours of the merest stuff that was ever uttered in a county court. Judge Bell was present, and had the pleasure of hearing him, but could not stay out his speech. Wirt followed. He is a good deal of a lawyer, and has very quick perceptions, and handsome power of argument; but he seemed to treat this case as if his side could furnish nothing but declamation. He undertook to make out one legal point on which he rested his argument, namely, that Dr. Wheelock was not founder. In this he was, I thought, completely unsuccessful. He abandoned his first point, recited some foolish opinions of Virginians on the third, but made his great effort to support the second, namely, that there was no contract. On this he had nothing new to say. The old story of the public nature of the use—a charter for the ultimate benefit of the people—in the nature of a public institution—like towns, &c. He made an apology for himself, that he had not had time to study the case, and had hardly thought of it, till it was called on.

Upon the whole, no new matter or reasoning was brought forward; and, in my opinion, the argument upon the law of the case on our side is not answered. Mr. Hopkinson made a most satisfactory reply, keeping to the law, and not following Holmes and Wirt into the fields of declamation and fine speaking. One pleasant thing occurred; Holmes said, that "really, for his part, he could not see how nine could be a majority of twenty-one." Hopkinson looked up with much good-nature, and said aloud, that "he could make that out if any body could."

I believe I may say that nearly or quite all the bar are with us. How the court will be I have no means of knowing. I shall write you again before I leave the place.

Ever yours,

D. Webster.

MR. WEBSTER TO CHIEF JUSTICE SMITH.

Washington, March 14, 1818.

Dear Sir,—Our college cause has been argued, and its present posture is stated in the Intelligencer. I have no accurate knowledge of the manner in which the judges are divided. The chief and Washington, I have no doubt are with us. Duval and Todd perhaps against us; the other three holding up. I cannot much doubt but that Story will be with us in the end, and I think we have much more than an even chance for one of the others. I think we shall finally succeed.

I opened the case with most of the principles and authorities on which we relied at Exeter. Your notes I found to contain the whole matter. They saved me great labor; but that was not the best part of their service; they put me in the right path, and conduct, as I think, to an irresistible conclusion. On some parts of the case, I have varied my views a little. The rogues here in congress, complain that the cause was put on grounds not stated in the court below. There is little or nothing in this. I labored the point that it was a private corporation, a charity. Eleazar Wheelock, its founder, as such, entitled generally by law to be visitor; all the power of visitor assigned, in law, by him to the trustees, &c. The only new aspect of the argument was produced by going into cases to prove these ideas, which indeed lie at the very bottom of your argument. My talk occupied nearly a whole sitting. Holmes followed. He spoke three or four hours. His points were: 1. No jurisdiction' because parties live in same State. 2. All corporations abolished by Revolution; and this never revived by constitution of New Hampshire. 3. Charter, not a contract, a mere appointment to office; trustees agents of government; property in fact given to the people. 4. If a contract, not impaired; only nine more assistants in their public duties, &c. Holmes did not make a figure. I had a malicious joy in seeing Bell sit by to hear him, while every body was grinning at the folly he uttered. Bell could not stand it. He seized his hat and went off. Mr. Wirt followed Holmes. He denied: 1. That Eleazar Wheelock was founder; said he never gave any thing; read Belknap, &c. not in the words of course. 2. Not a contract because not beneficial; here came in all the New Hampshire opinion. 3. Not impaired (as Holmes) being only officers, the acts only gave them assistance, &c. &c. Wirt has talents, is a competent lawyer, and argues a good cause well. In this case he said more nonsensical things than became him. Hopkinson, in concluding, confined himself strictly to replying, and acquitted himself with ability. We finished with the third day. The next morning, yesterday, the chief justice told us the court had conferred; that there were different opinions, and that some judges had not formed opinions; consequently, the cause must be continued. When I began this letter, I supposed some little account of what I have now mentioned was in the Intelligencer of this morning; but I since see that it is not. Bullard *v.* Bell has not come on. The court will rise this day. I depart to-morrow.

Yours,

D. WEBSTER.

MR. WEBSTER TO MR. MASON.

Boston, March 22, 1818.

My dear Sir,—I arrived last evening from Washington, having left the great city this day week. Of course I have little news to tell you. On the subject of the college cause, you know all I have to say. I send you your brief, and Judge Smith's; you may both probably need those hereafter. I believe it is fully expected that a case, raising the question in the amplest form, will be presented at the circuit court. I have given some reason to expect this, and, unless for good causes, should be mortified if it were not so.

Nothing seems likely to be done at Congress this session about the judiciary. I am rather glad of it; for, upon consideration, I am exceedingly doubtful on the constitutional point. Others are the same way of thinking; at least the objection would be plausible.

I conferred with very few on this subject. In general, I found what I thought to be a sincere desire to accomplish an object particularly important to myself and others. One reason why nothing is likely to be done this session is, that members of congress, at least some of them, are willing enough not to be excluded from the list of candidates. I think this weighs with certain Senators of Rome.

Mrs. Webster is not very well. She has had a fair trial of her nursing talent, and is obliged to yield the point.

We are procuring a wet-nurse for the child. When she is obtained, I have little doubt Mrs. Webster will enjoy full health.

I send you three or four seed potatoes.[1] I brought them in my trunk from New Jersey. The species is lately imported from England, and is a great favorite where known.

Be good enough to plant them in your garden, and raise enough to see what they are.

Mrs. Webster desires her love to Mrs. Mason, and beg to add my regards.

Yours, truly,

D. Webster.

[1] "Lady fingers," afterward well known in New Hampshire.

MR. WEBSTER TO MR. BROWN.

Boston, March 30, 1818.

Dear Sir,—I received yours of the 14th or thereabouts, which had gone to Washington for me, and was returned hither by Mr. Hopkinson. I am glad an action is brought, and hope it will come on regularly at the May term. I doubt whether Judge Story will incline to give an opinion, and rather think he will prefer that the case should go directly to Washington. In this particular, however, he must take his own course. My reasons for thinking he would prefer deferring an opinion till next winter in the Supreme Court, are only general. I do not expect to be at Haverhill in May. I understand that Judge Story and Mr. Mason will both be there. It would be advisable, I think, that you should be personally at Portsmouth at the Circuit Court. In relation to what transpired at Washington, I do not know that I have any thing new to say. I believe I gave you in a letter from that place a general account of the trial.

I have seen with particular regret some advertisement about dividing the society libraries; what good can come from entertaining or talking of such purposes? The course for yourself and friends, and the students under your care, seems to be, to act as if you expected a favorable result. If it should turn out otherwise, it will be time enough then for adopting such measures as the exigency may require.

Do you expect to be this way this spring?

I am, dear Sir, yours,

D. Webster.

P. S. I do not know whether I shall have any occasion to go to Portsmouth at the Circuit Court. If I should not, I will send to Mr. Mason my minutes, if he wishes it, that he may get any thing out of them if he can, to assist him in the argument of the cause. He, however, as well as Judge Smith, was, as you know, well prepared. I shall write Mr. Mason.

Yours, D. Webster.

MR. WEBSTER TO MR. BROWN.

Boston, April 12, 1818.

Dear Sir,—Yours of the 7th came this morning, and as the mail returns, I believe to-morrow, I answer it this evening. Mr. Marsh miscalculates the probable delay of the actions.

There is very little business in the Circuit Court in New Hampshire, and I have no great doubt the cause will be disposed of in some way within the first three days of the term. If Mr. Marsh intends seeing his counsel, he has no time to lose. He would do well to be at the court. If he is not, you must be there if possible. A client's presence is of no small importance on such occasions.

I do not know that I shall have any business which will take me to Portsmouth, at the Circuit Court, and therefore shall not attend on account of these causes, unless you and your friends should have a distinct desire that I should so do ; I do not think it of the least importance.

If you are this way you can look at my minutes, and such notes as I took at Washington of the arguments of others.

You must not be too sanguine of ultimate success. All I would say is, that I think our chance now quite as good, if not a little better, than it ever was before.

Yours, D. Webster.

MR. WEBSTER TO MR. MASON.

Boston, April 23, 1818.

My dear Sir,—The plaintiff in the Edson cause requested my attendance at Portsmouth at the Circuit Court. I have agreed to go on his performance of certain conditions precedent; and probably it rests on this, whether I shall attend the court. As to the college cause, I cannot argue it any more, I believe. I have told you very often that you and Judge Smith argued it very greatly. If it was well argued at Washington, it is a proof that I was right, because all that I said at Washington was but those two arguments, clumsily put together by me. I do not mean to hold you answerable for any deficiencies; but in truth have little right to claim the merit, if there be any, in the opening of our case. Since I came home, a young man in my office has assisted me to copy my minutes, and I have been foolish enough to print three or four copies. I committed this folly principally on the motion of some friends here, who were anxious to know something of the grounds of our case, of which they have been most deplorably uninformed. These copies are and will remain, except when loaned for a single day, under my own lock and key. They are hastily written off, with much abbreviation, and contain little else than quotation from the cases. All the nonsense is left out. There is no title or name to it. These precautions were taken to avoid the indecorum of publishing the creature. If I have a safe conveyance, I shall send one to you. You must not let Farrar see it, because he would wish to show it to President Brown and all. And perhaps I should do better to burn it, than to send it at all. Judge Story has been recently in town. I have no doubt he will incline to send up the new cause in the most convenient manner, without giving any opinion, and probably without an argument. If the district judge will agree to divide without argument, *pro formâ*, I think Judge Story will incline so to dispose of the cause. A special verdict is the most convenient mode, I think. The verdict in the other cause I think very right, and from the same minutes one can be drawn in the present case. I shall be at Portsmouth whether I hear from Edson or not, unless I should be engaged at Ipswich.

Mr. Prescott is judge, a very good thing for the county of Suffolk, and not so bad a thing for himself as it might at first seem. He will receive about three thousand dollars per annum. He does not wish and has repeatedly declined a seat on the other bench, on account of its great labor, and being willing to leave the bar pretty soon, this seems to be an eligible retirement. We shall endeavor to get along without him at the bar, and bear our loss as well as we can.

We expect Mrs. Mason to see us next month, and she has partly promised to bring her husband.

Yours truly, D. WEBSTER.

MR. WEBSTER TO MR. JUSTICE STORY.

Boston, May 14, 1818.

Dear Sir,—Among those who have applied for the appointment of an appraiser under the late law, is Mr. Isaac P. Davis. He thinks the aid of your neighbor, Mr. Silsbee, to whom he is well known, would be useful to him. The object of this is, if you should see Mr. Silsbee to-day, to beg of you the favor of suggesting the thing to him, that if he should see fit he may address a line to any of his friends at Washington. There have been many previous applications, and some of them, and as far as I know all, by very fit and proper men. I think Mr. Davis's chance of success not great; but it would be gratifying to himself and friends that he should be well recommended. You, yourself, can best judge whether it would be worth while for you to give him a letter. I say this confidentially; because as there is no great prospect of success, you might incline to think that your name and influence should be reserved for a more promising occasion. It will be time enough to think of this part of the case after you arrive here. In the mean time, if you should have occasion to see Mr. Silsbee, and should suggest to him Mr. Davis's wish, it would oblige him and his friends.

I am, dear Sir, as always, with great regard yours,

D. Webster.

MR. WEBSTER TO MR. MASON.

Ipswich, April 28, 1818.

Dear Sir,—Mr. March's account of the probable disposition of the college actions, seems to leave no occasion at all for my being at Portsmouth, and my engagements here render it truly considerably inconvenient. I could not leave at all till Friday evening; and your court will probably rise on Saturday.

I saw Judge Story as I came along. He is evidently expecting a case which shall present all the questions. It is not of great consequence whether the actions or action, go up at this term, except that it would give it at an earlier standing on the docket next winter.

The question which we must raise in one of these actions, is, "whether, by the general principles of our governments, the State legislatures be not restrained from divesting vested rights?" This of course, independent of the constitutional provision respecting contracts. On this question I have great confidence in a decision on the right side. This is the proposition with which you began your argument at Exeter, and which I endeavored to state from your minutes at Washington. The particular provisions in the New Hampshire Constitution no doubt strengthen this general proposition in our case; but on general principles, I am very confident the court at Washington would be with us.

If so, then nothing will remain but this: "Are the powers, privileges, or authorities of the trustees under this charter rights, within the meaning of the proposition? Are they franchises, liberties, or privileges, such as the law protects, or are they merely disinterested duties, or official services." I cannot state this question very accurately, but this is the general idea. If we get up one of these cases in due form, we shall defeat our adversaries.

I shall come and stay a week with you, as soon as our Circuit Court is over. One reason for not going now, is that Mrs. Webster cannot go, and I could not stay. I want to make a bargain with you for a summer trip somewhere this year; say Albany, &c., or Montreal, &c. Think of these things a little. The robbery trial commences to-morrow morning.

Yours, D. WEBSTER.

P. S. Judge Story goes down in the stage-coach on Friday morning.

MR. WEBSTER TO CHIEF JUSTICE SMITH.

Boston, July 2, 1818.

DEAR SIR,—President Adams has expressed a wish to see Chalmers's opinions of eminent men, and I have promised him a sight of it. If you will have the goodness to send the volumes up, they will be much at your service another time, if you should need them. I suppose he wishes to see them now, as he is writing on colonial affairs. They will come safely by the driver of the stage-coach, I believe, if no other mode offers. If they can be left at Langmaid's, to be brought by the driver of the mail stage-coach, I shall get them without difficulty.

Yours as ever,

D. Webster.

[Note. On the next page of the sheet on which the above letter was written, is a sketch of Judge Smith's answer, in the last part of which there is something so characteristic of him, that it was thought best not to resist the inclination to transcribe it.]

Exeter, July 7, 1818.

Dear Sir,—I did not receive yours of the 2d till last evening. I shall endeavor to send the books this evening to Langmaid's for the mail stage-driver, and will bribe him to fidelity, the only way to make a stage-coach man honest. On the subject of colonial ambiguities, there are so few capable of illustrating them, that every attempt of that sort deserves encouragement. I hope the old gentleman will persevere to the end and leave the world some fruits of his long and laborious life. It is a provoking thing to have knowledge, which, God knows, the living need, covered up in the grave with these vile bodies.

MR. WEBSTER TO MR. BROWN.

Boston, July 16, 1818.

Dear Sir,—You are not much accustomed, I believe, to forget your duties; and some apology would seem necessary for reminding you of things, which in all probability you have fully attended to. There are two topics, however, upon each of which I will repeat the expression of a wish. The first is the letter to Mr. Hopkinson; the second, care to prevent any public use being made of our argument. Mr. Gilbert informs me that a copy has been given to the students, and I am fearful their zeal in a good cause may lead them possibly to make an indiscreet use of it. I rely on you for safety against such evils. I am quite satisfied our course is right. The argument will cease to do good, if used in any other way than that in which we have used it. Pray caution the students against publishing it, or any part of it. The printer also should be admonished not to say any thing about it.

We have nothing new about the final result. As far as I learn, those who have paid attention to the question are more and more convinced that we have the right side.

Very truly yours,

D. Webster.

MR. D. PUTNAM TO MR. WEBSTER.

Brooklyn, Conn., July 17, 1818.

Sir,—I have read with deep interest and great satisfaction an article in the North American Review, vindicating the character of General Putnam and his conduct on the 17th of June, 1775. If the attack was violent and unexpected, the defence has been valiant and effectual to the satisfaction of the public mind. For the distinguished part which your love of justice has contributed towards it, I pray you to accept the grateful thanks of the family, and my own individual acknowledgment of obligation, greater than it will ever be in my power to repay.

It is due however to the relation I stand in to General Putnam, to maintain with modesty what he always asserted with confidence, that the command on Bunker Hill was his. If this could not be done without taking from the gallant and deserving Prescott, any part of the glory which always has and I hope ever will be awarded by his grateful country, for the persevering valor with which he defended the principal objects of assault, I should be among the last to make the claim, in favor even of a father.

But this business has been candidly and I hope satisfactorily stated in the last of a series of numbers in the Centinel, which do honor to the head and heart of the writer, and give to Putnam and Prescott the commendation appropriately due to each; leaving nothing for the friends of either to wish or regret.

I have the honor to be, most respectfully, Sir,

Your most obedient and much obliged servant,

Dan'l Putnam.

MR. WEBSTER TO MR. JUSTICE STORY.

Boston, August 16, 1818.

DEAR SIR,—I have been looking over a file of English newspapers, in order to learn the proceedings of Parliament, at its late session, on the subject of redressing abuses in charities. The measure originated with Mr. Brougham. The complaint was, that funds given to charitable purposes, especially such as were connected with education, were often abused, unproductive, &c. &c. The remedy proposed was a commission to inquire into the state of such charities. What was to be done in the end was not provided for in the bill. The object of the bill was merely to obtain information. The universities and the great schools were excepted out of the provisions of the bill. When it got to the House of Lords, it met with opposition, on several grounds. In its progress, Lord Eldon took occasion to say something on the right of legislative interference. I send you herewith the paper which contains his remarks. In the further progress of the bill in the House of Lords, it was amended by excepting from its operation "all charitable endowments having special visitors;" thus amended, it passed both Houses with Lord Eldon's concurrence.

As nothing but inquiry was proposed, I do not see any great objection to the bill, as it was, but I think its history shows, 1. That the English lawyers recognize a difference between charities having visitors, and such as have none. Indeed, I did not observe, till lately, that the commissions, issued under the statute of Elizabeth, do not extend to charities with visitors. 2. I think we may see that Parliament is not supposed to have the power of new-modelling, and directing to new uses, at its own pleasure, charitable funds, arising from donations of individuals, and by them subjected to the *forum domesticum*. I do not find the debate in the House of Lords, when the amendment stated above was introduced. If I should light upon it, I will preserve it.

According to your wish, I send you a copy of such memoranda of cases, &c., as I have met with, relative to the college question. They are of small importance.

Yours, with the greatest regard,

D. W.

MR. WEBSTER TO MR. JUSTICE STORY.

September 9, 1818.

DEAR SIR,—I send you five copies of our argument. If you send one of them to each of such of the judges as you think proper, you will of course do it in the manner least likely to lead to a feeling that any indecorum has been committed by the plaintiffs. The truth is, the New Hampshire opinion is able, ingenious, and plausible. It has been widely circulated, and something was necessary to exhibit the other side of the question.

I have read the article on "Maritime Law" with the highest delight. There is a great deal that is new to me, and will be most useful to the profession. Your compliment to Chancellor Kent was happily turned, and well deserved. His brother, Moss Kent, of Albany, is a personal acquaintance of mine, and not knowing how many copies of the North American Review might be taken in Albany, I yesterday sent one to him. I think this Number a very good one.

To-day I have been at work for Wheaton, although I have not seen the book yet. Whatever I write must pass your revision. Very truly, your obedient servant,

D. WEBSTER.

MR. WEBSTER TO MR. BROWN.

Boston, November 9, 1818.

DEAR SIR,—I received yours yesterday. It will not be necessary to decide on the subject of other counsel until I see you. You do not appear to apprehend my reasons exactly, and I can explain them better *ore tenus;* suffice it to say, at present, that, although if nothing should be necessary in the way of argument but a reply, Mr. Hopkinson, or myself, might do that, yet if it should be necessary to go over the whole ground again, some new hand must come into the cause. My own impression is to apply, in case of need, to some gentleman there on the spot. Let this rest till January.

As to money and compensation, &c., I hardly know what to say about it. As to myself, considerations of that sort have not added greatly to my interest in the case. I am aware also, that others, whose labors are more useful than mine, are obliged to confer gratuitous services. The going to Washington, however, is no small affair, and is attended with great inconvenience to my practice here. My other inducements to attend the ensuing term are not great, not so much so as last year, while the sacrifice here will be greater.

As to Mr. Hopkinson, he has put the case on such ground, that nothing can be done about his compensation till a final decision. If that should be as we hope, something honorable must be done for him; towards which I expect to contribute in proportion to my means, and in common with other friends. I hope you will be here a little sooner than January 15, as I hope to be able to set off by that time. I rely on you for all necessary knowledge of Moore's Charity School; not caring, however, so much about it as you seem to. The cause has gone too far to be influenced by small circumstances of variance.

I hear nothing unfavorable. Our friends say sometimes that the university people abate nothing of their confidence, which, I confess, a little surprises me, as I think they cannot but observe the general tendency of professional opinion. Mr. Hough says, a hundred and fifty copies of our argument have been printed at the Patriot office and distributed. I hope they will do no hurt.

Yours, very truly,

DAN'L WEBSTER.

P. S. I wish you to understand that if I go to Washington, and am paid for it, anything necessary for new counsel there, I shall pay. It is not my intention that any arrangement of this sort shall increase expense. I am not certain that a new argument will be ordered, and am still more doubtful whether a new opening on our side will be called for. But this is possible, and if so, some gentleman must repeat our view, and add what he or we may have obtained new. This event or course of things is not probable, but possible.

MR. HOPKINSON TO MR. WEBSTER.

Washington, November 17, 1818.

MY DEAR FRIEND,—On my arrival here I received your letter of the 9th instant, just as I was about to write to you on the same subject. In my passage through Baltimore, I fell in with Pinkney, who told me he was engaged in the cause by the present University, and that he is desirous to argue it, if the court will let him. I suppose he expects to do something very extraordinary in it, as he says Mr. Wirt "was not strong enough for it, has not back enough." There is a wonderful degree of harmony and mutual respect among our opponents in this case. You may remember how Wirt and Holmes thought and spoke of each other. On receiving this information from Mr. Pinkney, I seriously reflected upon the course it would be proper for us to take; and I assure you most truly, I decided precisely in favor of that suggested by you. It cannot be expected we shall repeat our argument merely to enable Mr. Pinkney to make a speech, or that a cause shall be re-argued, because, after the argument has been concluded, and the court has the case under advisement, either party may choose to employ new counsel. I think if the court consents to hear Mr. Pinkney, it will be a great stretch of complaisance, and that we should not give our consent to any such proceeding; but if Mr. Pinkney, on his own application, is permitted to speak, we should claim our right of reply. The court cannot want to have our argument repeated; and they will hardly require us to do it for the accommodation of Mr. Pinkney. However, we shall have an opportunity to consult more fully on these matters.

We shall have the message, I presume, to-day, and I shall send you one. Interesting matter is looked for; but this is usual. As to the bankrupt law, I shall feel about, and if I discover any chance of success, I shall make another effort for it. Perhaps it will be advisable to get another vote upon it, without again discussing the whole subject at large, as it is the same congress.

God bless you, yours truly,

J. Hopkinson.

MR. WEBSTER TO MR. BROWN.

Boston, December 6, 1818.

Dear Sir,—I was very glad to receive yours, as I wished to know something of your health, having heard of your indisposition. I trust you will by no means expose yourself until your recovery is complete. As to money concerns, I am of opinion, which I speak freely, that little is to be accomplished here without you. If the professors, &c. can employ the vacation in recruiting for the immediate wants of the college government, each in that region of the country where he may have most friends, it may be very well. This quarter, I think, had better be left till you shall be able to visit it. As far as relates to any provision for the expenses at Washington, &c., I would have every thing remain as it is, unless you should be able to come down, and would by no means have you come unless your health should be altogether restored. I must try to get along with things as well as I can. However, if you should think fit to try what can be done here without yourself, I think it would be useful, if practicable, to join such a man as Mr. Payson or Mr. Olcott with such a man as Dr. Payson.

I am as yet not well informed on the topics connected with the will, and with the school. I hope your health will enable you to give me some view of this subject. It will save me both labor and time; the latter of which I shall have little to spare between this and the 15th January. I have read the will. The general impression I took from it was not at all unfavorable to our general doctrine. Perhaps a second reading might enable me to see something else. As to the school, if you wish the act of 1807, in the verdict, which is perhaps admissible, I think you had better write to Judge Smith on the subject soon. I think I heard that all papers were to be furnished, so as to make up the case by January 1. I do not think it will be easy, perhaps not possible, to get the court to say any thing about the school. They will think that "sufficient," &c. At the same time I should not expect much difficulty about the school, if the question should be decided right with the college.

Let me hear from you every week, respecting your health. If any thing further occurs to me I shall write again. Writing lately to Dr. P. to acknowledge a copy of his "Eulogy," I took occasion to ask whether Mrs. W. intended to enter her appearance voluntarily in the suit now at Washington. If not, I am inclined to give her notice so to do.

Yours truly,

D. WEBSTER.

MEMORANDA

OF MR. WEBSTER'S PROFESSIONAL FEES FOR TWO YEARS, 1818 AND 1833.

[Mr. Webster, until the latter years of his life, kept a regular account of his professional receipts in small memorandum-books, finishing one with each year. Some members of the Suffolk bar, who had seen these memoranda, have suggested that their publication would prove interesting, especially to gentlemen of the profession.

Accordingly, the contents of two of these books are given, being neither the first nor the last, nor showing the largest or the smallest amount of such receipts.]

Receipts 1818 to 1819.—August 14.

1818.		
Aug. 15.	Of Mr. Odiorne, in his patent cause	$80 00
" 20.	Of Salem Bank, in cause *v.* Gloucester Bank	30 00
	Of Messrs. Torrey, Warner, and Co., for advice respecting guarantee	15 00
" 24.	Of Messrs. Munson and Barnard, for opening in case of Acct.	25 00
" 28.	Of Arthur Gilman	20 00
" 29.	Of Mr. Dearborn in lottery case	150 00
Sept. 3.	Of Mr. R. Crowninshield, in case Sturgis *v.* Crowninshield	150 00
" 4.	Of Mr. B. Smith, for advice, on will of Abiel Smith	20 00
	Of Mr. Noyes, in Robinson's business	25 00
" 6.	Of S. T. T., fee in case T. *v.* Skinner	30 00
" 9.	Of Samuel Wait in dispute with Mill corporation, retainer	50 00
	Of Wm. Tucker, retainer in action *v.* Weld	40 00
		$635 00

1818.	Brought over	$635 00
Sept. 11.	Of Cline and others, indicted for riot .	20 00
	Of Mr. Barnard, fee in Penniman *v.* Barnard	25 00
	Of B. Eaton, Jr., in Simpson *v.* Eaton	20 00
Oct. 15.	Of United States in action *v.* Lyman .	250 00
	Of S. Hubbard, retained in Richardson causes	50 00
" 25.	Of Jas. Otis	50 00
" 28.	Of H. G. Otis, Jr., in case respecting bridge	30 00
	Of Capt. Tracy, in case respecting Galen	20 00
Nov. 2.	Of Mr. Gray, advice about Bond *v.* Essex Bank	25 00
	Of Mr. Marsh, fee in Harmon *v.* March, C. P.	40 00
	Of Silas Bullard	100 00
" 3.	Of Mr. Foster's Ex'rs at Salem . .	70 00
	Of John Paine, in Page *v.* Paine, in Essex	50 00
	Of Caleb Smith, in tobacco cause, Cir. Court . -	25 00
" 9.	Of Bryant and Sturgis, in Paul Jones	100 00
	For opinions about Spanish dollars .	20 00
" 10.	Of Exr's of George Crowninshield, for case on will, and retainer in "Bonds"	150 00
" 13.	Of defendant, in case Stanwood *v.* Stanwood Essex	50 00
	Of Salem Bank *v.* Gloucester Bank .	70 00
	Of Col. Little, in Little *v.* Bradstreet .	20 00
	Of Dr. Thomas Sewall	100 00
	Of Mr. McIntyre, in Poole *v.* McIntyre	30 00
	Of J. J. Jackson, retainer in N. Hamp. case	40 00
" 14.	Of Mr. Barker, in Calis *v.* Barker .	30 00
		$2,020 00

1818.	Brought over	$2,020 00
Nov. 17.	Of Mr. McIntyre, for the fees, in Poole against him	20 00
" 19.	Of Mr. Webb, retainer in causes *v.* Capen	20 00
" 24.	Of Dr. J. S. Stoughton, retainer in The Industrier	100 00
" 24.	Of James Rundlet, in factory cause *v.* Winkley	180 00
" 26.	Of Mr. Dillaway, in Boardman *v.* him	40 00
	Of Isaac Danforth, in Lovejoy *v.* Lyman	30 00
" 27.	Of W. Taggart, in Taggart *v.* Lewis .	20 00
Dec. 2.	Of Mr. Tucker, retainer Armstrong *v.* Gray	50 00
	In case of Neal and Walton . .	100 00
	Of Mr. Baxter, retainer in E. V. Baxter's case	20 00
" 11.	Of Mr. Henry, in Jenkins *v.* Henry .	45 00
	Of Mr. Malagamba, in the case from R. J.	200 00
	Of Mr. Touro, sometime since, in Goddard's case	20 00
	Of Mr. Barker, in Curtiss *v.* Barker . .	100 00
	Of Mr. Chesley, in Mill Corporation *v.* Chesley	20 00
	Of Mr. Bryant, in the causes *v.* him .	50 00
	Of Mr. Brackett, in Niles *v.* Brackett .	20 00
" 15.	Of Natha'l Russell and Company, in the Herring causes	30 00
		$3,085 00
1819.		
Jan. 2.	Of Mr. Pearson, in case *v.* Goodrich .	110 00
	Of Mr. Otis, Jr., retainer in Pet. abt. Bridge	100 00
	Of Mr. Laurence, fees in Searle *v.* Williams	70 00
	Of *Casus extraordinarius* . . .	400 00
" 14.	Of Mr. Blake, for fees in Hughes case .	500 00
	Of William Sullivan, for Dr. Stoughton	250 00
		$4,515 00

1819.		Brought over	$4,515 00
Jan.	14.	Of Mr. Hamilton, retainer in Amory *v.* him	20 00
		Of Coolidge and Deblois, retainer .	40 00
		Of Mr. Prince, in The London Packet cause, at Washington . . .	200 00
		Of Mr. Crowninshield, in Sturgis *v.* Crowninshield	100 00
		Of S. Brown, in Yazoo case . .	150 00
		Of R. D. Lawler, in Harvey *v.* Richards	550 00
		Of Mr. Bulfinch, in case about Whitcomb's will	20 00
		Of Mr. Peabody, in Osgood *v.* Breed .	50 00
		Of Mr. Hubbard, in the Richardson causes	100 00
		Of Mr. Warner	50 00
		Of Mr. Tucker, balance fees in Armstrong *v.* Gray	30 00
"	25.	At New York, of Mr. Prince . .	50 00
"	28.	At Baltimore, of Mr. McCullough, in the Bank cause	500 00
Feb.	12.	Of Mr. Bell's son, at Washington .	200 00
Mar.	13.	Of Dr. Haywood's son, for his father .	30 00
"	21.	Of Mr. Munson, for proprietors of Rowe's wharf	20 00
"	25.	Of Mr. Whitney	166 00
		Of Mr. Holker	100 00
		Of Mr. Waddington, N. Y. retainer .	100 00
		Of John S. Sullivan, retainer in Patent causes	150 00
		Of Mr. Mitchell of Bridgewater, retainer	50 00
		Of Mr. S. Dilloway, paid Mr. Bliss .	35 00
April	7.	Of Bank of United States, Balance of fees	1,500 00
		Of Mr. L. Tappan, in Barrell *v.* Gilman	50 00
		Of George Sullivan, Esq. in James *v.* Rogers	160 00
			$8,936 00

1819.		Brought over	$8,936 00
April	8.	Of Nathan Hale, Esq. in Guild *v.* Hale Executors	70 00
"	9.	Of R. Crowninshield, Esq. retainer	100 00
"	10.	Of Messrs. A. and A. by Mr. Peters, acceptance	2,000 00
		Of Mr. Farley	20 00
		Of Mr. Potter, in N. E. Bank *v.* him	50 00
"	13.	Of Mr. Parkman, by Mr. Gallison	50 00
"	14.	Of Dedham Bank, balance of account	100 00
		Of Theodore Ely, retainer by R. D. Tucker	50 00
		Of Mr. Hooper	250 00
"	19.	Of Mr. Gardiner, advice about marriage articles	20 00
		Of Mr. T. L. Winthrop and Mr. R. Sullivan, Trustees under Mr. Bowdoin's will	100 00
		Of W. Mitchell, Jr., in Allen and Mitchell's causes	50 00
		Of Mr. Lovering, Jr., retainer in Herrick *v.* Gilman, &c.	50 00
"	26.	Of Benjamin Eaton, Jr., in settlement of Halliburton cause	40 00
"	29.	Of Mr. Tucker, through Mr. Hubbard, balance in Weed suits	100 00
May	1.	Of Jas. Holmes, retainer in New Orleans cause, C. C. New Hampshire	50 00
"	6.	Of State bank, by J. T. A., in case *v.* Baxter and Boardman	50 00
"	7.	Of F. & M. Insurance office, account	150 00
		Of John Jacob Astor, retainer	50 00
"	17.	Of Mr. Balch, retainer for owners of The Prometheus	50 00
"	18.	Of Mr. Welch, in Dr. Shattuck's action	25 00
"	22.	Of Mr. Hooper	1,000 00
		John Richards, in Maury's case	540 00
June	1.	Of Mr. Vaughan, in Hallowell Bank case	30 00
			$13,931 00

1819.		Brought over	$13,931 00
June	1.	Of Messrs. R. and S., advice in slander case	20 00
"	3.	Of Mr. Gilchrist, retainer . . .	20 00
"	4.	Of Mr. Eaton, in the Bradley cause .	50 00
"	5.	Of the Charlestown committee . .	200 00
		Of R. D. Tucker and Company, retainer, in United States Bank *v.* Brown .	50 00
		Of Benjamin Hale, for writ against Manning	20 00
		Of Munson and Barnard, in M. and B. *v.* Amory	20 00
July	2.	Of C. J. Catlett, retainer . . .	100 00
"	3.	Mr. Wait	40 00
"	5.	In Holker's cause with Mackay . .	100 00
		Of Mr. Maury, deducting error in first credit	210 00
		Of Mr. Russell, in New York, say in his account in Ledger	50 00
June	11.	Of Mr. Bradbury, on settlement of Mr. Astor's case	90 00
"	22.	Of Executors of John Brooks . .	40 00
		Of Messrs. Gurney and Putnam, retainer paid Mr. Bliss.	50 00
		Of R. D. T., as fee, for advice in their business and concerns one year from this time	50 00
		Of Mr. Brigham, retainer for Samuel Williams	50 00
		Of R. Freeman, in behalf of Sandwich	20 00
Aug.	11.	Of Mr. Clarke, balance of fees in Capen causes	50 00
"	12.	Of Mr. Briggs, Esq., by H. Hace, Esq. .	20 00
			$15,181 00

I have omitted several small affairs and sums under ten dollars. D. W.

1832.		
Oct. 8.	Of Merchant Ins. Co., for retainer for two years to come	$200 00
	Of Suffolk office, retainer up to Dec. 1, 1833	100 00
	Of Mr. Dewolfe, in Dodge *et als. v.* Dewolfe	200 00
	Retainer for Dr. Nott, patent causes, through Mr. Codman	100 00
" 23.	In case of Bradbury Cilley's will . .	100 00
Nov. 12.	Of P. P. and Co., retainer . . .	100 00
	Of D. Sears, Esq., for Jackson Co. .	100 00
	Of N. E. Ins. Co. and Boston Ins. Co., fee in The Dover	400 00
	Of Washington Ins. Co., annual retainer	100 00
	Of N. E. Ins. Co., annual retainer .	100 00
	Of Boston Ins. Co., annual retainer .	100 00
" 20.	Of Messrs. Baring, Brothers and Co., annual retainer through Mr. Ward .	100 00
Dec. 4.	Of Wm. Savage, Esq., balance fee due	100 00
	Of Rob. Fuller, Esq., retainer . .	50 00
" 7.	Received of John A. Lowell, $100, as an additional retainer for Locks and Canals, which is to serve as a retainer in all cases	100 00
" 12.	Of W. Phillips $30, retainer in Revere *v.* Copper Co.	30 00
" 18.	Of Messrs. Black and Co., Smyrna, retainer against suit of Mr. McTier .	50 00
	Of S. A. Welles, retainer	100 00
" 21.	Of John R. Willis, in behalf of Orthodox Quakers	250 00
1833.		
Jan'y 1.	Of Thos. P. E. of Arkansas, for opinion	100 00
	Of Mr. Avery of North Carolina, through Mr. Badger	200 00
Feb'y	Of Col. White	250 00
	Of Mr. Tomlinson, for Mr. Davenport .	100 00
		$3,030 00

1833.	Brought over	$3,030 00
Mar. 3.	Congress pay	992 00
" 25.	Of Mr. Johnson, balance fee	50 00
	Of Mr. Blount, fee in Danish claim	190 00
	Of Mr. Payne and Mr. Donelson, fee for Mr. Wheaton, in his cause *v.* Mr. Peters	500 00
" 27.	Of Mr. Griswold, retainer	100 00
	Of same, on account French claims	500 00
" 29.	Of J. H. Clarke, in controversy with Field	50 00
April 5.	Of Dr. Van Rensselaer, retainer	500 00
	Of T. W. Ward, for divers professional services	500 00
	Of Mr. Gifford	100 00
	Of Mr. Lawrence, at Worcester	200 00
	Of Mr. Sergeant, through Mr. Snelling	100 00
May 9.	Of Isaac D., retainer, in behalf of his patent baker	100 00
	Of Mr. Loring, for Mill Corporation *v.* Railroad	100 00
Aug. 3.	Of Mr. Curtis, in Daggett *v.* Barney, *finale*	150 00
	Of Mr. Jones, on Corporation *v.* him	50 00
" 7.	Of Edward Curtis, *de bene esse*	250 00
	Of Stephen White, general retainer for three years	300 00
	Of Newark people, in May	200 00
Sept. 5.	Of Mr. Chever, through Mr. Choate, in Stone *v.* Chever	50 00
	Of B. and L., retainer	100 00
" 9.	Of Mr. G. and Mrs. T.	100 00
		$8,212 00

Sept. 9, 1833.—Thus done and concluded, Sept. 9.—A very poor year's work. Nullification kept me out of the supreme court all last winter.

D. WEBSTER.

MR. WEBSTER TO MR. BROWN.

Boston, January 10, 1819.

DEAR SIR,—A letter came to me to-day, addressed to you, bearing the Hanover postmark. As it was not superscribed in a lady's hand, I presumed it might relate to the common cause, and might be intended to communicate information important for me to have. I therefore opened it. It was from Mr. Shurtleff, containing some little account of movements on the other side. I do not think it necessary to send it back to you.

I have nothing new to say. No public or general opinion seems to be formed of the opinion of any particular judge. I hope no judge, if he has formed an opinion, will communicate it, or hint what it is; inasmuch as it would commit him, which would be likely to make him more tenacious, and so be worse for us, if his opinion should be against us, or it might diminish the weight of his opinion upon others, if it should be in our favor. I hope the judges will come together without its being known at all what opinions any particular judge may have formed.

I have received the records from Mr. Farrar, and I believe am prepared with all necessary papers. The book of memoirs I shall not carry. Dr. Perkins can lend me one, if I should want it.

If any thing new occurs before I leave home, I shall write you. You may expect early and frequent intelligence from Washington.

Very truly, yours,

D. WEBSTER.

MR. WEBSTER TO CHIEF JUSTICE SMITH.

Washington, February 2, 1819.

MY DEAR SIR,—I have the pleasure to tell you that the college cause has been decided in our favor. The Chief Justice, Washington, Livingston, Johnson, and Story, Justices, *concurrentibus;* Duval, Justice, *dissentiente; absente*, Todd. The opinion was delivered by the chief. I believe other judges also drew up opinions, which I hope to see published.

With all reasonable congratulation and rejoicing, I am, dear Sir, Yours,

D. Webster.

DANIEL WEBSTER TO EZEKIEL WEBSTER.

Washington, February 2, 1819.

My dear Ezekiel,—All is safe. Judgment was rendered this morning, reversing the judgment in New Hampshire. Present: Marshall, Washington, Livingston, Johnson, Duval, and Story. All concurring but Duval; and he giving no reason to the contrary. The opinion was delivered by the Chief Justice. It was very able and very elaborate; it goes the whole length, and leaves not an inch of ground for the University to stand on.

Yours affectionately,

D. Webster, in court.

MR. WEBSTER TO MR. BROWN.

Washington, February 2, 1819.

My dear Sir.—All is safe and certain. The Chief Justice delivered an opinion this morning, in our favor, on all the points. In this opinion, Washington, Livingston, Johnson, and Story, Justices, are understood to have concurred. Duval, Justice, it is said, dissents. Mr. Justice Todd is not present. The opinion goes the whole length, and leaves nothing further to be decided. I give you my congratulations on this occasion; and assure you that I feel a load removed from my shoulders much heavier than they have been accustomed to bear.

Very truly, yours,

D. Webster.

MR. HOPKINSON TO MR. BROWN.

Washington, February 2, 1819.

DEAR SIR,—I have the pleasure of enclosing you a letter informing you of great matters. Our triumph in the college cause has been complete. Five judges, only six attending, concur not only in a decision in our favor, but in placing it upon principles broad and deep, and which secure corporations of this description from legislative despotism and party violence for the future. The Court goes all lengths with us, and whatever trouble these gentlemen may give us in future, in their great and pious zeal for the interests of learning, they cannot shake those principles which must and will restore Dartmouth College to its true and original owners. I would have an inscription over the door of your building, "Founded by Eleazar Wheelock, Refounded by Daniel Webster."

I wish you, Sir, much happiness and success in promoting the usefulness of the institution, and proving to the world that it has changed hands. Most respectfully,

Your obedient servant,

JOS. HOPKINSON.

MR. WEBSTER TO MR. BROWN.

Washington, February 23, 1819.

MY DEAR SIR,—In the action The Trustees *v.* Woodward, judgment is entered, *nunc pro tunc*, as of last term. This relieves us from any difficulty that might arise from Mr. Woodward's death. The other causes are not yet reached, but I am inclined to think they will take this course, namely: They must, in any event, go back to the Circuit Court for judgment. Of course, in that event, if other material facts exist, the parties would have an opportunity of establishing those facts. You understand that the cause comes here, not for judgment, but for a direction to the Circuit Court what judgment to give on the verdict in that court. But after having received direction what judgment to give on that verdict, the circuit might, in its discretion, give the party an opportunity of altering the state of facts, if he could. This is but the common case of granting a new trial, which is frequent. I do not see that it would do us any good to get a direction from the court here to the Circuit Court what judgment to render on this verdict, because, the parties say, they have new facts, and they may, for aught I know, be permitted to prove these new facts in this very cause. As to arguing the case here, upon admissions of new facts, it is out of all question. They will state one fact, we shall state an inconsistent or repugnant fact, what judgment can be formed on such materials? The impossibility of this will be seen just as soon as we approach the question. If, therefore, the other side have an argument here, it must be on precisely the old facts. Now I think Mr. P. and Mr. W. having seen the opinions of the court, will hardly attempt that. It will therefore come to this. The cause will be sent back without further discussion here. These verdicts will be set aside, so far as to admit proof of other pertinent facts. They will then, if they please, offer proof of a particular fact. We shall object on the ground that that fact is not material, or pertinent. The judge will decide this, and if they do not like the decision, they will tender a bill of exceptions. Of all the courses which offer themselves, this seems to be the most safe and easy for us. All this goes on the ground that there should remain a serious intention of further litigation. But I am of opinion, *inter nos*, that any such intention will be abandoned, that counsel here will be willing to be rid of it, and do not wish to argue it again. For the moment there is fermentation in New Hampshire; I suspect it will go off with the election; and when the case is printed, I do not think any counsel will advise to any further contest. At any rate, the course above indicated seems to me the natural one for the business to take. I am persuaded it will take it. You will not, therefore, probably hear of any new arguments at this term. I hope to get away from this place in season to get home by March 10 or 15.

I am, dear Sir, yours,

D. WEBSTER.

MR. WEBSTER TO MR. BROWN.

Washington, February 25, 1819.

DEAR SIR,—Yours I received last evening. The new causes will be disposed of as I mentioned to you in my last. I am quite satisfied with this arrangement, and do not expect much further trouble in the case. We shall get a judgment, I trust, at May term, even if the friends of the University should be advised that it is worth their while to attempt to renew the contest. I hope they will be better advised, both for their own sake and yours. You need the use of the buildings, and I hope they will admit you to possession without further inconvenience or delay. I am quite confident that there can be no reasonable expectation of changing the decision; and though it may be inconvenient to you, it can do no good to the other side to continue the contest.

I hope to be at home by the 15th March. I should be glad to see you at that time; some things which must be done, may better be done then than afterwards. I shall carry with me the materials for the book, and if it is made, it ought to be put to press without a day's delay. Let me at least find a letter from you at Boston on my arrival, say the 13th. The sooner after that that you are there, the better.

Very truly yours,
D. WEBSTER.

MR. WEBSTER TO MR. BROWN.

Boston, April 14, 1819.

MY DEAR SIR,—I am happy to hear that Mrs. Woodward is so well advised as to be disposed to surrender the property according to agreement. I should be equally happy to see the President of the University wise enough to deliver the books and apparatus, and retire from the contest without giving anybody further trouble. His own reputation and character, I should think, would be as much benefited by that course as your convenience. If he thinks otherwise, however, he has a right to judge for himself. I do not know any thing which is necessary to be done by way of preparation. I have written to Mr. Mason repeatedly. Mr. Olcott must be there; his presence will be essentially necessary on many accounts. I wish him to bring with him your affidavit of the notice given by you to Mr. Allen and Dr. Perkins, of our intention to proceed to final judgment in these causes this term, and the time of giving such notice. Mr. Mason has given notice to the counsel. I flatter myself the cause will not be put off to October term without reason.

The University folks should understand, very distinctly, that we are resolved to bring this controversy to an immediate end, and that they are to have no delay, except such as they can obtain by law. There is a fable of the old man and the boy who stole his apples, which it would be edifying for the gentlemen connected with the University to read.

I think of nothing necessary to be done by the trustees particularly.

As to the proposals, I hear little of them. Mr. Lamson of Exeter was here, and finding nothing done, attempted gratuitously to do something; and I helped him as I could. Nothing effectual will be done from Portsmouth on that subject.

MR. WEBSTER TO MR. BROWN.

Boston, April 14, 1819.

Dear Sir,—I write this to add that I think it would be very fortunate if President Allen, Dr. Perkins, and their friends, should be at Portsmouth.

I have reason to think they would learn that the new grounds upon which they wish to put their case, would not change the opinion of the judges, or any of them, in any respect. Perhaps, however, you could not suggest this to them; I think you cannot. But if they should attend of their own heads, it would be well.

Yours, D. Webster.

MR. HOPKINSON TO MR. WEBSTER.

Bordentown, April 19, 1819.

My dear Friend,—It is but time and labor thrown away to attempt to do that which we know to be impossible. This proposition seems to me to be so clear that nobody but Luther Martin, who delights in amplitude, or P. Barbour, whose logical head disdains to take any thing for granted, would give a moment to prove it. I shall presume that you admit it, and proceed to say that this is precisely the case, in relation to making up either the speech I did make or one I did not make, in our college cause, from the notes which served well enough to guide me through the argument at the time of the trial. The chain of connection, the whole course of thought, are now so entirely lost and gone with the things "beyond the flood," that they are as much out of my power as Noah's ark, or Jacob's ladder. All I can do is to give good counsel instead of a bad speech, to wit, that it be stated in its proper place in the big book, that the argument of Mr. Hopkinson at large could not be obtained, but that it consisted of a repetition of the principles opened by Mr. Webster, enforcing and illustrating them by various cases and arguments; and giving full and satisfactory answers to the arguments urged by the counsel on the other side. Something of this will answer all the purpose.

I will write to you shortly on our matter of business.

God bless you,—yours,

J. Hopkinson.

P. S. I have heard you Boston folks brag that the codfish we get are not the thing; but you have a certain animal called a "Dun fish," much superior. Can you procure me a box, and send it to Philadelphia? Cost and charges will be cheerfully paid by J. H.

MR. WEBSTER TO CHIEF JUSTICE SMITH.

Boston, May 12, 1819.

Dear Sir,—I send you by Judge Peabody your argument and Mason's, bungingly put together by me. Right or wrong, I have done the deed. So great, and how great you know, was the want of information on this subject by our best men, that I could endure it no longer. Some few copies are printed, not to be published, but to be read by those who ought to understand the subject a little. I shall take all care I can not to let the things get much abroad. It is, as you see, nameless; and it may go "unclaimed of any man." I have been more than usually silly on this occasion; ascribe it to having been six weeks at Washington. Mr. Wells has received a few new books; not yet opened. If you wish any particular book which he is likely to have, I will look out for it, if you let me know soon. I believe he has the latest reports.

Always very truly yours,

D. Webster.

MR. WEBSTER TO MR. BROWN.

Boston, May 30, 1819.

Dear Sir,—James T. Austin, Esq., in behalf of the University, presented the new facts to Judge Story on Thursday. They were what we expected and no more. The judge said, he saw nothing to vary at all the case, as it had been considered and decided. None of these "facts," if true, changed the ground; nor did he see any the least contradiction between any of these facts and the recitals of the charter. He was willing, however, to take the papers and read them attentively, to the end that he might fully ascertain whether they presented any new point which could be material. He accordingly took home the papers, and to-morrow or the next day, will probably announce his final decision. There is no doubt about it. These new facts, whether true or false, have nothing to do with the question; and you may expect judgment and execution in the causes in the Circuit Court, June 10, as by arrangement made at Portsmouth. I am glad you have made a bargain for the house, provided it is a good bargain. The house, I think, will suit your purpose, and a house you needed. If in order to furnish it, you have occasion to order any articles from here, you will do me a favor by directing the venders to present their bills to me; I will pay them, and be reimbursed at your convenience.

Very truly yours,

D. Webster.

P. S. I trust you will write me before you leave Concord, and let me know what temper you find prevalent there.

MR. WEBSTER TO MR. MASON.

Boston, June 28, 1819.

Dear Sir,—I received yours of the 13th, and have felt in too much spleen to answer it. Whoso meddleth with type-setters gets into trouble. You have narrated the progress, present state, and prospects of our book, in a manner to make one's blood run cold.

It appears to me as desperate as it does to you, and I believe the safest way is to make up our minds that we shall have no book; none at least in this generation. I wrote to Mr. Farrar, have got his answer, and written again. He thinks the book will be out at Commencement. If it should not be well printed, and on our good paper, it will not sell, and a new book will be published. I have so stated to Mr. Farrar, and he may be assured it is true.

I suppose you go to Haverhill about this time. My wife and I have made up our minds to a journey, which will occupy us till toward the end of July. We shall go to the North River, and perhaps to the Springs. We expect to leave here about the 5th July. I am sorry to inform you that Mr. Gore is ill again. His other knee has become affected. It is now some time since this was the case, and I have heard within a day or two of his being a little better, still he is quite unwell. We have no news here, nor is any thing doing.

It is very much my wish that you would not decline the

trusteeship. It will give great satisfaction this way, and by staying a single year, you can do a great deal of good. Judge Story is going to Commencement, with his wife. We will make a party, and go your way, and take you and Mrs. Mason.

Yours,

D. Webster.

MR. WEBSTER TO MR. MASON.

Boston, August 10, [1819.]

My dear Sir,—We have at length returned from an unexpectedly long journey. Our trip extended to Philadelphia, and on our return, we went up the North River as far as Albany, from which place we came home without finding it necessary on account of health to drink the Spring waters. Mrs. Webster is for the present satisfied with riding and will not think of going to Hanover; I believe I shall attempt it. As you have been somewhat stationary through the summer, I hope you will come up. I propose to go from here in such season as to be at Concord or Boscawen on Sunday evening. It is then an easy day's ride to Hanover; I shall go up in my chaise, and should be particularly glad to meet you at Concord. I do not think Judge Story will go up; he has engagements here which he cannot well leave. I shall ask the driver of the stage-coach to deliver you this, and to take an answer, if you have one. It will be very gratifying if I should learn that you contemplate this expedition.

Mrs. Webster and myself desire our best respects to be given to Mrs. Mason.

Yours truly, D. Webster.

P. S. I possibly may go from here on Friday morning, and so shall not get your answer unless you send it to-morrow by the driver.

MR. WEBSTER TO MR. BROWN.

Boston, September 26, [1819.]

My dear Friend,—I have received yours this moment, and shall be most happy to give you and procure for you all letters in my power. Be good enough to let me know when it will be seasonable to write you at Hanover, and when you may probably go. It will give me the most sincere gratification to give you letters to my friends in Philadelphia, Charleston, Washington, and Savannah; but as in some of these places my acquaintance is not great, I shall be happy to find you letters from other gentlemen. Have the goodness to say what places you may be likely to visit, and in the mean time I shall be preparing letters to gentlemen in the places where I have acquaintance. I will obtain letters, as I am sure I can, from Judge Story and Dr. Kirkland.

I rejoice in every amendment of your health, and am most truly,

Your friend,

D. Webster.

P. S. Please let me hear from you by return of mail.

MR. WEBSTER TO MR. BROWN.

Boston, October 5, 1819.

My dear Sir,—I have paid Mr. Lang's draft, eighty dollars, and have also given him one hundred dollars for you. For the balance, three hundred and twenty dollars, you can either draw your bill, or order, in such sums as suit you, and at times convenient, on your journey, as you may direct me to send it to you, at New York or Philadelphia; in either of which cases your commands will be obeyed. If you prefer the money to be sent you, write me to that effect before you leave Hanover. Mr. Professor Haddock, being himself a traveller, can tell you what will be most convenient for you in that respect. Mr. Lang's departure is to be so soon that I shall not be able, with entire convenience, to send up the balance by him. I can easily, however, cause it to meet you, either in Philadelphia or New York.

I send you a few letters, and hope to have some from Dr. Kirkland to meet you in Philadelphia. I shall send them to the care of Charles Chauncey, Esq., counsellor at law, Walnut street, to whom you have a letter. I have asked Mr. Dwight for letters, which he has kindly furnished, and which I enclose. I hope you will see Mr. Wolsey in New York, a brother-in-law of the late President Dwight, and an excellent man.

I have written two letters to Charles March, Esq., New York. He is a merchant, a son of Dr. Clement March, deceased, Greenland, New Hampshire. One is a letter of introduction, the other you will see and use or not use according to your occasion. I will only add that you must omit nothing beneficial to your health on account of expense. If the "ways and means" fall short, write to me from any place, at any time, and some way or another we will see your necessary funds forthcoming.

May God bless and preserve you and yours,

D. Webster.

Mr. C. March is now here, and I told him you would call on him, probably in New York. He will be glad to see you.

☞ Since writing I enclose fifty dollars.

MR. WEBSTER TO MR. MASON.

Boston, Saturday evening, 8 o'clock, October, 1819.

My dear Sir,—Enclosed you have a letter from Mr. Gore. Mrs. Webster and I have been there to-day, where we had the pleasure of meeting Mr. King. Mr. King expressed a great wish to see you; said he had thought of going as far as Portsmouth, but could not well go there, without going further, and it would not be convenient at this time to go to Maine. The object of this is to join Mr. and Mrs. Gore, and Mr. King, in the wish that you and Mrs. Mason would come up next week and make us a visit. Mr. King will probably stay at Mr. Gore's until the latter part of next week. I hope you and Mrs. Mason will find it convenient to come up, as it will give us great pleasure to see you, and it will also gratify Mr. Gore and Mr. King. Our household is now well. We have a chamber, as usual, for you, and shall depend on your coming directly here. The circuit court sits here next week; there is nothing to do in it; it is as lean as your Exeter circuit court, and, as far as I now know, will not engage me a single day. On all accounts it would be pleasant to have a visit from you now. I send this by the driver, in order to anticipate a day, as the mail for to-morrow is closed. Please favor me with a line to-morrow afternoon, in answer to this, and be kind enough to say that you will be here on Tuesday.

Mrs. Webster desires me to say to Mrs. Mason that she must come; and that, you know, is the end of a lady's argument.

In the hope of seeing you,

I am yours,

D. WEBSTER.

N. B. As I always choose to end my own arguments, I take the liberty to fill this little space in my husband's letter, my dear Mrs. Mason, to beg that you and Mr. Mason will gratify us with a visit next week. We are quite alone, and I am ready to attend you any where, being very much at leisure, and shall be very much disappointed if you do not come. With much love,

Truly yours,

G. WEBSTER.

MR. WEBSTER TO MR. MASON.

Boston, Sunday evening, [1819.]

DEAR SIR,—I send the creature, and commend it to your discreet use. I hope you will find that I have not abandoned the old ground, notwithstanding the high authority of a newspaper. I already repent of having this thing printed, but must make the best of it now.

There is one point on which I have suspected that my opinion differs from Judge Smith's; I think that the trustees are most clearly visitors, and that this lies at the bottom of our case, and as visitors, I think they are not answerable in any court, while acting within the scope of their visitatorial power. I should be glad you would think of this a little. If I am in an error, it is a pretty important error.

I think I shall be at Portsmouth, but am not absolutely certain. If I can go without a good deal of sacrifice, I will present myself. I will write you again on this point. Mrs. Webster must put off her journey to another occasion, on account of my expected detention. She acquiesces in this the more cheerfully, as she expects the pleasure of seeing Mrs. Mason this way soon.

Ever yours,

D. Webster.

DANIEL WEBSTER TO EZEKIEL WEBSTER.

(Extract.)

Boston, August 17, 1820.

Dear Ezekiel,—

* * * * * * *

As to a president, I have weighed the subject very much in my own mind, and conversed on it on every occasion with the friends of the college. My mind is not made up in favor of any candidate. The gentleman whom you and I thought most of when I saw you, is not, I fear, in all respects the most eligible. I learn that he has not much energy of character, and as to scholarship, not more than respectable. And if as much fitness for the office could be found in a man ten years younger, it would be much better. The more I think of it, the more I incline to a younger man. At fifty, not enough of life remains to acquire much; whereas at thirty or thirty-five a man is young enough to form himself to be president. I cannot yet fix on any body. Mr. Spring of New York, son of the late Dr. Spring, has been mentioned by some. I think Mr. Lord's fitness should be considered. On the whole, my opinion at present is, that you should fill up the board, and postpone the appointment of president for the present.

I have been industrious to collect the opinion of our best and most intelligent friends in Essex, and it seems to be against the appointment which you contemplated as most probable. I am willing you should show this letter to Mr. Thompson, Mr. March, and Mr. Payson, or other friends. The trustees can inquire and correspond through the autumn, on this important subject, and when they come to a conclusion, a quorum can meet, and make the appointment.

I hope, therefore, you will on all accounts take further time. It is not only an important question, so far as the college itself is concerned, but it is of importance also, generally, to show that a college not under legislative control can flourish. I believe I may say that all our friends this way recommend further consideration.

As to the LL. D., I thought best to speak directly to the gentleman concerned. I saw him day before yesterday, and he thinks so recent are certain things, that a compliment of that sort to him had better be deferred to next year. I told him I would give you this hint. I am, on the whole, of the same opinion.

I hope your board will remember Mr. Wood. He at least deserves well of the college, having sent a hundred of us, such as we are, to be educated in it.

[The remainder of the letter is wanting.]

MR. WEBSTER TO MR. JUSTICE STORY.

Philadelphia, January 3, 1821.

My dear Sir,—I am not content to wait till I get to Washington, without giving you some account of myself and my travels. I left Boston in the mail stage-coach Saturday noon the 29th, with Mr. Perkins, T. Parsons, and William Gardiner. We kept with the mail to New Haven, where we found ourselves Sunday, 3 o'clock. Here we remained through that day, and finding an accommodation stage-coach going the next day to New York, we took it to ourselves, and reached that city early the evening of the same day. From New York we came hither in a new line of stage-coaches, called the Union line, which we are bound to speak well of. It gave us a whole coach for forty dollars, and allowed us to take our own hours.

We left New York at three or four o'clock Tuesday afternoon, lodged at New Brunswick, and arrived here to dine Wednesday, yesterday. Our journey was safe and expeditious. I mention these circumstances for your benefit, knowing that in three weeks you are to be on our track, although I am well aware that Mrs. Story would scold me, if she could scold, for adverting to such a disagreeable topic.

Everybody is in expectation here of receiving your opinion in the case of "The Young Eugenie." It must come out, and that soon. I beg you to tell Mason either to publish it at once in a pamphlet, or to let Hale publish it in the paper. I last evening referred some gentlemen to the case of "The Amedie, which they had overlooked. In relation to this case of The Amedie," I was very negligent, which I confess with shame. I quoted it only from the note in Dodson; whereas the whole case is in Acton, and there is there one pretty strong expression of Sir W. Grant, not found in the note in Dodson. I mention this lest my unpardonable negligence may have misled you; for not hearing your judgment, I do not know whether you cited the case as from Acton. I think Judge Davis's suggestion, of publishing with the opinion a summary of the English cases, a very good one. Here I find Hopkinson up to his neck in business. He seems to have stepped right off into deep water. He has an interesting charter case, in which he says he made some use of a little bit of an opinion about Dartmouth College.

Adieu, my dear Sir; I shall write you again from Washington, where I hope also to hear from you.

I am, both at home and abroad, yours truly,

D. Webster.

DANIEL WEBSTER TO EZEKIEL WEBSTER.

Boston, June 17, 1821.

Dear Ezekiel,—I have received yours of Friday. Mr. Olcott wrote me on this same subject of the overseers. I am very doubtful whether any good would come of the project. Who would the Board be? Every thing depends on that. It would be injurious, I think, to propose to take this important alteration in the charter before the ground was well explored, and some security obtained that the concession should not be abused.

On the whole, it strikes me that the project, so far as it relates to getting money, is impracticable, and the whole of it not without danger.

I hope to be able to leave here about the 25th. It depends on the adjournment of the court, which is still sitting, and I know not exactly when to expect its adjournment.

Your governor seems to have made a pretty good speech; certainly better than the average of such things. He talks against false economy very justly, and as if he had never shared in the benefit derived from the currency of opposite sentiments. I think you will have a pleasant session. Your house has good men enough in it to prevent great mischief, even if you shall not effect much positive good; and it is a great thing, nowadays, to keep things from growing worse.

Yours, D. WEBSTER.

MR. WEBSTER TO MR. EVERETT.

Boston, July 9, 1821.

DEAR SIR,—I think this No.[1] exceedeth all its predecessors in glory. I have read three articles. 1. Yours, in answer to the new magazine, of which I do most honestly admire both the right spirit and the able execution. 2. Florida, by which I am greatly edified and instructed. 3. St. Pierre, which is a very entertaining romance.

I verily think we have had nothing so good as this number. *Sic itur ad astra.*

Thine, D. WEBSTER.

[1] The number of the North American Review for July, 1821.

MR. WEBSTER TO MR. JUSTICE STORY.

Boston, September 24, 1821.

My dear Sir,—I am happy to hear that you are coming up to-morrow, to dine with the commodore. Mr. Baker, the British consul-general, is in town. He called on me to-day, and expressed a wish to see you. I have invited him to pass an hour with me to-morrow evening, and have promised him your company; and he has accepted, on the strength of that promise.

Will you be kind enough to bring up with you the last Dodson. I wish to look at the recent case about the slave-trade. I very much fear my Lord Stowell has missed a figure. However, I suppose, as usual, he has given plausible reasons.

We shall have some interesting questions here on this subject, and that shortly.

Very truly yours,
D. Webster.

P. S. I am greatly delighted at this notion of going to Worcester. I know nothing of that county, where so many venues were laid, and I think we shall meet some good men. Bainbridge means to go with us.

DANIEL WEBSTER TO EZEKIEL WEBSTER.

Boston, October 4, 1821.

Dear Ezekiel,—I like your project of a course of proceeding for the trustees very much. I have no doubt something like that would be very judicious. I think it of great importance that you should come down here before you go to Hanover, if you can possibly. Judge Story and Mr. Mason will probably both be here on the 15th, and they both feel a strong wish that the Board should take a right course. If you can possibly come, I hope you will, in the stage-coach on Saturday, the 13th. I have no doubt, by putting all our heads together, we can do something. I would go up and see you if it were not almost impossible, and if it were not much more advantageous that you should be here, where you can confer with many others. Please let me hear, by the earliest mail, whether you can probably come.

Yours affectionately,
D. WEBSTER.

MR. WEBSTER TO MR. JUSTICE STORY.

Boston, November 7, 1821.

DEAR SIR,—I am puzzled to know how the law stands respecting appeals in equity cases, from circuit court to supreme court by defendants. Must the defendant in all cases give bond to fulfil the final decree? I know not what construction to put, in this respect, on the provisions of the act of March 3, 1803. On looking to the only case of the kind in which I have been concerned, namely, Gilman *v.* Brown, I find no such bond given. When you have read this, will you say in two words, how it is? I suppose it is somewhere settled. A line this afternoon or to-morrow morning will greatly oblige

Your often obliged,
D. W.

DANIEL WEBSTER TO EZEKIEL WEBSTER.

Boston, Sunday evening, [1821.]

DEAR EZEKIEL,—Judge Story has written a letter to Judge Paine. I enclose it by this mail, to the care of Mr. Olcott. Mr. Mason has not been here, but is expected on Tuesday. I had a good deal of conversation with him in the summer, on the subject of the college, and I have no doubt he agrees with the rest of us, who think the safe way is to proceed very slowly, in relation to the next appointment. My own opinion is most decidedly in favor of postponing any choice till next spring. I will thank you to mention that such is my opinion to Mr. March and Mr. Payson. We can lose no great advantage by delay, and a better choice can in all probability be made. I assure you it is the universal sense of all the friends of the college here whom I have spoken with, and I have spoken with many, that the prudent course is to put off the appointment.

I shall be particularly anxious to know the result of your meeting.

Affectionately yours,
DANIEL WEBSTER.

PRESIDENT JOHN ADAMS TO MR. WEBSTER.

Montezillo, December 23, 1821.

DEAR SIR,—I thank you for your discourse, delivered at Plymouth on the termination of the second century of the landing of our forefathers. Unable to read it, from defect of sight, it was last night read to me, by our friend Shaw. The fullest justice that I could do it, would be to transcribe it at full length. It is the effort of a great mind, richly stored with every species of information. If there be an American who can read it without tears, I am not that American. It enters more perfectly into the genuine spirit of New England, than any production I ever read. The observations on the Greeks and Romans; on colonization in general; on the West India Islands; on the past, present, and future in America, and on the slave-trade, are sagacious, profound, and affecting in a high degree.

Mr. Burke is no longer entitled to the praise—the most consummate orator of modern times.

What can I say of what regards myself? To my humble name, "*Exegisti monumentum ære perennius.*"

This oration will be read five hundred years hence, with as much rapture as it was heard. It ought to be read at the end of every century, and indeed at the end of every year, for ever and ever.

I am, Sir, with the profoundest esteem, your obliged friend, and very humble servant,

JOHN ADAMS.

The Honorable Daniel Webster.

CHANCELLOR KENT TO MR. WEBSTER.

Albany, December 29, 1821.

My dear Sir,—Be pleased to accept my thanks for the receipt and perusal of your Plymouth discourse, which came by yesterday's mail. The reflections, the sentiments, the morals, the patriotism, the eloquence, the imagination of this admirable production are exactly what I anticipated; elevated, just, and true. I think it is also embellished by a style distinguished for purity, taste, and simplicity.) Excuse me for this once, and I will not trespass in this manner again. I am proud to be able to trace my own lineage back to the Pilgrims of New England, and prouder still that I have been thought deserving of the esteem and friendship of some of the brightest of their descendants.

Permit Mrs. Kent and me to unite in presenting our best respects, and the compliments of the season, to Mrs. Webster, and be assured of the constant esteem and regard of your friend and most obedient servant,

James Kent.

Honorable D. Webster.

MR. WEBSTER TO MR. JUSTICE STORY.

Washington, January 14, 1822.

My dear Sir,—I am much obliged to you for yours of the 8th, which I have just received. I came on very safe and sound, and am lodged comfortably, but not on the Capitol Hill; which, for some reasons, I regret. I learn that somebody has made provision for the court at, or near, the old spot. I will, however, speak to Mr. Caldwell.

There is much stir and buzz about Presidential candidates here. Mr. Clay's friends are certainly numerous; whether it be because his is the most recent nomination, or for what other reason, the fact is he is just now much talked about. I think it will be a busy winter, in talking and electioneering. My own opinion is, but I would not intimate it to others, that

Mr. Clay considers himself a candidate, and means to run the race. More hereafter on these subjects.

Mr. Hopkinson desired me to beseech you to give him a day, as you come on. I promised him to write you, and mention his request. He wishes much to see you, and to give some of his friends that pleasure. If, on your arrival, you contrive to send him notice, to No. 196, Chestnut street, he will esteem it a great favor.

I am glad your opinion is coming out. It is much asked for.

Mr. Johnson of Kentucky, has to-day, I learn, made a long speech in favor of his proposed amendment. He has dealt, they say, pretty freely with the supreme court. Dartmouth College, Sturgis and Crowninshield, *et cetera*, have all been demolished. To-morrow he is to pull to pieces the case of the Kentucky betterment law. Then Governor Barber is to annihilate Cohens *v.* Virginia. So things go; but I see less reality in all this smoke than I thought I should, before I came here.

I hope you will call and see my wife, and my boys, what few there are of them; not forgetting Miss Julia.

Give my love to Mrs. Story, and believe me, most truly

Yours,

D. Webster.

MR. WEBSTER TO MR. JUSTICE STORY.

Washington, August 6, 1822.

My dear Sir,—This gentleman, the Rev. Mr. Gurley, comes recommended by our friends at the South, on the subject of the Colonization Society. He has with him some very interesting publications of the African Institution in London, as well as the reports of the society here, and appears to be a very agreeable and intelligent man.

I feel inclined to do whatever duty requires on this subject. You know that my opinion has not been the most favorable, and yet I would wish to pay proper deference to such excellent men as Judge Washington and Mr. Kay.

Mr. Gurley will probably be in this neighborhood till Commencement, and if you think it proper that some bread should be cast on the waters in this case, I am willing to follow the example.

While I cannot, conscientiously, very confidently recommend the cause of this society as being a great attainable good, I am still willing to confide in those good men, who have more confidence, so far as to contribute my own little mite to the object in view.

At any rate, my dear Sir, you have discharged your duty before God and man, on the subject of African slavery; and you must not be surprised if more should be expected from him who has done so much and so admirably.

With perpetual regard, dear Sir,

Yours, DANIEL WEBSTER.

COLONEL PERKINS AND OTHERS TO MR. WEBSTER.

[Mr. Webster's first nomination to Congress from Massachusetts.]

Boston, October 18, 1822.

DEAR SIR,—We, the undersigned, having been chosen at a meeting of delegates from all the wards, held at Concert Hall on Thursday evening last, a committee to acquaint you, that at that meeting you were unanimously selected to be recommended to the support of their fellow-citizens, to represent the District of Suffolk, in the next Congress of the United States; and having been, by your absence from town, unable to wait upon you personally, have the pleasure to address you, to communicate the above fact; and we beg you to be assured, that in the performance of this duty we experience a peculiar satisfaction, which will be greatly enhanced by the knowledge of your consent to conform, upon this occasion, to the wishes of your friends, in the number of which we hope to be considered, and with the highest respect and esteem remain,

Your obedient servants,

T. H. PERKINS,
WM. SULLIVAN,
BENJ. RUSSELL, } Committee.
WM. STURGIS,
J. W. T. APTHORP,

MR. WEBSTER TO MR. JUSTICE STORY.

Boston, November 13, 1822.

Dear Sir,—I went to Salem yesterday rather unexpectedly; a cause in which I was concerned having been called on. I found myself too unwell to try it, and so got delay, and returned last night. I feel pretty well while I am quiet and keep house, but I am not able to make any effort without pain, and renewing a half feverish feeling. My wish now is to remain at home till Saturday, go on that day to Providence, and I believe I shall take my wife with me, and get well enough, if I can, to try the Gold cause on Monday. I am afraid, however, that parties will be prepared on Friday, and that, on account of the number of witnesses, any delay will be inconvenient. In this case the cause must go on without me.

I am desirous to see you as you pass along to-morrow, and the particular object of this is to inquire, at what time and what place I may hope to find you in this town to-morrow. The bearer will take your answer, and bring it to me.

I saw Dr. Warren on my return last evening, and he has put me on a regimen for three days with medicine, &c. I hate all physic.

Yours, D. Webster.

DANIEL WEBSTER TO EZEKIEL WEBSTER.

Washington, March 25, 1823.

Dear Ezekiel,—I am detained here still by the affairs of the Commission, and do not expect to leave before ten or fifteen days. It is our expectation to go to Dorchester for the summer, and I intend to move the second day of May. Soon after that I hope you will come down, as I shall want to see you very much on more accounts than one.

You have accomplished a great affair in New Hampshire. I know not whether it is a triumph, but it is at least a change, and for the present it seems for the better. I have seen the returns, and it is clear enough which way the Federal votes went.

As to the great Presidential question, my opinion is, that it was never more uncertain than now who will succeed. It is time to prepare public opinion in our quarter, for certain contingencies which may arise.

Who would New Hampshire be for, in your opinion, if it were certain that Mr. Adams would not succeed, or who would she prefer next to him? I wish you would write me an answer to this question, with or without the reasons on which your opinion rests, so as to reach me here by the tenth or twelfth of April. This can be done, if you will sit right down to it, on receipt of this. I would thank you also to express your own preference.

Yours always,
D. WEBSTER.

P. S. You will probably hear from Portsmouth soon, on another subject.

EZEKIEL WEBSTER TO DANIEL WEBSTER.

April 3, 1823.

DEAR DANIEL,—I received yours this morning. Of all the candidates named for the Presidency, the people of New Hampshire would undoubtedly prefer Mr. Adams. Mr. Adams being out of the question, I think Mr. Calhoun would be their choice. I think neither Jackson, Crawford, nor Clay could ever obtain the votes of this State. They would prefer to have a Northern man for the President, and I think would vote for Mr. Clinton, if there should be any prospect of his being chosen. It seems to me there is among us a pretty strong local feeling, something like a very general wish that the next President should be from the North. There is a kind of presentiment that, after this election, we may give up all further expectation.

Of all the persons named I reply Calhoun. Yet, if a prominent man from New England, New York, or Pennsylvania should be put in nomination against him, I think he would obtain the electoral vote.

Consulting my own feelings and wishes at this time, I should put the candidates in this order, Adams, Calhoun, Clinton. I am, however, very incompetent to judge correctly of their qualifications.

For the time we had to labor we did something. Every department of the government will be what is called here anti-Hill. Some good will result from the change, not immediately perhaps, but in time.

The result of the election was one of the most unexpected, and yet one of the most natural events that could be imagined. Here is a paradox, I give no more.

I intend to be in Boston the 3d day of May, as I have some engagements after the 10th that will require me to be at home.

Yours affectionately,
EZEKIEL WEBSTER.

MR. WEBSTER TO MR. MASON.

Washington, April 10, 1823.

DEAR SIR,—Mr. John D. Williams of Boston informs me that he has written requesting you to go to Portland, at the Circuit Court, and argue his cause against Mr. Reed. I hope you will be able to go. He is a very worthy man, and an exceeding good client. He will satisfy you well; and his case you will easily understand. Mr. Greenleaf, who is in the cause for the plaintiff, Williams, is a very correct and able lawyer of his age, and will have the case duly prepared. It is a case of some importance and some expectation; and I would not for a good deal, as we say, that any thing should prevent your attention to it. I cannot be home in season to rest and then go to Portland. I have no other engagements there, and do not intend practising in that court. You are sixty miles nearer the court than I am, and I am sure you would find it much to your advantage to attend regularly.

When you see Judge Story, ask him to show you a letter which I wrote him about the appointment of a judge.

I grow very anxious to get home. The commissioners are here yet, and will remain probably ten days longer.

I have got through the bulk of all the cases committed to my care, and hope now to have a little repose. I shall be ready for any scheme of play which you can get up.

Yours very sincerely,

D. WEBSTER.

MR. WEBSTER TO MR. JUSTICE STORY.

Boston, May 12, 1823.

MY DEAR SIR,—It will give us great pleasure to go to Portsmouth, especially in company with you and Mrs. Story. I believe there is very little to do in the Circuit Court. For myself I have next to nothing. There will probably be one capital trial, as I learn from Mr. Blake, which he thinks must be postponed for a short time from the commencement of the court; so that on the whole there will probably be no inconvenience in adjourning the court over next week.

I never felt more down sick on all subjects connected with the public, than at the present moment. I have heretofore cherished a faint hope that New England would some time or other get out of this miserable, dirty squabble of local politics, and assert her proper character and consequence. But I at length give up. I feel the hand of fate upon us, and to struggle is in vain. We are doomed to be hewers of wood and drawers of water; and I am prepared, henceforth, to do my part of the drudgery, without hoping for an end. You know I am not disappointed at the result of the election for governor. My "agony" was over before the election took place, for I never doubted the result. Indeed, on the grounds on which the controversy was placed, I could have enjoyed the triumph of neither party. What has sickened me beyond remedy is the tone and temper of these disputes. We are disgraced beyond help or hope by these things. There is a Federal interest, a Democratic interest, a Bankrupt interest, an Orthodox interest, and a Middling interest, but I see no national interest, nor any national feeling in the whole matter.

I am, dear Sir, your true but despairing friend,

D. WEBSTER.

MISS ——— TO MR. WEBSTER.

Columbia, May 29, 1823.

SIR,—You have probably before this time entirely forgotten that you ever had an acquaintance by the name of Fanny. It is a long time since I have heard any thing of you. I lately, by accident, heard that you were settled in Boston, and in affluence. Very different is my situation. I live in this town with my aged parents, who are unable to do any thing towards supporting themselves. I have one sister; we have nothing but our hands to support our parents and a helpless brother. As a help towards doing this, I took an orphan child under my care. I was to receive six dollars per month for board and tuition; I have kept the child two years, and received but forty dollars, and have no expectation of ever receiving more. His guardian has failed and fled to parts unknown. I agreed with a merchant in this vicinity for some of the necessaries of life, expecting to receive payment quarterly, and pay it to him; he now calls loudly for his pay, and I have nothing to pay with; I expect he will take the steps of the law; in that case you know how dreadful would be the situation of a poor defenceless female. I can do nothing towards paying the debt unless some of my rich friends will help me. The debt due to me is about eighty dollars, and the debt which I owe about fifty dollars. Should you feel able and willing to bestow some pecuniary assistance, you will please to send by mail. I live in Columbia, Brooklyn County, Connecticut. Should you not find it convenient to assist me, I should be glad to hear of your health and happiness and that of your dear ones. If you could make it convenient to answer this the first mail after receiving it, you would much oblige

Your unfortunate friend.

P. S. Where is Hervey Bingham, and what is his situation? Do you correspond with him? Perhaps you would be willing to state my condition to him. My great anxiety to do all in my power to render the few remaining days of my parents in some measure comfortable, is all the apology I can offer for thus troubling you.

MR. WEBSTER TO MR. BINGHAM.

Boston, June 9, 1823.

Dear Bingham,—I this morning received this from our old acquaintance. I have never heard of her before, since we left college. She seems to be in want and trouble. I have sent her a little money, and, according to her request, enclose the letter to you.

You seem to have given up the good custom of an annual visit this way. We should be very glad to see you and your wife.

Yours always,

D. Webster.

MR. WEBSTER TO MR. EVERETT.

Boston, November, 1823.

I am sure, my dear Sir, Lord Coke never looked so gay before;[1] but this is only another proof how much the most obsolete subjects are improved in passing through your hands. I shall certainly cultivate his acquaintance in some interval or intermission of the Waverley Novels, and will hereafter tell you what I think of him. For the present accept my thanks.

It will rejoice my heart that you should come to Washington. If nobody does it who can do it better, I shall certainly say something of the Greeks. The miserable issue of the Spanish Revolution makes the Greek cause more interesting, and I begin to think they have character enough to carry them through the contest with success. Let me know when you are coming to Washington, and in the mean time let me hear from you. You cannot do me so great a favor as to suggest to me any thoughts that occur respecting matters and things in general.

Adieu, yours always,

D. Webster.

[1] A set of Lord Coke's Reports.

MR. WEBSTER TO MR. EVERETT.

New York, November 16, 1823.

I have found leisure here, and not until now, to read your admirable article[1] on the Greeks. Since I left Boston, also, we have had important information from them. I feel a great inclination to say or do something in their behalf early in the session, if I know what to say or to do. If you can readily direct me to any source from which I can obtain more information than is already public respecting their affairs, I would be obliged to you so to do.

I have not yet seen Wheaton, nor other wise men of Manhattan. Yours always,

D. W.

DANIEL WEBSTER TO EZEKIEL WEBSTER.

Princeton, November 20, 1823.

Dear Ezekiel,—I left New York yesterday, having remained there two or three days, which was long enough to learn the strange confusion and division of opinion which exists there in relation to prominent public subjects. It seems to be generally believed that Mr. Crawford's friends have no longer any reasonable hope of success in that State. This point being agreed, every thing else is controverted. I was altogether astonished at the confidence which the friends of Mr. Clinton expressed, of their ability to secure to him the votes of that State. It is certain that his popularity has experienced a sudden and most extraordinary revival, so much so as to inspire unlimited expectations. The canal has done this. It is said also, with great confidence, that Ohio is better inclined towards Mr. Clinton than any body else. On the other hand, the friends of Mr. Adams, Mr. Calhoun, and Mr. Clay, say that although Mr. Clinton may be gaining strength, it is impossible he can obtain the votes of New York, and impossible at all events that he can be President. The friends of Mr. Calhoun, especially, regret that Mr. Clinton should be brought forward, apprehending it may have

[1] North American Review, October, 1823.

the effect of reuniting the fragments of the old republican party, in favor of Mr. Crawford, through the operation of strong feelings of dislike towards Mr. Clinton. As far as I could understand, the friends of these two gentlemen in that State are inclined to no mutual hostilities, but willing to leave public sentiment as between those two to declare itself.

In the mean time it is thought Mr. Adams has a very large, though not an increasing number of friends. I should not be at all surprised if the reaction, which has begun evidently to take place in Mr. Clinton's favor, together with the canal and other local considerations, should give him the State. It seems undoubted that the legislature, which assembles in January, will send the election to the people, on a general ticket, and then, I presume the friends of the parties will array themselves. Many of the Federalists in the western district, it is supposed, favor Mr. Adams; otherwise, in the city and its neighborhood.

This State of New Jersey is thought likely enough to be in favor of Mr. Calhoun, unless it should be inundated by an overflow of Mr. Clinton's popularity from New York.

We have got along thus far without accident, and shall resume our journey immediately.

Yours, affectionately,

D. WEBSTER.

MR. WEBSTER TO MR. MASON.

Washington, November 30, [1823.]

DEAR SIR,—We arrived here on Wednesday evening safe and well, after a journey which, on the whole, was pleasant and agreeable. Our lodgings were ready and are very comfortable.

The attendance of members is uncommonly large, and we shall have a quorum, no doubt, to-morrow. Mr. Clay arrived last evening. He will doubtless be Speaker, although I understood Mr. Barbour's friends intend to run him. It will not go. Mr. Clay's popularity as Speaker is great, and he is in many respects a liberal and honorable man. His health is not good, but I fancy not so bad as to induce him to decline the chair.

Although I think him tolerably liberal, and not unfriendly in his general feeling, yet I do not suppose that, in the organization and arrangement of the affairs of the House, he will venture to disregard old lines of distinction.

Mr. King has arrived, but I have not seen him. Both your senators are here.

I have not seen much here yet to add to my stock of knowledge on the subject of the Presidential election. It looks to me, however, at present, as if it might happen that Mr. Crawford would ere long be given up, and his friends go off in a direction to Mr. Clay.

It appears to me to be our true policy to oppose all caucuses; so far our course seems to me to be clear. Beyond that I do not think we are bound to proceed at present. To defeat caucus nominations, or prevent them, and to give the election, wherever it can be done, to the people, are the best means of restoring the body politic to its natural and wholesome state.

Mrs. W. sends a great deal of love to you all.

Yours, most truly,

D. Webster.

P. S. I hope you have not abandoned an idea which you intimated to me at Dorchester. I think you will do exceedingly right to take that step, and am sure you will not regret it.

It will excite no jealousy or suspicion here, at all; and you have reasons which will allay any that might arise at home.

DANIEL WEBSTER TO EZEKIEL WEBSTER.

Washington, December 4, [1823.]

Dear Ezekiel,—I have received yours, covering three letters, to-day. My information as to what Mr. H. said in New York, was from the editor of the Statesman; but I suppose he would not wish to have it known. He is now here; I shall see him and will endeavor to put him in the right way. Mr. Parrot lodges in the same house with us. He said to-day, speaking of New Hampshire affairs, that if there were any objection to Governor W., he could not be chosen; that Mr. Morrill was talked of, but he thought that would hardly do, and that if Judge L. were a candidate, he probably might and would succeed.

One thing I hold to be material—get on without a caucus. It will only require a little more pains. It is time to put an end to caucuses. They make great men little, and little men great. The true source of power is the people. The Democrats are not democratic enough. They are real Aristocrats. Their leaders wish to govern by a combination among themselves, and they think they have a fee-simple in the people's suffrages.

Go to the people, and convince them that their pretended friends are a knot of self-interested jobbers, who make a trade of patriotism and live on popular credulity.

We have as yet done little or nothing here. The choice of Speaker should be considered as indicating nothing but a sense, in the House, of Mr. Clay's fitness for that place. He had nearly all the northern votes. How he will discharge the important duties of the chair, in arranging the business of the House, we shall know to-morrow. I have no doubt of the liberality of his feelings, and can hardly persuade myself that he will be afraid to shake off trammels. Yet in the present condition of things, he may perhaps keep on the safe side, as he may think it. We shall see.

Nothing very new and important has transpired in relation to the Presidential election. I remain of opinion the choice must come to the House.

I shall write you often, and should be glad to hear from you twice a week. These are interesting times, and we ought to keep awake. What think you of doing or saying something in favor of the Greeks?

Mr. Longfellow has not yet arrived. I note your request, and will see him. Yours, faithfully,

D. W.

MR. WEBSTER TO MR. EVERETT.

Washington, December 5, 1823.

My dear Sir,—I have gone over your two manuscripts with the map before me, and think I have mastered the campaigns of 1821–1822, historically and topographically. My wonder is, where and how your most extraordinary industry has been able to find all the materials for so interesting and detailed a narrative. I hope you will send me a digested narrative of the events of this year, so far as they are to be learned from the last accounts.

I have spoken to several gentlemen on the subject of a motion respecting Greece, and all of them approve it. The object which I wish to bring about, and which I believe may be brought about, is the appointment of a commissioner to go to Greece. Two modes present themselves. A motion to that effect, and a speech in support of it, giving some account of the rise and progress of the Greek revolution, and showing the propriety and utility of the proposed mission. The other is to raise a committee on the subject, and let there be a report containing the same matter. The first would be the easier to be done; the last would be the more grave and imposing. Whichever may be adopted, your communications are invaluable; and I wish you would tell me frankly how far I can use them without injury to your January article in The North American.

We can wait until that article is out if you think best, but my impression is we should do well to bring forward the subject within ten or twelve days from this time, while the House is not yet much occupied, and while the country feels the warmth communicated by the President's message. I intend to see, in the course of this day and to-morrow, Mr. R. King, Mr. Clay, and perhaps the President, and learn their views of this matter.

I shall send you every thing in the shape of a document that is printed this session. These are interesting times; let us improve them. Yours, most devotedly,

DANIEL WEBSTER.

MR. WEBSTER TO MR. EVERETT.

Washington, December 6, 1823.

MY DEAR SIR,—There was, as I believe, a meeting of the members of the administration yesterday, at which, *inter alia*, they talked of Greece. The pinch is, that in the message, the President has taken, as is supposed, pretty high ground as to this continent; and is afraid of the appearance of interfering in the concerns of the other continent also. This does not weigh greatly with me; I think we have as much community with the Greeks as with the inhabitants of the Andes, and the dwellers on the borders of the Vermilion sea.

If nothing should occur to alter my present purpose, I shall bring forward a motion on the subject on Monday, and shall propose to let it lie on the table for a fortnight.

If you can find any tolerable map of modern Greece, I wish you would send it to me for Mr. Calhoun. I write this at his request, who desires me to say to you that he is as friendly to the Greeks as yourself.

I am glad to see that you publish, in the Daily, your narrative. It will be well received, and do much good.

There seems to be here a good-natured and liberal spirit on all subjects. Yours, most sincerely,

D. WEBSTER.

MR. WEBSTER TO MR. BLAKE.

Washington, December 20, 1823.

MY DEAR SIR,—I believe Mrs. W. is meditating a letter to Mrs. B. to-day; but as she told me this morning it was uncertain whether engagements of business would allow her time to write, she directed me to indite a line to Mrs. B. to be inclosed in this, which I told her I was about writing to you.

The object of this is to call your attention to Mr. Fuller's resolution respecting the law of 1814, that partial and odious act. The resolution is now before our committee. We shall act upon it soon, and probably report a bill to repeal the act of 1814; probably in twelve days we shall be acting on the matter in our House. I wish you, therefore, to do two things: First, to write to me, giving me your ideas, and any information which you may think useful; and, secondly, to write to Mr. Mills to look after the matter if it should get to the Senate.

I have a belief, perhaps it is unfounded, that it will pass our House. I shall be very glad, if the first thing I do here, in addition to its being just and proper, shall also be something not unfavorable to you.

As to the business of the court, I have not yet paid much attention to it. My Spanish claims have called for all the time at my command. They are now pretty much finished, at least so far as not to be extremely burdensome on my time.

As to great political affairs, we, who are not in secrets, know here very little more than is known in Massachusetts. Some say there is to be a caucus, and some say there is not. I think it yet uncertain whether there will be one or not. I suppose the members of the House have all their preferences, but, so far, there is great abstinence in the House from all topics connected with the election. I hope this will last.

I write this in the House, not now in session, and your friend, Mr. Buchanan, is here, and he desires me to make his remembrances to you and Mrs. Blake. He means to write to you soon, and he just now says, "Mr. Blake is one of the most agreeable men I have ever known." What a poor judge of such matters he is! If he always judges so wrong he will not do to be followed!

Pray let me hear from you soon, and believe me, most truly,

Yours, always,

DANIEL WEBSTER.

MR. WEBSTER TO MRS. BLAKE.

Washington, December 20, 1823.

MY DEAR MADAM,—It is Mrs. Webster's intention to write you immediately, in her proper person, in answer to yours of the eleventh. Not to suffer, however, so great a favor to remain altogether unnoticed, even for a short time, she commands me to write to you to acknowledge its receipt, and to assure you of the pleasure it gives us to hear from you. It is true that we find objects here which may well enough fill up the attention for a time; and, truth to tell, I really think Mrs. Webster likes Washington tolerably well. Nevertheless, we need your and Mr. Blake's society very much. There is nobody here to come in of an evening, and pull off his overshoes, coats, and handkerchiefs, and sit down to a regular social talk, like your husband. For my part I would give something just to see that blue handkerchief. Our evenings are sometimes not a little lonesome. However, I occasionally, though seldom, take a nap; and as you speak of dreaming away the long nights, you hit me on a tender point, since I am always accused, very unjustly of course, of no little love of the good thing, sleep. However, I will not altogether deny it, and in respect to good dreams, I am, I am sure, surpassed by nobody; I believe I have a talent that way. Our evening parties are not yet numerous; we have been but to two, one at General Brown's, the night before last, and one at Mrs. Adams, ten days ago. Report runs that the drawing-room at the White House will be opened on New Year's day, and afterward as usual. There are several handsome female faces here that I have not seen before; especially two or three ladies from the South. We may be in some danger, my dear lady, of losing the reputation of the North, if you do not come on to sustain us against this southern competition. You must remember that our northern forces are much weakened since your beautiful friend Miss Dickinson stays out of the combat. For this, as well as other reasons, I hope you will allow me to entreat you to accompany your husband.

You have a great friend here in the person of Master Edward. He desires all sorts of affectionate remembrance. I think both he and his sister may speak well of the bread and butter of the Potomac. I will thank you to remember me to Miss Helen. I regret that you are so soon to lose her pleasant society. Give our love to George. Mrs. Webster will probably write you in a day or two.

Yours with most sincere regard,

DANIEL WEBSTER.

MR. WEBSTER TO MR. EVERETT.

Washington, December 21, 1823.

MY DEAR SIR,—Two days ago I received your Greek statistics, and to-day your letter of the 13th. I pray you not to think my engagements are such as to make your correspondence inconvenient. In the first place, I write you only when I can with convenience, and as to my duties in the judiciary committee, most of the topics coming up there are pretty familiar to me, and are consequently disposed of without great labor.

As to the Greek subject, the resolution will be taken up

to-morrow fortnight, not yesterday fortnight, as mentioned in yesterday's Daily Intelligencer. I believe there will be a good deal of discussion, although, if any, pretty much on one side. While some of our Boston friends, as I know, think this resolution even Quixotic, leading to crusade, it will be objected to strongly by many, on account of its tame milk and water character. The merchants are naturally enough a little afraid about their cargoes at Smyrna; besides, Greece is a great way off, &c.

I find your communications of the utmost utility. In regard to the history of the campaigns, I could have done nothing without your aid.

My intention is to justify the resolution against two classes of objections, those that suppose it not to go far enough, and those that suppose it to go too far. Then, to give some little history of the Greek revolution, express a pretty strong conviction of its ultimate success, and persuade the House, if I can, to take the merit of being the first government, among all the civilized nations, who have publicly rejoiced in the emancipation of Greece.

There will be speeches enough, some of them no doubt, tolerably good. Whatever occurs to you, if it be but a scrap, in season to be sent here, pray forward it. Mr. Calhoun is greatly obliged to you for your map.

I hope to hear from you a short word at least every day or two. Yours always truly,

D. Webster.

P. S. I feel now as if I could make a pretty good speech for my friends the Greeks, but I shall get cool in fourteen days, unless you keep up my temperature.

[The following lines, with prefatory note by Mr. Webster in his own handwriting, were found among his papers. Ed.]

THE LAST NIGHT OF THE SESSION.

The following lines, so descriptive of the condition of the two Houses of Congress at the end of the session, were written at the termination of the session of 1823–1824, by the late Governor Lincoln of Maine, then a member of the House. Of the six persons mentioned, three, as well as the writer, have paid the debt of nature.

D. W.

> "What guardian power my country's glory keeps,
> When Senates doze, and e'en her Webster sleeps?
> When Clay, out-watched, forsakes the empty chair,
> And Warfield winks, amidst the dusky air?
> Thro' the dim hall the wandering echoes stray
> And yawning messengers look out for day.
> Cutt's laboring tongue can scarce pronounce the bills,
> And Cocke himself forgets his country's ills.
> Sigh answers sigh, and snore resounds to snore,
> Like billows bursting on some dreary shore.
> With lazy pace, the long, long hours return,
> While worn-out Sibley cries, "Adjourn, adjourn."

MR. WEBSTER TO MRS. LANGDON ELWYN.

Washington, January 2, 1824.

The season approaches, my dear Madam, in which we may be allowed to expect the pleasure of seeing you and Miss Langdon Elwyn, in this place. I have accordingly been looking out for your commands. Although you may be very much interested and delighted in Philadelphia, you must remember that this great city is the national capital, and that the court is here. I assure you, my dear Madam, that you are very much needed here. The North needs reinforcements, as well in your department as in ours. There is a brilliant circle of beauties from the South, while that from the North, if not less brilliant than usual, is yet less than usual.

We all went yesterday to the President's, and had a very splendid New Year. Mrs. Webster, I perceive, lays it up against Messrs. Gales and Seaton, that in their account of the matter, in the paper of this morning, nothing is said of the ladies. That, certainly, was a capital omission. Mrs. Monroe was not well enough to be seen, but the honors of the occasion were well performed by Mrs. Hay.

Mrs. Webster begs me to make her love to yourself and Miss Emily. I pray, also, to be remembered; and, in the hope of soon being able to pay my respects in person,

I am, Madam, with true regard, your obedient servant,

DANIEL WEBSTER.

MR. WEBSTER TO MR. EVERETT.

Washington, January 2, 1824.

DEAR SIR,—I send you the answer to the call for information respecting the Greeks. If I mistake not, it will, with the country, very much raise the Greek stock. As to the danger, from my motion, of offending the Turk, I think we may disregard that, when we see the Secretary of State corresponding with a Greek agent in London, wishing him and his nation all success, and publishing the correspondence.

It is possible my motion may be put off till we get an answer to Mr. Mallory's motion, so as to debate our whole foreign relations at once. We shall have the nation; and if Mr. Monroe does not do speedily as much as I have suggested, he will soon be obliged to do more.

I mean to say as much to him, this day or to-morrow.

D. W.

MR. WEBSTER TO MR. JUSTICE STORY.

Washington, January 4, 1824.

MY DEAR SIR,—I am in great trouble and perplexity on this subject of the courts; and often wish I was almost any where rather than where I am. There are difficulties, inherent in the subject; there are others, more formidable, arising from the state of men's opinions.

In the first place, I cannot get over my own objections to separating your bench entirely from the circuits. I trust you know, that so far as that course would be convenient to the members of the court, it would be most desirable to me to follow it. But my convictions of the public interest are the other way, and are very strong. Suffice it for the present to say, that if we separate your bench from the circuit, and reduce it to five, I should expect to see it, in a very few years, the most unpopular tribunal that ever existed.

In the second place, I cannot persuade others to come into my views, which would be to appoint circuit judges for some circuits. The objection is, that this mode would have the effect of producing anti-equality. Some circuits would have a supreme judge, others a subordinate judge; and that this inequality, which is offensive, and touches feeling, would be necessarily permanent; as when a vacancy should happen on the supreme bench, an appointment to fill it must be made with reference to the circuit duties performed by the last incumbent. It is impossible, at least it seems so, to procure the support of the West to this system; and, as the West alone is much interested in the change, nothing of course will be done which they are not reconciled with.

One suggestion is, to elevate the condition of the district judges, give them better salaries, &c., and to make circuit courts by the association of district judges. This, in my mind, is liable to the first objection, it disconnects your court from the circuits.

I wish you would now tell me, just as strongly as you feel them to be, what and how great would be the disadvantages of increasing your bench to nine?

Some of them are obvious; such as the difficulty of commanding the attention of nine men to a cause, particularly as in cases of equity and admiralty, where evidence is to be examined, &c. There are many others which occur to me; and more will occur to you. And yet I confess I cannot make so strong a case against that measure as I thought I could when it was first suggested. On interesting constitutional questions, I rather think it would be an advantage.

My impression is that, with such increase, we could get along probably for twenty years, or forever; for I am inclined to think there will be a gradual and progressive improvement in the district courts, and that so far as the business becomes incapable of being performed by the nine supreme judges on the circuit, the duties of the circuit court will be devolved on the district judge. We shall not in my opinion be likely to have intermediate circuit judges. Suppose, for example, we should lose the district judge of New Hampshire; we would try to get Mr. Mason appointed, lop off New Hampshire from your circuit, and make him a circuit court.

I think we should get pretty good judges if appointments were now to be made. I mean, of two on your bench. There is no doubt Judge Woodbury would be one, and he is as sound a man as I know of. It is said Mr. Burnet, of Ohio, would be the other.

On all these subjects do pray write me, and tell me what to do. I have not heard a word from you.

I am quite well, except that the winding off the Spanish commissions has made me write my fingers off. Before you get through this long epistle, you will wish that were true.

Yours always,

D. Webster.

MR. I. P. DAVIS TO MR. WEBSTER.

Boston, January 6, 1824.

My dear Sir,—I feel greatly obliged by your kind attention in sending the canvas-back ducks. They arrived in excellent order, in a very short passage from Baltimore. I made the distribution as you directed. Your club met with Mr. Dutton, and they made a very favorable report of the good quality of the birds. Gorham, who is now called an excellent judge, decides them to be the very best ever seen this side of Havre de Grace.

I was so fortunate as to have them in season for my club to feast on them. Callender and Perkins had their wing a-piece. We drank your health and a happy New Year in a bumper of "Black top." I sent a very fine pair to our friend Blake. As he leaves this to-morrow for Washington, he will make his own report.

I should be greatly delighted to visit Washington in February, and think Bliss is quite disposed; if I can make any excuse I shall certainly do it. A party propose going on in a few days; Messrs. J. Russell, Codman, and Lee, if they are not discouraged by a cold storm.

Mr. Lowell has been writing on the subject of the Greeks; his signature is "A Calm Man." It appears to me he is the only one that is not perfectly so among us. The rich are not much disposed to aid by giving money, and the merchants have some fears of the trade at Smyrna. Perkins writes in the Daily Advertiser the piece signed "A Merchant."

We are pleased to have a good report of Jeannette, and I hope she will continue to deserve it. The token you enclosed for her sister was received and delivered. My wife's love to you and yours, and many happy returns of a New Year, in which I most heartily join.

Yours as ever,

I. P. Davis.

MR. WEBSTER TO MR. EVERETT.

Washington, January, 1824.

Dear Sir,—You are in a long confabulation—a short word to write when one is in a hurry—with the Secretary of State, and my coachman complains of the tempestuous night. Good-bye. Give my love to your wife.

I shall send my speech[1] along forthwith, in multitudes, "like which the populous North," &c.

Can you leave me the French author? I will send it by Mr. Coolidge, if needful, three days hence.

Your documents shall go regularly, and also any letters that may come to me for you. I hope the inclemency of the weather may induce you to postpone your departure another day. If so, pray let me see you or hear from you in the morning. Adieu.

Yours,

D. W.

MR. HOPKINSON TO MR. WEBSTER.

Philadelphia, January 23, 1824.

My dear Sir,—The report of your speech, meagre as it is, shows the foot of Hercules; but we want the whole body and

[1] Speech on the Revolution in Greece, January 19, 1824.

soul, and trust you will give it to us. Mr. Hempbill wrote me it was the best he ever heard. I published his letter in Walsh's Gazette.

I scribbled some New Year's rhymes, you know what such things are, for Poulson's paper, and am struck with some coincidences in our notions about the Holy Alliance, and the Greek cause. I enclose you a copy, not because the verses are worth a farthing as poetry, but because I now think they have some value as far as they are coincident with your views. In my rhymes of the former year, upon the same subject, I stated that it was a combination of all kings against all people; and suggested the hope you also entertain, that the time is approaching when the moral and intellectual power of man will be united with his physical force, and overthrow the unnatural and degrading slavery that now oppresses him. I confess this hope is considerably darkened by the late events in Italy and Spain.

Most truly yours,

JOS. HOPKINSON.

EXTRACT FROM THE ADDRESS.

Not so the Greeks, who still maintain their right,
And bravely meet their tyrants in the fight;
Still keep undaunted the embattled field,
Where they may perish but will never yield.
What nobler cause can fire the human breast,
Than thine, O! Greece, so long, so low opprest?
What is there sacred in the heart of man,
Dear to his soul since life and light began,
That meets not in your cause, afflicted race,
And recommends it to the Throne of Grace?
Religion, Liberty, Home, Children, Life,
All hang suspended on this awful strife;—
May Heaven afford the aid which Man denies,
And crown your efforts with the hard-earn'd prize.
Christians of Europe! Burn ye not with shame?
Christians ye are not, only in the name;—
The Turk, exulting, mocks your God and creed;
Beneath his sabre, hosts of Christians bleed;
And ye look on and coldly count the cost,

The policy of battles won and lost.
Your monarchs meet and hold a grave debate,
Weighing this cause against some trick of state;
Find it is best the Crescent should prevail,
And sink the bleeding Cross—O shameful tale!
The Turk himself can scarce believe it true;
He would not thus abandon Turk to you.
Holy Allies—your flag is now unfurl'd,
No longer can you cheat and mock the world;
Ambition, power, and avarice, are the ties
That bind these generous, great, and good Allies.

MR. HOPKINSON TO MR. WEBSTER.

Philadelphia, February 1, 1824.

MY DEAR SIR,—Now that your Greek resolution, like poor Fidele, is laid in its tomb, decked with flowers of every hue, I hope you will have time to think of your living friends in Philadelphia, who never cease to think of you. By your letter to our friend Walsh, I find you are preparing a proper publication of your speech. I pray you to take pains with it. You are generally too careless of yourself and your reputation; and, content with doing a thing well, you have too little solicitude about the proof of it to the world. Your views of the character, object, and extent of the Holy Alliance have particularly attracted public attention for their strength and novelty in many particulars. Develop yourself fully on this subject; it is of vast interest, and may be illustrated with great force by their declarations and conduct for the last two years. It is, in one respect, a misfortune for a man to obtain a high eminence of character; he is required always to maintain it, and this calls for a constant vigilance and effort which are not always convenient. Besides, few have judgment to know of what a subject is capable, and expect to see the same power displayed, whether an oak is to be uprooted, or a rose plucked from its bush. I agree with Mr. Randolph in his surprise that you should find so much to be well said on your resolution. It is only a mind of great resources, with a genius creative and prolific, that could have connected it with so much important and interesting matter. Not one of your opponents has met you fairly on your own ground. Some have treated the resolution as an abstract Declaration of War, and others have assumed that it would certainly lead to war; and thus mounted on a monster of their own creation, they have gone off at full speed, spreading devastation and terror in their path. It is thus with men who must speak, and can't argue. Of this *genus*, I have seen so many, especially in the great hall of Congress, that I know them from the first jump they take.

I saw our friend Judge Story during the short time he gave us in Philadelphia, and was delighted to find him in high health and spirits. He is ready for a tough campaign; but on his return, I shall look for paler cheeks and dimmer eyes. Your duties with the court, commission, and congress will now be heavy; but nobody is more able to bear them. God bless you and yours ever and forever.

Truly yours,

Jos. Hopkinson.

DANIEL WEBSTER TO EZEKIEL WEBSTER.

Washington, January 27, 1824.

I have omitted for a long time to write to you, principally because I have had nothing important to say, and partly because I have had little leisure. I shall send you my Greek speech in a pamphlet form, in a few days. You notice the occurrence between Mr. Speaker and Mr. Bartlett. I am inclined to think Mr. Bartlett will find it necessary to do something, in consequence of what happened, by way of obtaining a pacific explanation. He will, as you see, get no explanation in the House, and yet it would seem he is bound to obtain explanation. I presume some friends will undertake to set matters right.

I have conversed about the mail contracts. There is the best disposition at the department to do what is right, but the question is, how? The contracts are not out till next year, and if a law were to pass excluding printers, still, printers' friends would bid. Some one else must offer lower, there is no other remedy.

* * * * * * *

The Presidential question is still in the clouds. We know no more here than you do, and such as you and I have nothing to do but keep quiet.

I think your course is right about your next governor. Take care to open the door, and let the people say who shall go in. For certain reasons, I should wish Mr. Livermore might be chosen. For certain others, I should not regret Mr. Morrill's elevation. Let us know how things are going on.

Of all your representatives I have seen most of Mr. Plumer, and am thus far quite well pleased with him.

Yours always,

D. W.

MR. WEBSTER TO MR. EVERETT.

Washington, February 13, 1824.

Mr. Bliss can furnish you the report of the commissioners under the Louisiana Treaty; there is a copy in my drawer in the office.

I have sent you sundry speeches; if you think it worth while, you may send one to any friend on the other side the Atlantic. There is no export duty; it is *casus omissus* in the new tariff. On this same tariff we are now occupied; it is a tedious, disagreeable subject. The House, or a majority of it, are apparently insane, at least I think so. Whether any thing can be done to moderate the disease, I know not. I have very little hope. I am aware that something is expected from me, much more than I shall perform. It would be easy to make a speech, but I am anxious to do something better, if I can, but I see not what I can do.

The caucus is to-morrow; I intend to learn what transpires in it, and write a line to Mr. Hale, after it is over, in the evening.

Thine, D. W.

DANIEL WEBSTER TO EZEKIEL WEBSTER.

Washington, February 22.

Dear Ezekiel,—I will send you the book you wish.

I imagine that New Hampshire, Rhode Island, Connecticut, and Georgia, have always chosen on a general ticket. Vermont and New Jersey sometimes, but not always. The rest of the States probably never. But I will make some inquiries among the members and inform you of the result.

The caucus has hurt nobody but its friends, as far as I can now judge. Mr. Adams's chance seems to increase, and he and General Jackson are likely to be the real competitors at last. General Jackson's manners are more presidential than those of any of the candidates. He is grave, mild, and reserved. My wife is for him decidedly.

We are going on in debating the tariff. The result is uncertain; with some modification the bill would pass, and probably may as it is.

I think your friend Governor W. will probably be reëlected for want of some one to be set up against him.

Yours, D. W.

P. S. We shall beat our adversaries, I trust, in the Steamboat cause.

DANIEL WEBSTER TO EZEKIEL WEBSTER.

Boston, Saturday Morning, [1824.]

Dear Ezekiel,—The matters of business I wrote you about in my last, have all been attended to on my part.

As to politics, we are all in a ferment, as you will see. By the way, Governor Morrill has been in town, and I have heard of his saying that he should favor the election of General Miller and yourself. That he should give his support to the gallant general is easy enough to be believed; but how he should happen to think so well of you as to say, voluntarily, that he should support your election, can be accounted for only on the principle of the near approach, or actual arrival, of the "era of good feeling."

But to advert to matters that come nearer home; Mrs. Webster wants half a dozen barrels of your best potatoes sent down by the boat; the flour has arrived, &c.

Yours, in haste,

D. WEBSTER.

DANIEL WEBSTER TO EZEKIEL WEBSTER.

Washington, March 14, 1824.

DEAR EZEKIEL,—I fully agree with you that it is unfortunate that Judge Smith should be set up for Governor, but, as it is all over by this time, it is in vain to repine. I feel confident from all accounts, there will be no choice, and incline to think M. and W. will be the highest candidates; in which event, I presume the former will be chosen. It may be as well to try him. I hope to see a number of good men chosen into the Legislature.

The tariff is yet undecided. It will not pass, I think, in its present shape, and I doubt if it will pass at all. As yet I have not interfered much in the debate, partly because there were others more desirous to discuss the details than I am, and partly because I have been so much in the court. I have done, however, with the court, and the whole tariff subject is yet open. I shall be looking after it, although I should prefer it should die a natural death, by postponement or other easy violence. We shall not do much with the judiciary, and yet we shall do something.

As to President, Jackson seems to be making head yet, Arbuthnot and Ambrister notwithstanding. The truth is, he is the people's candidate in a great part of the southern and western country. I hope all New England will support Mr. Calhoun for the Vice-Presidency. If so, he will probably be chosen, and that will be a great thing. He is a true man, and will do good to the country in that situation.

The court will sit a week longer. My engagements in it this term have not been few nor small, and have kept me pretty busy. The Spanish affairs are nearly through.

Mrs. Webster sends her love to you and the children. She will write you shortly, and I believe is expecting a communication from you.

Yours always,
D. Webster.

MR. WEBSTER TO MR. JUSTICE STORY.

Washington, April 10, 1824.

My dear Sir,—I am happy to hear, through Mr. Paige, that you were at home so seasonably and so safe; and I hope to learn soon from yourself, that you had the pleasure of finding Mrs. Story and the children well. I have not had an earlier opportunity of writing to you, although I wished to call your attention to two or three things, in regard to which you promised me the benefit of your opinions. We have had a busy time of it since you left us. For myself, I am exhausted. When I look in the glass, I think of our old New England saying, "As thin as a shad." I have not vigor enough left, either mental or physical, to try an action for assault and battery. However, the fine weather has come on, I have resumed the saddle, and hope to "pick up my crumbs" again soon. You see the condition of the tariff. The great struggle has been on the iron; and our majority yesterday was unexpectedly great. The speeches on the side of the bill have been very impressive and captivating on the general question; on the ability of protecting domestic industry, raising prices of agricultural products by manufactures, working up our own materials, &c. Accompanying sentiments of this sort, we have had much from the Philadelphia school, of the adverse balance of trade, exportation of specie, loss of foreign markets, &c. But I think some impression has been made against arguments of this class. For myself, I have really wished some proper and reasonable bill to pass, that the business might be settled. I would not oppose the bill, I think, if hemp should be struck out, and some other minor amendments made. The molasses, I presume, will come out. The minimum ought to be struck out of the woollens. And if possible, there should be a change in a variety of provisions about hardware. It is a great object to settle the concerns of the community; so that one may know what to depend on. I am apprehensive, however, that our vote yesterday has made the bill so unacceptable to its friends, that it is very probable they may abandon it.

I shall call up some bills reported by our committee, as soon as possible. The gentlemen of the West will propose a clause, requiring the assent of a majority of all the judges to a judgment, which pronounces a state law void, as being in violation of the constitution or laws of the United States. Do you see any great evil in such a provision? Judge Todd told me he thought it would give great satisfaction in the West. In what phraseology would you make such a provision?

As to the bankrupt law, pray give me your ideas of an outline, as I must bring forward some resolutions on that subject before the end of the session. I know how much you are employed, but still I must have one half hour.

Mrs. Webster desires her best regards to Mrs. Story and yourself. I will also beg to be remembered to Mrs. Story. I hope you will allow me to hear from you soon.

With constant regard, yours,

D. Webster.

P. S. *Sunday Morning.*—I hardly know what our votes of yesterday indicate, as to the final decision on the tariff. My impression rather is, that the bill will hardly get through our House. It certainly would not, if there were not so many members who vote on the judgment of their constituents, not on their own.

DANIEL WEBSTER TO EZEKIEL WEBSTER.

Washington, April 18, 1824

Dear Ezekiel,—Mr. Clay's speech is printed; mine is in press, and both shall be sent to you in pamphlet.[1]

I hope to get away by 12th May, and to be at home in season to see you at Dorchester the week before the General Court meets at Concord. The ensuing summer I shall do nothing

[1] Speech on the Tariff, April 1 and 2, 1824.

but move about and play. I shall certainly spend a fortnight with you at Boscawen, and the rest you must spend with us. August we will pass together on Cape Cod. My wife wants some one to ride about with her, while I am shooting, &c.

The tariff will not pass the Senate without great amendment.

We have struck a mortal blow on the tariff principle. If it were not for instruction and other nonsense, two thirds nearly of our House would be against it. It would be a noble thing for Mason, Haven, and yourself, to draw up resolutions that should be just and sensible on that subject, and pass them through the New Hampshire Legislature.

There is nothing new about President, except that I think Mr. Adams's prospects have grown more favorable for a few weeks.

I enclose you three letters by way of samples of my correspondence. I shall answer none of them. If you see my "old friend D. Dyer," I have no objection to your telling him that I remember him, and that I wished you to make him a present of a few dollars in my name, if he be poor as represented. I have many more letters equally interesting. My wife and children are well, and send their love to you and yours.

D. W.

MR. WEBSTER TO MR. JUSTICE STORY.

Washington, May 4, 1824.

Dear Sir,—We had the Supreme Court before us yesterday, rather unexpectedly, and a debate arose which lasted all day. Cohens *v.* Virginia, Green and Biddle, &c. were all discussed. Most of the gentlemen were very temperate and guarded; there were, however, some exceptions, especially Mr. Randolph, whose remarks were not a little extraordinary. Mr. Barbour re-argued Cohen's case; Mr. Letcher and Mr. Wickliffe did the same for Green and Biddle; I said some few things, *eo instanti*, which I thought the case called for. The proposition for the concurrence of five judges will not prevail. This morning I have submitted my own proposition, which I apprehend will receive very general assent.

Just as I was getting out of other troubles, this business of Mr. Edwards came upon me. I could not avoid it.

This fine weather passes off without my knowing whether it rains or shines. From nine in the morning till eleven at night, I am shut up either in the House or the committee rooms. I am, however, remarkably well for me; and have, I believe, in a month picked up some pounds *avoir du pois* of flesh.

My wife sends her love to you and yours. We are "dreadful homesick."

Yours always, D. WEBSTER.

GOVERNOR GORE TO MR. WEBSTER.

Waltham, May 11, 1824.

MY DEAR SIR,—I thank you for an excellent speech, lately received, on the tariff, replete in my estimation with true principles and sound doctrines, which, if acted upon, would promote the individual objects exclusively intended to be fostered, at the same time that the other great interests of the community would be preserved.

No one rejoices more sincerely than myself at witnessing your advance in the public mind. There is hardly cavil and carping enough to relieve you from the denunciation pronounced against him of whom all speak well.

Governor Eustis will ride triumphantly into the chair of State, and has the cheering prospect of being buried under arms; that, to a minister of war, and one who has been in the field of Waterloo, must brighten his setting sun.

I owe a bill to Gales and Seaton for The Intelligencer from some time in 1822 or 1823. Be so good as to pay the amount and to the end of the current year of my subscription. I will repay you on your return.

With great regard, I remain, my dear Sir, your affectionate friend, and obedient servant,

C. GORE.

MR. WEBSTER TO MRS. BLAKE.

Washington, June 9, 1824.

My dear Madam,—Mrs. Coyle has granted me the honor of franking a letter to you, which, in her opinion, contains something which in its perfect state a good deal resembled yourself. I presume on the further liberty of writing this, just to inform yourself and husband that I am yet alive, and do not hope to be quite forgotten. I have been as far as Philadelphia with Mrs. Webster; there we parted, and I suppose she will have the pleasure of seeing you next week. I am yet busy, with little to do; and hope to leave a P. P. C. with the whole of Washington in four or five days.

You will not expect me to say how suddenly and how really all things seemed changed here, when you and your husband departed. No talks, no music, no rides, no little suppers on the light stand, no birthnight balls. And now, since Mrs. Webster and Julia, and that good-for-nothing Ned, are gone, it is lonely enough.

I pray you tell Mr. Blake, that after I get home, if I ever should do so, I expect to find him ready for play the residue of the summer. I am yet not so reduced but that I could walk with a bit of iron on my shoulder. Truth to tell I am extremely homesick; and I shall reckon it a happy day, when I set my face northward.

I hope George has become quite well, and that he has kept a controlling eye on Master Daniel, during his vacation. You have done the said master a great favor by allowing him a shelter.

I pray you, my dear lady, to make my love to your husband, and to believe me with great truth and regard,

Yours, Daniel Webster.

MR. WEBSTER TO MR. BLAKE.

Washington, June 16, 1824.

My dear Sir,—I have been thinking a good deal of you for the last three days. It is very unhappy to associate the idea of one's friend with anything disagreeable, ugly, or abominable. And yet, my dear Sir, that unluckily happens to me. And what disagreeable or abominable thing do you think it is which brings you to my mind, and keeps you there? Simply our old enemy, the east wind. Here he is, however little you might suspect it, in great strength and true character. I have tasted it for three successive mornings. It has its old flavor. I have never known certainly such weather here, at this season. It was cold enough yesterday morning for a frost. I am here yet on a certain committee. We hope to get through the evidence to-day, and then to wind up our labors soon. I am, in the mean time, trying to get along with a few Spanish claims, in which I have made some little progress. All that I can do here, I wish to do, while I have the aid of Mr. Jaudon, and all the papers. I have, for this reason, dispersed what I have received as fast as possible among those to whom it belongs, saving a little to buy a few articles that may be necessary about August.

I trust I shall get away before the week is out. I am homesick—homesick—homesick. I learn that Mrs. Webster was to embark yesterday from New York for New Haven. I presume she will be in Dorchester by the time you receive this.

We have no news here worth communicating. Pray give my most profound regards to Mrs. Blake. If I live to get home, I shall be glad.

Yours, D. W.

P. S. Have you been at Cohasset or Chelsea Beach? Are you ever found riding with an umbrella[1] in your chaise?

MR. WEBSTER TO MR. MASON.

Boston, November 6, 1824.

MY DEAR SIR,—I was about writing to you this morning, when I received your letter. I assure you few things of the kind have given me more uneasiness than my failing to visit

[1] Mr. Blake used to call his fowling-piece, when in its case, as he was driving, his umbrella.

you on my return from New Hampshire. But truly, we could not do it. There were strong reasons why I should come by way of Dunstable, or go there after I got home; and I found I could not have time for the latter. I came home from Washington so late, that there has been no summer. But I am still more disappointed at your abandonment of the intention of coming here. I beg you to reconsider that matter. It is yet a fortnight before you are wanted at Concord. Pray come over the ensuing week, and stay a day or two, if no more. I shall be at home, as I expect, every day, and with no engagement of business. By the 16th or 17th, I must be off. If you are afraid to come to Boston, I will meet you, any day, except Friday, at Salem, on a little notice. But it will be no more trouble for you to come here. You need see nobody, unless you choose. We are in town, safe and snug; and can give you a bed. Pray come if you can, and write me on Monday to let me know if we may look for you.

I am quite astonished at New Hampshire votes. From the Concord and the Keene papers, I should think probably that Ezekiel Webster is chosen, though by no means certain; but at any rate, the result shows some new movements and workings in the public mind.

I shall write to Mr. Haven next week, unless I learn that you are coming up. You certainly do very right to go to Concord. My brother has been here this week; he thinks there are very good prospects of a pleasant session. Interested individuals may pretend that the result of the late voting proves only a surprise on the old democratic party, I think otherwise. It appears to me to indicate a diminution of party feeling, and a growing regard to personal character.

Yours always, with much love from Mrs. Webster to you and yours. I shall hear from you by Tuesday; I hope, that you are coming; don't disappoint us.

Yours always,
Daniel Webster.

MR. WEBSTER TO MRS. WEBSTER.

Washington, December 4, 1824.

My dear Love,—I have made an engagement to take lodgings at a Mr. McIntire's, Pennsylvania Avenue, between Mrs. Peyton's and Brown's on the opposite side. It is a new house, and the people seem to be good people. I have a large room in front to myself, and a very comfortable lodging-room. There are some other persons living in the house, but my establishment is all to myself. Charles is to be my servant; I am to take possession to-morrow, and present prospects are favorable.

I dined to-day at Mrs. Coyles. Her house is not yet full. She says she has never had so much difficulty in making up a mess. Mr. Williams, Mr. Baylies, Mr. McKee, and Mr. Storrs, are there, and nobody else at present. You will hardly be sorry to hear that poor old Mary is dead. She was sick all summer, and Mrs. Coyle says she was a perfect slave to her many months; not an unjust retribution. She died a month ago.

I am going up this evening to see the President.

Yours always, D. Webster.

P. S. I have your letter of Thanksgiving day and William's from New York.

MR. WEBSTER TO MRS. WEBSTER.

Washington, December 6, 1824.

My dear Love,—I am so happy as to have received yours of the 2d instant, and to hear of the health and happiness of you all.

For two days I have been busy in getting into my new lodgings; and by to-morrow evening hope to have all things in order. I am a good deal like Robinson Crusoe; I have an outer room, and an inner one for retreat, and a man Friday; and except Friday, am quite alone.

Thus far every thing looks well. The keepers of the house seem to be very obliging, neat, good people; and for convenience of work and business, I have never been better off here. I am sorry to find that my books have suffered much. They look as if they had all been tumbled into the cellar together. However, I hope in a day or two to get the mould off, though the scratches and bruises are likely to remain.

Mrs. Brown gave her first party last night. Having occasion to go to the President's, I called on my return. It was the assemblage pretty much of a Washington party of last year. Mrs. Johnston was there and spoke of you with great kindness, and inquired for you very particularly. Her youngest boy is six weeks old. Many other ladies, and gentleman also! asked after your welfare with much apparent interest, and one of them pronounced you a favorite of the whole city. Mr. Vaughan is unbounded in his thanks for what he calls our kindness at Boston, and by way of proof has invited me to a small dinner on Monday. Mrs. Lowell has a party on Friday, and this I believe is all the Washington news I have.

I thank Julia for her very good and kind letter, and Master D. for his imitation of an obedient medal. Whatsoever is properly obedient I hope he will continue successfully to imitate.

I shall write Julia soon. I hope Edward will not suffer me much longer to languish for a letter from his pen. A single one of his delicate and delightful scrawls would give me pleasure.

Adieu, my dear Grace, give my love "to all the house."

D. W.

MR. WEBSTER TO MRS. WEBSTER.

Washington, December 8, 1824, Friday evening.

My dear Love,—I am happy to have a letter to-day from Uncle William, under a Boston date. He seems to have had a rapid passage home, and informs me you were all well Monday morning.

I am at length pretty well settled in my new abode, and well pleased with it.

Together with this, I send a little box, in which, when you have taken all the papers off and opened it, you will find two little bits of articles[1] designed as presents. One of them, if you like it, you will place in your own cap; and the other in Col. Paige's ruffle. Give him a box on the ear, and tell him to be a good boy. The one intended for him is that with a single stone and pillar. If you do not fancy yours, you can return it to me in the same little box, and the proprietor will take it back again. If he does not fancy his, tell him he is no true man. Intending to put a thing of this kind in the Colonel's shirt, I sent for one, and the jeweller sent me two, to make a choice from. They both seemed pretty; and Mr. Wallenstein thought the one with three stones would be very proper for a lady; so I send both.

Mrs. Lowell has a party to-night, and if I am not too sleepy at eight o'clock, I intend to go.

I hope to hear from you to-morrow, as I have no letter to-day.

Adieu, with love to all.

Yours always, D. W.

MR. WEBSTER TO MR. HADDOCK.

Washington, December 23, 1824.

My dear Charles,—I have received your letter, and under present circumstances, you must expect only a brief answer.

I hope you will write your oration for the Phi Beta Kappa. The subject you speak of is a good one; but will lead you, I fancy, to this result, that is, that the period of literature "most adapted to form the character of those who are to bear a part in our future transactions," is the present period. This is an age of free, powerful, and intense thinking, rather than an age of fine writing. The wits of Anne's time were fit to polish the age, perhaps more than to advance it in positive acquirement. If I have leisure, I will sometime give you my thoughts on this matter at large, but I am so poor a manager of the great

[1] Two diamond pins.

treasure, time, that I never have on hand any stock to disburse. And this metaphor brings me to the other part of your letter, on which I have to say, that if you think you can do any thing useful with a thousand dollars, you may have that sum in the spring, or sooner if need be, on the following conditions: 1. You must give a note for it, with reasonable security. 2. The interest must be payable annually, and must be paid at the day without fail. And so long as this continues to be done, the money not to be called for, the principal, under six months' notice.

I am thus explicit with you, because you wish me to be so; and because, also, having a little money, and but a little, I am resolved on keeping it. My days of hard work have been many, too many to be repeated. I must now live, principally upon what I have got; and though I am willing to loan to my friends in preference to other modes of investment, in some cases, yet in no case can I do so on other conditions than as above.

Your hard-hearted uncle,

DANIEL WEBSTER.

EZEKIEL WEBSTER TO DANIEL WEBSTER.

December 28, 1824.

DEAR DANIEL,—The Concord Register, under its editorial head, gives a pretty correct account of the closing scene in our Senate. The Journal of the same day, last Saturday, has a statement under the hand of Mr. Haven. I think our Senate are in a promising way to be as immortal as the New York seventeen.

If a majority of our Senate are to be believed, Mr. Mason was chosen. When you have the facts, I should like very well to have an article appear in the National Intelligencer, on the extraordinary conduct of a majority who denied the inquiry into the mistake, &c. It should appear as editorial. If it could not appear in the Intelligencer, it might perhaps be inserted in the National Journal. A well-written article would count here.

Our object now is to secure such a Senate and House as will elect Mr. Mason next June. We feel the importance of having such a man of talents and integrity in our national councils.

We shall make an effort from a sense of duty. If you notice any thing which will have a favorable bearing, please to forward it.

We had a campaign of seven weeks. We kept our armor buckled on and slept upon our arms, and the New Hampshire troops never did themselves more credit since they fought at Bunker Hill and Bennington.

Yours, &c., E. WEBSTER.

MRS. WEBSTER TO MR. WEBSTER.

[Boston,] December 28, 1824.

I HAVE a great desire to write to you, my beloved husband, but I doubt if I can write legibly, as I can hold my pen but in my fingers.[1] I have just received your letter in answer to William, which told you that dear little Charley was no more. I have dreaded the hour that should destroy your hopes, but trust you will not let this event afflict you too much, and that we both shall be able to resign him without a murmur, happy in the reflection that he has returned to his Heavenly Father pure as I received him. It was an inexpressible consolation to me, when I contemplated him in his sickness, that he had not one regret for the past, nor one dread for the future; he was patient as a lamb during all his sufferings, and they were at last so great, I was happy when they were ended.

I shall always reflect on his brief life with mournful pleasure, and, I hope, remember with gratitude all the joy he gave me; and it has been great. And oh! how fondly did I flatter myself it would be lasting.

> "It was but yesterday, my child, thy little heart beat high;
> And I had scorned the warning voice that told me thou must die."

Dear little Charles! He sleeps alone under St. Paul's. I cannot express how much I regret that it did not occur to any one of us to have the dear remains of Grace removed. I thought much of it when the tomb of Mr. Sullivan was opened for Mrs. Sullivan's little boy. I regretted you were not here to consult upon

[1] Mrs. Webster had received an injury on the thumb of the right hand.

the subject. Oh, do not, my dear husband, talk of your own "final abode;" that is a subject I never can dwell on for a moment. With you here, my dear, I can never be desolate! O may Heaven in its mercy long preserve you! and that we may ever wisely improve every event, and yet rejoice together in this life, prays your ever affectionate

G. W.

I ought to mention William's unwearied attention and kindness to dear little Charles. His grief is great at the loss. Poor Nancy came last Friday; she is much afflicted that she did not come in time to see the dear little boy once more. She begs you to accept her sympathy and love.

MR. WEBSTER TO MR. MASON.

Washington, December 29, 1824.

My dear Sir,—We have heard of the adjournment of the Legislature of New Hampshire without having effected a choice of Senator. Seeing, towards the close, that the Senate were equally divided, I had some hope that a choice might be made. But, on a general view, the result is more favorable than there was reason to expect. So decisive a feeling in the House, and an equality in such a Senate, were circumstances showing very solid strength. I am sure, my dear Sir, you have no reason to regret the occurrences of the session. They have shown to the public your personal weight and consideration with the State; and they have also given an opportunity for the people of the State to learn your standing with the community generally. Public opinion, whenever expressed, has been uniformly in your favor. Here, I may assure you, all considerable men, of all parties and all associations, have felt and expressed the same wishes. Mr. Parrot is generally respected, and while he was of the number of candidates, being the present incumbent, a desire to have you here was naturally a little mitigated by a feeling of unwillingness to dispossess him. But, he being out of the case, if there were any who did not wish your success, there were none who ventured to express such feelings. Looking at the matter at a distance, and judging only from the operation of general causes, I should think your election was only postponed; nothing else can happen, certainly, if the House, now soon to be elected, be like its predecessor. I should not think it of first importance to turn out those Senators; if the House remain of the same opinion, the Senate must come to it.

I have been home from Virginia a week. My intention was to go to Richmond and Norfolk, from Monticello, but intelligence from home induced me to return, without accomplishing that part of my intention. We were two days at Mr. Madison's. He was very agreeable, and treated us with much hospitality. He keeps alive a stronger interest in passing events than his more advanced friend. Mrs. Madison is in perfect health, and remembers all her Washington acquaintances. At Mr. Jefferson's, we remained five days. This was something longer than our intention, but there came rains, which prevented our departure. Mr. Jefferson is a man of whom one may form a very just account, as to person and manners, from description and pictures. We met him in the road, and I knew him at once, although he was on horseback, something straighter, and freer from the debility of age than I had expected. We found him uniformly pleasant, social, and interesting. He talked less of present things than might be expected, although in the intercourse with gentlemen under his own roof, he did not keep back his opinions on men or things. But if I were to say what appeared to be the leading topics with him, and those to which his mind habitually turned itself, I should mention three: early anecdotes of revolutionary times; French society, politics, and literature such as they were when he was in France, and general literature; and the Virginia university. On these three general topics he has much to say, and he says it all well.

Since I returned here, I have not been in the way of hearing much said on the election of President. It would be difficult, in my opinion, to say which of the two leading candidates has the best chance, but if I were to express an opinion, such as it is, it would be at this moment that Mr. Adams's chance is best. New England, 6; New York, Delaware, Virginia, Georgia, North Carolina, Ohio, Louisiana, Illinois, out of these 14, I think it not unlikely Mr. Adams may get 13. He may also get New Jersey. It seems to me that there is, at this moment, rather a reaction against General Jackson; a feeling somewhat adverse to giving the Presidency to mere military character.

I propose to do nothing this session myself but a few useful and necessary things; such as to provide for the punishment of some crimes, now unprovided for, &c. My health is very good. You see what Mr. Randolph said about his letter. He had talked with some of the committee, and told a story, material or immaterial, which he thought they would confirm. I had not been spoken to; it occurred to me at the moment to be the right course to put the main question to him, coolly and quietly, and let him answer or evade it, as he chose. His course was open enough to remark, but I did not wish to have a quarrel, or to go further than the strict necessity of self-defence. Whether I judged right or not, I cannot tell.

I should be glad to hear from you, now that you have returned from your Concord expedition. Give my remembrance, affectionately, to your family, and believe me truly,

Yours,

DANIEL WEBSTER.

DANIEL WEBSTER TO EZEKIEL WEBSTER.

Washington, December 29, 1824.

DEAR EZEKIEL,—I have not heard from you for a long time, nor had much leisure to write since my return from Virginia. The information which has reached me from home[1] must have reached you sooner. I think of this loss with great grief; but I think also that you lost all your little boys; and I hope to sustain myself with the consciousness, that my blessings are still much more numerous than my afflictions. I wish you would sometimes write to my wife, it would give her great pleasure, as I think her affection for you is pretty much her first feeling out of her own family.

I had a pleasant journey, on many accounts, in Virginia. Saw many things and some men, and had a pretty fair opportunity of learning what Virginia is. In the ensuing month, I must pay

[1] Of the death of his youngest son, Charles.

some little attention to the public business. There is nothing of great importance or peculiar interest in which I expect to be concerned. February must be devoted to the court, and early in March I hope to be home.

I have seen your legislative proceedings through. You have come out about where we expected, except that having got unexpectedly half the "committee on the change of names," you unexpectedly, I should think, failed to get one more.

Every thing now depends on the new House. If that remains firm and strong, no matter who the Senators are they must come in. I do not see but you must go once more into the House, though I regret it, as I had laid out for a journey next June. Constancy to Mr. Mason seems to require it. I should like to know what you think of your congressional chance.

Does the law confine the votes to you and Mr. Healey?

Will this struggle for Senator make a pretty active election, and will that help or hurt you? You have districted the State. Does Merrimac County form precisely one district?

I wrote you, some time ago, for your and Mr. Mason's opinion about Bunker Hill; you have not given it to me. In hopes of hearing from you soon, I am, Yours,

D. WEBSTER.

MEMORANDUM

OF MR. JEFFERSON'S CONVERSATIONS.

[In December, eighteen hundred and twenty-four, Mr. Webster, with a party of friends, visited Mr. Madison and Mr. Jefferson at their respective residences in Virginia. He afterward noted down portions of the conversations, during the visit to Mr. Jefferson, which, as they are very entertaining and instructive, are subjoined.]

December, 1824.

Mr. Jefferson is now between eighty-one and eighty-two, above six feet high, of an ample, long frame, rather thin and spare. His head, which is not peculiar in its shape, is set rather forward on his shoulders; and his neck being long, there is, when he is walking or conversing, an habitual protrusion of it. It is still well covered with hair, which having been once red, and now turning gray, is of an indistinct sandy color.

His eyes are small, very light, and now neither brilliant nor striking. His chin is rather long, but not pointed. His nose small, regular in its outline, and the nostrils a little elevated. His mouth is well formed and still filled with teeth; it is strongly compressed, bearing an expression of contentment and benevolence. His complexion, formerly light and freckled, now bears the marks of age and cutaneous affection. His limbs are uncommonly long; his hands and feet very large, and his wrists of an extraordinary size. His walk is not precise and military, but easy and swinging. He stoops a little, not so much from age as from natural formation. When sitting, he appears short, partly from a rather lounging habit of sitting, and partly from the disproportionate length of his limbs.

His dress, when in the house, is a gray surtout coat, kerseymere stuff waistcoat, with an under one faced with some material of a dingy red. His pantaloons are very long and loose, and of the same color as his coat. His stockings are woollen either white or gray; and his shoes of the kind that bear his name. His whole dress is very much neglected, but not slovenly. He wears a common round hat. His dress, when on horseback, is a gray straight-bodied coat and a spencer of the same material, both fastened with large pearl buttons. When we first saw him, he was riding; and, in addition to the above articles of apparel, wore round his throat a knit white woollen tippet, in the place of a cravat, and black velvet gaiters under his pantaloons. His general appearance indicates an extraordinary degree of health, vivacity, and spirit. His sight is still good, for he needs glasses only in the evening. His hearing is generally good, but a number of voices in animated conversation confuses it.

Mr. Jefferson rises in the morning as soon as he can see the hands of his clock, which is directly opposite his bed, and examines his thermometer immediately, as he keeps a regular meteorological diary. He employs himself chiefly in writing till breakfast, which is at nine. From that time, till dinner, he is in his library, excepting that in fair weather he rides on horseback from seven to fourteen miles. Dines at four, returns to the drawing-room at six, when coffee is brought in, and passes the evening till nine in conversation. His habit of retiring at that hour is so strong, that it has become essential to his health and comfort. His diet is simple, but he seems restrained only by his taste. His breakfast is tea and coffee, bread always fresh from the oven, of which he does not seem afraid, with sometimes a slight accompaniment of cold meat. He enjoys his dinner well, taking with his meat a large proportion of vegetables. He has a strong preference for the wines of the continent, of which he has many sorts of excellent quality, having been more than commonly successful in his mode of importing and preserving them. Among others, we found the following, which are very rare in this country, and apparently not at all injured by transportation: L'Ednau, Muscat, Samian, and Blanchette de Limoux. Dinner is served in half Virginian, half French style, in good taste and abundance. No wine is put on the table till the cloth is removed.

In conversation, Mr. Jefferson is easy and natural, and apparently not ambitious; it is not loud, as challenging general attention, but usually addressed to the person next him. The topics, when not selected to suit the character and feelings of his auditor, are those subjects with which his mind seems particularly occupied; and these, at present, may be said to be science and letters, and especially the University of Virginia, which is coming into existence almost entirely from his exertions, and will rise, it is to be hoped, to usefulness and credit under his continued care. When we were with him, his favorite subjects were Greek and Anglo-Saxon, historical recollections of the times and events of the Revolution, and of his residence in France from 1783–4 to 1789.

[In the course of the evening when the preceding was written, from Mr. Webster's dictation, the following anecdotes from Mr. Jefferson's conversation were recalled and written down:—]

PATRICK HENRY.

Was originally a bar-keeper. He was married very young, and going into some business, on his own account, was a bankrupt before the year was out. When I was about the age of fifteen, I left the school here, to go to the college at Williamsburgh. I stopped a few days at a friend's in the county of Louisa. There I first saw and became acquainted with Patrick Henry. Having spent the Christmas holidays there, I proceeded to Williamsburgh. Some question arose about my admission, as my preparatory studies had not been pursued at the school connected with that institution. This delayed my admission about a fortnight, at which time Henry appeared in Williamsburgh, and applied for a license to practise law, having commenced the study of it at or subsequently to the time of my meeting him in Louisa. There were four examiners, Wythe, Pendleton, Peyton Randolph, and John Randolph; Wythe and Pendleton at once rejected his application. The two Randolphs, by his importunity, were prevailed upon to sign the license; and having obtained their signatures, he applied again to Pendleton, and after much entreaty and many promises of future study, succeeded in obtaining his. He then turned out for a practising lawyer. The first case which brought him into notice, was a contested election, in which he appeared as counsel before a committee of the House of Burgesses. His second was the Parsons cause, already well known. These and similar efforts soon obtained for him so much reputation, that he was elected a member of the legislature. He was as well suited to the times as any man ever was, and it is not now easy to say what we should have done without Patrick Henry. He was far before all in maintaining the spirit of the Revolution. His influence was most extensive with the members from the upper counties, and his boldness and their votes overawed and controlled the more cool or the more timid aristocratic gentlemen of the lower part of the State. His eloquence was peculiar, if indeed it should be called eloquence; for it was impressive and sublime, beyond what can be imagined. Although it was difficult when he had spoken to tell what he had said, yet, while he was speaking, it always seemed directly to the point. When he had spoken in opposition to my opinion, had produced a great effect, and I myself been highly delighted and moved, I have asked myself when he ceased: "What the d—l has he said?" I could never answer the inquiry. His person was of full size, and his manner and voice free and manly. His utterance neither very fast nor very slow. His speeches generally short, from a quarter to a half an hour. His pronunciation was vulgar and vicious, but it was forgotten while he was speaking.

He was a man of very little knowledge of any sort; he read nothing, and had no books. Returning one November from Albemarle court, he borrowed of me Hume's Essays, in two volumes, saying he should have leisure in the winter for reading. In the spring he returned them, and declared he had not been able to go further than twenty or thirty pages in the first volume. He wrote almost nothing—he could not write. The resolutions of '75, which have been ascribed to him, have by many been supposed to have been written by Mr. Johnson, who acted as his second on that occasion; but if they were written by Henry himself, they are not such as to prove any power of composition. Neither in politics nor in his profession was he a man of business; he was a man for debate only. His biographer says that he read Plutarch every year. I doubt whether he ever read a volume of it in his life. His temper was excellent, and he generally observed decorum in debate. On one or two occasions I have seen him angry, and his anger was terrible; those who witnessed it, were not disposed to rouse it again. In his opinions he was yielding and practicable and not disposed to differ from his friends. In private conversation, he was agreeable and facetious, and, while in genteel society, appeared to understand all the decencies and proprieties of it; but, in his heart, he preferred low society, and sought it as often as possible. He would hunt in the pine woods of Fluvannah, with overseers, and people of that description, living in a camp for a fortnight at a time without a change of raiment. I have often been astonished at his command of proper language; how he attained the knowledge of it, I never could find out, as he read so little and conversed little with educated men. After all, it must be allowed that he was our leader in the measures of the Revolution, in Virginia. In that respect more was due to him than any other person. If we had not had him we should probably have got on pretty well, as you did, by a number of men of nearly equal talents, but he left us all far behind. His biographer sent the sheets of his work to me as they were printed, and at the end asked for my opinion. I told him it would be a question hereafter, whether his work should be placed on the shelf of history or of panegyric. It is a poor book written in bad taste, and gives so imperfect an idea of Patrick Henry, that it seems intended to show off the writer more than the subject of the work.

Throughout the whole Revolution, Virginia and the four New England States acted together; indeed, they made the Revolution. Their five votes were always to be counted on; but they had to pick up the remaining two for a majority, when and where they could.

About the time of the Boston Port Bill, the patriotic feeling in Virginia had become languid and worn out, from some cause or other. It was thought by some of us to be absolutely necessary to excite the people; but we hardly knew the right means. At length it occurred to us to make grave faces and propose a fast. Some of us, who were the younger members of the assembly, resolved upon the measure. We thought Oliver Cromwell would be a good guide in such a case. So we looked into Rushworth, and drew up our resolutions after the most pious and praiseworthy examples. It would hardly have been in character for us to present them ourselves. We applied therefore to Mr. Nicholas, a grave and religious man; he proposed them in a set and solemn speech; some of us gravely seconded him, and the resolutions were passed unanimously. If any debate had occurred, or if they had been postponed for consideration, there was no chance that they would have been passed. The next morning Lord Bottetourt, the governor, summoned the assembly to his presence, and said to them: "I have heard of your proceedings of yesterday, and augur ill of their effects. His Majesty's interest requires that you be dissolved, and you are dissolved." Another election taking place soon afterwards, such was the spirit of the times, that every member of the assembly, without an individual exception, was re-elected.

Our fast produced very considerable effect. We all agreed to go home and see that preachers were provided in our counties, and notice given to our people. I came home to my own county, provided a preacher, and notified the people, who came together in great multitudes, wondering what it meant.

Lord Bottetourt was an honorable man. His government had authorized him to make certain assurances to the people here, which he made accordingly. He wrote to the minister that he had made these assurances, and that, unless he should be enabled to fulfil them, he must retire from his situation. This letter he sent unsealed to Peyton Randolph for his inspection. Lord Bottetourt's great respectability, his character for integrity, and his general popularity, would have enabled him to embarrass the measures of the patriots exceedingly. His death was, therefore, a fortunate event for the cause of the Revolution. He was the first governor in chief that had ever come over to Virginia. Before his time, we had received only deputies, the governor residing in England, with a salary of five thousand pounds, and paying his deputy one thousand pounds.

When Congress met, Patrick Henry and Richard Henry Lee opened the subject with great ability and eloquence. So much so, that Paca and Chase, delegates from Maryland, said to each other as they returned from the House: "We shall not be wanted here; those gentlemen from Virginia will be able to do every thing without us." But neither Henry nor Lee were men of business, and having made strong and eloquent general speeches, they had done all they could.

It was thought advisable that two papers should be drawn up, one, an address to the people of England, and the other, an address, I think, to the king. Committees were raised for these purposes, and Henry was at the head of the first, and Lee of the second.

When the address to the people of England was reported, Congress heard it with utter amazement. It was miserably written and good for nothing. At length Governor Livingston of New Jersey, ventured to break silence. After complimenting the author, he said he thought some other ideas might be usefully added to his draft of the address. Some such paper had been for a considerable time contemplated, and he believed a friend of his had tried his hand in the composition of one. He thought if the subject were again committed, some improvement in the present draft might be made. It was accordingly recommitted, and the address which had been alluded to by Governor Livingston, and which was written by John Jay, was reported by the committee, and adopted as it now appears.

It is, in my opinion, one of the very best state papers which the Revolution produced.

Richard Henry Lee moved the Declaration of Independence, in pursuance of the resolutions of the assembly of Virginia, and only because he was the oldest member of the Virginia delegation.

The Declaration of Independence was written in a house on the north side of Chestnut street, Philadelphia, between third and fourth, not a corner house. Heiskell's tavern, which has been pointed out as the house, is not the true one.

For depth of purpose, zeal, and sagacity, no man in Congress exceeded, if any equalled Sam. Adams; and none did more than he to originate and sustain revolutionary measures in Congress. But he could not speak; he had a hesitating, grunting manner.

John Adams was our Colossus on the floor. He was not graceful, nor elegant, nor remarkably fluent; but he came out, occasionally, with a power of thought and expression that moved us from our seats.

I feel much alarmed at the prospect of seeing General Jackson President. He is one of the most unfit men I know of for such a place. He has had very little respect for laws or constitutions, and is, in fact, an able military chief. His passions are terrible. When I was President of the Senate he was a Senator; and he could never speak on account of the rashness of his feelings. I have seen him attempt it repeatedly, and as often choke with rage. His passions are no doubt cooler now; he has been much tried since I knew him, but he is a dangerous man.

When I was in France, the Marquis de Chasteleux carried me over to Buffon's residence in the country, and introduced me to him.

It was Buffon's practice to remain in his study till dinner time, and receive no visitors under any pretence; but his house was open and his grounds, and a servant showed them very civilly, and invited all strangers and friends to remain to dine. We saw Buffon in the garden, but carefully avoided him; but we dined with him, and he proved himself then, as he always did, a man of extraordinary powers in conversation. He did not declaim; he was singularly agreeable.

I was introduced to him as Mr. Jefferson, who, in some notes on Virginia, had combated some of his opinions. Instead of entering into an argument, he took down his last work, presented it to me, and said, "When Mr. Jefferson shall have read this, he will be perfectly satisfied that I am right."

Being about to embark from Philadelphia for France, I observed an uncommonly large panther skin at the door of a hatter's shop. I bought it for half a Jo (sixteen dollars) on the spot, determining to carry it to France to convince Monsieur Buffon of his mistake in relation to this animal; which he had confounded with the cougar. He acknowledged his mistake, and said he would correct it in his next volume.

I attempted also to convince him of his error in relation to the common deer, and the moose of America; he having confounded our deer with the red deer of Europe, and our moose with the reindeer. I told him that our deer had horns two feet long; he replied with warmth, that if I could produce a single specimen, with horns one foot long, he would give up the question. Upon this I wrote to Virginia for the horns of one of our deer, and obtained a very good specimen, four feet long. I told him also that the reindeer could walk under the belly of our moose; but he entirely scouted the idea. Whereupon I wrote to General Sullivan of New Hampshire. I desired him to send me the bones, skin, and antlers of our moose, supposing they could easily be procured by him. Six months afterwards my agent in England advised me that General Sullivan had drawn on him for forty guineas. I had forgotten my request, and wondered why such a draft had been made, but I paid it at once. A little later came a letter from General Sullivan, setting forth the manner in which he had complied with my request. He had been obliged to raise a company of nearly twenty men, had made an excursion towards the White Hills, camping out many nights, and had at last after many difficulties caught my moose, boiled his bones in the desert, stuffed his skin and remitted him to me. This accounted for my debt and convinced Mr. Buffon. He promised in his next volume to set these things right also, but he died directly afterwards.

Madame Houdetot's society was one of the most agreeable in Paris when I was there. She inherited the materials of which it was composed from Madame de Terrier and Madame Geoffrin. St. Lambert was always there, and it was generally believed that every evening on his return home, he wrote down the substance of the conversations he had held there with D'Alembert, Diderot, and the other distinguished persons, who frequented her house. From these conversations he made his books.

I knew the Baron de Grignon very well; he was quite ugly, and one of his legs was shorter than the other; but he was the most agreeable person in French society, and his opinion was always considered decisive in matters relating to the theatre and painting. His persiflage was the keenest and most provoking I ever knew.

Madame Necker was a very sincere and excellent woman, but she was not very pleasant in conversation, for she was subject to what in Virginia we call the "Budge," that is, she was very nervous and fidgety. She could rarely remain long in the same place, or converse long on the same subject. I have known her get up from table five or six times in the course of the dinner, and walk up and down her saloon to compose herself.

Marmontel was a very amusing man. He dined with me every Thursday for a long time, and I think told some of the most agreeable stories I ever heard in my life. After his death, I found almost all of them in his memoirs, and I dare say he told them so well because he had written them before in his book.

I wish Mr. Pickering would make a radical lexicon. It would do more than any thing else in the present state of the matter, to promote the study of Greek among us. Jones's Greek Lexicon is very poor. I have been much disappointed in it. The best I have ever used is the Greek and French one by Planche.

DANIEL WEBSTER TO EZEKIEL WEBSTER.

Washington, January 13, 1825.

I AM much obliged to you for yours of the 10th. It gave me much information that I wanted. I trust you have not forgotten to write me again, having seen Mr. Mason at the court.

I hope you will pay all proper attention to your approaching election. The Patriot man, I perceive, is very angry, and will be very active. If you save the House you will save all. I hope that public opinion everywhere for Mr. Mason, will have some effect on the people of New Hampshire.

As the 9th February approaches, we begin to hear a little more about the election. I think some important indications will be made soon. A main inquiry is, in what direction Mr. Clay and his friends will move. There would seem at present to be some reason to think they will take a part finally for Mr. Adams. This will not necessarily be decisive, but it will be very important. After all, I cannot predict results. I believe Mr. Adams might be chosen if he or his friends would act somewhat differently. But if he has good counsellors, I know not who they are. If Mr. Clay's friends should join Mr. Crawford's, it would probably put him ahead of Mr. Adams, the first ballot, and, that being done, I know not what might follow.

I should like to know your opinion of what is proper to be done in two or three contingencies.

1. If on the first or any subsequent ballot Mr. Adams falls behind Mr. Crawford, and remains so a day or two, shall we hold out to the end of the chapter, or shall we vote for one of the highest?

2. If for one of the highest, say Jackson and Crawford, for which?

3. Is it advisable, under any circumstances, to hold out and leave the chair to Mr. Calhoun?

4. Would or would not New England prefer conferring the power on Calhoun, to a choice of General Jackson?

On these and other similar points, I want your full opinion by the first of next month.

I shall write you again in a day or two.

Yours, D. W.

DANIEL WEBSTER TO EZEKIEL WEBSTER.

January 15, 1825.

I HAVE written to the boys,[1] that I will help them a little, if you are satisfied it would do them good. I have told them that one of them would do well to come to Boscawen. I am willing to give them outright what I can afford; or to help them in any other way you may think best. If two hundred dollars each would certainly pay their debts, it is pity they should not have it. Please write them an encouraging word; and if they come down let them have what you think proper; preferring, if it can be done, to make a small gift rather than a large loan. I would be willing to give them one hundred dollars each.

Yours, D. W.

MRS. WEBSTER TO MR. WEBSTER.

Saturday Morning, January 22, 1825.

MY DEAR HUSBAND,—I was sitting alone in my chamber reflecting on the brief life of our sainted little boy, when your letter came enclosing those lines of yours, which to a "mother's eye" are precious. O! my husband, have not some of our brightest hopes perished! "Our fairest flowers are indeed blossoms gathered for the tomb." But do not, my dear husband, do not let these afflictions weigh too heavily upon you; those dear children who had such strong holds on us while here, now allure us to Heaven.

"On us with looks of love they bend,
For us the Lord of life implore,
And oft from sainted bliss descend,
Our wounded spirits to restore."

Farewell, my beloved husband! I have not time to write more, only to say I regret you have lost the pleasure of Mr. and Mrs.

[1] Nephews residing in Canada.

Ticknor's society, which you so much need. I fear Mrs. Dwight is not much benefited by her voyage, so the last accounts appear; though at first they thought her better.

The children are tolerably well, though not free from colds.

Your ever affectionate, G. W.

LINES ON THE DEATH OF HIS SON CHARLES, BY MR. WEBSTER.

My son, thou wast my heart's delight,
Thy morn of life was gay and cheery;
That morn has rushed to sudden night,
Thy father's house is sad and dreary.

I held thee on my knee, my son!
And kissed thee laughing, kissed thee weeping;
But ah! thy little day is done,
Thou'rt with thy angel sister sleeping.

The staff, on which my years should lean,
Is broken, ere those years come o'er me;
My funeral rites thou shoulds't have seen,
But thou art in the tomb before me.

Thou rear'st to me no filial stone,
No parent's grave with tears beholdest;
Thou art my ancestor, my son!
And stand'st in Heaven's account the oldest.

On earth my lot was soonest cast,
Thy generation after mine,
Thou hast thy predecessor past;
Earlier eternity is thine.

I should have set before thine eyes
The road to Heaven, and showed it clear;
But thou untaught springs't to the skies,
And leav'st thy teacher lingering here.

Sweet Seraph, I would learn of thee,
And hasten to partake thy bliss!

And oh! to thy world welcome me,
As first I welcomed thee to this.

Dear Angel, thou art safe in heaven;
No prayers for thee need more be made;
Oh! let thy prayers for those be given
Who oft have blessed thy infant head.

My Father! I beheld thee born,
And led thy tottering steps with care;
Before me risen to Heaven's bright morn,
My son! My Father! guide me there.

MR. WARFIELD TO MR. WEBSTER.

(CONFIDENTIAL.)

Washington, February 3, 1825.

MY DEAR SIR,—I am induced from the good feelings which I trust have always existed between us, to make to you this communication. The approaching presidential election gives me great anxiety. I am peculiarly situated; for although directly and indirectly I have been applied to, at least, I am sure, in a hundred instances, I have never expressed to a human being the vote I intend to give. The representation, as you know, is composed of nine members from Maryland; every member except myself has expressed his opinion. The awful responsibility of the vote of that State may devolve on me. Nay, more, situated as the votes of the different States are, Maryland may make the President on the first ballot. Now, Sir, I am oppressed with this difficulty. Those with whom I am in the habit of associating in Maryland, are for the most part called Federal, and they constantly express to me their apprehensions that, should Mr. Adams be the President, he will administer the government on party considerations; that the old landmarks of party distinction will be built up; that an exclusion of all participation in office will be enforced with regard to those who have hitherto been denominated Federals. I cannot for my own part believe that such a course would be pursued. I should trust that Mr. Adams's administration would be conducted on liberal and independent grounds; and that, regardless of names, he would not deny to talent, integrity, and competency a due participation. For in truth I consider all the old party distinctions to exist only in the name. I shall feel particularly obliged if you will give me your candid opinion on these points.

I am with true esteem, yours,

HENRY R. WARFIELD.

MR. WEBSTER TO MR. WARFIELD.

House of Representatives, February 5, 1825.

MY DEAR SIR,—I have received your note of yesterday, and reflected on its contents, and am very willing to answer it, as far as I can, without incurring the danger of misleading you in the discharge of the delicate and important trust belonging to your present situation.

I must remark in the first place, that my acquaintance with Mr. Adams, although friendly and respectful, I hope, on both sides, certainly so on mine, is not particular. I can say nothing, therefore, on the present occasion, by any authority derived from him.

Being in a situation, however, not altogether unlike your own, I have naturally been anxious, like yourself, to form an opinion as to what would be his course of administration, in regard to the subject alluded to by you. For myself, I am satisfied, and shall give him my vote, cheerfully and steadily. And I am ready to say that I should not do so, if I did not believe that he would administer the government on liberal principles, not excluding Federalists, as such, from his regard and confidence.

I entertain this feeling not because I wish to see any number of offices, or any particular office, given to those who have been called Federalists; nor because there is a number of such individuals, or any one, that I particularly desire to see employed in the public service; but because the time is come, in my opinion, when we have a right to know whether a particular political name, in reference to former parties, is, of itself, to be regarded as cause of exclusion.

I wish to see nothing like a portioning, parcelling out, or distributing offices of trust among men called by different denominations. Such a proceeding would be to acknowledge and to regard the existence of distinctions; whereas my wish is, that distinctions should be disregarded. What I think just and reasonable to be expected, is, that by some one clear and distinct case, it may be shown that the distinction above alluded to does not operate as cause of exclusion. Some such case will doubtless present itself, and may be embraced, probably, in proper time and manner, if thought expedient to embrace it, without prejudice to the pretensions or claims of individuals. The government will then be left at liberty to call to the public service the best ability and the purest character. It will then be understood that the field is open, and that men are to stand according to their individual merits. So far as this, I think it just to expect the next administration to go. At any rate, it is natural to wish to know what may probably be expected in this regard.

While with these sentiments, which, my dear Sir, are as strong in my breast as they can be in yours, I am willing to support Mr. Adams, and to give him my vote and influence, I must again remind you that my judgment is made up, not from any understanding or communication with him, but from general considerations; from what I think I know of his liberal feelings, from his good sense and judgment, and from the force of circumstances. I assure you, very sincerely, that I have a full confidence that Mr. Adams's administration will be just and liberal towards Federalists as towards others; and I need not say that there is no individual who would feel more pain than myself, if you and the rest of our friends should ever find reason to doubt the solidity of the foundation on which this confidence rests.

NOTE. I read this, precisely as it now stands here, to Mr. Adams, on the evening of February 4. He said, when I had got through, that the letter expressed his general sentiments, and such as he was willing to have understood as his sentiments. There was one particular, however, on which he wished to make a remark. The letter seemed to require him, or expect him, to place one Federalist in the administration. Here I interrupted him, and told him he had misinterpreted the writer's meaning.

That the letter did not speak of those appointments called cabinet appointments particularly, but of appointments generally. With that understanding he said the letter contained his opinions, and he should feel it his duty, by some such appointment, to mark his desire of disregarding party distinctions. He thought either of them, if elected, must necessarily act liberally in this respect. In consequence of this conversation, I interlined, in this letter, the words, "in proper time and manner." I made no other alteration in it.

DANIEL WEBSTER TO EZEKIEL WEBSTER.

February 4, [1825.]

We have a little excitement here, as you will see; but there is less than there seems. Mr. Clay's ill-judged card has produced an avowal, or sort of avowal, which makes the whole thing look ridiculous. Mr. Kremer is a man with whom one would think of having a shot, about as soon as with your neighbor, Mr. Simeon Atkinson, whom he somewhat resembles.

Mr. Adams, I believe, and have no doubt, will be chosen, probably the first day.

Judge L. means to go home so as to be at Haverhill, C. C. P. He has received Mr. Kelly's letter, and expresses, in general terms, friendly feelings towards him.

How do you come on in your various matters?

Yours, D. W.

DANIEL WEBSTER TO EZEKIEL WEBSTER.

Washington, February 16, 1825.

Dear Ezekiel,—You are acquainted with all the particulars of the election. The appointments are now under consideration. Mr. Clay will be Secretary of State; Mr. Southard, &c. will remain. For the War, De Witt Clinton, John W. Taylor, and Mr. McLean, the present Postmaster-General, are spoken of.

For Treasury, Mr. Cheves. I know not now how these appointments will go; but, perhaps, may know before evening. If there is any faith in man, we shall have a liberal administration. I think it not unlikely that if it were pressed, there might be a Federalist in the cabinet, but our friends are not at all satisfied that such a measure would be discreet at this moment. No doubt the true course at present is to maintain the administration, and give it a fair chance. We may be deceived, but if we are, it will be gross deception.

I have strong hopes that Mr. Mason will be elected, unless your spring elections should go very bad. He will stand as a friend to the government and the new elected President, and his principal opponent will be *e contrà*. In this state of the question causes will then act strongly which last session only acted feebly. Mr. Dinsmore will not be chosen, I predict. It will lie between Mr. Mason and Mr. Parrott.

I see by the New Hampshire papers that the State is getting a little excited. I should like to hear how things look, and to know whether every body acquiesces in the election quietly.

Yours,

D. W.

Evening,—I have more to say than a P. S. will suffice for. Go on; support Mr. A. Get elected if you can. There is no great danger of Mr. Mason; there is more time in his case. Every thing looks well.

D. W.

MR. MADISON TO MR. WEBSTER.

Montpelier, February 25, 1825.

DEAR SIR,—I must not let the session of Congress close without returning my thanks for the printed documents for which I was indebted, as appeared, to your friendly politeness. Though they find their way to me through the daily vehicles, there is an advantage in possessing them in a more compact as well as less perishable form. Among the characteristic attributes of our government is its frankness in giving publicity to proceedings, elsewhere locked up as arcana of state; and it will always be happy when they will so well bear the light; or rather, so much contribute to the reputation of our own country and the edification of others.

Be pleased to accept, Sir, assurances of my high esteem and cordial respect.

JAMES MADISON.

DANIEL WEBSTER TO EZEKIEL WEBSTER.

(EXTRACT.)

Washington, March 15, [1825.]

DEAR EZEKIEL,—I expected a letter from you to-day, with regard to the election. As it has not come, I infer that you have little good to communicate; an inference in which I am strengthened by seeing the disagreeable result in Portsmouth.

I still believe that this is but the last gasp of selfishness and party, and that better days are coming. At any rate, he who loses only an office, loses nothing that he need break his heart about. I should have been glad that we should have been here a year or two together, but it is not essential to the happiness of either of us.

* * * * * * *

I am busy, very busy, in the court, and shall be to the moment of my departure.

Yours truly, as always,

D. WEBSTER.

MR. WEBSTER TO JUDGE STORY.

April 8, 1825.

MY DEAR SIR,—I enclose you a letter I received yesterday, for you, from Mr. Palfrey.

You will have heard of the bloodless duel; I regret it very much; but the conduct of Mr. Randolph has been such that I suppose it was thought that it could not longer be tolerated. We have had something like it in the House of Representatives, but not so bad. In truth, the manner of debate adopted by certain gentlemen in both Houses, is without a parallel in the history of this country.

We have done nothing since you left. The bankruptcy has not been called up. The Senate do little or nothing. Mr. Randolph occupies about three hours every day, be the subject what it will; and then the Senate adjourns. I know not what will be the result, but public business has come pretty much to a stand. I intend to report a bankrupt bill to our House this week.

The Senate has agreed to Rowan's amendment to the judiciary bill. I presume we shall reject it; and if the Senate adhere, I trust the bill will be lost. If it passes, I think the appointments will be satisfactory. We hope to finish Panama in our House by Wednesday.

The Massachusetts claim has been discussed. Some heats were created, but in general the claim has gained much by the discussion. Almost all, or quite all, of the active opposition, has come from a certain quarter, and has been made, no doubt, with a view to certain effects.

Mrs. Webster desires her remembrance; and your friend Edward is particular in his love to Judge Story.

Yours, always truly,

DANIEL WEBSTER.

MR. WEBSTER TO MR. ISAAC P. DAVIS.

April 11, 1825.

DEAR SIR,—I shall be very glad to get something done for your cordage if I can. If Mr. De Wolfe's bill comes down from the Senate, we will do what we can for it.

I have grown very tired, and want to go home. I cannot think of failing to hold the Sandwich court, at the usual season.

Mrs. Webster, and the children, and Jeanette are all well, and all send their love to Mrs. Jackson, Mrs. Davis, and yourself and boys. Ned, however, says he has sent so much love to every body, that he has none left.

Notwithstanding the mildness of the winter, March has been cold, and the spring is backward. I hope we shall rise by the 10th or 12th of May. I know not what to say about the tariff, except that there is an increased probability that it will not pass, even through our House. There are members who are influenced by their instructions, or afraid of their constituents; otherwise there would be, I have no doubt, a decided majority for giving the bill its repose upon the table.

Yours always,

D. W.

MR. WEBSTER TO CHANCELLOR KENT.

Boston, May 23, 1825.

MY DEAR SIR,—You know Judge Smith of New Hampshire, at least in his public and professional character. I wish to recommend him to you, on the score of private worth and social qualities. There are few men in the world I think more to your taste.

I entertain for him the highest regard, and true gratitude. When I came to the bar, he was chief justice of the State. It was a day of "the gladsome light" of Jurisprudence. His friends, and I was one of them, thought he must be made governor.

For this office we persuaded him to leave the bench, and that same "gladsome light" cheered us no longer. *Ponto nox incubat atra.* I need not continue Virgil, nor say how the east wind, and the north wind, and the stormy south wind, all rushed out together, and what a shipwreck they made both of law and parties.

Judge Smith has since occasionally practised the law, but for some years has lived entirely, I believe, with his books and his friends. He knows every thing about New England, having studied much its history and its institutions; and as to the law, he knows so much more of it than I do, or ever shall, that I forbear to speak on that point.

Indeed, I am ashamed to find myself commending to you one so well known to you and all other good men; but hearing he was about to visit your city, I could not resist the temptation afforded by the occasion of mentioning my regard for him, and of recommending him to the regard and friendship of yourself and friends.

Yours, always truly,

DANIEL WEBSTER.

MR. WEBSTER TO MRS. GEORGE BLAKE.

Niagara Falls, July 15, 1825.

My dear Mrs. Blake,—It is one of my most agreeable duties, before leaving this place, to write to you, to tell you how much we have admired the great spectacle here, and how sincerely we have lamented every hour that you were not with us, to partake and increase our pleasure. This is the third day of our being here; the weather has been uniformly fine, and we have seen the Falls under all advantages. You have of course read many accounts of this Fall, to which no account can do justice; and although I am disposed to say something on the subject, I expect no better success than others who have undertaken the description.

The Niagara River, at the moment of leaving Lake Erie, is one mile in width. It runs nearly directly north with a rapidity of six miles and a half an hour. We crossed it from the east side to the west, at the village of Black Rock, two miles and a half below the end of the lake. Here its current is less rapid, running probably about four miles an hour. This river, being fed from such vast reservoirs above, is subject to little variation in the height of its waters. Its annual rise does not exceed a foot; and it may give some idea of the immense distance through which its waters have flowed, to mention that the spring "fresh" is not felt here till July. It is now just about the time of high water. It is truly a noble river; rapid, but smooth and glassy; always full, but never overflowing:—

"Tho' deep, yet clear; tho' gentle, yet not dull;
"Strong, without rage; without o'erflowing, full."

We passed down its western shore, along the bank close to the water's edge, and over a level road. Lake Erie is 330 feet higher than Lake Ontario; but in descending the river from Lake Erie, one perceives no very considerable or great descent, although the current is all the way rapid, till we get nearly down to the Falls. A little below the village of Black Rock, perhaps about five miles from Lake Erie, the river divides into two channels, forming a large island in the centre, called Grand Isle, about twelve miles long, and in some places six or seven broad. This island terminates, and the two channels unite again, just at the head of what are called The Rapids, a mile or a mile and a half above the great Falls. These Rapids are a succession of cascades, spreading over the whole river, of different and various heights and appearances, rendering the whole breadth of the stream, which is here not less than two miles, white with foam. They would form a fine object, if there were nothing near which called the attention another way. Midway of these Rapids is Goat Island, which divides the river into two unequal parts, about one third in breadth being on the Eastern, or American side, and two thirds on the Western, or British. This island runs down to the very brink of the Falls, and there terminates in a perpendicular precipice, or wall of rock, which is part of the same great declivity over which the river pours. This island thus divides the river, so that it falls over the precipice in two sheets. The length of the Fall on the American side is estimated at 380 yards,—then the distance across the end of Goat Island, 330 yards,—and the length of the fall on the British side, 700 yards. On the east side of Goat Island, is another small island; I know not its name, but it is separated from Goat Island by twenty or thirty yards of water, which pours over here and makes a beautiful object by itself, being wholly separate and distinct from the two great Falls. The Fall is reckoned to be highest on the American side, being there 165 feet; and on the British side 150. Vastly the greatest portion of water, I should think three fourths or even more, runs over on the British side.

I have seen no description which correctly represents the line of these Falls. I, also, shall fail in attempting to describe it to you; but, nevertheless, I will make the attempt. But, in the first place, you must remember that the land, or country, does not descend, or fall off, at the Falls. From the end of Lake Erie to Lewiston, which is seven miles below the Falls, the surface of the earth is uncommonly level; but here, at Lewiston, is a great descent, from the level of Lake Erie to that of Lake Ontario. Therefore, as you come along down the river from Lake Erie, when you get to the Falls, the river seems to fall away from your feet, and to pitch right down into the earth. Many miles before you reach the Falls, you see the mist or spray rising up like a cloud. But this does not seem to be rising from the earth into the air, so much as from the centre of the earth to the surface. It appears to be coming out of the ground. From the bottom of the Falls to Lewiston, seven miles, the whole channel of the river is one great trough, 100 or 150 feet deep, with sides of perpendicular rock. This has given currency to the opinion that the Falls were once seven miles lower down than they now are; and that the force of the water, in time has worn away the rocks and forced the Falls back to their present position.

Now, as to the line of the Falls, as it appears to me, at the moment of writing this, from the upper rooms in Forsyth's Hotel. The American Fall may be said to be straight. There are some little inequalities in the line, but on the whole it is very regular; next comes the little island, near Goat Island, a little advanced beyond the great American Fall; then the little separate Cascade, a little more advanced; then the end of Goat Island, about on a line with the little Cascade; and then the great British Fall. The line of this Fall, leaving the point of Goat Island, advances, makes a bend forward, a sort of gentle sweep or graceful arch, perhaps two hundred yards in length, then retreats again till it gets a little further back than the point of the island, where it set out, and making now an angle or rather a curve, it goes downward, and across the river, and joins the western bank at Table Rock, which is a good deal below the end of Goat Island. This last-mentioned bend or curve in the line of the Falls, is commonly called the Horseshoe; for no reason, that I know of, except that a horseshoe is a ready figure to express any curving line. On the earth at the bottom of the Falls, among the rocks, I succeeded, with a walking-stick six feet long, in drawing pretty accurately the line of the Falls. I cannot do it on paper. The enclosed is as near as I can come.

But I wish now to state something which I have seen mentioned in no printed account, but which is absolutely essential to any correct understanding of the subject. At the very foot of the Falls the whole river turns suddenly to the right; and runs off in that direction. So that the water which falls over on the British side, runs along at the foot of the American Fall. The American Fall faces, exactly and completely, the western bank of the river. As you walk along down from the Table Rock, you have the American Fall precisely in front. Just at the bottom of the American Fall is the ferry. We land at the very edge of this Fall. But, on the other side, we set out near half a mile below the Table Rock. The whole, I think, may be understood, by bearing in mind that, at the very Fall, the river makes a sudden turn to the right, so that all the Fall, out of the Horseshoe, and especially the American Fall, fronts not down the river, but directly across it.

I am afraid, after all, my dear lady, that you are little the wiser for this attempt at description. I can draw nothing; but if I find you in the dark on the subject when I get home, I think, with a piece of shingle and a penknife, I may explain my ideas.

The Falls are seen from many different points, and the views are very various. I write this, in an upper parlor, in Forsyth's Hotel, on the Canada side; the entire line of the Falls is in my view, but the whole is below me. The view, however, of the great curve, or Horseshoe, is very good from this spot; I think as perfect as from any point. I can see the water as it pours over, nearly all round the semicircle. The sheet has all appearances of being very thick; probably, it is thought, fifteen or twenty feet. Its surface, as it falls over, is streaked with alternate white, caused by the foam, and the most brilliant emerald.

In descending to get a nearer view, we go down a steep hill, or what may be called the upper part of the bank, about 100 feet. This is about as much descent as the river makes in the Rapids above the Falls, so that, having come down this distance, we are on the level of the water at the head of the Falls. Here are several acres of flat land, between the foot of this hill and the water's edge, thickly covered with trees and shrubbery. A planked walk leads along towards the river, and I do not know that my attention has been more strongly arrested by any thing than by the view which occurs, as we walk along this path. The water is seen rather suddenly and unexpectedly through a vista, or avenue of trees. It is nearly, and seems to be quite, on your own level. Great and unbroken ridges of billows come hastening and bounding along, and rush forward to the precipice, which, as yet, the spectator does not see. The magnitude, the strength, and the hurry of the mighty stream, create deep and instant consternation. Proceeding onward, and turning a little down the stream, we come to the water's edge, at the top of the Fall. The water is even with the bank, and we can wash our hands in safety in the river. Going along, now, on the Table Rock, we have what is generally thought the best view of the whole Falls.

Fronting us is the American Fall, and the little Cascade; further to the right Goat Island, and the commencement by it of the British Fall; and further to our right is the great circular Fall, or Horseshoe, which will hardly allow the eyes to be withdrawn long enough to look at any thing else. You may stand by the water just where it falls off, and if your head does not swim, you may proceed to the brink of Table Rock, and look down into the gulf beneath. This is all foam, and froth, and spray. As you stand here, it looks as if all the water of the globe was collected round this circle, and pouring down here into the centre of the earth. As we stood to-day at noon, on the projecting point of Table Rock, we looked over into this abyss, and far beneath our feet, arched over this tremendous aggregate of water, foam, and vapor, we saw a perfect and radiant rainbow. This ornament of heaven does not seem out of place, in being half-way up the sheet of the glorious cataract. It looked as if the skies themselves paid homage to this stupendous work of nature. From Table Rock, or a little further down, a winding staircase is constructed, down which we descend from the level of Table Rock, 95 feet. This brings us to the bottom of the perpendicular rock, and from this place we descend 50 or 60 feet further, over large fragments of rock and other substance, down to the edge of the river. We went this afternoon a little lower down the river than the upper staircase, almost indeed down to the ferry, and getting out on a rock, in the edge of the river, we thought the view of the whole Falls the best we had obtained. If, at the bottom of the staircase, instead of descending further, we choose to turn to the right, and go up the stream, keeping close at the foot of the Table Rock, or the perpendicular bank, we soon get to the foot of the Fall, and approach the edge of the falling mass. It is easy to go in behind, for a little distance, between the falling water and the rock over which it is precipitated; this cannot be done, however, without being entirely wet. From within this cavern there issues a wind, occasionally very strong, and bringing with it such showers and torrents of spray, that we are soon as wet as if we had come over the Falls with the water. As near to the

Fall in this place as you can well come, is perhaps the spot on which the mind is most deeply impressed with the whole scene. Over our heads hangs a fearful rock, projecting out like an unsupported piazza. Before us is a hurly-burly of waters, too deep to be fathomed, too irregular to be described, shrouded in too much mist to be clearly seen. Water, vapor, foam, and the atmosphere, are all mixed up together, in sublime confusion. By our side, down comes this world of green and white waters, and pours into the invisible abyss. A steady, unvarying, low-toned roar, thunders incessantly upon our ears; as we look up, we think some sudden disaster has opened the seas, and that all their floods are coming down upon us at once; but we soon recollect, that what we see is not a sudden or violent exhibition, but the permanent and uniform character of the object which we contemplate. There, the grand spectacle has stood, for centuries, from the creation even, as far as we know, without change. From the beginning, it has shaken, as it now does, the earth and the air; and its unvarying thunder existed before there were human ears to hear it. Reflections like these, on the duration and permanency of this grand object, naturally arise, and contribute much to the deep feeling which the whole scene produces. We cannot help being struck with a sense of the insignificance of man and all his works, compared with what is before us.

> "Lo! where it comes, like an eternity,
> As if to sweep down all things in its track!"

I shall not, my dear Mrs. Blake, attempt any full description of this scene; and still less to represent its whole effect on the mind. It must be seen; it is something which speaks to the senses; no description can set it forth.

The ferry, as I believe I have already stated, leaves the British shore near half a mile below the Fall on that side, and passes over to the American shore just at the lower edge of the Fall there. The view of the whole Fall, from the boat, is very perfect; as much so, perhaps, as from any spot. From the landing-place on the American side, a new and well-built staircase brings us up, close along by the falling water, to the top of the bank. We there walk along up the river, and see that the American branch is not only less wide but much less deep than the British. The Cascades, however, are beautiful on this side.

About half a mile above the Fall a good bridge is thrown over to Goat Island. This is a charming place, containing sixty or seventy acres of ground covered with large and handsome trees. We may walk all round it, and see the Rapids to great advantage, in both divisions of the stream. Its lower end also presents some good views of the Falls. We see here that the American Fall is not so straight as it seems from the other side, but has various projections and indentations. The little stream, running at the east corner of Goat Island, and forming, as it falls, the little Cascade, is quite accessible, and might almost be waded over. In the morning the bow is very fine, from this point. I saw one this morning caused by the spray from the American Fall. It seemed to spring up from the little house in which the ferry-man lives, on the British side, and swelling up along the Bank it came down again near the Table Rock. The depth of the water in the river below the Falls, is very great. It is said to have been lately sounded, by public authority, where the ferry is, and found to be more than 300 feet. It would seem to be dangerous, where the boat passes, but I believe it is not so. The water is a good deal agitated, but it does not run with any current too strong to be encountered.

The rock over which the waters of the Cataract fall is limestone. No doubt the same sort of rock underlies this whole country, for a great extent. The banks of the river, and the wall over which the Falls run, show great regularity of formation. In building the stairs, on the American side, lately, the workmen have blown away the rock in the side of the bank, for some distance, to make room for the staircase, and here the successive strata are seen, generally from six inches to three feet thick, laid up with the precision of masonry.

We have been here now the whole or a part of three days; and although our eyes are not satisfied with seeing, yet some of us complain of weary limbs, from walking about so much, and going down and climbing up the banks so often.

We shall leave probably to-morrow. It will not be without pain that I part from the Falls.

And now, my dear Mrs. Blake, let me repeat how much we lament that you and your husband have not been with us on this visit. Our whole party desire their best respects to you both. Mrs. Webster particularly sends her love to you, and thinks you will deserve well, if your patience holds out through this long letter. However that may be, I assure you I have had much pleasure in writing it, and, if I could think of any thing more to say on the subject, should write still longer. But be not alarmed, I am through; and have only to add that I am, most affectionately, Yours, always,

DAN'L WEBSTER.

MR. WEBSTER TO MRS. GEORGE BLAKE.

Niagara Falls, July 17, 1825.

MY DEAR MRS. BLAKE,—Before leaving here I wish to say an additional word or two on the subject of the Falls, by way of explaining or correcting some things in my letter.

In the first place I said, I think, that Goat Island was midway of the Rapids. This may lead to an erroneous opinion. The Rapids in fact, commence precisely at the head of Goat Island. We may stand at the head of the island, and look up and see a mild and even surface. The shore is level to the water, and we may amuse ourselves by throwing in sticks, and speculating on their course, either to the British or American Fall.

In the next place, I am convinced that I over-estimated both the breadth of the stream and the amount of water on the American side. I think the stream is not more than one fourth as wide as on the other side; and the proportion of water still less.

In the last place, when saying that the rock over which the river falls is limestone, I ought to have added that this limestone constituted but a part of the bank or wall. The first, or upper fifty feet, is limestone, lying in regular strata, as I have mentioned; the next hundred feet is a soft slate stone, which yields in some measure to the action of air, frost, and water. It comes off in small parcels, and is easily picked out of the sides of the bank. I pulled off a piece six feet long, as straight as a walking stick, and not much larger. As these pieces fall down they become pulverized, and turn to a sort of earth. The wearing away of this slate stone necessarily lets fall the limestone from above. Table Rock is the projecting platform of limestone.

The slate stone underneath it is already worn away a great depth into the bank; and Table Rock will one day doubtless precipitate itself into the river.

At the bottom of this course of slate stone, just about even with the surface of the river, commences another kind of stone. It seems to be a red sandstone, lying in very thin layers. It is of so bright a color that it may sometimes be seen, forming the bottom of the river, where the water is very deep.

You will excuse me, my dear Mrs. Blake, for adding these remarks to my long and tedious letter. It is doubtful whether I shall ever see the Falls again. You will be here at some time, and I hope soon. I will not promise myself, that, as you view the scene, you will find any great correspondence between the view itself and my account of it; but I trust you will call to mind those who have been over the spot before you, and be willing to remember even this unsuccessful attempt to describe it to you by

Your affectionate and faithful,

D. Webster.

P. S. We set out this morning for home.

MR. WEBSTER TO MR. PAIGE.

Utica, July 8, 1825.

Dear William,—You perceive that our flight is not very rapid. We arrived here evening before last, at the moment of the arrival of your letter, which, you may be assured, it gave us no small pleasure to receive. Yesterday we went to visit Trenton Falls, a famous lion, fifteen miles from this place. It is a succession of cascades, or water falls, in a stream called "West Canada Creek," for a mile and a half or two miles. On either side, for the whole distance, is a wall of rock nearly perpendicular, and varying in height from one hundred to one hundred and fifty feet. The passage to view the Falls is at the bottom of this bank of rocks, and at the very edge of the torrent. It is difficult, and in some places I think dangerous; there are however chains fastened in the rock in the most critical spots, to hold on by. Our ladies accomplished the object of getting a full view, although it rained like a torrent, and to have fallen over would not have soaked them more thoroughly. We find all the inns, and all the roads, full of travellers, many of them from Boston. This country is all alive; it is new, growing, and highly excited. A universal competition prevails in every thing; carriages, public houses, boats, all much more abundant than would seem strictly necessary, and all competitors. We leave this morning at nine, if our party should wake up by that time; I intend going forty or fifty miles to-day.

It will be Sunday before we reach Canandaigua, where we hope to find some of your letters. We often wish some of our friends were with us, when we see the great sights. We dined on very fine trout, caught in the Falls, where some are found weighing five pounds. We have heard of nothing very good in Mr. Blake's particular line.

I do not know whether Mrs. Webster has any thing to send, but love. I presume she is dreaming about you all. Give my own to the children, and to Mr. and Mrs. Blake, and believe me,

Truly yours,

D. WEBSTER.

MR. WEBSTER TO MR. PAIGE.

Niagara Falls, American side, July 16, 1825.

MY DEAR WILLIAM,—I believe Mrs. Webster wrote you from Buffalo. We found letters from you at Utica, Canandaigua, Buffalo, and two here. At Canandaigua, we got them Monday morning, the moment of our departure. I believe we have received all that you have written. We came down from Buffalo on Wednesday, on the west side, stayed at Forsyth's until yesterday, when we came across to this place. We have all been greatly delighted with the Falls; they have exceeded our expectations. I have written a long and poor account of the matter to Mrs. Blake. I presume you will find twenty others, much more full and accurate, though I do not remember to have seen any description, which I now think just. Many people are disappointed at not finding the Falls appear higher. This is very natural; one hundred and sixty five feet, when applied to a great object, is no very vast height of itself, and the great breadth of the Fall, the magnitude of the volume of water, and the circumstance that you generally see it first from the top, all conspire to make you incredulous as to the reputed height. But there is no mistake as to the height. A line dropped from Table Rock to where it strikes below, will convince any one. Or, when we are down at the water's edge, we look up to the bottom of the staircase, then compare that distance with the height of the staircase, which we know to be ninety-five feet, we shall be satisfied that the distance through which the water falls has not been overstated.

We have examined the Falls from all accessible points of view. Yesterday afternoon, we crossed from this side over to Goat Island, on a bridge, and had a fine ramble. Here is a small village, and on the rapids above and below the bridge, are some little mills. By the enclosed, you will see that the proprietors of the shores on this side would be glad to dispose of the water power of Niagara Falls, what little there is of it, to "Eastern capitalists."

To-day we have made a ride down the river two or three miles, to a place called the "Whirlpool." It is a fearful eddy; we look upon it from a height, I suppose, of two hundred and fifty feet. No man can approach it; the whole river is in a whirl. It is said that trees and logs, getting in there, will sometimes be carried round for days and weeks before they get out of the eddy. They are tossed about in all directions, sometimes standing up perpendicularly, and going down, and reappearing. I regretted that I had not a glass, that I might better have examined this great boiling caldron. Just below this is another place, called the "Devil's Hole." It is a kind of cut, made into the bank, on this side. In the French war, a party of English were stationed on the bank here to guard the portage round the Falls; they were surprised by a party of French and Indians, all surrounded, and pushed off. Of course they were all killed, except one drummer; he caught by his belt, upon some limb of a tree, running out from the bank, or as some say, fell on his drum. At any rate he survived the fall, and, as I understand, was living in Canada ten years ago.

But enough of Niagara and story-telling. It has taken us so long a time to get here, and must take us so much to get home, that I despair of Canada. I fancy we shall go to Rochester,

Utica, Lake George, Burlington, home; but this is only my private opinion. We shall set off East to-morrow, and shall soon determine our course. I will write to you again, say from Rochester. Yours,

D. Webster.

P. S. I am going to try to wet a line at the foot of the Falls.

Saturday 5, P. M., and all well; 23 days out, no news; calicoes wet and heavy.

MR. MADISON TO MR. WEBSTER.

Montpelier, August 12, 1825.

Dear Sir,—I have received the copy of your oration delivered at Bunker Hill, on the occasion presented by the 17th of June last. It merits all the praise which has been bestowed on it; and I tender you many thanks for the pleasure it has afforded me. With assurances of my distinguished consideration,

I am yours truly,

James Madison.

MR. WEBSTER TO MR. HADDOCK.

Boston, October 13, 1825.

Dear Charles,—Your Mr. Perkins called here this morning, at a moment when I happened to be so much occupied with gentlemen in the office, that I could not even read your letter through. Unfortunately, his engagements were so stringent, that he could not flatter me with a hope of another call tomorrow morning. If any auspicious changes in his affairs should enable him to call again, or if your next agent should be willing to wait till I could catch my breath even, I shall endeavor to comply with your wishes. If no other arrangement occur, draw on me for the sum, say $500, at three days' sight, and as soon as convenient send me such a note as you propose.

I had true pleasure in reading your Bible Society speech. Certainly I think it the best, far the best, which I have seen. We hear much of your Commencement oration. When are we to see it? Print it by all means; especially if it be half so good as report makes it. The tendencies of a college life are doubtless drowsy; and you deserve therefore the more praise for showing signs of life. It is not always that a pulsation manifests itself in those sons of leisure, who, having no absolute engagements for the future, refer to the blank of to-morrow whatever might have made to-day something better than a blank.

Yours most truly always,

DAN'L WEBSTER.

MR. WEBSTER TO DR. WARREN.

November 17, 1825.

MY DEAR SIR,—I am highly pleased with the idea of a gymnasium; it is a subject which has often occupied my thoughts, and in relation to which it has appeared to me that the fashion of the times needs to be changed. Those who have the charge of education seem sometimes to forget that the body is a part of the man. The number of young men who leave our colleges, emulous indeed, and learned, but with pale faces and narrow chests, is truly alarming. The common rustic amusements hung about our literary institutions for a long time; but they at length seem to have been entirely abandoned, and nothing, at least nothing useful, has succeeded them. If it be desirable that there should be cultivated intellect, it is equally so, as far as this world is concerned, that there should be also a sound body to hold it in.

I shall most gladly assist in your endeavors; thinking that I do some service when I aid any measure calculated to enforce on the rising generation a sense of the invaluable advantages of temperance and exercise.

I am, dear Sir, most truly yours,

DAN'L WEBSTER.

LAFAYETTE TO MR. WEBSTER.

La Grange, December 28, 1825.

My dear Sir,—I have had the pleasure to receive your letter by the Reverend Mr. Palfrey, of whose church in Boston I am one of the oldest parishioners; nor have I been a little surprised after I had left him in his pulpit, to see him on a sudden entering my room in Paris. He has since favored us with a visit at La Grange, and went to Geneva on his way to Italy.

You are by this time at Washington, with many others of my friends, occupied in the day with concerns most interesting to me, and spending every evening in those parties which I have happily enjoyed last winter. I wish I could again, some time in the session, share with you in that most pleasing way of life; and this not being the case, my best mode of existence, on this side of the Atlantic, is to be on my farm with my family and kind visitors; yet I will be obliged by the middle of January to go to the city for two or three months, with my children and grandchildren, however partial they are, along with me, to our retirement of La Grange. Here we have been threatened with the greater calamity by the illness of one of my granddaughters; she is now recovered. The less happy Mr. Clay has been more severely treated in his parental fondness.

From every quarter you will hear the great news of the death of the Emperor Alexander; from each quarter a different story about the mode of his exit; the most natural in that family is murder. How it may affect the concerns of general freedom is the important point. Nothing worse can be apprehended in a state of things, when the main object with every European, continental, and insular cabinet, is to stifle the spirit of freedom in this, and to introduce, if they can, aristocracy and monarchy in the better hemisphere. Should they quarrel together, something new may come out of it. It is said the King of Portugal cannot live long; let Don Pedro be sent to succeed him, and Brazil be raised to the dignity of a Commonwealth. At Panama, good and candid advice will be very seasonable. So it would be in Greece, whose situation appears to be now better than it was reported to be some weeks ago, and where the jealousies between Russia and Great Britain may give rise to new combinations. I hope the two frigates building at New York will be gone before you receive this letter. I wish our steamboat plan may have succeeded. There is in their moral influence upon the political civilization of mankind, something very gratifying and honorable to the character of the United States.

My brother officers of Massachusetts and Connecticut have communicated to me a proposed application to Congress relative to the pension law and their pecuniary situation, of which you are the better informed, as you will probably be one of its supporters. You know, my dear friend, how far I am from availing myself of my happy situation, honored as I am with a precious share of popular affection, to launch into political improprieties. But in this particular case it seems to me that the very favors of which I have been the object, one of them peculiarly added to my community of services and fraternity with those gallant and beloved companions in arms, entitle me to express more of my opinion and wishes, than it would be proper to do in any other instance. I took the liberty to write to the President and the Secretary of War, as I do now to you, my dear Sir; and indeed, the more bounteous Congress have been to me, the more happy I will be if they do something in explanation of the bill to confer additional comfort, where so much merit is acknowledged.

I am eagerly waiting for news from Washington. The President's "Message," the Greek business, the resolutions respecting my excellent friend Colonel Monroe's statement, combine to make me very anxious to hear and read. Be pleased, my dear Sir, to present my affectionate respects to Mrs. Webster, Mr. Boyd and families, to Mr. Everett, to all friends about you. My son begs to be remembered, and so would Le Vasseur, if he was at La Grange.

I don't know what business had the ministerial papers of England to encourage the French government not to pay the American claims. Madame De la Rue and her husband, my former aid-de-camp, came to see me, and was very desirous to obtain a declaration from Congress, stating what you consider, I think, as a matter of fact, that the President is entitled to make their claim an object for negotiation with the French cabinet along with the business of American reclamation, when they cannot be effectuated.

Adieu, my dear Sir, believe me forever your affectionate, grateful friend,

LAFAYETTE.

P. S. Your Bunker Hill has been translated in French and other languages, to the very great profit of European readers. My gallant and eloquent friend, Foy, has lived long enough to enjoy it.

Permit me confidentially to mention an object for which I hope there will be no occasion. It came round to me that some friends had contemplated moving Congress for an appropriation, relative to a compensation due by me to the proprietors of The Cadmus, which they have hitherto declined to receive, as it would be in fact paying more money on my account. You must feel the impropriety of the proposal, and will of course prevent it, if it did chance to be made. But would consider it as an additional service, if Mr. W—— may be prevailed upon by our common friends to accept from me this debt to him.

MR. WEBSTER TO JUDGE STORY.

Washington, December 31, 1825.

DEAR SIR,—By direction of our committee I brought in to-day a resolution for a bankrupt law. I think there is some chance for it if we get a good bill. I must call it up on Monday, the 16th instant, by which time I hope to hear from you. What say you to the following:—

" Resolved, that all merchants, &c. (using the common terms,) committing an act of bankruptcy, shall be liable to a commission, at suit of creditors, &c.; and that other persons, not merchants and traders, who shall file a voluntary declaration of insolvency, shall be subject to the law," &c.

Unless we make some provision for the non-traders, we cannot possibly carry along the bill.

I shall call up the judiciary bill to-morrow. I know not what will be its fate. I was for two judges, but a majority of the committee were for three. A great majority in committee were against separating your court from the circuit. I shall consent to it, if nothing else can be done, but shall give my feelings on the subject fully to-morrow. I hope I shall commit no contempt.

An opposition is evidently brewing. It will show itself on the Panama question. When that discussion comes on, you will probably see reason to think that the government has decided wisely about the mission. The nominations are yet before the Senate. As soon as they are confirmed, if they shall be so, a proposition will be made in our House for an appropriation, and then we shall have a grand debate.

My health is good, never better, not having yet worked off the strength obtained at Niagara, and at Sandwich. Mrs. Webster sends a great deal of love to Mrs. Story and yourself. Pray let me hear from you by the 16th.

Yours truly, DAN'L WEBSTER.

DANIEL WEBSTER TO EZEKIEL WEBSTER.

Washington, January 29, 1826.

DEAR EZEKIEL,—Nearly two months of the session have passed away, without producing much of particular interest. I think I have never known a session, in which there seemed more reluctance to go early to work. Indeed, there is not a great deal that is absolutely necessary to be done.

The judiciary bill will probably pass the Senate, as it left our House. There will be no difficulty in finding perfectly safe men for the new appointments. The contests on those constitutional questions in the West, have made men fit to be judges.

After a week's squabbling about the appropriation bills, I suppose we shall have a debate of a week on Mr. McDuffie's constitution-amendment-motion. Probably the subject will end with the debate. The Panama mission is yet undecided in the Senate. It is supposed to furnish some plausible grounds for opposition, and there will be a rallying of forces on the occasion. We do not know, of course, what takes place in the secret sessions of the Senate, but it is understood that the subject is to be debated next Wednesday.

I have no doubt the mission will be approved, and the nominations confirmed by a large majority. Perhaps it might have been desirable, that the new government should have held no Congress, or should not have invited the presence of ministers of the United States; but when the correspondence is seen, it will probably be generally thought that the President decided right. We expect to have the matter discussed in our House publicly, on the question of the appropriation to pay the expense.

The bankrupt bill will be introduced, and has a fair chance of being passed. I hope it will be first brought into the Senate, but if it does not soon make its appearance there, I shall begin the business in the House. The late revision of the English system has greatly facilitated our labors.

The political aspect of things here is well enough. A good degree of civility and kind feeling prevails, and I cannot help hoping that time and event may abate the malignity that still rages in some quarters. I have not had the pleasure of making the acquaintance of your new members from New Hampshire. There are so many new members in the House, it requires a great while to find them out. The new senator keeps pretty close; a little inclined to oppose, as is thought, but perhaps not quite certain how it might turn out. I believe Mr. Bell is sincerely friendly to the President, and much more inclined to act and think generously and liberally than he has heretofore been supposed to be.

I seldom see a New Hampshire paper, and hear nothing of New Hampshire politics. If there be any thing passing worth telling of, please write about it.

As to domestic matters, we get on tolerably well. Fletcher lives at Dr. Sewall's, and goes to school. The other two children are with us. Julia has been a little unwell, but is better, and the rest of us have good health. We beg to give our love to your wife and children, and hope to hear from you.

Yours always,

DAN'L WEBSTER.

LAFAYETTE TO MR. WEBSTER.

La Grange, March 12, 1826.

MY DEAR SIR,—While you are on the duties of congressional business, I make some escapes from town to my farm, and, having no public task to perform, I am active in the thought of what is probably going on in Washington, in my enjoyment of usual prosperity; and in my anticipations of every circumstance which can maintain and forward the felicity and dignity of the United States, placed as they are at the head of human civilization, their moral influence cannot but be confidently exerted for the instruction and happiness of mankind.

The arrival of Mr. Palfrey has been welcomed with the feelings of a faithful parishioner and friend. He is now in Italy, and I much wish he may embark from France, as he will then favor us with another visit at La Grange.

By the last accounts from Washington, the Panama mission was still debated in the Senate. Sorry I would be to think the former Spanish colonies, now independent and well disposed republics, have been deprived of the only honest advice they can expect. On none of the European governments can they depend. They, all of them, are determined to favor a creeping of monarchy and aristocracy into those countries, and the Court of Brazil is by them considered as the head-quarters of their plots, corruption, and intrigues. Nothing, of course, seems to me more desirable, than to see the United States maintain their hold in the confidence of the Southern Republic, and the Empire of Brazil converted into a good democratic commonwealth.

Is it not very amusing to find, that while the Russian autocrat was watching, advising, lecturing about the possibility of plots and insurrection wherever he had no right to meddle, he was himself surrounded with a vast conspiracy of his own nobles and favorites? It is to me a daily diversion to pursue the contrast between a presidential election, under a representative democracy, and the succession to the throne, in the bosom of the most complete monarchical good order, supported by all the blessings of aristocracy, without the encumbrance of any thing like a nation. It seems that jealousy and selfishness have worked the Western governments, and Austria herself, to a degree, into a better mood with respect to the Greeks than could have been produced by a sense of honor, compassion, or Christianity. As they are afraid to see Emperor Nicholas carried away by his troops into a war against the Ottoman empire, which might give him a supremacy over the people and the territory of Greece, they now incline towards an arrangement favorable to Grecian independence; an inadequate substitute, in their minds, to a total and speedy destruction of the insurgents, but where as little of republican freedom as possible should be admitted. There are already popping out from every country candidates for the sovereignty over this gallant people, whom nature has, still more especially than any other, marked for a republican confederacy. Here, I confess, comes again my proud sense of the moral influence of the United States. I hope Commodore Rodgers's squadron will be seen in those seas; and I much lament the frigates, that were building in New York, are not yet arrived. From the European governments, without exception, not one honest feeling nor one disinterested advice can be by them expected. Not so with private persons. The day before I left town, an express arrived from Missolonghi to the French committee, announcing a want of ammunition and other necessaries in that fortress, upon which twelve thousand dollars were sent the same night to Leghorn, to purchase and ship off those articles.

I have not heard the result of the position of the revolutionary officers; but from my happy knowledge of the feeling toward them, and of the disposition of Congress in their favor, and my grateful experience of what they have done for one of them, I fondly hope my beloved comrades will not have been disappointed.

Be so kind, my dear Sir, as to present my best respects to Mrs. Webster and family, and to your brother, to our friends at Washington and Boston. I hope the President and family are well. My son and Le Vasseur beg to be remembered. Has our friend Everett tried his splendid talents in the House of Representatives? His brother and Mrs. Everett I expect to see before long, as Mr. Adam Smith has gone to Madrid, and he will, it is said, improve the first moment he can properly devote, to a visit to the North. Most truly and forever

Your affectionate friend, LAFAYETTE.

CHIEF JUSTICE MARSHALL TO MR. WEBSTER.

Richmond, April 3, 1826.

DEAR SIR,—I had the pleasure of receiving a few days past, under cover from you, the documents accompanying the late message of the President to the House of Representatives on the Panama mission. We anticipate a tolerably animated discussion of this subject. I thank you very sincerely for this mark of polite recollection, and beg you to believe that I remain with sincere regard,

Yours, JOHN MARSHALL.

MR. WEBSTER TO MR. JUSTICE STORY.

Washington, May 8, 1826.

MY DEAR SIR,—I have received your letter written at Portland, and will not fail to attend to the subject of it. I had already found my attention turned towards the proposed law, which I very much dislike, and shall take care to oppose.

The fate of the judiciary bill is quite uncertain. The Senate show much pertinacity in regard to their amendment; and it is doubtful whether the House will ever consent to it. You will have noticed the proceedings thus far. If the Senate decline a conference, the bill is certainly lost. If they agree to a conference, and in that conference consent to abandon that part of their amendment which does not relate to the districts, it is possible, and only possible, the bill may finally pass. The real truth is, the gentlemen in the Senate who are called the Opposition, do not wish the bill to pass; even those of them who are from the West have but a cool desire for it. I suppose the reason is, they do not wish to give so many important appointments to the President. I think we stand pretty well, either way. If the bill passes, well; if not, we have made a fair offer, and the court will remain at seven some years longer. Judge Trimble's nomination is not yet acted on.

There remain no very important measures now before congress, although there is a mass of subordinate business, and of private bills.

My plan is to leave here on the 15th; to send the horses along three or four days earlier, so as to proceed rapidly ourselves to New York. I shall hardly be more than seven or eight days going home; so that I intend to be in your court, the second week of its sitting. I believe I have very little to do there, and I shall write to Mr. Bliss to postpone to next term, at once, all that can be so disposed of. After the second week of the court comes election week, a week not convenient for courts; so that I think the business of the term had better be wound up, if practicable, the second week. I shall write to Mr. Blake to that effect, as well as Mr. Bliss. My health is good; but still I am not anxious to go immediately to much hard work when I get home. From the first day of December, I have not been an inch from my place till Saturday, when I rode a few miles on horseback. I need motion and air, more than a court. If any thing occurs to change my present purposes, respecting the time of my departure, &c. I shall give you timely notice; this letter I direct to Salem. Very probably I may write you again in a day or two, under cover to Mr. Bliss.

Mrs. Webster joins me in love to you, and we both join in one other thing, that is the most affectionate remembrance to Mrs. Story.

Yours truly,

DAN'L WEBSTER.

CHIEF JUSTICE MARSHALL TO MR. WEBSTER.

Richmond, May 20, 1826.

DEAR SIR,—I returned yesterday from North Carolina, and had the pleasure of finding your speech on the mission to Panama, under cover from yourself. I had previously read it with deep interest, but was not on that account the less gratified at this polite mark of your attention. I can preserve it more certainly in a pamphlet form, than in that of a newspaper.

Whatever doubts may very fairly be entertained respecting the policy of the mission, as an original measure, I think it was not involved in much difficulty when considered as it came before the House of Representatives.

I congratulate you on closing a most laborious session, and am with great and respectful esteem,

Your obedient servant,

J. Marshall.

LAFAYETTE TO MR. WEBSTER.

La Grange, July 26, 1826.

I have been happy to hear from you, my dear Sir, and to welcome Mr. Bond at La Grange. My family have shared in the gratification, and I was preparing to offer at some length my acknowledgments, when I am informed this evening that Mr. Bigelow must have my letters to-morrow in town. I must therefore this time content myself with a few lines, in the hope they will speedily reach Boston. I wish I could say the like of the writer.

It is superfluous to tell you I have with patriotic eagerness followed your long congressional debates; nor can you doubt my having been highly gratified to read your eloquent and substantial observations, particularly when you have claimed the credit due to the people of the United States, their representatives, and the chief magistrate of the Union, for the eminent service rendered to the cause of South America and Mexico. My friend President Monroe's message did evidently put an end to the plots of the Holy Alliance, and drag the government of Great Britain into an immediate recognizance of the American republics.

Notwithstanding the disaster of Missolonghi, and the abominable conduct of the European cabinets, the affairs of Greece wear a better aspect than had been, even by many of their friends, anticipated. They have found a providential auxiliary in the internal convulsions of the Ottoman Empire soon after the British policy had succeeded in quelling the co-religionary sympathies of Russia. The ardor of the Greeks is far from being abated. The most lively interest in their cause pervades every community, particularly in France, and it is not the only complete contrast between the governors and the governed in this side of the Atlantic. Lord Cochrane's private expedition in the service of Greece promises great deal. I ardently wish the frigates built in New York may arrive in time for assistance. I want the people of the United States to have as much credit as possible in this so very interesting cause of Greece; it is with unspeakable pleasure and a due sense of pride, that I have a few days ago taken by the hand Captain Allen, a gallant citizen of New York, who, after having served four years in the United States navy as a midshipman, went to Greece a few days after my arrival in America, and since that time has been highly serviceable, being now flag captain to Admiral Miaulis and his intimate friend. He has been on a mission to London, but found time to stop a few hours at La Grange.

Be pleased to present my affectionate regards to Mrs. Webster, your brother, Mr. and Mrs. Boyd, and our other friends in Boston. I must, to my great regret, leave you to-day; but not before I have mentioned my son and Le Vasseur.

Most cordially and forever your affectionate friend,

LAFAYETTE.

P. S. Present me very affectionately to my old friend John Adams, when you see him. I wish it may be in the power of the President to pay him a visit this summer; should he and his lady be with you when you receive my letter, mention me most affectionately to them.

MR. QUINCY TO MR. WEBSTER.

Boston, August 3, 1826.

MY DEAR SIR,—Your perfect success yesterday ought to be as satisfactory to you as it is to your friends. I think nothing has ever exceeded or perhaps equalled it.

In consequence of a controversy I had yesterday with a friend, I deem it an act of friendship to draw your attention to one part. If it be as I understood it, there can be no possible objection. But if it be as he and I find others understood it, then it is desirable that it should be well considered in the aspect in which it may be viewed.

I understood you, in that part in which you give an imaginary debate, relative to the expediency of a declaration of independence, to represent Hancock as the presiding officer; an objector not prepared for the declaration addressing him, in opposition to it; but I did not understand you as intending to attach those arguments against independence, to any person whatsoever, particularly not to Hancock; because, being in the chair, he could not have partaken in that debate. To this state of the scene there can be no possible objection.

I find, however, that the general, and I believe the universal impression, is that the argument against the declaration was put by you into the mouth of Hancock, and intended to attach to his character; and that, in point of form, it was bringing Hancock and J. Adams on the arena in direct opposition to each other on this point.

As my own impressions at the time of delivery were different, I have no difficulties in the case; all was perfectly satisfactory to me. But, if I am mistaken, and the general impression concerning this part of your discourse be correct, then permit me, in that deep sentiment of respect and affection which I entertain for your name, fame, and influence, all which I would have as spotless as it is brilliant, to inquire—

1. Is there any fact in history which justifies the attaching more doubt or hesitation, at that moment, to the character of Hancock than to that of Adams. If not, why should Hancock be made the channel for the communicating the timid and temporizing policy in argument, as though it was his opinion. In sketches of fancy, to which the names of great men are attached, we owe to them a scrupulous justice. If Hancock did not take that ground, it ought not to be attached to his memory.

2. If he did, and in his anxiety to prevent the declaration, he abandoned the chair, and took the ground of opposition, still, I respectfully inquire, is it worth while to keep that fact in memory against him, by a formal register of a speech made on that ground? Will not the effect be just as strong, by representing the speech in opposition to have been made by some nameless individual, who may be considered as concentrating in his own argument, whatever may be urged in opposition, without making any individual responsible for it? I stated to you, in the beginning, this was my understanding of your

speech. But I find both clergymen and lawyers, and, I am certain, the multitude, received it otherwise.

The argument of Adams was noble and characteristic. The point of the objection you will see. If there be any grounds for it, I wish you to consider it. If, as I believe, there is none, then I have nothing to say except that now as ever I am

Yours, JOSIAH QUINCY.[1]

MR. WEBSTER TO MR. HADDOCK.

Boston, October 14, 1826.

DEAR SIR,—I do not know that I am acquainted with any sources of information, on the subject mentioned in your letter which are not probably known to you. We do not know as much of the first settlers of New Hampshire as of those of Massachusetts. The two colonies came for different purposes and under different auspices. Dr. Belknap found out a greater part of what is to be learned of the New Hampshire settlers. He was a very thorough and diligent searcher among all the early legislative and judicial records of the province. Possibly some of the old families in Portsmouth may have valuable materials, but I doubt it. Mr. Adams, in his annals of Portsmouth, has been able to add but little to the stock of knowledge. Before the peace of Paris, 1763, the settlements in New Hampshire were very limited. Concord and Charlestown were the frontier. When, by that peace, the Indian hostilities were terminated, new settlements spread over the State. These settlers were most of them from Massachusetts and Connecticut. The original settlers, therefore, are only those who planted themselves on the Piscataqua, and its branches; and I doubt whether there remain any unexplored sources affording information as to their early history. Your industry, however, will glean something, and the subject is a proper one for research and discussion.

It would give us much pleasure to see you here with your wife, and to receive a good visit from you. Your stops here are are all too short; at least we think them so.

I am, my dear nephew, yours affectionately,

DANIEL WEBSTER.

1 Mr. Quincy's understanding of the remarks was the correct one. No such reference to Mr. Hancock was intended by Mr. Webster.

P. S. In regard to the moral character generally of our ancestors, the settlers of New England, my opinion is that they possessed all the Christian virtues but charity; and they seem never to have doubted that they possessed that also. And nobody could accuse their system or their practice but of one vice, and that was religious hypocrisy, of which they had an infusion without ever being sensible of it.

It necessarily resulted from that disposition which they cherished, of subjecting men's external conduct, in all particulars, to the influence and government of express rule and precept, either of church or state. That always makes hypocrites and formalists; it leads men to rely on mint and cummin. A man thought it an act of merit, if we may take the blue laws of Connecticut for authority, not to walk within ten feet of his wife in their way to church; as some parents, nowadays, think it a merit to restrain their daughters from a village dance; one is quite as sensible and as much to do with religion as the other. Indeed, it is the universal tendency of strong religious excitement, a tendency of our infirm nature, growing out of our weaknesses and our vices, to run into observances, and make a strong merit of external acts. Our excellent ancestors did not escape the influence of this propensity; but they had so many high and pure virtues, that this spot should not give offence. They were a wonderful people. This very failing, of which I have spoken, leaned so much on the virtues of decision, sense of duty, and the feeling that will bear no compromise with what it thinks wrong, that I forgive it to them. The determined spirit with which they resisted every approach of what they thought evil, was itself a great virtue. "Of itself it is harmless, but it leads, or may lead to evil." This was their answer, and perhaps there is something in it; but then it may be said of almost everything. The vice of the argument, as an argument, is, that it proves too much. Eating, drinking, sleeping, conversation, are all equally under its condemnation. But though indefensible as a rule of conduct, some general consequences followed from the spirit which accompanied it, which consequences are extremely useful. It sharpened the sight for the discovery of political evils. The tea tax, for example, was not oppressive, as a tax; it was too small for that. It was opposed on principle. "It led or might lead to other taxes." Our fathers acted on system; and the inquiry with them was, not whether the thing was bearable, but whether it was right. I verily believe, although I do not like creeds in religious matters, that creeds had something to do with the Revolution. In their religious controversies, the people of New England had always been accustomed to stand on points; and when Lord North undertook to tax them, they stood on points also. It so happened, fortunately, that their opposition to Lord North was a point on which they all united.

But enough of this postscript.

MR. WEBSTER TO JUDGE STORY.

Washington, December 26.

Dear Sir,—I rose this morning with a resolution not to let the day pass without writing you one word, although it should be but one. I have long intended, every day, to do the same thing, but something has constantly happened to prevent it. Thus far, I have been laboring hard to get the Spanish claims off my hands, so as to be able to attend, without distraction, to my other duties. But these things together, and some new engagements for the court, leave me quite too little time for correspondence. The private affairs with which a member from a large town is necessarily charged, are very numerous. To be a public man, I ought to represent one of the inland counties of my good native State, or else a borough.

You will have seen in a late National Intelligencer, the report of last year, respecting the courts. Something undoubtedly will be done on that subject this session. What shall we do? Shall we increase your bench by two? Shall we relieve your bench from all circuit duties, and establish a uniform system of circuit courts? Shall we provide circuit judges for the western districts?

I must entreat your sentiments fully on these matters. I feel great objection to either of the first two propositions; others have objections to the last. They make a kind of point of honor to have supreme judges in the circuit courts, if other circuits have such.

My plan, if it deserve the name, would be to appoint three or four circuit judges in the West; to provide also, if we could, for the appointment of a circuit judge contingently in the East, in the next vacancy.

My object, in short, would be to provide, that all the judges of the supreme court should perform some circuit duty; and as much as they could conveniently; that there should be circuit judges enough to perform the rest; and that such arrangements should be made in this respect, as, when vacancies occur on your bench, giving the opportunity, two supreme judges should be allotted to the West; in other words, that the West should have two judges on the supreme bench.

Is this a right object? If it be, tell me how I shall accomplish it. By the middle of the next month, I must report some plan. Pray sit down, think, and write. We are all well; my wife is very happy. We have good rooms, good fires, good company, and good spirits, *in quomodo sensu, intelligitur.* Mrs. Webster sends her love to Mrs. Story and yourself. I beg to make a large addition to it, as it passes through my hands.

Yours always,

D. W.

MR. WEBSTER TO MR. EVERETT.

Washington, December 31, 1826.

Dear Sir,—Mr. Vaughan called here yesterday, and invited me to dine with him to-morrow, *en famille*, and particularly requested me to see you and your ladies, and beg of you and them the favor to be of the party. Mrs. Bankhead will be there to keep your wife and Miss Brooks in countenance. If you will signify to me, through the bearer, your good inclinations in regard to this matter, I will make them known.

It was so cold yesterday that I could not persuade myself to leave my room, or I should have called at your house. As near as I recollect, though my memory is a good deal chilled, it is now about a week since I was warm, out of bed.

Yours, however, very warmly,

Daniel Webster.

MR. WEBSTER TO MR. SPRAGUE.

Washington, January 10, 1827.

My dear Sir,—I am quite obliged to you for your letter, although I confess it has caused me some uneasiness. I cannot persuade myself that the legislature, under present circumstances, will omit to reëlect Mr. Mills. Here, I assure you, we are all of one mind on the subject. We think there is nothing in his health to make it improper, and that every thing else is in favor of it. If the legislature will not agree to that, I hope the election may be postponed. For mercy's sake, do not weaken our power in the Senate. When all the Philistines are against us, do let us have all the strength we can have. If Mr. Mills lives, he is second to no man in the Senate among our friends. Why then should he be now superseded? We shall know more of his health in June; and June is early enough for the election. But, as I will answer for it, that he will not hold the office any longer than he is able to discharge its duties, I should hope he would be now reëlected.

Having so settled an opinion as to what is fit to be done, namely, to reëlect Mr. Mills, or postpone the choice, I really have not thought of what would be best in case neither of these two things can take place. Of that, my dear Sir, you can better judge than I. I only say that if you are governed by a disposition to sustain Mr. Adams, and help on the public business, you will, in all events, elect a man of the very best talents which are at your disposal. I pray you let no local, nor temporary, nor any small consideration induce you to refrain from electing the fittest man that can be found, and that can possibly be prevailed on to take the place. The present moment, be assured, is a crisis in the affairs of Massachusetts and all the North.

I am, dear Sir, very truly yours,

Daniel Webster.

EZEKIEL WEBSTER TO DANIEL WEBSTER.

Londonderry, January 17, 1827.

Dear Daniel,—I came here yesterday. My wife has been here a fortnight with Alice, who has been ill. She is gaining slowly, and it will probably be another fortnight before she will be able to go home. Governor Bell and his friends took the course I anticipated. They called, by a printed notice, a meeting of the Republican friends of the administration at the court house. This adjective was inserted before deliberation or consultation. I did not attend, feeling myself excluded by the terms of the invitation. The meeting was large, and many speeches were made by Governor Bell, Bartlett, Governor Morrill, Richard Bartlett, and Speaker Hubbard. The object of all the speakers, except Governor Bell, was to prove Mr. Adams to be a democrat, his administration strictly democratic, and more purely and actively so than Monroe's, Madison's, or Jefferson's. They vindicated him from the charges of being a Federalist, or inclining to favor the Federalists. This was the substance of their speeches. After the meeting, Governor Bell wished to see me, and I called upon him. He said the manner of calling the meeting might not be satisfactory to me; he hoped it would be upon reflection; that he and his friends had determined to have resolutions introduced into the House approving the measures of the administration, and hoped that the Federalists would support them. He repeated very much his former conversation, renewed his declarations of good feeling, &c., &c. In reply, I calmly told him that, in our former conversation, I had suggested to him the course which I thought the republican friends of the administration ought to pursue; but I was willing that he and his friends should adopt the principles on which they would support the administration in this State; and, as far as I was concerned, they might support it on their own principles as well as they could. But if those principles were exclusive, or proscriptive of the Federalists, they could not complain if they had not the aid or assistance of the Federalists. I remarked that he knew that the course of the Federalists had been honorable in New Hampshire, and marked by the strictest integrity; that in all divisions of the republican party, whether upon men or measures, the Federalists had voted for the best men and the best measures; that when gentlemen of the republican party were candidates for office, they were very desirous to appear to have no intercourse with Federalists; but they had no objection to the receiving of federal votes, and federal support. At other times, the Federalists were treated as outcasts and aliens. I referred him to the conduct of the Federalists in this very legislature, in the organization of the House and in the choice of commissary-general. I reminded him that the friends of the administration had represented to us that the political salvation of Portsmouth, certainly, and perhaps that of the State, depended upon this election, insignificant as was the office; that it was made a party question; that on this vote the Jackson men were to rally, and if Nelson, their candidate, succeeded, it would give such confidence to the friends of Jackson in Portsmouth, that they would carry every election in the town ever afterwards. Such was their representation to us, and they courted the influence and solicited the votes of the Federalists; and the Federalists did give their votes, to a man, for their candidate, and elected him; yet, in two days, these gentlemen, in express terms, declared that they would not admit us to the meeting of the friends of the administration. I told him that I considered this treatment of the Federalists from the republican friends of the administration as ungenerous and unjust; and such as Federalists, who had any self-respect, would not submit to. I inquired of him why the friends of the administration did not support that administration in New Hampshire on their own principles, and whether they expected the aid of Federalists in other States, when they proscribed them in this? He said, in reply, that his own feelings were liberal, and that the time would certainly come when there might be a union with Federalists, on the principles mentioned by me; but as yet, the public sentiment was not ripe. I replied, that, on that point, I differed from him; that I believed the public sentiment to be in favor of such a union at this moment; that it was not the sentiment of the people that needed to be corrected, but the sentiments of those who affected to be leaders of the people; and that, in my opinion, the public feeling would be right, in this respect, whenever he and his friends wished to have it so; that this was a matter altogether with him and his friends; that whenever they were willing to unite with the Federalists, they might expect their aid, and not before, whether in favor of their resolutions or any other measure. We parted under a good deal of excitement. The resolutions, I suppose, will be introduced on Monday; and if they should be, a motion will be made to postpone them indefinitely, for which I shall vote, if no other man does. My present intention is to have the resolutions postponed; and if it becomes necessary in the debate on that question, to give to the House the true reasons plainly and frankly for the motion, I shall do it. If that motion fail, and we are obliged to act upon them, I shall endeavor to amend them, giving them force and character, and then advocate their passage, giving my hearty and zealous support to the administration on its own principles, and not on those of its exclusive friends in this State.

We are glad to hear of Mrs. Webster's recovery.

Let us know the appearances of things in New York, &c.

Yours truly,

E. Webster

MR. WEBSTER TO MR. MASON.

Boston, April 10, 1827.

My dear Sir,—You will have heard from Mary, since her arrival here. We had a pleasant passage, and I was glad of her company. Since I have been at home, my attention has been occupied with various matters, private and professional. I have, nominally, some little business yet in the State courts; although my long absences have very much severed me from them. In the neighboring counties, where courts are held at seasons when I am at home, I have also an occasional engagement, and these affairs have required my attention since my return.

The business in the State court at Washington was heavy, as you have seen; and my participation in it greater than usual. We got on with the Virginia cause famously; you will see, when you see the report, that our friend Judge Story laid out his whole strength and made a great opinion. The attorney-general argued the cause with me. It was not one of his happiest efforts. By the aid of your brief, I got on tolerably well, and took the credit, modestly, of having made a good argument;

at any rate, I got a very good fee; and although I shall not send you your just part of it, I yet enclose a draft for the least sum which I can persuade myself you deserve to receive.

I was sorry not to be able to get good materials from you, in the lottery case, also. But we got along with the cause, and hope sometime to get the money.

As to political matters, I wish to say something, but hardly know where to begin. A survey of the whole ground leads me to believe, confidently, in Mr. Adams's reëlection. I set down New England, New Jersey, the greater part of Maryland, and perhaps all Delaware, Ohio, Kentucky, Indiana, Missouri, and Louisiana for him.

We must then get votes enough in New York to choose him, and I think cannot fail of this. It is possible we may lose four votes in Kentucky, but I do not expect it. At the same time it is not impossible that Pennsylvania may go for Mr. Adams. Beyond doubt, public opinion is taking a very strong turn in that State, and it is not now easy to say how far the change may proceed. That there is a change, and a great change, is too clear to be questioned.

In New York, affairs wear the common complexion of New York politics. Mr. Clinton and some few of his friends have the credulity to think that he has yet some chance of being President two years hence. They flatter themselves that General Jackson's friends will abandon the General, and take him up. You will think none can be so weak or so ill-informed as to entertain such a hope, but, in truth, there are such men, and Mr. Clinton is himself one of them. The choice is with the people in districts, and unless some change takes place, Mr. Adams will get a majority, perhaps a large one.

You perceive how local questions have split up our good people here. You see the worst of it. In truth, right feeling very generally prevails, and nothing but prudent conduct is necessary to manifest it. Measures are in train, in relation to the ensuing choice of representatives, which I think will show that Boston is yet Boston. Care will also be taken to induce other towns to send good, and a good many, members to the general court. We shall have a Senator to elect. Our difficulty will be to find a man fit for the place, and with popularity to carry the election.

I had a great deal of conversation with Mr. Bell, in the course of the session, respecting the state of affairs with you. I have confidence in his good dispositions, but I do not think his policy bold enough. He understands my opinion, and guesses at yours, on that point. Experience, one would think, must have taught him by this time that there is but one course; and that is to rally, as administration men, without reference to bygone distinctions.

I wish you could see and converse with him, about the 19th or 20th. I shall go up to Boscawen to see my brother. If I can persuade him to accompany me, I would return by way of Portsmouth, to pass a single day with you. It seems, that without his consent or knowledge, he is chosen to the State legislature. He is so much displeased and dissatisfied with the course adopted by Mr. Adams's republican friends, in New Hampshire, that I know not whether he can be persuaded to do any thing. I have, however, thought it would be worth considering whether he should not bring forward resolutions, approving the conduct of the administration, and disapproving that of the opposition, and supporting them by a good strong speech. This would, perhaps, have two good effects; it would, in the first place, compel Mr. Adams's friends to act with him, and, in the second place, it would oblige Mr. Hill's friends to take their side. All this, however, is for future consideration.

When you have time, not better employed, I shall be glad to hear from you. If I should not return from Boscawen by your way, I shall take another early opportunity to go to Portsmouth.

To-morrow, Thursday, I am going down to dine with the judge. Yours, always truly,

DANIEL WEBSTER.

MR. MILLS TO MR. WEBSTER.

New York, June 9, 1827.

MY DEAR SIR,—I have just learned the result of the choice of Senator, on the part of the House of Representatives, and I assure you, with the utmost sincerity, that it is as gratifying to me as it is creditable to the House, and will be beneficial to the Commonwealth and the nation.

I regret, however, that I had not known your views in season to prevent any votes being thrown away upon me. I should certainly have done so, had I not been assured, by an extract of a letter, read to me as coming from you, that you would not consent to be a candidate; and that the choice would probably fall on Mr. John Mills. This I was willing to prevent, I confess; and in consequence of all this, I now appear before the public as an unsuccessful candidate for an office which, Heaven knows, I sincerely wished not to hold, and as having incurred an implied vote of censure for my past services. I have the vanity to believe, however, that this was not intended, and that I shall have credit for honest intentions and pure motives in the discharge of my public duties, and of having served the State, which has so long honored me with its confidence, with fidelity and zeal, and a sincere desire to promote its honor and interests, however inadequate my capacity may have been to accomplish the object. The consciousness of this will, at any rate, be a source of no small gratification to me through life.

My health is gradually improving, and I hope to reach home in the course of next week. I shall leave New York on Monday, and probably stop a few days in New Haven.

With great regard and esteem, I am, dear Sir, very respectfully,

Your obedient servant,

E. H. MILLS.

MR. WEBSTER TO MR. SPRAGUE.

[PRIVATE.]

Boston, June 20, 1827.

MY DEAR SIR,—I must not omit longer to thank you for all the kind things you have said and done in connection with recent events.

I beg you to be assured that I am not and shall not be insensible to the effect which your good wishes and good efforts have produced. I hope to have a long memory for friendship and kindness, as I desire a short one for injuries and acts of injustice; none of which last, however, have I ever received at your hands.

They appear to go on nobly in New Hampshire, except in one respect. They confined their call for an administration meeting to "Republicans" exclusively; thereby shutting out more than one third of the legislature, and nearly all men of talents, though all well disposed. Mr. Bell means well, but he is yet afraid of Hill.

I rejoice that you are going to Harrisburg. It will be an excellent thing, both for you and the public. I mean to persuade my brother, who is appointed to go from New Hampshire, to accept the appointment. I venture to say you will be pleased with him, as a man of sense and information. I hope to see you before your departure. Mrs. Webster has been quite ill. She is now well enough to ride, and I propose taking a journey with her, and then I go to the court at Nantucket, from all which, however, I expect to be home by the 10th or 15th of July, which will be before you set off.

Yours, very truly,

DANIEL WEBSTER.

DANIEL WEBSTER TO EZEKIEL WEBSTER.

Boston, July 20, 1827.

DEAR EZEKIEL,—I have received yours from Londonderry. You cannot disapprove and dislike the party proceeding at Concord, more than I do. I hold it equally unjust and impolitic. I would not support the administration one hour if I supposed it countenanced such a narrow and bigoted policy. Of this sentiment I make no secret. Governor Bell means well, as I believe, but I do think he has made a great mistake. It is miserable, it is miserable indeed, if those who are inclined to support the administration, find it or think it necessary to make an apology for such an act as the appointment of Mr. King.

If you find it necessary, for your own justification, to speak on these subjects, tell the whole truth, right out, plainly, and go at once to the people; they will be with you. I hope, however, the resolutions may be of a character so liberal as that you can support them. I am more and more persuaded that the true way was for you, or some of your friends, to have introduced the resolutions yourselves.

I am glad you go to Harrisburg. It will be both useful and pleasant to you. I shall of course see you here a day or two, on your way. By all means go. Make some arrangement of your Concord court business. Make Mr. Mason attend to it, or Brother Stevens.

The meeting, I hear, is now expected to be on the 30th July. It is precisely the season to see Pennsylvania. Mrs. Webster is getting well. At the end of this week I take her to Sandwich; thence I go to Nantucket court, return by Plymouth court, and get home the 10th August.

All is well in New York. We can do without New Hampshire, if narrow counsels make it necessary to give her up. Yet I should be ashamed if our native State should act foolishly.

Yours,

D. W.

MR. WEBSTER TO MR. SILSBEE.

New York, December 1, 1827.

My dear Sir,—I am kept here by a concurrence of unfortunate circumstances. Mrs. Webster's health was not entirely good when we left home, but still, such as to allow the hope that we should be able to travel with ordinary speed. Our unfortunate passage from Providence increased her debility, and since she has arrived here, an accidental cause has contributed to make her case worse. From this last, however, she is now fast recovering, and I trust will be able to travel on Monday. To-day I have myself a very painful attack of rheumatism, occasioned, I suppose, by a violent cold I took on the way; and am not now able to leave my room. This will be better, however, I trust soon; so that my present hopes are to set forward on Monday. We shall not make a moment's stop for any purpose not connected with health. I hope I may not be needed before I can arrive with my family. But if it were likely that I should be, I would leave them, at whatever inconvenience, and proceed by the most rapid conveyance, if my own health should be such as to allow of it. You will receive this on Monday, and I will thank you to write me, addressed to Philadelphia, saying whether any thing is expected to occur, in which my vote may be essential. I am fully aware of the general importance of every member's presence at this moment in the Senate; and I feel extreme anxiety in consequence of my own unavoidable absence, even for a single day. Still, I am desirous of keeping my wife and children with me, if possible; as I should otherwise be obliged to return for them. Let me hear from you as above requested. I write this not without great inconvenience. I can neither walk nor sit upright.

Yours, DAN'L WEBSTER.

MR. MILLS TO MR. WEBSTER.

Northampton, December 3, 1827.

MY DEAR SIR,—If you will put the enclosed in a way of speedily reaching Mr. Barrell, you will confer a favor on both him and me. If time permitted I should probably give you some further trouble, but must postpone it for a day or two. At present, I can only say that my health is considerably improved since I left Boston, although the cold weather has shut me up, I suppose for the winter, if I live through it. My professional pursuits are entirely suspended, and all continued efforts of the lungs forbidden. I congratulate you, my dear Sir, on your preservation through the perils of your steamboat passage, and most sincerely hope you experienced a continuance of the same providential protection through your journey, and are now safely located with your family in comfortable quarters. Although I truly rejoice that I am not obliged to mingle in the strifes and debates of the Capitol, I am very anxious to hear how they are managed and how they terminate. Should your multiplied engagements allow you to drop me a few lines occasionally, I assure you they will contribute much towards rendering my solitude less dreary. I am so well acquainted with most of your fellow-laborers that all their movements possess with me no little interest. Even the solemn foppery of Colonel K. and the mock-heroics of Governor B., ridiculous as they are, afford me amusement when higher matter fails. But I am already trespassing upon the mail hour. Mrs. Mills unites with me in cordial regards to Mrs. Webster and family, and believe me,

Dear Sir, yours truly,
E. H. Mills.

MR. WEBSTER TO MR. PAIGE.

New York, December 5, 7 P. M. 1827.

Dear William,—I must now write you more fully upon the afflicting state of Mrs. Webster's health. Dr. Post, a very eminent physician and surgeon, has to-day been called into consultation with Dr. Perkins. Their opinion, I am distressed to say, is far from favorable. I believe they will recommend her return to Boston as soon as convenient. They seem to think that it is very uncertain how fast or how slow may be the progress of the complaint; but they hold out faint hopes of any cure. I hope I may be able to meet the greatest of all earthly afflictions with firmness, but I need not say that I am at present quite overcome. I have not yet communicated to Mrs. Webster what the physicians think. That dreadful task remains. She will receive the information, I am sure, as a Christian ought. Under present circumstances, I should be very glad if you could come here, although I would not wish you to put yourself to too much inconvenience. I should be very glad myself to go to Washington, though it were but for a single day, but I should not do that unless in the mean time Mrs. Webster could be on her return. I shall now make no move until I hear from you in answer to this letter. If you come on, I think the best way will be to take the mail stage-coach, with the chance of finding an evening boat at New Haven. You must let Fletcher know, without alarming him too much, that his mother's health is precarious, and that she will probably return home. I am not yet able to write, as you see, though I think I am getting better.

Yours truly,
Dan'l Webster.

P. S. 8 o'clock.—I would fain hope that the foregoing is of too alarming a character. I have since seen Mrs. Webster and told her the doctors' opinions. She says she still has courage. If you can come on so as to accompany Mrs. Webster home, it will not be necessary that you should set out the very day you receive this. But I shall not myself go to Washington until I hear from you that you can come to take Mrs. Webster home, if need be.

MR. WEBSTER TO MR. SILSBEE.

New York, December 9, 1827.

My dear Sir,—I am sorry not to be able to give you a better account of myself, and especially that I am obliged to speak so unfavorably of Mrs. Webster's health. I have not yet been able to leave the house, nor indeed was I able to quit my own room till yesterday evening. I am getting better, however, and if the weather were not so particularly unfavorable, I should have hopes of setting forward in a day or two.

My great affliction is the state of Mrs. Webster's health. Whether it is best for her to return to Boston, or to remain some time here, with a hope of being able hereafter to proceed to Washington, is a question difficult to decide. She is very unwilling to return; and the physicians do not encourage her further progress South. I am now in the hourly expectation of the arrival of her brother, Mr. Paige, when we shall determine on something. It is most probable, I think, that she will return to Boston with Mr. Paige, and that I shall proceed South without her. It is possible, however, she may stay here, in the hope of being able to accompany Mr. and Mrs. Story, some three weeks hence, to Washington, as I have already said.

Yours, with most true regard,

Dan'l Webster.

DANIEL WEBSTER TO EZEKIEL WEBSTER.

Washington, December 17, 1827.

Dear Ezekiel,—I arrived here but last night, and have first to say that I left my wife sick at New York. Her complaint, which is partly local, has been of some time standing, but we did not think much of it till lately. I fear now it is dangerous. She was much more comfortable when I left New York than she had been for a fortnight; but whether permanently better I know not. Mr. Paige is now there with her, at Dr. Perkins's. If she should get so well as to be able to travel, I shall go back for her. On the other hand, if she grow worse, I must go and stay with her. I know not how Providence will dispose of this threatening case; but at present it fills me with the keenest anxiety.

I find here two letters from you, and have received another to-day. As soon as I have been here long enough to learn what is the state of things, I will write you on political matters. I find our friends here not despairing.

Yours as ever,
D. Webster.

MR. WEBSTER TO JUDGE STORY.

Washington, December 18, 1827.

My dear Sir,—Yours of the 13th, addressed to New York, has followed me hither. My own health was so far restored, that on Thursday, the 13th, I ventured to set forth, and arrived here Sunday evening, the 16th, without inconvenience, and with far better health than I had when I left New York. I do not now write myself an invalid.

I left Mrs. Webster at New York. Her health was bad, though better than it had been. I know not whether you are acquainted with the nature of her complaint; though Dr. Warren or Mr. Ticknor will readily explain it to you. My last letter, December 16, says she is on the whole "better than any time before since she came to New York." I am still in great hopes of her being able to join me here. Mr. Paige is now with her, and will stay till Christmas. If she should be able to travel, I expect to go for her and bring her along. I desired Mr. Paige to keep you informed.

Our rooms I found all ready and in order; and notwithstanding Mrs. Webster's illness they will be kept for her, and for you and Mrs. Story. Our good landlady has done all in her power to prepare for us; and if my poor wife had health, I should look forward to a happy session. And as it is I hope for the best. You say you shall set out by the 29th. I have given that information this morning to Mr. Silsbee's and Mr. Crowninshield's families, and they hope only that it may be earlier. I am sure Mrs. Story will find herself pleasantly situated here. As to political affairs, I have not been here long enough to learn much. I find our friends not discouraged. Virginia appears to be showing great strength for the administration, and many hopes are entertained of her final vote that way The weather has been so bad, I have as yet seen very few persons, since I came here.

I am glad Mason succeeded in The Argonaut. It is a good cause, whatever Judge P. may think of it, and must finally prevail It would not give rise to a serious doubt in any other part of the Union, at least I think so.

I shall write you again shortly; and in the mean time am, with all my heart,

Yours, D. Webster.

P. S. Remember my regards to Mrs. Story.

MR. WEBSTER TO MR. MILLS.

Washington, December 19, 1827.

My dear Sir,—I arrived here only on Sunday evening, the 16th instant. You are acquainted probably with the causes of my detention for a fortnight in New York. I left Mrs. Webster there still quite unwell. My last letters represent her as much more comfortable and free from pain than she had been, but I feel the greatest anxiety as to the original cause of her illness.

I found here your letter of the 3d, and despatched its

enclosure to Mr. Barrell. It gave me great pleasure to hear from you, and to know that thus far you are getting along through the winter with less inconvenience than was expected. I hope we shall have little weather more severe than was experienced the latter part of last month.

As yet I feel new and strange in the Senate. My habits have become conformed to the course and manner of things elsewhere; and it will require time to enable me to feel at home where I now am. According to present appearances, there will be little for me to do. Our adversaries undoubtedly have a majority, and I think the true course is to let them exercise it, as seems to them good. Why should we be responsible for what we cannot control?

To-day we have heard Colonel Johnson's "Annual" on abolition of imprisonment; sound, practical, systematic, and coherent!

The good Deacon Bradford is here, a sort of agent for the revolutionary officers. He has, as you will see, trusted their cause in the Senate to Mr. Woodbury. Be it so. No considerable debate has arisen yet in either House. P. P. Barber's resolution, to sell out of the bank, is expected to be called up to-morrow.

The Senate room is transmogrified since last session. The Vice-President sits opposite the main door, and faces his former seat. The seats are crowded, and altogether the arrangement is not good. My place, Hobson's choice, is nearest the chair on its left hand. It was left by forty-seven wiser heads than mine, and yet I believe it the best seat in the chamber.

Mrs. Adams's first drawing-room was last night; I was not there, but believe she is not at all well. The President is tolerably well, and Mr. Clay also, whose faith and courage still hold out. I hear he has thought it necessary to put forth another publication on the combination question, which is expected soon to appear. I regret it; though I am told it is very satisfactorily done. This, I believe, is not yet a public matter.

It will be one of my most agreeable duties, my dear Sir, to write to you, and to forward you any thing to occupy your hours; it will be still more gratifying to be useful to you in any more important respect.

When you have leisure and strength, I shall be happy to hear from you.

Yours always truly,
DAN'L WEBSTER.

MR. WEBSTER TO MR. PAIGE.

December 25, Christmas noon, 1827.

DEAR WILLIAM,—Your letter of Sunday has this moment reached me, in which you say Mrs. Webster would be glad if it should be quite convenient for me that I would come to New York to meet Judge Story, and I certainly shall do so. I cannot go for a day or two, because my cold is too severe; but there is nothing to prevent my setting off so soon as I am quite well. Judge Story wrote me that he should probably set out about the 29th, which is next Saturday.

Possibly I may not leave here before Monday, the 31st; but even then I shall be in New York as soon as the judge. On receipt of this, I will thank you to write me, saying whether Mrs. Webster wishes me to bring any of hers or the children's things along with me. Your letter, if written on Friday morning, will be here on Sunday, so that if I happen to stay till Monday, I shall get it. Probably I shall go off before Monday; this will depend a little as well on the weather and the state of the public conveyances as on my getting rid of my cold.

I hope, if it be not too inconvenient, you will stay till I come, and then we can talk about Grace's going to Boston, or Washington. The tone of your letters, for three or four days, has been so much more favorable than before, that I feel encouraged. It will be dull to her, I fear, to be left again by me, after you are gone; but then I must come here, despatch some few things, and return to her again. I shall let no business, public or private, prevent attention to her, as the first duty.

My cold is better to-day, but still I am not quite well. Indeed, so much of rheumatism, and then so severe a cold, have rather reduced this corporeal system of mine to some little degree of weakness. Two or three days of good weather, which I know not when we shall see again, would do me a great deal of good.

You will of course send this to Grace, as I shall not write another to-day.

Yours always truly,

D. WEBSTER.

P. S. Again to-morrow.

My Christmas dinner is a handful of magnesia, a bowl of gruel.

MR. WEBSTER TO MR. MASON.

Washington, December 26, 1827.

MY DEAR FRIEND,—I cannot write you now a political letter, but must tell you something about me and mine. I came here the 17th, pretty free of rheumatism, but have since had a violent and obstinate cold, which finally has brought me to keep house. It is now, I think, better; but it will be two or three days before I shall be well again, at best. Mrs. Webster, as you know, I left in New York, quite sick. She has been perhaps, on the whole, from the time of my departure to the date of my last letter, a good deal more comfortable and free from pain than for the fortnight I was in New York. I cannot say that her substantial cause of illness is better; but Mr. Paige writes on the 23d that he thinks more favorably of the future progress and final result of the complaint than I did, when I left New York. It is a tumor of rather anomalous character, and the best surgeons look upon it with much fear of consequences. It seems to have a tendency to break out; this they dread, and try to disperse it; although its real character, perhaps, can only be fully known when that shall take place. I would not alarm myself or my friends, unnecessarily; but, to say the truth, my dear Sir, I fear the worst. I shall leave here, if I am well enough, on Saturday, for New York. There I expect to meet the Judge and Mrs. Story. Whether I shall return hither with her, or stay at New York, or endeavor to get Mrs. Webster home, must be decided by the state of things which I shall find existing when I get there. If it should be probable, which the surgeons somewhat incline to suppose, that my wife may remain for a considerable time without essential change, I do not see that the superior duty of being with her must not lead to the vacation of the situation which I fill here. I should be very glad to hear from you, directed to New York, care of Dr. Perkins, Fulton street.

I am, dear Sir, most truly yours,

DANIEL WEBSTER.

MR. WEBSTER TO MR. SILSBEE.

New York, January 4, 1828.

MY DEAR SIR,—I arrived here yesterday at eleven o'clock, after a very tolerable journey, and without having added any thing to my cold. Indeed, I think it is better than when I left Washington.

I find Mrs. Webster more comfortable, on the whole, than I expected. She has now enjoyed more rest and repose, and more freedom from pain, for three days together, than in any equal time since we came here, six weeks ago. She has lost flesh since I left her, however, and is now feeble.

As to the original cause of her illness, I do not know exactly what to think of it. Some symptoms are certainly a little more favorable. I cannot help getting a little new hope, on the whole; though I fear I build on a slight foundation.

I find here Judge Story and his wife. They are in very good health. He has not looked so well for a long time. It is a great thing to get him out of his study. They set off this afternoon, being anxious to get over the Chesapeake before the boat stops. They will take possession of the rooms at Mrs. McIntyre's, where I hope to join them soon. Mr. Paige went to Boston yesterday. As soon as he shall be able to return, which I think will be in a few days, I shall return to Washington, if Mrs. Webster remains as comfortable as at present.

I am, my dear Sir, with most true regard, yours,

DANIEL WEBSTER.

P. S. Mr. Clay's address seems to meet with universal approbation.

MR. WEBSTER TO MR. SILSBEE.

New York, January 8, 1828.

My dear Sir,—I thank you for your letter of the 4th, and for the friendly manner in which you applied for my leave of absence.

Mrs. Webster remains essentially the same as when I wrote you last, except that I think she had not quite so comfortable a night last night.

* * * * * * *

Of the three physicians who have attended her here, (Dr. Perkins, Dr. Post, and Dr. Hosack,) the former only thinks he ever saw such a case before. A description of it, made out by Dr. Perkins, has been sent to Dr. Physick, and also to Dr. Nathan Smith of New Haven, for their opinion and advice. I have written an urgent letter to Dr. Warren, to come to New York, to consult with the physicians here.

My own health is mending, and if we could have a little clear weather, I think I should soon be well.

We have no news here. The thick weather is supposed to have kept back the packets. That of November 24, is not yet arrived.

Yours very truly,

Daniel Webster.

P. S. I suppose Judge Story will be with you nearly as soon as you receive this, unless he stopped in Philadelphia.

DANIEL WEBSTER TO EZEKIEL WEBSTER.

New York, January 8, 1828.

Dear Ezekiel,—I came here from Washington on Friday the 4th. There are so many friends to write to on the subject of Mrs. Webster's health, that I fear I may neglect some; and hardly know how long it is since I wrote you. William, however, has written occasionally to his friends in your vicinity.

I cannot say any thing new in regard to Mrs. Webster. Her case is most serious. It is one of rare occurrence; no physician here, but Dr. Perkins, thinking he ever saw one like it. The tumor has not yet broke out, but threatens it, and will, doubtless, soon. Its character will be then better known, and I fear the worst. Dr. Nathan Smith, Dr. Physick, &c. have been written to for opinions and advice; and I have written an urgent letter to Dr. Warren to come here. After all, the case is very much out of the reach of medical application, or surgical aid. The tumor is so large, so situated, embracing so many muscles, nerves, and blood vessels, that an operation is not to be thought of. Internal remedies do not reach it, and external applications have little effect. The result must be left with Providence; but you must be prepared to learn the worst. For three or four days, she has been more free from pain than for some time before; but yesterday she was a good deal distressed again. William Paige went home the day I came. He thinks he can return in a week or ten days, and stay till I make a visit to the court at Washington, if Mrs. Webster should be so as to allow of my leaving her. You will, of course, not alarm your wife and Mrs. Kelly, and Nancy, too much in regard to Grace. There is yet a hope; but I have thought it best to tell you my real opinion.

My own health has suffered from continued colds and catarrhs. Though not quite well even yet, I have no dangerous or bad symptoms. I feel no inflammation of the lungs, or soreness of the chest, nor any febrile symptoms. An epidemic cold is all about here, and I partake in it; but it appears to be getting better, and I have no doubt that two or three clear days would finish it. Julia and Edward are pretty well; they go to school. Grace and the children desire their best love to Mrs. Webster and the little girls, as well as to you.

Yours always truly,

DANIEL WEBSTER.

MR. WEBSTER TO MR. MASON.

New York, January 15, 1828.

MY DEAR SIR,—I thank you for your kind and friendly letter, and wish I could feel justified in confirming those favorable hopes which your friendship leads you to form, in regard to my sick wife. Would to God I were able to encourage my own hopes, and yours also. But I fear, greatly fear, that Providence has not so ordered it. Although she is better one day than another, that is, more comfortable, more free from severe pain, yet I do not see any material change in that which has occasioned her illness. The tumor remains as hard and unmanageable as ever. It seems altogether beyond the reach of human art. Nothing removes, nothing softens it. In the mean time, so much pain and illness begin to affect the general health, and some indications appear of what I have all along feared, since I formed any notion of the disease, of an affection produced by it on the chest and lungs. For the last two days there has been less of acute pain in the limb, but more of stiffness and numbness; I mean in the whole limb below the tumor. She has complained also of weakness of the breast, and manifested considerable difficulty in breathing. Large glandular swellings appear also in other parts of the body, especially about the abdomen. On the whole, though there is less of suffering, I think the danger is plainly increased. The tumor itself has not yet broken through the skin, and does not look quite so much threatening to-day as it did yesterday.

After all, my dear Sir, we have a ray of hope. I try to keep up my courage, and to strengthen hers; but it is due to our friendship that I tell you the whole truth. I have endeavored to prepare myself for that event of all others the most calamitous to me and to my children.

I thank you for your advice as to myself, and shall certainly follow it. In all probability, I shall stay here for some time yet. I fear circumstances will not be such as that I can leave, even after Mr. Paige comes, nor am I very anxious to do so. There seems nothing important in Congress; and I must try to make some arrangement of my business in court.

My health, though not entirely confirmed, is daily improving. I have the remnant of an epidemical cold, a little loose cough and catarrh; no soreness of breast, nor inflammation of the lungs, nor any feverish tendency. Be assured, my dear Sir, I shall take all possible care of my own health.

Ten o'clock P. M. Mrs. Webster is now asleep, and is free from severe pain, but breathes not easily. She is a good deal inclined to sleep. I leave a space to tell you how she may be in the morning.

Wednesday morning, eight o'clock.—Mrs. Webster passed rather a comfortable night. She had less cough than I apprehended, and seems calm and quiet this morning. She thinks she breathes a little easier than yesterday. Her voice is faint, but natural in its tones.

DANIEL WEBSTER TO EZEKIEL WEBSTER.

New York, January 17, 1828.

My dear Brother,—I cannot give you any favorable news respecting my wife. She is no better, and I fear is daily growing weaker. She is now exceedingly feeble. Dr. Perkins thinks she has altered very much the last three or four days.

The prospect nearly confounds me; but I hope to meet the event with submission to the will of God.

I expect Mr. Paige to-morrow morning. He or I will write you again, soon.

Yours affectionately,

Daniel Webster.

Monday Morning, January 21.

Dear Brother,—Mrs. Webster still lives, but is evidently near her end. We did not expect her continuance yesterday, from hour to hour.

Yours affectionately,

D. W.

MR. WEBSTER TO MR. MASON.

Monday Morning, 9 o'clock.

My dear Sir,—Mrs. Webster still lives, but cannot possibly remain long with us. We expected her decease yesterday, from hour to hour.

I received Mrs. Mason's letter, but could not communicate it.

Yours, D. Webster.

DANIEL WEBSTER TO EZEKIEL WEBSTER.

Monday, ½ past 2 o'clock.

Dear Brother,—Poor Grace has gone to Heaven. She has now just breathed her last breath.

I shall go with her forthwith to Boston, and on receipt of this, I hope you will come there if you can.

I shall stay there some days. May God bless you and yours,

D. Webster.

MR. WEBSTER TO MRS. LEE.

Monday, ½ past 2 o'clock.

My dear Eliza,—The scene is ended, and Mrs. Webster has gone to God. She has just breathed her last breath. How she died, with what cheerfulness and submission, with what hopes and what happiness, how kindly she remembered her friends, and how often and how affectionately she spoke of you, I hope soon to be able to tell you; till then, adieu.

Yours, D. Webster.

P. S. We shall all proceed immediately to Boston.

MRS. LEE TO MR. WEBSTER.

Tuesday Morning, January 22, 1828.

My dear Friend,—Before this reaches you, our beloved friend must be beyond the want of our care or our alleviations. She is happy! Oh, that we might soon go to meet her, where there is no more sorrow. I should not write to you at such a moment, for I know that the deepest sympathy cannot lessen your affliction, but I wish to ask you to let the children come to me, when you think best to send them to Boston; and to let Julia remain with me, as long as it is agreeable to you and to her. My husband joins in this request. My dear friend once said to me, that if she should be called to leave her children, she should feel happy in leaving them to my care. But this might have been the feeling of the moment, and you know, my dear friend, her last wishes on this subject. If I can in any way lessen your cares on this account or any other, you know my heart and you will trust to it. Poor Daniel, I fear, did not reach New York to see his mother. Give my love to the children, and to William. He must feel this very much. When I think of you and of them, my own loss seems as nothing; but I feel that it is irreparable, and that no one else can fill the place to me.

I am always yours,

ELIZA LEE.

SKETCH

OF MRS. G. F. WEBSTER BY MRS. E. BUCKMINSTER LEE.

January 23, 1856.

MY DEAR FLETCHER,—I very gladly comply with your request, to furnish you with some memorials of your mother and of your sister Grace, in order to assist your too early and indistinct recollection of those precious relatives; for although they are to me beings of the shadowy past, they can never fade from their place in my memory, where the individuality and beauty of their characters are as fresh as when retouched every day by their presence. And indeed, to borrow the thought of another, when the precious memories of youth revive, the present seems to vanish and become indistinct, and the long past to be the only reality.

But it will be impossible for me to think or speak of your mother apart from the relation she held to your father. Her being was inwrought with his. The tender and silken thread of her life was inwoven with his "purple and gold." She not only lived in his shadow, but her pulses seemed to "beat double" with his and her life.

My earliest recollection of your father is when he came to Portsmouth in 1808 to open his law office. His appearance was very striking. Slender, and apparently of delicate organization, his large eyes and massive brow seemed very predominant above the other features, which were sharply cut, refined, and delicate. The paleness of his complexion was heightened by hair as black as the raven's wing.

I will mention a little anecdote connected with his first appearance. He had arrived in Portsmouth at the close of the week, and the next day being Sunday, the sexton, as was the custom in those days, introduced the stranger to the minister's pew. My eldest sister was at church, and when she came home she said "there had been a remarkable person in the pew with her, that he riveted her attention, and that she was sure he had a most marked character for good or for evil." After a short time we became acquainted with Mr. Webster, and there was no longer a problem connected with him.

Mr. Webster took lodgings very near our house, and we soon saw enough of him to appreciate in some degree, young as we were, his extraordinary genius, and the noble qualities of his character. The genial and exceedingly rich humor that he so often exhibited, was perhaps at this time more prized by us than any other of the diversified talents we admired in him. He soon formed a circle around him of which he was the life and soul. We young people saw him only rarely in friendly visits. I well remember one afternoon that he came in, when the elders of the family were absent. He sat down by the window, and as now and then an inhabitant of the small town passed through the street, his fancy was caught by their appearance and his imagination excited, and he improvised the most humorous imaginary histories about them, which would have furnished a rich treasure for Dickens, could he have been the delighted listener, instead of the young girl for whose amusement this wealth of invention was expended. Hon. Mr. Mason of Portsmouth, who delighted in the rich humor so often displayed by Mr. Webster, used to say, "that there was never such an actor lost to the stage as he would have made had he chosen to turn his talents in that direction."

My father, Dr. Buckminster, took the liveliest interest in Mr. Webster, and as he remarked at this time the apparent frailty of his constitution, he urged upon his young friend his sure remedy for slight indisposition. This was half an hour of wood-sawing before breakfast, with a long two-handed saw, himself holding the end opposite to that of his young friend. We young people were always delighted when this strong medicine was taken before breakfast, for however disagreeable in itself, Mr. Webster appeared at our breakfast afterwards with his genial humor unimpaired.

The following June your father left Portsmouth for a visit, as we thought, to his native place, without communicating, previously, a word of his intention. He did not come back alone; and, with no change in the domestic arrangements, the wife he brought with him added the charm of her presence to our society.

Grace Fletcher was the daughter of the Rev. Elijah Fletcher of Hopkinton, New Hampshire. The clergy of New Hampshire were at that time a class of superior men. It was before the parishes had been rent asunder and divided into a multitude of religious sects, and, together with the rest of the clergy of New England, they included in their ranks, men, who in any age would have been marked for their talents and learning. Living as they did, with the frugal simplicity characteristic of the early days of New England, without worldly possessions, they were every where honored as guides in religious faith, and as the guardians of the best interests of society. It is true that the cultivation of the female intellect scarcely entered into the range of their duties, yet their daughters could not dwell, even in the atmosphere of their scanty libraries, or listen to the conversation of their clerical visitors, without attaining a certain mental development; and the desire for improvement was then answered by the best authors of England, rather than with the miscellaneous ephemera of the circulating library. Mrs. Webster's mind was naturally of a high order, and whatever was the degree of culture she received, it fitted her to be the chosen companion and the trusted friend of her gifted husband.

She was sincerely and deeply religious, and to this divinely operating principle was it to be attributed that she was never elated, never thrown off the balance of her habitual composure, by the singular early success of her husband, and the applause constantly following him. I remember a remark of the Rev. Dr. Parker of Portsmouth, "that it was a striking peculiarity of Mrs. Webster that she was always equal to all occasions; that she appeared with the same quiet dignity and composed self-possession in the drawing-room in Washington, as in her own quiet parlor;" it was only when an unexpected burst of applause followed some noble effort of her husband, that the quickened pulse sent the blood to her heart, and the tear started to her eye. Uniting with great sweetness of disposition, unaffected, frank and winning manners, you will readily believe that no one could approach your mother without wishing to know her, and no one could know her well, without loving her.

When Mr. Webster had brought this interesting companion

to Portsmouth, the circle that gathered around them became more intimate and was held by more powerful attractions. There certainly was never a more charming room, than the low-roofed, simple parlor, where, relieved from the cares of business, in the full gayety of his disposition, he gave himself up to relaxation.

Those who only knew Mr. Webster in the later years of his life can never believe how gracefully, and with what infinite humor he could lend himself to the amusement of the hour. There were other evenings given to more serious occupation, when he would read parts of the plays of Shakspeare to a circle of young friends, or keep them enchained by the eloquent charm of his own conversation.

The happiness of these Portsmouth days was within two years increased by the birth of a daughter, who bore her mother's name. I can hardly trust myself to speak of this child, so little to be relied on are the reports of precocious children. But as I recall some of the peculiarities of this little girl, she certainly appears, at three and four years old, wonderfully intelligent, and a most agreeable companion. There was no one so much in demand as the little Grace; her mother's friends constantly sending for her, and delighting themselves with her sweet simplicity, and, if such an expression can be allowed, her infantile sagacity.

Her young soul seemed to dwell very near the author of her being. Her mother once said to a friend, "I wish I could feel the presence of God as little Grace seems to feel it. Not only did "Heaven lie about her in her infancy," but she knew that God was always near her.

Another peculiarity was the tenderness she felt for the poor and unhappy. Beggars were frequent at this time. There were few relief societies, and begging from door to door was not forbidden. Grace would never consent that an asker of charity should be sent away empty. She would bring them herself into the house, see that their wants were supplied, comfort them with the ministration of her own little hands, and the tender compassion of her large gray eyes. If her mother ever refused, those eyes would fill with tears, and she would urge their requests so perseveringly that there was no resisting her.

But God's hand soon beckoned her away. Her parents in

the mean time had left Portsmouth for their residence in Boston, and Mr. Webster had gone the second time from New Hampshire to serve a session in Congress, when that insidious disease, to which delicate organizations so often become a prey, began to impair the health of the little Grace. The progress of the disease was so rapid, that her parents had only time to hasten from Washington to their house in Boston, where their child, whose short life had been lived, as it were, on the threshold of heaven, passed with gentle and painless steps within the veil which hides from us the great mysteries of the future. Grace woke from a sweet sleep, and asked for her father. He was instantly called, and placing his arm beneath her, he drew her towards him, when a smile of singular love and sweetness passed over her countenance and her life was gone. Mr. Webster turned away from the bed, and great tears coursed down his cheeks. I have three times seen this great man weep convulsively. Another time was when death deprived him of that brother, so tenderly loved, with whom, as we learn from the autobiography, and from his own lips, there was so close a union, that till both of them had families which drew them from each other, there had been between them but one aim, one purse, one welfare, and one hope.

Mr. Webster says in his autobiography, that after he had finished his session in Congress from New Hampshire, he came to Boston and gave himself with diligence to the business of his profession.

He was now thirty-five years old, and certainly in the perfection of all the powers of body and mind. The majestic beauty of his countenance was never more striking than at this period. There is a miniature taken at this time which gives a most agreeable impression of his features, but which those who knew him only in the later years of his life, would hardly accept as a perfect likeness. The noble expansive brow, and deep set melancholy eyes, do justice to those features; but the tender, flexible lips, although expressing the sweetness of his character at that period of his life, have not the expression of intense firmness, which afterwards gave such character to his countenance.

As I had the privilege of being often a visitor in his family, a recapitulation of the course of his every day life may be more interesting to you than any thing else.

Mr. Webster was always an early riser. There is an eloquent letter which expresses his true feeling upon the influence of the morning hours. Like most of the great and good men we read of, the hours of the early morning were the most cheerful of the day. The drowsy in his own house were awoke by his joyous voice singing some cheerful carol, such as,

"The east is bright with morning light."

"Uprose the king of men with speed," &c.

At breakfast, before the cares of business began, he was cheerful but thoughtful, courteous and genial towards every one; listening to the prattle of the children, and kindly attentive to all their little requests. When he returned, at two or three o'clock, weary from the courts, or from his office, the promptly ready service of Hannah, a woman who had been in his family many years, was always welcome. She knew the sound of the door when opened by Mr. Webster, and it was scarcely closed before she was at his side. He was dependent upon services prompted by affection, and loved those spontaneous offerings which came from the heart.

After dinner, Mr. Webster would throw himself upon the sofa, and then was seen the truly electrical attraction of his character. Every person in the room was drawn immediately into his sphere. The children squeezing themselves into all possible places and postures upon the sofa, in order to be close to him; Mrs. Webster sitting by his side, and the friend in the house, or social visitor, only too happy to join in the circle. All this was not from invitation to the children; he did nothing to amuse them, he told them no stories; it was the irresistible attraction of his character, the charm of his illumined countenance, from which beamed indulgence and kindness to every one of his family. In the evening, if visitors came in, Mr. Webster was too much exhausted to take a very active part in conversation. He had done a large amount of work before others were awake in the morning, and in the evening he was ready for that sweet sleep which "God gives to his beloved."

At the period I now speak of, the children of Mr. and Mrs. Webster were four. The youngest, Charles, was taken from them in the winter of 1825. This lovely child, at three years old, indicated singular attractiveness of mind and character. His illness was short, and had hardly impaired the fresh beauty of his countenance; but shortly after his death, when the round contour of the cheeks had a little fallen away, his face and head were like a perfect miniature cast of his father. No marble bust can ever present a more perfect likeness of his noble father.

Mrs. Webster was the most tender of mothers. Many persons thought, that devoted as she was to her husband and children, the whole tenderness of her nature was absorbed by her home and its exacting duties. It was not so. She had much to give to many. She loved to collect around her a small number of intimate friends, when, without form, or etiquette, they could enjoy the pleasure of each other's society. Mrs. Webster never appeared so truly charming as when thus the centre of a circle of intimate and trusted friends.

I would fain linger a little longer upon the memory of your mother, and upon those bright and happy years before the clouds gathered, and that fatal disease began to show itself, which made all those who loved her tremble.

But while they trembled she was firm, and those lessons of faith and submission, which in her days of joy she had learned with Christian docility, were now to be tried and tested, and they did not fail. She had determined to go with her husband in the winter of 1828 to Washington, but her disease made such fearful progress, that she was arrested in New York; where in the midst of devoted friends, with husband and children around her, she passed beyond the reach of our affection, but forever followed by tender regrets and blessed memories.

E. Buckminster Lee.

MR. JUSTICE STORY TO MR. WEBSTER.

Washington, January 27, 1828.

My dear Sir,—I received in the course of the mail your letter announcing the melancholy news of the death of Mrs. Webster. It has sunk Mrs. Story and myself in deep affliction. And prepared as we were for the heavy intelligence, it yet came, at last, with a most distressing power over our minds. We do, indeed, most sincerely and entirely from our whole hearts sympathize with you, and partake largely of your sorrows. We have long considered Mrs. Webster one of our best and truest friends, and, indeed, as standing to us almost in the relation of a sister. We have known her excellent qualities, her kindness of heart, her generous feelings, her mild and conciliatory temper, her warm and elevated affections, her constancy, purity, and piety, and her noble disinterestedness, and excellent sense. Such a woman, and such a friend, must be at all times a most severe loss, and to us, at our age, is irreparable; we can scarcely hope to form many new friendships, and our hope, our dearest hope, was to retain what we had. We have so hoped in vain. I can say with Young, in deep humiliation of soul,

> " Our dying friends come o'er us like a cloud,
> To damp our brainless ardor, and abate
> That glare of life, which sometimes blinds the wise."

Of the loss to you, I can and ought to say nothing. I know that if we suffer, your sorrows must be unspeakable. And I can only pray God to aid you by His consolations and to suggest to you, that, after your first agony is over, her virtues and your own admirable devotion to her cannot but be sources of the most soothing recollection to you. I know well that we may do mischief by intermeddling with a heart wounded by grief; and it must be left to itself to recover its powers, and to soften its anguish. What some of us think of the dead, you may read in the National Intelligencer of Saturday.

In going to Boston, and attending the funeral obsequies, I entirely agree with your own judgment. I should have done the same under the like circumstances, as most appropriate to my own feelings and to public propriety. We have in spirit followed your wife to the grave with you.

I do not urge your immediate return here. But yet, having been a like sufferer, I can say, that the great secret of comfort must be sought, so far as human aid can go, in employment. It requires effort and sacrifices, but it is the only specific remedy against unavailing and wasting sorrow; that canker which eats into the heart, and destroys its vitality. If you will therefore allow me to advise, it would be that you should return here as soon as you can gather up your strength, and try professional and public labors. Endeavor to wear off that spirit of despondency which you cannot but feel, and which you will scarcely feel any inclination to resist. Saying this, I have said all that I ought, and I know that you can understand what is best, better than I can prescribe.

Mrs. Story desires her most affectionate regards to you and the children, and I join in them, being always affectionately,

Your friend,

JOSEPH STORY.

MR. WEBSTER TO DR. PERKINS.

Boston, Monday, January 28, 1828.

MY DEAR SIR,—You have learned by Mr. Paige's letter, that we reached Boston on Friday evening, and on Saturday committed Mrs. Webster's remains to the tomb. We used the occasion to bring into our own tomb the coffin containing the remains of our daughter Grace, who died January 23, 1817. My dear wife now lies with her oldest and her youngest; and I hope it may please God, when my own appointed hour comes, that I may rest by her side.

Mrs. Bryant came immediately to see me and the children, and manifests the kindest sympathy in the calamity which has befallen us. She is an excellent woman, and one whom Mrs. Webster very much regarded and loved. All our friends have received us with a sincerity of condolence and sympathy which we can never forget. The children are well. Daniel will resume his usual residence and occupation in a day or two. Mrs. Lee, (Eliza Buckminster,) Mrs. Ticknor, Mrs. Hale, Mrs. Appleton, and others, have offered, in the most friendly manner, to take care of Julia and Edward, for the winter. We have not yet decided how we shall dispose of them.

I pray you to give my most affectionate regards to Mrs. Perkins. I never can express how much I feel indebted to her kindness and friendship. If Mrs. Webster had been her sister, she could have done no more.

In a few days, I intend to set out for Washington. If there should come a flight of snow, so as to make sleighing, I shall immediately improve the occasion to get over the hills to New Haven. I am, dear Sir, most truly,

Yours, always,

DANIEL WEBSTER.

MR. WEBSTER TO MR. MASON.

Boston, January 29, 1828.

MY DEAR SIR,—I thank you for your kind letter of yesterday. It would give me great pleasure to see you, but I do not expect you to make a journey hither, at this season. I know also that your engagements must be pressing. I am at present at Mr. Blake's, with the children. My brother came down yesterday. It is my purpose to stay till towards the end of this week, or to the first of next, according to the weather, and then proceed South. My own health is pretty good, although I feel in some measure fatigued and exhausted. I shall travel slowly, and must necessarily stay two or three days in New York.

As to my children, I think I shall dispose of them in this town for the present, without inconvenience. Daniel is perfectly well disposed of where he is. Mrs. Lee (Eliza B.) lays claim to Julia, of right, and would be glad of Edward; also Mrs. Ticknor, Mrs. Hale, Mrs. Appleton, and others have kindly offered to take them. I feel a reluctance to separate these two little ones, but still incline to think the best thing will be to let Julia go to Mrs. Lee's, and turn Edward, for the winter, into Mrs. Hale's little flock.

As far as I have thought at all on my future arrangements,

my inclination is to make no more change in my course and mode of life than the event necessarily produces.

I think I shall leave orders to have the furniture put up, in the house, with a view of taking home the children when I return, and, with the aid of Mr. Paige, keeping the family together. Except, perhaps, that it may be best that Julia should stay principally with Eliza, or in some other family, where there is a lady. Very probably both the little children may pass the summer at their uncle's.

I pray you give my most affectionate remembrance to Mrs. Mason. Mrs. Webster spoke of her often, and always with the strongest sentiments of esteem and affection. Her last letter was received, I think, before Mrs. Webster's death; but when she was not in a condition to read it, or hear it.

In regard to this calamity, my dear Sir, I feel that every thing has conspired to alleviate, as far as possible, the effects of the calamity itself. All was done that could be done; the kindness of friends had no bounds; and it is now continued, also, towards me and the children. The manner of the death too, was, in all respects, such as her dearest friends would have wished.

Adieu, my dear Sir,

Yours, always truly,

DANIEL WEBSTER.

DANIEL WEBSTER TO FLETCHER WEBSTER.

Senate Chamber, Tuesday, February 17, 1828.

MY DEAR SON,—I have received a letter from you to-day, before I have found time to answer your last. That gave me singular pleasure, as it contained a very gratifying report from Mr. Leverett. I have nothing more at heart, my dear son, than your success and welfare, and the cultivation of your talents and virtues. You will be, in the common course of things, coming into active life, when, if I live so long, I shall be already an old man, and shall have little left in life but my children, and their hopes and happiness. In contemplation of these things, I look with the most affectionate anxiety upon your progress, considering the present as a most critical and important period in your life.

Such reports as that last received, give me good spirits; and I doubt not, my dear son, that the consciousness that your good conduct and respectable progress in your class, and among your fellows, gives me pleasure, will stimulate your affectionate heart, with other motives, to earnest and assiduous endeavors to excel. I pray Heaven to bless you and prosper you.

At present my time is exceedingly occupied between the Senate and the court, and I suppose it will continue so to be, till the 3d of March. It is very cold here; much the severest winter I ever experienced at Washington.

Yours, most affectionately,

D. WEBSTER.

MR. HADDOCK TO MR. WEBSTER.

Dartmouth College, March 12, 1828.

MY DEAR UNCLE,—My last interview with you was a painful one, more painful than I can express. But I did not feel at liberty to revive in your mind ideas and feelings which had already but too much oppressed you. In your loss I suffered deeply; in all your sorrows I was afflicted. To that dear aunt I had long cherished a fond attachment. Her sickness I did not suppose so severe, or so dangerous as it really was, until just before the intelligence of her death arrived. I received it at Concord. It was too late for me to reach Boston, before the funeral solemnities. It would have been grateful to my feelings to have joined in the sacred duty to one so dear to me, and of whose kind regard I had received so many demonstrations. How pleasant, how inexpressibly precious, in the seasons of reflection upon this event, is the conviction, which we cherish, that she is as the "angels of God which are in heaven." It takes away the keenest sting of affliction. It may be unjust to the society of the Saviour, and the communion with God, in which the sacred writers place so much of the happiness of heaven, but I cannot resist the feeling excited anew by every victory of death among my Christian friends, that we shall derive no inconsiderable part of our eternal happiness from the renewal of earthly friendships. I know not why this feeling should strengthen as I grow older, unless it may possibly be, that the heart feels more sensibly its dependence upon the few whom nature, or youthful love, has bound to us, as death rapidly narrows the little circle. It may seem misanthropic, I know not that it is common or just, but, though not greatly disappointed, indeed, on the whole, remarkably favored by the approbation of those whose approbation I have sought, I have a horror of depending for my social happiness on persons to whom I have felt no natural ties, and with whom I have formed no early habits of affection. So that I feel, when a friend dies, that another hold on life is broken, another reason for wishing to live, removed. Could I feel, in my own heart, in the same proportion, prepared to meet death, and the momentous scenes after it, it would give me the truest joy. I hope, dear uncle, that on this subject you have obtained a state of mind, for which I look, but which I have imperfectly, if at all, enjoyed. I am satisfied from the cases of Job, Joshua, Stephen, Paul, and others, and from the strong language of the New Testament, that there must be a strong Christian faith and confidence attainable. It is worthy of the heart's desire and prayer.

With sentiments of the highest respect and affection, I am, dear uncle, Your nephew,

CHARLES B. HADDOCK.

MR. WEBSTER TO MR. PAIGE.

Washington, Sunday Evening, 1828.

DEAR WILLIAM,—I found divers letters of yours here yesterday, and have another to-day; for all which I thank you. A line from you, as often as you can write one, will always give me pleasure and satisfaction. I sometimes feel as if I were troubling you too much, with so much care of the children, and so much attention to my concerns. But I trust you will not suffer me to wear out your patience and kindness. Notwithstanding the blessed spirit that has so long been the common bond of union between us, is now on earth no more, you will ever be to me one of the nearest and dearest objects in life; nearer and dearer, indeed, from this very calamity. Enough!

I find Judge Story and his wife very well. Mrs. Story has had the company of Mrs. Laurence, and has not been therefore lonely. But, alas! it is not such a winter as she promised herself. I have not been out of the house to-day. A great many people have been to see me. To-morrow, I shall probably go into court. Yours, dear William,

Most faithfully,

D. WEBSTER.

MR. WEBSTER TO MR. PAIGE.

Wednesday Evening, Washington, 1828.

DEAR WILLIAM,—I have received to-day your letter of Saturday, which makes me feel a good deal better. I have seldom been five days before without hearing from home; and although I have lost what mainly made home dear to me, there is yet that in it which I love more than all things else in the world. I could not get along without cherishing the feeling that I have a home notwithstanding the shock I have received. You must try to make the children write, when you cannot, so that I may hear from some of you; one every two or three days at least.

This morning was devoted to General Brown's funeral; and I went into court at one o'clock. For some days to come, indeed, as long as the court continues, I expect no leisure. Time has been when I should not have cared much about it; and as it is, I shall get through somehow or other. Mr. Belknap will not be tried probably till next week.

The arrangement you suggested some time ago, as to the children's all dining with you on Sunday, and occasionally with our other friends, pleases me very well. I hope they are happy. Edward, I am sure, is as well off as he can be, and since you cannot spare him, I am content he should remain where he is.

Riley's trunk is here. I shall send it the very first opportunity. He will receive it, I trust, in a week or two. I am sorry to hear Mary is sick, and hope her illness will not be of long duration.

Remember me kindly to Mr. Blake. I would write him if I had time to-night, but must put it off for a day or two.

Give my love to all the children. I wish I had one of them here.

Good-night. D. WEBSTER.

MR. WEBSTER TO MRS. E. B. LEE.

Washington, March 15, 1828.

DEAR ELIZA,—I return you Mr. Parker's letter, which I have read, as you may well suppose, with great pleasure. Nothing is more soothing and balmy to my feelings, than to dwell on the recollection of my dear wife, and to hear others speak of her, who knew her and loved her. My heart holds on by this thread, as if it were by means of it to retain her yet here. Mr. and Mrs. Parker were always kind to us, and are among those Portsmouth friends whom time and distance never separated from our acquaintance and affection. Mrs. Webster had very high esteem for them both.

I hear from Mr. Paige, and from Julia, and from Edward, that you are well. Julia has told me all about your party, and how long she sat up. I hear from others, as well as herself, that she is happy as possible under the protection of your care and kindness. You will love her, I know, for her mother's sake, and I hope for her own also; and I trust she will make herself agreeable to your husband. You are kind enough to say, that concern for Julia need not lead me to forbear any purpose which I might otherwise have, of crossing the water. It would be unpleasant, certainly, to leave the children, and especially a little girl of Julia's age, but I should not feel uneasy about her at all, while under your guardianship. There are other considerations, however, which are well to be weighed before I am water-borne. Even if what you allude to were supposed to be at my own option, and however desirable it might be in itself, times and circumstances may nevertheless be such as "give me pause." This is all I can say about it at present; except that I am now too old to do any thing in a hurry. I believe this is almost the only time that I have alluded to the subject, to any one; and would not wish to be quoted as having said one word respecting it.

Mrs. Story left us the day before yesterday. The Judge goes in a day or two. I shall be sorry to lose him, though quite willing to have the court break up.

I have a very kind letter indeed from Mrs. Everett, respecting the name of her youngest daughter; I wish uncle would carry Julia out to see her.

Is your husband a document reader? I should be glad to send him some of our papers, speeches, &c., but have been afraid he would vote it a bore. Pray give my love to him, and believe me, as

Ever yours, DAN'L WEBSTER.

DANIEL WEBSTER TO EZEKIEL WEBSTER.

Washington, March 20, 1828.

DEAR BROTHER,—I wrote you yesterday. The object of this is more private and personal. I want you to tell me what you think best for the administration, and for me in relation to a subject upon which the newspapers continue to be loquacious.[1] Give your advice without favor or affection, and as a man who is "looking before and after."

Yours, as always,
DAN'L WEBSTER

MR. WEBSTER TO MR. HADDOCK.

Washington, March 21, 1828.

MY DEAR NEPHEW,—I thank you for your kind and affectionate letter, and assure you its suggestions are all in strict accordance with my own feelings. It does not appear to me unreasonable to believe that the friendships of this life are perpetuated in heaven. Flesh and blood, indeed, cannot inherit the kingdom of God; but I know not why that which constitutes a pure source of happiness on earth, individual affection and love, may not survive the tomb. Indeed, is not the prin-

[1] A report that Mr. Webster was to be sent minister to England.

ciple of happiness to the sentient being essentially the same in heaven and on earth? The love of God and of the good beings whom he has created, and the admiration of the material universe which he has formed, can there be other sources of happiness than these to the human mind, unless it is to alter its whole structure and character? And again, it may be asked how can this world be rightly called a scene of probation and discipline, if these affections, which we are commanded to cherish and cultivate here, are to leave us on the threshold of the other world? These views and many others, would seem to lead to the belief that earthly affections, purified and exalted, are fit to carry with us to the abode of the blessed. Yet it must be confessed, that there are some things in the New Testament which may possibly countenance a different conclusion. The words of our Saviour, especially in regard to the woman who had seven husbands, deserve deep reflection. I am free to confess that some descriptions of heavenly happiness are so ethereal and sublimated as to fill me with a strange sort of terror. Even that which you quote, that our departed friends "are as the angels of God," penetrates my soul with a dreadful emotion. Like an angel of God, indeed, I hope she is, in purity, in happiness, and in immortality; but I would fain hope, that in kind remembrance of those she has left; in a lingering human sympathy and human love, she may yet be as God originally created her, a little lower than the angels.

My dear nephew, I cannot pursue these thoughts nor turn back to see what I have written.

Adieu, D. W.

DANIEL WEBSTER TO EZEKIEL WEBSTER.

Washington, March 23, 1828.

Dear Ezekiel,—I have received yours of the 17th, and am glad you propose to write Governor Bell. If you have not already done so when you receive this, lose no time in accomplishing your purpose.

I cannot listen for a moment to what you say about not being a candidate. I never shall consent to your declining, if you have a fair opportunity. Be assured it will do you much good to be here a year or two, and you will lose nothing by it. I beg of you by no means to come to a different conclusion, at least till I come home.

The New Hampshire election has produced vastly more impression here than I had expected from it. It seems quite certain that a pretty strong confidence of success was entertained by General Jackson's friends. I was told to-day that Mr. Harvey, shortly since, expressed the strongest belief that New Hampshire would go for the military candidate.

I send you to-day a militia document. The preface and notes, &c., are understood to have been drawn up by Mr. Storrs, though I suppose if this be so, it it intended to be kept private. I think you will find it a thing to make the people think; I shall send you several copies.

We need much a list of names, in Mr. Harvey's district, of intelligent people, to whom this and other documents can be sent. Who is there in Warren, Sutton, Fisherville, Hancock, Henniker, &c. &c., to whom the New Hampshire members might send something calculated to enlighten the people and to give them the truth? I really feel it a duty to give the people light, in regard to the present state of public affairs.

We have every reason to think the tide has turned in New York, and is setting the other way with prodigious force. Something of the same nature is visible in Kentucky. Depend upon it, with proper exertions, we may yet save the country.

Yours, always truly,

D. WEBSTER.

P. S. I am anxious for your answer to my last.

EZEKIEL WEBSTER TO DANIEL WEBSTER.

March 31, 1828.

DEAR DANIEL,—I have written Governor Bell to-day. I have stated to him my opinion of our present condition. It is the best opinion I can form. I suggested to him both the importance and necessity that our representatives in Congress should make an address to the people of this State under their own signatures. They should speak out. Something of this kind is certainly needed. It should be published in a pamphlet form of thirty thousand copies at least. The people want information, light, knowledge of the character and measures of the administration.

I may say to you what I may to no person here, we cannot carry the election next November without the greatest exertions. Bold and manly measures only can defeat the Jackson party in this State. It is necessary that every man should put into the support of the good cause all his talents, all his personal character, personal influence, and exertions. The contest must be made to resemble the ancient battle, where every man grapples with his adversary. The crisis is extraordinary. The contest is extraordinary. Both the crisis and the contest call for extraordinary efforts. Let our representatives give us the example; let them make an appeal to the good sense of the people and warn us of our dangers. Let them lead, and there will be enough to follow. The public sentiment, enlightened and informed by the address itself, will support them, and carry them and the State triumphantly through the contest.

The present delusion is astonishing; no man who does not witness it, can believe it.

Mr. Healy can do more in those towns you mention, than any other man. He should have documents plentifully. He knows to whom it would be useful to send, better than any other person.

I have received the militia document. I think an edition of it will be printed in this State.

Yours always,
E. Webster.

DANIEL WEBSTER TO EZEKIEL WEBSTER.

Washington, April 4, 1828.

Dear Ezekiel,—I send you Mr. Davis's tariff speech, and shall send you others. Having some numbers of an English newspaper published in Paris, for the benefit, I presume, of English residents there, I enclose them to you, as you will find in them full accounts of the late ministerial changes in England, Mr. Brougham's speech on the laws, &c., &c.

I believe what you advise in relation to a certain question is right, and I presume the matter will have that termination.

I have had a good deal of conversation here about the Hampshire matters, with certain friends. I think a good disposition prevails, and that a satisfactory arrangement in regard to future proceedings may be made in June. But you will find it indispensable to this arrangement, that you be a candidate for a seat here. To that there will be no objection, I imagine, but on the contrary, a hearty assent. Other propositions would or might create difficulty. For one I shall never agree to let you off.

It is quite uncertain whether any tariff bill will pass. Nothing new has developed itself for a week in regard to the subject.

Yours always, D. WEBSTER.

MR. WEBSTER TO MRS. E. B. LEE.

Washington, May 18, 1828, Sunday Evening.

MY DEAR FRIEND,—Your very kind letter of the 12th was received to-day. I cannot sufficiently thank you for your goodness and affection towards Julia. Certainly you come nearer to supplying her loss than anybody else. I believe she loves you best of any; and it is my wish, my dear friend, that you should make her as much your own as your feelings prompt you to do. She cannot be better than with you, and I incline to leave it very much to your choice, how much she shall be with you, and when it is best for her to be elsewhere. You have a right to her, if you choose to have, which nobody else will ever divide. You have been among our dearest friends from the day of our marriage, and, as Julia is left motherless, I know not what to do for her so well as to leave her with you, whenever it is agreeable to you to have her with you. If you think her education would not suffer, I should be quite willing she should be with you most of the summer; though I hope to have her with me some of the time.

I thank you, my dear friend, for all your kind remembrance and good wishes. Your regard and friendship are among the objects which make me willing to live longer, and which I shall never cease to value while I do live. You say Mr. Sullivan thought me depressed. It is true. I fear I grow more and more so. I feel a vacuum, an indifference, a want of motive, which I cannot well describe.

I hope my children, and the society of my best friends, may rouse me; but I can never see such days as I have seen. Yet I would not repine; I have enjoyed much, very much; and if I were to die to-night, I should bless God most fervently that I had lived.

Adieu, my dear friend; I hope to be in better spirits when I see you.

DAN'L WEBSTER.

DANIEL WEBSTER TO EZEKIEL WEBSTER.

Boston, June 19, 1828.

MY DEAR EZEKIEL,—I hardly know what to say, in reply to yours, about going to Boscawen. I had firmly resolved to go up last Saturday with Mr. Paige, Julia, and Edward, but was persuaded to give it up, and to stay and argue a cause here in the Supreme Court, on Tuesday last. For the rest of this week I have nothing to do; but by the middle of next week shall be obliged to go to Nantucket, as I expect. That is the only professional engagement which I expect for the summer. It will occupy me sometime, and perhaps I cannot calculate on being back till the 10th of July. I should be glad to have the children, especially Edward, pass some time with you, during the hot weather. Julia will be very well for some time at Mrs. Lee's, at Brookline. We are now in our own house, and comfortably situated.

I wish to make a little journey on to Connecticut River this season. If you would join me, I would go to Cabot, if Uncle Ben. should be living. I could be at your house July 15, go to Cabot, return to Hanover, and proceed further down the river or not, according to circumstances.

One thing more. I shall not probably go to Sandwich, because there is no one to go with us; but if your wife and daughters will come down and go and stay there, while you are holding your August court, I and the children will go with them.

I will write you further before I go to Nantucket. I resisted going there for a long time; but it was of some importance to my employers, and they made it of some importance to me.

You say nothing of what is done, or doing at Concord, except that all is by this time done; I hope well done.

Yours, D. W.

CHIEF JUSTICE SMITH TO MR. WEBSTER.

Exeter, August 10, 1828.

Dear Sir,—The trustees of the academy have usually convened on Wednesday noon, this year 22d, to attend examination; and for business, Thursday morning.

It is understood this year that the Principal intends to resign before the meeting with his friends on Thursday. Under these circumstances, I have supposed it proper that the trustees should meet Wednesday morning, for business, so that Thursday may be devoted to the *fête*. The examination and the exhibition in the academy are to be dispensed with; I hope we shall have the pleasure of your attendance on the going out and coming in of Mr. Prince to the trustees, not a mere ceremony. Colonel Bell will not attend, and circumstances may, without you, prevent a quorum.

I am, as always, with sincere regard yours,

Jeremiah Smith.

MR. TUDOR TO MR. WEBSTER.

Rio Janeiro, August 26, 1828.

Dear Webster,—I had at length the pleasure of receiving a letter from you a few days since, and being one of the most placable of men, forgot the preceding enormous neglect. In the events that tried you last winter, I need not tell you I sympathized, not only from affection towards you, but towards her whom you lost. After wrestling for a time with feeling, and gaining a partial victory by aid of time, placed as you are, a man is obliged, out of regard to her he laments, to supply her place with some one to watch over the pledges she left him. To this conclusion you must come at last; and, strange as it may seem, though the last person in the world to be a matchmaker, there is a young native woman of New Hampshire, who I thought would be a suitable person. I would have wished you had gone to St. James, for your own gratification, your further preparation for being the person hereafter to approve the laws instead of making them, and for the advantage of the United States. But I suppose you cannot be spared for a year or two; but at any rate you must get a run through London, Paris, and Edinburgh, some vacation, instead of going to Sandwich; you may do it all in four months out and home; Perkins would say, in less time.

I do not like to express myself about our opposition, lest it might possibly be the result of any interested feeling, which I cannot detect after self-examination. I see but few of their papers, and seldom read them when seen; but I will say, nothing more indecent, mischievous, flagitious, than the gang that has conspired together to make use of the poor General's name, ever disgraced a free country. That T. T. L. should have waded deliberately into such a slough, is strange, though it always seemed that there was a want of heart to keep the head he has in a right course, but I hope it is only a transient error, and that he will get out, take a warm bath, and again be able to mix with gentlemen.

As to my affairs here, they have caused me considerable anxiety, being with people who, from a complication of weaknesses, vanity, presumption, timidity, &c., are difficult to manage, and especially involved as they are, or rather have been, for they are now about being relieved, in a maze of difficulties, growing out of this stupid war. Their object was to turn, to double, and delay, to gain time if possible. The short-course process, that of force, we might have used very effectively; but the danger was, that they are so feeble, we could not have handled them without breaking their shell. Our intercourse is too considerable and too fast increasing not to be fostered and put on a good footing. I hope I shall be able to effect this in season to be submitted to you this winter; they seem to me to be really desirous of making a treaty, and of being on good terms. I shall try to strengthen these inclinations.

If I can get through the business intrusted to me in season to have the treaty ratified this winter, I propose to ask the President to give me leave to resign, being tired of South America. There are many sacrifices to be made, beside that of health, in a long residence. This country about Rio, its magnificent bay, surrounding mountains, all forming the most varied and picturesque outline, a landscape painter would be in ecstasy at the endless number of studies it offers; but the society is nothing. Besides, it is hard to live here on our salary; and as promotion is very uncertain, the service with us not being regular, commanders-in-chief being in most instances taken from the militia, there is little motive to stay abroad on a bare subsistence, though in a respectable station; and though I have not a very pleasant prospect before me in returning, a very dismal one if my mines in Peru do not yield something, I hope to see you early next summer. Never having had an opportunity before, I must trouble you to make my affectionate compliments to Mrs. S. Lee.

Yours sincerely,
W. Tudor.

MR. TUDOR TO MR. WEBSTER.

Legation of the United States of America, August 29, 1828.

Dear Webster,—The Macedonian has been delayed, waiting to carry the news of peace, the preliminaries of which I think were signed yesterday, though I do not know it certainly. I made a sortie from the heaps of papers, in which I am obliged to burrow, to breathe a freer air, and write a postscript to what I have already addressed to you, by this same frigate.

I forgot to touch upon a subject I had in my mind. If opposition can go on in the unprincipled manner it has done the last four years, for a few years longer, in my opinion they will break down the government by the mere weight of filth they will heap upon it.

There seems to be a concerted plan to destroy every branch of the public service. I believe that the greatest abuses of our government are now to be found in Congress, and that they are getting into more vicious courses every day. It will eventually, if unchecked by public opinion, become only an arena, where every profligate demagogue will attempt to court public applause by doing his uttermost to blast, rather than to sustain, the government. I touched upon the subject, in a moment of vexation, in an article in The North American Review, the only scrap I have written for type since I left home. I think either in that or Walsh's, a powerful article, written with temper, energy, and knowledge of the subject, as a kind of appeal to the nation, to pounce upon the recent conduct of their servants, in the two Houses who have sacrificed their duty in the mad career of faction would be salutary, and would have its effect.

The disregard of the interests of the country in an endeavor to embarrass the administration by want of timely legislation in the United States question; the attempt to break down the army by abolishing the poor office of a solitary major-general; the keeping down the navy by the refusal to appoint flag officers; the excessive mischief that has been caused by refusing to make a quarter's advance in the appropriations for the navy until the present year, a chairman of a naval committee declaring that merchant captains might be taken as they should be wanted to command our ships of war! which is either ignorance or treachery without example, and fifty other items that I cannot particularize, but of equal, or greater moment; the making the tariff bill as bad as they could avowedly; the patronage of ruffians in the capitol, like the editors of The Telegraph, &c., &c., &c. Pray have this matter thought about by those who are capable.

You alluded to what I hastily wrote you on the subject of conveying back the commerce of the western side of this continent to Panama. It would take a quire to develop the subject, but be assured it is the most important object that can be effected for the increase of our foreign commerce. This point, that of settling the West India's question, with the English, (I think I shall be able to make Brazil a potent ally against the colonial system,) the obtaining payment for the claims on France, and the restoring Spain to her former prosperity and power by persuading her to recognize South America, are the great desiderata, in my humble opinion, of our foreign policy.

The preliminaries of peace are undoubtedly signed. I expect to be able to communicate officially, though I only know it as yet second hand from Sir Robert Otway, the English admiral. Excuse a very hurried epistle from

Yours, truly and affectionately,

W. Tudor.

MR. WEBSTER TO REV. MR. BRAZER.

Boston, November 10, 1828.

Dear Sir,—I part with Whately, not without regret, as I have not had leisure to go through him regularly, although I have had some good snatches here and there. It is a good book. If it were not for an appearance of self-conceit, I would say that I have found in it twenty things which I have thought of often, and been convinced of long, but never before saw in print. He shows sense, especially in the prominence which he gives to perspicuity and energy, as qualities of style. I like his hatred of adjectives, his love of Saxon words, and his idea of the true use of repetition; this last might be much further explained than it is done by him. There is something which may be called augmentative repetition, that is capable sometimes of producing great effect. "The author of the murder stood by the side of his victim, wet, bathed with the blood he had shed," or, "the murderer stood by the side of the slain, his sandals wet with the blood, the warm, gushing blood of his victim." In this last case, by the way, adjectives do their office; they add definite ideas.

What Mr. Whately says upon the effect of particularization, is just, especially as applied to pathetic description. The skilful, and apparently natural enumeration of particulars, is certainly, in its proper place, one of the very best modes of producing impression. All the standard works are full of instances of this sort of composition.

Perhaps the very best and most touching, is in the 12th verse of the 7th chapter of Luke. Here are comprised, in one short and single paragraph:—

A death; a funeral; the death of a young person, for his mother was living; the death of a son; the death of an only son; the son of a living mother; that mother a widow.

You remember, much better than I do, what a burst Massillon has, at the opening of his sermon on this text. This fine passage would have been tame enough, if, sinking all particulars, it had only recited, that, "when he came to the city, he met the funeral of one who had died under very afflicting circumstances."

Additional effect is given to the incident, by fixing so nearly the place where it was, nigh to the gate of the city. This minute statement of place, as well as of time, gives great naturalness to narrative compositions. Homer and De Foe, I regard as the greatest masters of this part of their art, always excepting the Scriptures.

Mr. Whately's rejection of expletives and epithets, shows his just perception of strength and beauty. Yet, particularization is sometimes out of place. There are cases in which comprehension or generalization is altogether preferable. Suppose one should say, "The distinction of the Christian revelation is, that it is addressed not only to Englishmen, but also to Frenchmen, Spaniards, Germans, Italians, Russians, Prussians," &c., &c. This would be feeble. Better thus. "The distinction of the Christian revelation is, that it reveals important truths, not to a few favored individuals, but to all the race of men; not to a single nation, but to the whole world." A book might be written on this little question, "When is effect produced by generalization; when by particularization?" At least, a book might be filled with opposite instances of both kinds, from our English classics, especially the Scriptures, Shakespeare, and Milton. An accurate writer should avoid generalities sometimes, not always; but when, it would require a treatise to expound. I rejoice to see one Rhetorician who will allow nothing to words but as they are signs of ideas. The rule is a good one, to use no word which does not suggest an idea, or modify some idea already suggested. And this should lead writers to adopt sparingly the use of such words as "vast," "amazing," "astonishing," &c. For, what do they mean? Dr. Watts, who by the way, I do not deem altogether a bad poet, somewhere speaks of the flight of an angel as being with "most amazing speed." But what idea is conveyed by this mode of expression? What is "amazing speed?"

It would amaze us, if we saw an oyster moving a mile a day. It would not amaze us to see a greyhound run a mile in a minute.

On the other hand, see with what unequalled skill Milton represents both the distance through which, and the speed with which, Mulciber fell from heaven:—

> From morn
> To noon he fell, from noon to dewy eve,
> A summer's day; and with the setting sun,
> Dropt from the zenith, like a falling star.

What art is manifest in these few lines! The object is to express great distance, and great velocity, neither of which is capable of very easy suggestion to the human mind. We are told that the angel fell a day, a long summer's day; the day is broken into forenoon and afternoon, that the time may seem to be protracted.

He does not reach the earth till sunset; and then, to represent the velocity, he "drops," one of the very best words in the language, to signify sudden and rapid fall, and then comes a simile, "like a falling star."

Excuse, my dear Sir, this very hurried and very presumptuous letter. You have, I hope, leisure to study rhetoric by investigating its principles. I have given little time, for I have had little time to give, to the systematic authors; but I have observed something of the effect of speaking and writing, and have endeavored to analyze "the causes of effects." "After all," says Cobbett, "he is a man of talent that can make a thing move." And after all, say I, he is an orator that can make me think as he thinks, and feel as he feels.

And I pray you, my dear Sir, both to think and to feel, that I am, with much regard,

Your obedient servant,

DANIEL WEBSTER.

EZEKIEL WEBSTER TO DANIEL WEBSTER.

January 9, 1829.

My dear Brother,—The legislature adjourned on Saturday last, the 3d instant, after having a very long session and doing a good deal of business. You will see by the papers that a nomination was made of candidates for Congress. To be frank with you, I did not wish nor intend to be a candidate myself. My only wish is to lead a quiet and peaceable life in domestic happiness and peace. But circumstances left me no choice; they did not permit me to consult my own feelings and wishes. My friends determined to act for me, and thought I had no right to act for myself. And so I am up. The result of the election is pretty doubtful, and especially in regard to my own. There are, I have no doubt, a good many Republicans in the administration party who will not vote for a Federalist, and they, of course, will strike off my name.

I should like to learn the aspect of things at Washington as soon as you have leisure. How is Mr. Clay's health?

Yours truly,

Ezekiel Webster.

DANIEL WEBSTER TO EZEKIEL WEBSTER.

Washington, January 17, 1829.

Dear Ezekiel,—The enclosed will give you a brief of all that is to be said of the state of things here.

I came here on the 12th, after a severe cold journey. But three judges are yet here; we expect a fourth to-night, and I must go into court on Monday. Not much is doing in the Senate. Mr. Wickliffe's motion about the mode of choosing officers of the House, which was intended mainly to affect the choice of printer, was to-day laid on the table by a majority of seven or eight votes.

You did right to go on the ticket. I showed Mr. Bell your letter. He says your fears, that republicans will strike off your name, are groundless, and that you will get as many votes as any of the rest. I believe you will all be chosen. Let me know from time to time how the prospect is. Mr. Moore's remark in a late journal is true; it is the most important election in New Hampshire since the adoption of the Constitution. I hope our friends will not lose it for want of attention.

Let me hear from you. D. W.

[Inclosed in letter dated January 17, 1829.]

General Jackson will be here about 15th February.

Nobody knows what he will do when he does come.

Many letters are sent to him; he answers none of them.

His friends here pretend to be very knowing; but be assured, not one of them has any confidential communication from him.

Great efforts are making to put him up to a general sweep, as to all offices; springing from great doubt whether he is disposed to go it.

Nobody is authorized to say, whether he intends to retire after one term of service.

Who will form his cabinet is as well known at Boston as at Washington.

The present apparent calm is a suspension of action, a sort of syncope, arising from ignorance of the views of the President elect.

My opinion is, that when he comes he will bring a breeze with him. Which way it will blow I cannot tell.

He will either go with the party, as they say in New York, or go the whole hog, as it is phrased elsewhere, making all the places he can for friends and supporters, and shaking a rod of terror at his opposers.

Or else he will continue to keep his own counsels, make friends and advisers of whom he pleases, and be President upon his own strength.

The first would show boldness where there is no danger, and decision where the opposite virtue of moderation would be more useful. The latter would show real nerve, and if he have talents to maintain himself in that course, true greatness.

My fear is stronger than my hope.

Mr. Adams is in good health, and complains not at all of the measure meted out to him.

Mr. Clay's health is much improved, and his spirits excellent. He goes to Kentucky in March, and, I conjecture, will be pressed into the next House of Representatives. His chance of being at the head of affairs is now better, in my judgment, than ever before.

Keep New England firm and steady, and she can make him President if she chooses.

Sundry important nominations are postponed, probably to know General Jackson's pleasure.

The above contains all that is known here, at this time.

[Indorsed 1829.]

MR. WOOD TO MR. WEBSTER.

Boscawen, January 31, 1829.

Honored and dear Sir,—It is with pleasure that I perform an office in the object of which I am much interested. I say interested, because it gives me an opportunity to do that officially, which I have considered as incumbent on me to do as an individual.

I present you the enclosed, as expressive of the feelings of the friends, and especially the trustees, of Boscawen Academy.

You will perhaps ask after my health, as I was feeble when I saw you last. Sir, I have reason to be thankful that my health is such as that I am able to preach on the Sabbaths and to attend to some other duties. It is my prayer that you may have wisdom from on high to direct you in the important station which you are called to fill.

Your affectionate friend,

Samuel Wood.

Honorable Daniel Webster.

Voted, That the thanks of this Board of Trustees be presented to the Honorable Daniel Webster for his very generous donation of a suitable bell for our academy; and that the president communicate the same.

From the Record. Eben. Price, *Secretary.*

EZEKIEL WEBSTER TO DANIEL WEBSTER.

February 15, 1829.

DEAR DANIEL,—I do not write to you oftener for two reasons; one, I have nothing to say; the other, that you have no leisure to read letters that say nothing. I can give you nothing new in regard to affairs in New Hampshire.

The truth is that the people made such an effort last fall, were so disappointed in the result, and so disgusted with the conduct of Mr. Adams, that they have not any heart to make any exertions. They always supported his cause from a cold sense of duty, and not from any liking of the man. We soon satisfy ourselves that we have discharged our duty to the cause of any man, when we do not entertain for him one personal kind feeling, nor cannot, unless we disembowel ourselves, like a trussed turkey, of all that is human nature within us. During the last contest, this cause alone had no little effect in producing all its disasters.

If there had been at the head of affairs a man of popular character, like Mr. Clay, or any man whom we were not compelled by our natures, instincts, and fixed fate to dislike, the result would have been different.

People cannot have strong affections for the cause, and strong dislike for the man. The measures of his administration were just and wise, and every honest man should have supported them, but many honest men did not, for the reason I have mentioned.

At what time do you intend to be home?

We are anxious here to see the first movements of General Jackson, as this will indicate the course of his policy.

I hear from Boston often, and you, I suppose, every day.

Yours truly,

E. WEBSTER.

MR. WEBSTER TO MRS. E. WEBSTER.

Senate Chamber, February 19, 1829.

My dear Sister,—I must begin with apology; or let me rather say, with confession; for though I am willing to confess great and censurable omissions, I have little to urge by way of apology, and nothing which amounts to justification. Let me pray you therefore, in the exercise of your clemency, to adopt the rule which Hamlet prescribes for passing judgment on the players. Do not treat me according to my deserts, for if so, "who would escape whipping," but according to your own bounty and dignity; the less I deserve forgiveness, the more will forgiveness exalt your forbearance and mercy.

The children under your good superintendence have written me continually, day by day, very good letters. Mr. Paige also has been kind, as he always is. Your own letters have completed my circle of domestic correspondence, and I must say that it has been very punctual, and highly gratifying. And now what can I tell you worth hearing?

General Jackson has been here about ten days. Of course the city is full of speculation and speculators. "A great multitude," too many to be fed without a miracle, are already in the city, hungry for office. Especially, I learn, that the typographical corps is assembled in great force. From New Hampshire, our friend Hill; from Boston, Mr. Greene; from Connecticut, Mr. Norton; from New York, Mr. Noah; from Kentucky, Mr. Kendall, and from everywhere else, somebody else. So many friends ready to advise, and whose advice is so disinterested, make somewhat of a numerous council about the President elect; and, if report be true, it is a council which only "makes that darker, which was dark enough before." For these reasons, or these with others, nothing is settled yet, about the new cabinet. I suppose Mr. Van Buren will be Secretary of State; but beyond that, I do not think any thing is yet determined.

For ten or twelve days, our Senate has been acting with closed doors, on certain nominations to office by Mr. Adams What we have done is not yet known, though one day it will be probably.

The general spirit prevailing here, with the friends of the new

President, is that of a pretty decided party character. It is not quite so fierce as our New England Jackson men are actuated by, still, I think it likely to grow more and more bitter, unless, which is highly probable, the party itself should divide.

We have all read the dispute between Mr. Adams and the Boston gentlemen. Thus far I believe the universal feeling is, that Mr. Adams has the worst side of it. I hear, however, that he is about to reply in another pamphlet!!

The fashionable world is and has been full and gay. Crowds have come and are coming to see the inauguration, &c. I have been to three parties, to wit, Mrs. Adams's last, Mrs. Clay's last, and Mrs. Porter's last. Mrs. Porter, wife of the Secretary of War, is a fine woman, whom we visited at Niagara, when there four years ago. With these manifestations of regard for the setting sun and stars, I have satisfied my desire of seeing the social circles. If there should be a ball on the 22d, I shall attend as usual, to commemorate the great and good man born on that day.

Judge Story is well, and in his usual spirits. The court is deeply engaged, and as soon as I get rid of these secret sessions of the Senate, I have enough to do in it.

We are looking to New Hampshire. I shall not engage lodgings for you and your husband next winter, till I see the returns.

[Conclusion cut off.]

MR. WEBSTER TO MARY ANN WEBSTER.

Washington, February 23, 1829.

My dear Mary Ann,—I am exceedingly sorry that you are so ill that your thoughts cannot flow from your own pen. I trust, however, that your little fever, which the Doctor calls a slow one, will hasten off with a quickened pace. Your sister and Julia will, I hope, not fail to let me know, every day, how you get along, as I shall be anxious till I hear that you are quite well. You may safely tell Alice and Julia to do their best to run away from you if they can. You will overtake them when you get well. Tell them to fly on in music, dancing, and French. Give my love to mother and all the rest.

Your affectionate uncle,

Daniel Webster.

MR. WEBSTER TO MRS. E. WEBSTER.

Washington, Sunday morning, March 2, 1829.

DEAR SISTER,—I had letters yesterday from Mr. Paige and from Alice, which ought to have been received two days earlier. This, I suppose, is to be placed to the account of your great storm.

With less snow, we have very cold weather here. There has not been a warm day since I came here, although I have often seen the peach-trees in blossom in February. The ground is still covered with snow, the river hard frozen, and the weather steadily cold. It will make bad travelling for those who leave here the 4th.

Tuesday is the last day of the session of Congress. A special session of the Senate is called to meet on Wednesday, the 4th. I suppose it will not last beyond two or three days. General Jackson will then nominate his new cabinet, and make such changes in office as he sees fit. On this latter subject very little is known about his intentions; probably he will make some removals, but I think not a great many immediately. But we shall soon see.

The court will probably continue its session a fortnight longer, and then I shall set my face northward. I hope your patience will hold out. Consider how cold it must be up at Boscawen, and how busy your husband is now, and how soon he will come to Boston, after the 10th, either for congratulation or condolence. He will need a week in either case, and that will bring March so far along, that I trust you will be able to content yourself till I come.

My health is good, but I find, to confess the truth, that I am growing indolent. I would be glad to have more decisive volitions. I do nothing in Congress or the court, but what is clearly necessary; and in such cases, even, my efforts "come haltingly off." In short, I believe the truth is, that I am growing old, and age you know, or rather you have heard, requires repose.

Adieu, yours, with much affectionate regard,

DANIEL WEBSTER.

MR. WEBSTER TO MRS. E. WEBSTER.

Washington, March 4, 1829.

[First year of the administration of Andrew Jackson, and the first day.]

My dear Sister,—I thank you for yours, received to-day, and thank you both for the letter itself and for your pardon which it contains, and of which I stood in so much need. Your benignity is memorable and praiseworthy. To be serious, however, my dear sister, let me say once for all, that I have a very affectionate regard for you; that I am very glad you are my sister, and the wife of the best of all brothers; and that if, like him, I am not the most punctual of all correspondents, I am like him in sincerity and constancy of esteem. If you find in your connection with my own little broken circle but one half as much pleasure as you bestow, you will have no reason to regret it. Your presence with my children, through the winter, has relieved me from a pressing weight of anxiety.

To-day we have had the inauguration. A monstrous crowd of people is in the city. I never saw any thing like it before. Persons have come five hundred miles to see General Jackson, and they really seem to think that the country is rescued from some dreadful danger.

The inauguration speech you will see. I cannot make much of it, except that it is anti-tariff, at least in some degree. What it says about reform in office may be either a prelude to a general change in office, or a mere sop to soothe the hunger, without satisfying it, of the thousand expectants for office who throng the city, and clamor all over the country. I expect some changes, but not a great many at present. The show lasted only half an hour. The Senate assembled at eleven, the judges and foreign ministers came in, the President elect was introduced, and all seated by half-past eleven. The Senate was full of ladies; a pause ensued till twelve. Then the President, followed by the Senate, &c., went through the great rotunda, on to the portico, over the eastern front door; and those went with him who could, but the crowd broke in as we were passing the rotunda, and all became confusion. On the portico, in the open air, the day very warm and pleasant, he read his inaugural, and took the oath. A great shout followed from the multitude, and in fifteen minutes, "silence settled, deep and still." Every body was dispersed. As I walked home, I called in at a bookstore, and saw a volume which I now send you; it may serve to regulate matters of etiquette at Boscawen.

I hope to write Edward to-night. If not, I shall not fail to do so to-morrow.

Yours very sincerely and truly,

D. WEBSTER.

DANIEL WEBSTER TO EZEKIEL WEBSTER.

Washington, Sunday evening, March 15, 1829.

DEAR EZEKIEL,—The Senate will probably adjourn to-morrow, and I hope the court will rise, or at least will dismiss me by Wednesday or Thursday. I shall be immediately off. My books are in trunks. I shall hear from New Hampshire to-morrow, and dispose of them according to circumstances. If no change takes place in my own condition, of which I have not the slightest expectation, and if you are not elected, I shall not return. This, *inter nos*, but my mind is settled. Under present circumstances, public and domestic, it is disagreeable being here, and to me there is no novelty to make compensation. It will be better for me and my children that I should be with them. If I do not come in a public, I shall not in a professional character. I can leave the court now as well as ever, and can earn my bread as well at home as here.

Your company and that of your wife, would make a great difference. I have not much expectation that you will be returned. Our fortune is, as connected with recent and current political events, that if there be opposite chances, the unfavorable one turns up. You had a snow of five feet, which of itself might turn the election against the well-disposed and indifferent, and in favor of the mischievous and the active. I shall not be disappointed if I hear bad news.

I make my point to be home the first day of April, when I trust I shall meet you. We will then settle what is best to do with the children. I shall want Julia and Edward to stay a little while with me. Edward, I think, should then go to Boscawen. I hardly know what I shall think best to do with Julia.

Yours as ever,

D. Webster.

P. S. We have had one important cause here. It is from New York, respecting what is called the Sailors' Snug Harbor. I have made a greater exertion in it than in any other since Dartmouth College *v.* Woodward, or than it is probable I shall ever make in another.

MR. WEBSTER TO MRS. E. WEBSTER.

Boston, April 15, 1829.

My dear Sister,—We had a very good journey home, and arrived last evening at about eight o'clock. Mr. Paige is here; he reached home from New York on Sunday evening. No news reached him till he came into the house here. Julia has come home this morning; she seems well, except her usual cough. I think I shall consult Dr. Warren as to that. My losses have been such that I feel alarmed for every thing that remains.

Mary will put up your articles and Edward's clothes, and, perhaps, we may send them by the coach which carries this. I hear that Mrs. Ticknor and Mrs. Hale are well as usual.

Your house, my dear sister, is not alone solitary and melancholy. It is the same here.

Yours truly and affectionately,

Daniel Webster.

MR. WEBSTER TO DR. PERKINS.

Boston, April 17, 1829.

My dear Friend,—You will have heard of the sudden death of my brother. The event necessarily called me to Boscawen, from which place I returned a day or two ago. It has quite overwhelmed us all. Mrs. Webster and the oldest daughter were here, when it happened. The messenger brought us the news at three o'clock, on Saturday morning, the 11th instant. The death took place the previous afternoon at four o'clock. You will probably have seen some account of it. It seems to me I never heard of a death so instantaneous. He fell in an instant, without any effort to save himself, and without any struggle or sign of consciousness, after he reached the floor. On receiving the tidings, Mrs. Webster and her daughter, and myself and two sons, set off immediately, and arrived at Boscawen that evening at nine o'clock. The funeral was attended the next day. Mrs. Webster's constitution is feeble, and I knew not how she would get through the dreadful scene; yet she did get through. I left her far better than was to have been expected; and a letter received to-day says she continues so. It was not possible for me to stay long from home, on so sudden a call; but I must return in two or three days to Boscawen, to pay proper attention to the circumstances of the family. My brother has left two daughters, one fourteen and one twelve years old; and a wife, a fine woman, to whom he had been married about four years. He has left a competency to those dependent on him; but it will require care and oversight to preserve it, and make the most of it.

This event, my dear Sir, has affected me very much. Coming so soon after another awful stroke, it seems to fall with double weight. He has been my reliance, through life, and I have derived much of its happiness from his fraternal affection. I am left the sole survivor of my family. Yet I have objects of affection in my children, and I do not intend to repine; though I confess I cannot well describe the effect of this event on my feelings.

I ought to acknowledge the receipt of two letters from you, yet unanswered. It is probable, that but for this melancholy occurrence, I should have been in New York the first of May. Now, it is hardly likely I shall be there before the sitting of the court, on the 25th.

I pray you give our love to Mrs. Perkins. We know she sympathizes with us, in all our afflictions. Remember me also to Mr. Clarke's family, whom I had not the pleasure of seeing as I came home.

Yours always truly,

DAN'L WEBSTER.

MR. WEBSTER TO MR. MASON.

Boston, April 19, 1829.

My dear Sir,—I thank you for your kind letter. You do not and cannot overrate the strength of the shock which my brother's death has caused me. I have felt but one such in life; and this follows that so soon that it requires more fortitude than I possess to bear it with firmness, such perhaps as I ought. I am aware that the case admits of no remedy, nor any present relief; and endeavor to console myself with reflecting, that I have had much happiness in lost connections; and that they must expect to lose beloved objects in this world, who have beloved objects to lose. My life, I know, has been fortunate and happy beyond the common lot, and it would be now ungrateful, as well as unavailing, to repine at calamities of which, as they are human, I must expect to partake. But I confess the world, at present, has for me an aspect any thing but cheerful. With a multitude of acquaintance, I have few friends; my nearest intimacies are broken, and a sad void is made in the objects of affection. Of what remains dear and valuable, I need not say that a most precious part is the affectionate friendship of yourself and family. I want to see you very much indeed, but know not whether I shall be able soon to visit Portsmouth. You will be glad to know that my own health is good. I have never, for ten years, got through a winter without being more reduced in health and strength. My children also are well. Edward is at Boscawen, where he will probably stay through the summer, or as long as the family may be kept together there. Daniel hopes to go to college in August. Julia proposes to pass the summer, or part of it, with Mrs. Lee, and must afterwards be disposed of as best she may.

This occurrence is calculated to have effect on the future course of my own life, and to add to the inducements, already felt, to retire from a situation in which I am making daily sacrifices and doing little good to myself or others. Pray give my love to your family.

Yours affectionately and entirely,

Dan'l Webster.

MR. M'GAW TO MR. WEBSTER.

Bangor, May 1, 1829.

Dear Sir,—There are seasons, that sooner or later present themselves to us, which are too sacred to admit the presence of even dear friends. But these seasons are hallowed by the knowledge that the same friends share our griefs or our joys with us. My own experience leads to the conclusion that others possess these feelings in common with me.

How to approach the subject, with which my heart is full, and yours is overflowing, I do not know.

Bereavement of friends who were dear to you is not a new event, though the arrows of affliction have not fallen thick upon you, that I know of. If, however, your wounds had been quite numerous, few, very few of them could have been so severe as the one recently received.

A State has lost one of her most highly valued citizens, and the bar of New Hampshire one of its brightest ornaments; but some other citizen may supply his place to the State, and some other lawyer adorn the bar of which he was the pride. Would to God, it were possible that another brother, possessing equal excellence and equal love with him whom you have lost, could be granted you. I know that it is unavailing to utter such a wish, but it is a privilege to mourn in such cases.

The friends of my youth are pretty fast dropping off, and leaving me with few, and that number constantly diminishing, who are really dear to me; and though my heart clings close to those friends who remain, yet on the whole my desire of living becomes weaker and weaker every year.

Amid the vicissitudes and trials of life, there is consolation in the assurance that though no chastening for the present seemeth to be joyous, but grievous, nevertheless afterward it yieldeth the peaceable fruits of righteousness unto them which are exercised thereby.

That every dispensation of Divine Providence may bring you to the enjoyment of more of the smiles of our blessed Saviour, is the earnest prayer of,

Your friend,

Jacob McGaw.

[Mr. Webster, in connection with some other gentlemen, was interested in some wild land in the northern part of New Hampshire.

He paid little attention to the matter, apparently, and the occupier of the town of Dixville addressed him a remonstrance on the subject of the place, and its means of communication and transport, which, as it represents a not very flourishing state of things, in a good-natured style of reproach, I have thought might not be without amusement in its perusal.]

MR. WHITTEMORE TO MR. WEBSTER.

Dixville, June 22, 1829.

SIR,—The inhabitants of this town are now reduced to two; my children are all gone but my youngest daughter, and if there is no better prospect we must quit before winter. The roads are so bad there is but little travel. Last year the bridges were all carried off, and two large slides came down in the Notch. We did seventy days' work on the road before teams could pass; Mr. Parsons and others worked about twenty more; the prospect was so bad that my sons were determined not to winter here again. Mr. Gerrish told me the last time I saw him, that you and he had agreed not to sell any single lots, nor do any thing on the road. Now, Sir, if this is right, I ought not to complain, but I must hear some other reasons for its being just, before I can believe it. We have done at least five hundred days' work on the road, and the proprietors have done nothing. I am no beggar; all I ask is justice amongst men Your much lamented brother told me that Daniel would be willing to lay out a hundred or two dollars on the road, if that would satisfy me, but that you considered such sum only as an entering wedge for a larger sum; but I am not lawyer enough to see the propriety of such argument. Besides, two hundred dollars, well laid out, with what the people would do, provided that sum was promised to be paid those that should do the work, when done, under the superintendence of some good man that feels an interest in the road, would make it tolerable good, so that the reverse of curses would rest on the proprietors' heads. You can guess pretty near what men say, when they get their horses off the Notch, and have them lay in the gulf two or three days, which has several times been the case. I think it would be for your interest to sell the land by lots to settlers, and I should like good neighbors very much. Now, Sir, if you will assist in repairing the road, you will let me know how and when. General Town from Charlton has been here; if you see him, he can tell you my situation and that of the road.

I am your long neglected and very humble servant,

JOHN WHITTEMORE.

MR. WEBSTER TO MRS. LANGDON ELWYN.

Boston, September 8, 1829.

MY DEAR MRS. LANGDON ELWYN,—I have been long your debtor for two kind letters, received by me early in the season. I know not how to account for, much less excuse, so long a delay. But the summer has been running away, and occurrences happening which occupied my attention from week to week. My brother's death was an unexpected stroke, and has devolved on me, in addition to the pain arising from the loss of so good a brother, many new cares and duties. I have lived to be the last of a pretty large circle of brothers and sisters. It not only fills me with wonder, but with melancholy, to look round about the places of my early acquaintance. Every body is gone. While my brother lived, there was yet something to hold to; but now, the last attraction is gone. There was a large, valuable, and most pleasant farm which belonged to us, and which he had taken excellent care of for years, but it causes me great pain now to visit it. A new generation has sprung up around it, and I see nothing interesting to me but the tombs of my parents, and my brothers and sisters.

I have been from home but once, except to New Hampshire. Julia and I went to Brattleboro' in July, and intended to visit Lake George. I proceeded to Albany where I was to be joined by Mr. Hunt's family, of Brattleboro', and Julia, but Mrs. Hunt was taken sick, so that part of the journey failed, and I returned to Brattleboro' and thence home. I got home just in season to see your neighbor and my friend —— in the stage-coach, passing out of town on her return home. If all Boston talk be true, it is possible we may have the pleasure of seeing her again in this quarter. Some people's hearts, it seems, are not so cold as their occupations.

We have had sundry and divers good citizens of the South among us in the course of August; among others your neighbor, Mr. Biddle, was here just long enough to let us look at him. He is always most welcome, as he is always most agreeable; but, if instead of cashiers and other officials, he would bring fellow travellers of another kind with him, it would enhance our pleasure. Our Yankees have a great opinion of him. They think he takes good care of their money; although they do not see in him any of the marks of one of the children of Israel. He will have told you, that he had occasion to visit our town of Portsmouth. Mr. Mason was recently here, and expressed high satisfaction at the result of Mr. Biddle's visit, and much respect for him.

Of news in our circle, I dare say your daughters know more than I do. All that has come to my knowledge is, that Mr. Charles Adams and Miss Brooks are married, and saw their friends last evening; and that Mr. Gorham is engaged to Mrs. Coles. The latter fact I learn from Mr. Gorham himself, and the former I infer from having received a legal portion of wedding cake.

I send you a copy of Mr. Sprague's poem, which I did not hear, and have not read; but I subscribed for six copies, being told it was a poetical poem. I have seen no such production among us, lately, though I have met with several prose ones. Judge Story edified us with a good discourse, on his inauguration as professor.

What shall I say of your friend Mr. Blake? He has been very gay and gallant through the season of company, and is in fine health and spirits. I know not if he intends becoming a relative of yours, but I believe that when he goes out for a drive, if no special order be given, the coachman sets off, as of course, for Mrs. Eustis's.

I hear with much regret of the illness of Mrs. R., understanding she is in Portsmouth. I hope she will find an atmosphere somewhat less damp than that of New York, favorable to her. We saw little of Charles while he was here, everybody was engaged. I sought him diligently, to have his company at dinner with Mr. Biddle, but he had gone to carouse with the Phi Beta Kappa.

I pray you make my best respects to Emily and Matilda. For all I have heard of them lately, I am mainly indebted to Mr. Wallenstein, whom also I salute. Say to —— I have still in my eye the parting but reproachful shake of her finger through the coach window. She cannot say, I did it, "never shake," &c.

Yours always, very truly,
DANIEL WEBSTER.

DANIEL WEBSTER TO FLETCHER WEBSTER.

New York, December 14, 1829.

MY DEAR SON,—You have been informed that an important change in my domestic condition was expected to take place. It happened on Saturday. The lady who is now to bear the relation of mother to you, and Julia, and Edward, I am sure will be found worthy of all your affection and regard; and I am equally certain that she will experience from all of you the utmost kindness and attachment. She insists on taking Julia with us to Washington, thinking it will be better for her, and that she will also be good company.

We shall leave New York in about a week. I read your first letter, which gave me pleasure, and hope to have another from you before I leave New York. You will not fail to write me once a week, according to arrangement. The enclosed note you will of course answer. If you despatch your answer at once, without waiting for the keepsake, it will arrive here before our departure. Let it come enclosed to me. The "keepsake" is an elegant gold watch. You must send for it to Mr. Paige, by a careful hand. Mr. Paige will not be home under ten days from this time.

I hope, my dear son, that I shall continue to hear good accounts of you.

I am always, with much affection, your father,
D. WEBSTER.

MR. WEBSTER TO MR. DUTTON.

(Extract.)

Washington, January 15, 1830.

As to Washington occurrences I hardly know whether there be any thing of novelty. We have a plentiful parcel of persons here, many of them from Massachusetts, who having received commissions from the President since March, find it necessary to take care that they do not lose them. The great batch of appointments is not yet acted on in the Senate. Before particular cases shall be taken up, it is probable a general discussion will be had in open or secret session upon the course of the administration in regard to removals and appointments. I never did intend to trouble myself with another debate, on such questions, being as tired of them as I am of constitutional questions in the courts; but if I could see clearly what was the true ground, I fear I might break my resolution. The power of removal, as a distinct power, and as residing in the President alone, has been often exercised; but I confess I doubt its existence. It seems to me to be only incident to the power of appointment, and to belong therefore where that power belongs, that is to say, to the President and Senate. Pray, while you are making one turn in the Mall, give this subject one turn also in your thoughts.

The tariff sleepeth. It may be jogged a little during the session, but I think not awakened. Let them go on to spin at Lowell, with the persuasion that if their condition be not made better, it will still not be made worse. I think the duties on tea and coffee will be reduced; and that then reduction will stop. The general face of things appears here, I presume, much as it does with you. Mr. Van Buren has evidently, at this moment, quite the lead in influence and importance. He controls all the pages on the back stairs, and flatters what seems to be at present the Aaron's serpent among the President's desires, a settled purpose of making out the lady, of whom so much has been said, a person of reputation. It is odd enough, but too evident to be doubted, that the consequence of this dispute in the social and fashionable world, is producing great political effects, and may very probably determine who shall be successor to the present chief magistrate. "Such great events, &c. &c. &c."

Our good chief justice has not yet arrived, but is expected this evening, the convention at Richmond having agreed on a constitution, by a majority of ten, as the report is this morning. The court meantime is proceeding diligently with its docket of causes. Judge Story is well and in good spirits. The weather to-day is like May. Neither House sits. My wife is gone to the Capitol, House of Representatives, to hear Mr. Everett's address to the Columbia Institute. Julia is at her writing master's, and while a gentleman is occupying the attention of the court with the reading of a shocking long record, I have found time to write you a shocking long letter, which an apology would but further protract.

Yours always,

D. WEBSTER.

DANIEL WEBSTER TO MRS. E. WEBSTER.

January 17, 1830.

MY DEAR SISTER,—I have not heard from you since I left Boston, until this day, when I received a letter from C. B. Haddock. He informs me you are at Concord, where your mother is dangerously ill. I grieve for this new calamity. Providence has seen fit to let your sorrows and misfortunes come together. Be assured no one can feel for you more sympathy than myself, who know how much you have suffered for those dear to me. Your mother, however, has arrived at good old age, and her departure from this to a better state, would not and ought not to be so violent a disruption of strong ties as some that you have felt.

I parted with you, I think, the first day of October, not at all foreseeing what was to happen to myself in so short a time. I am now here, settled down for the session, with Mrs. Webster and Julia. When I left home, I did not expect to bring Julia further than New York. She was to have returned with Mr. Paige; but Mrs. Webster chose to have it otherwise, and I believe it is much better as it is. Julia seems exceedingly happy. Her health is better than I ever saw it, and she is much attached to her new mother. With this last personage, I am sure you will be pleased. You will find her amiable, affectionate, prudent, and agreeable; as these are good sober words, you must take them as used for what they ought to mean, and not as the rhapsody of a new husband. It will not be many months, however, I hope, before I shall bring her and yourself face to face, and then you can judge for yourself.

I hope you will write to me, and let me know how and where the children are. Send them my love, and remember me to Mrs. French.

I am, my dear sister, with unabated affection and regard, yours truly,

D. WEBSTER.

MR. WEBSTER TO MR. HADDOCK.

Washington, January 19, 1830.

MY DEAR NEPHEW,—If Messrs. Perkins and Marvin choose to run the risk of such a publication as you mention, I do not know as I can reasonably object to it; though, sure enough, I shall be ashamed to see the likeness of my face in the shop windows, as I go from my house to Court street.

As to any introductory notice, or family memoir, I shall leave that to your own good taste, with the reservation that I must see whatever is prepared before it is published. I hardly know what there is, not already known as mine, which it would be worth while to print. There are, however, some reviews, and an address to the Phi Beta Kappa, in 1806, which for a boy I thought pretty good; but I have not read it since it was delivered. I remember, among other things in it, I urged the necessity of forming agricultural and historical societies, when there were no such things in the State.

Joshua Coffin has looked up some genealogical dates, &c., as you will see by the enclosed letter, which you will please preserve. Major Bohonon sent me a minute of some dates, which might help you, in regard to the gravestones, but I left them in Boston. I think the best way is to send to Mr. Farley whatever is ready, and let him go on with that.

I am glad you are going to take an active part in the settlement of affairs at Boscawen. The faster things are adjusted the better. As to the farm, I would have you, of course, consider what will be best for your wards. It is not essential to sell before my return. I will buy, rather than suffer it to remain as it is, if it be thought best by you to sell it for what I can afford to give. I have no doubt what is for the children's interest, my only hesitation is, as to what I can afford to do myself. The whole farm would yield very little income to me, and yet I feel unwilling to sell it altogether; I wish you were rich enough to own it. Let me hear from you when you get your letter of guardianship, and as much sooner as you find it convenient.

I am affectionately yours,

DANIEL WEBSTER.

CHANCELLOR KENT TO MR. WEBSTER.

New York, January 21, 1830.

DEAR SIR,—I ought to have replied earlier to your letter of the 15th instant; but I have been diverted by a number of perplexing avocations, each of them, singly, petty in its nature; but conjointly such things make up the sum of the life of ordinary minds. And now to the purpose. I beg leave to decline any opinion on the question you state. 1. I have not time to do it justice and render any thing I could say worthy of you. 2. I am not going to undertake to instruct a Senatorial statesman, who has thought on the subject infinitely more than I have, for it comes officially before him.

Hamilton, in The Federalist, No. 77, was of opinion that the President could not remove without the consent of the Senate. I heard the question debated in the summer of 1789, and Madison, Benson, Ames, Lawrence, &c., were in favor of the right of removal by the President, and such has been the opinion ever since, and the practice. I thought they were right, because I then thought this side uniformly right. Mr. White of Virginia, was strenuously opposed to that construction. You will find the discussion in Fenno's United States Gazeteer for July or August, or September, 1789. Mr. Madison reasoned technically like a lawyer. Now, when I come to think on the subject, with my confirmed wary views of things, I pause and doubt of the construction, on account of the word "advice." That word is pregnant with meaning, and means something beyond consent to nominations, or it would not have been inserted. The consent, so it might be argued, applies to the individual named; the advice to the measure itself, which draws to it the whole ground of the interference. Again, it is a great and general principle, in all jurisprudence, that when there is no positive provision in the case regulating the principle, the power that appoints is the power to determine the pleasure of the appointment and the limitation. It is the power to reappoint; and the power to appoint and reappoint, when all else is silent, is the power to remove. I begin to have a strong suspicion that Hamilton was right, as he always was on public questions.

On the other hand it is too late to call the President's power in question, after a declaratory act of Congress and an acquiescence of half a century. We should hurt the reputation of our government with the world, and we are accused already of the Republican tendency of reducing all executive power into the legislative, and making Congress a national convention. That the President grossly abuses the power of removal is manifest, but it is the evil genius of Democracy to be the sport of factions. Hamilton said in The Federalist, in his speeches, and a hundred times to me, that factions would ruin us, and our government had not sufficient balance and energy to resist the propensity to them, and to control their tyranny and their profligacy. All theories of government that suppose the mass of the people virtuous, and able and willing to act virtuously, are plainly Utopian, and will remain so until the return of the Saturnian age.

Yours very sincerely,

JAMES KENT.

P. S. I never heard of any such book written by Mr. Wells, and I don't believe he ever wrote any such.

MR. WEBSTER TO MR. MASON.

Washington, February 27, 1830.

DEAR SIR,—The press has sent abroad all I said in the late debate, and you will have seen it. I have paid what attention I could to the reporter's notes; but, in the midst of other pressing engagements, I have not made either speech what it ought to be; but let them go. The whole matter was quite unexpected. I was busy with the court, and paying no attention to the debate which was going on sluggishly in the Senate, without exciting any interest. Happening to have nothing to do for the moment, in court, I went into the Senate, and Mr. Hayne, so it turned out, just then rose. When he sat down, my friends said he must be answered, and I thought so too, and being thus got in, thought I must go through. It is singular enough, though perhaps not unaccountable, that the feeling of this little public is all on our side. I may say to you that I never before spoke in the hearing of an audience so excited, so eager, and so sympathetic.

The appointments are not yet acted on, though I am expecting them to be taken up daily. Hill's chance is just about even. It depends on a single vote, or two at most, and they keep their own counsels, so that we shall never know till the time of voting comes. Decatur's chance is not equal. I think he will be rejected. I have some hopes that all the printers will be thrown out; but there is no certainty about it. Calhoun is forming a party against Van Buren, and as the President is supposed to be Van Buren's man, the Vice-President has great difficulty to separate his opposition to Van Buren from opposition to the President. Our idea is to let them pretty much alone; by no means to act a secondary part to either. We never can and never must support either.

While they are thus arranging themselves for battle, that is, Calhoun and Van Buren, there are two considerations which are likely to be overlooked, or disregarded by them, and which are material to be considered. 1. The probability that General Jackson will run again; that that is his present purpose, I am quite sure. 2. The extraordinary power of this anti-Masonic party, especially in Pennsylvania.

Judge Story has been ill, so as to be out of court for three or four days. He is now well again. Mr. Justice Baldwin is thought to give promise of being a very good judge. The other new judge, I fear, has his head turned too much to politics.

I have been written to, to go to New Hampshire to try a cause against you next August, brought by Mrs. Mellen *v.* Dover Company. Where is the August court holden? I suppose up at the Lakes. If it were an easy and plain case on our side, I might be willing to go; but I have some of your pounding in my bones yet, and don't care about any more till that wears out.

Yours ever truly, with regards to your family,

DANIEL WEBSTER.

MR. A. LAWRENCE TO MR. WEBSTER.

Boston, March 3, 1830.

DEAR SIR,—Permit me to indulge my feelings, after the banquet I have just had in reading your speech, by expressing to you my grateful sense of obligation, for the favor conferred on me, in common with every other son of New England, for your triumphant vindication of her character from the foul aspersions cast upon it by the South; and to assure you that my sense of the value and importance of this service, will only cease with the healthy exercise of my mind. I thank you as a citizen of Massachusetts, of New England, of the United States, not only for myself, but for my children. The vindication of New England is not more complete than is that of the Constitution of the United States, from the libels which these same citizens of the South would fasten upon it. The doctrines you have laid down are sound doctrines, and stated so plainly that all may understand them, and they will prove a safe political manual for our children after us.

Again I thank you. This humble tribute I pray you to accept with the assurance that I offer it, not less to gratify my own feelings, than from a sense of obligation for a great favor received by your unfeigned friend,

AMOS LAWRENCE

MR. WEBSTER TO MR. HADDOCK.

Washington, March 4, 1830.

Dear Charles,—I received duly yours of the 17th of February. Affairs at Salisbury may as well remain as they are, till I get home. We will then endeavor to meet in that region, and settle some arrangements. I am glad that Mrs. Webster and the children are with you, and pray you to remember me to them. We ourselves are all well.

As to my "Works," if a book is to be made, I should think the following might be selected:—

1. Plymouth Discourse; I think this the best of my efforts. 2. Bunker Hill. 3. Adams and Jefferson. 4. Greek Speech. 5. Tariff Speech of 1824. 6. Panama Mission. 7. Bank Speech. 8. Currency Speech, 1816, which I have caused to be copied and now send; but I have not read a word of it since it was delivered. Dinner Speeches, Boston. Faneuil Hall, Election Speeches. Two Speeches of this Session. Speech,—Revolutionary Officers; there are two of this description, pretty much alike. I do not know which is best; but one of them should be printed.

If any law speeches be printed, I think the following the best:—

Dartmouth College case, Steamboat case, and Prescott's defence; but I have never read this; I have quite forgotten it.

You speak of the Dedham speech; I do not know what you refer to. I defended Judge Haven on an indictment, growing out of an ecclesiastical dispute at Dedham; but the speech was never published, to my knowledge. The Address to the Mechanics' Association might be rigged up and put in for variety. I doubt whether there is any thing readable in what I said in Convention. Those debates might be looked to. I doubt whether it will be worth while to begin the work till I get home. A good deal of care should be bestowed upon it; and such a publication at the present moment will have so many bearings, that it must be well considered what it should contain. We can have no family memoir. As to biographical notices, if any, they must be exceedingly brief. If, however, it is matter of importance to the printers to begin earlier, you may let me know it. The picture is by Stewart; it is at Mr. I. P. Davis's. I suppose that he would suffer it to be used by a distinguished engraver, if it were thought best to have an engraving. If I could pick up what I said year before last to your boys at Hanover, and what I said last year to those of Amherst, they could be put together and make something which would eke out variety.

With regards to your family,

Yours, D. WEBSTER.

P. S. One volume would be enough in all conscience.

MR. WEBSTER TO MR. PLEASANTS.

[Draft of a letter found in Mr. Webster's handwriting.]

(PRIVATE AND CONFIDENTIAL.)

Washington, March 6, 1830.

DEAR SIR,—Soon after I had posted a speech to you this morning, I received yours of the 4th instant. I am glad you have written to me on general accounts; I need not say how much I am gratified to learn there are some in Virginia who think of my efforts without disrespect. To tell you the truth, I have sometimes felt that while political foes have dealt to me in your good State, a large measure of abuse, political friends have not always interposed a shield, under circumstances when perhaps it might have been expected by one engaged in the same general public cause. But I have no hard feeling in this respect. I knew there were reasons why some of us should bear abuse, without expecting to be defended. That time I hope has gone by; at any rate I should not hope to find myself in such a condition again. I am willing to correspond with you freely, but in entire and sacred confidence. Through life, thus far, I have been as much guarded as possible against the accidents of the post-office and other accidents attending confidential correspondence. Nevertheless, the times require occasional confidence, and that some hazards be run. I am willing therefore to write you an occasional letter, knowing that I shall be safe, even if I had secrets to communicate, which will not often be the case. I shall be glad also to hear from you often. You may rely on confidence on my side.

At present there is not much to be said, growing out of the state of things here. The most objectional nominations have not yet been acted on. It is quite uncertain how they will be disposed of. The Senate will be so nearly equally divided, that a vote or two will decide sundry nominations, and no one can say how these votes may be given. There will be close voting certainly in several cases. I agree with you, it is a balanced question, whether more good will flow from the rejection than from the confirmation. It would disappoint individuals, doubtless; but would it not, on the whole, rather strengthen the administration to send Hill, Kendall, &c. home? As to future operations, the general idea here seems to be this; to bring forward no candidate this year, though doubtless the general impression is that Mr. Clay stands first and foremost in the ranks of those who would desire a change. I do not think there is the least abatement of the respect and confidence entertained for him. As to the other Western gentleman whom you mention, he must not be thought of, for he is not with us. Depend upon it, there is a negotiation in train to bring him out as Vice-President, to run on the ticket with Mr. Calhoun. In my opinion he has very little weight or influence in the country, and that is fast declining. Our friends in the West will quit him, of course, in that event, as he must give up their interests. I write now to say, that two things are not to be omitted when we speculate on the future; first, that General Jackson will certainly be candidate again, if he live and be well; I say certainly, I mean only that I have no doubt of it. Second, that we cannot now foresee what events will follow from what is passing in Pennsylvania and New York on the subject of anti-Masonry; this matter, be assured, is not to be disregarded.

In the mean time it seems to me our course must be this. Expose the selfishness and pretence of the men in power, as much as possible; taking care to let the ministers be made responsible for at least their full share. The acts will be theirs in most cases; and therefore they ought to be responsible for them themselves.

Show ourselves uniform and just, by acting according to our principles, and opposing only such measures as deserve no support.

As to tariff subjects, we of the North must hold on where we are, and as to internal improvements, we also must go temperately and cautiously for them also.

Agree in all measures having in view the payment of the debt.

To hold ourselves absolutely aloof from Mr. Van Buren and Mr. Calhoun, and be ready to act for ourselves when the proper time comes, and to maintain our own men and defend our own friends.

Finally, cultivate a truly national spirit; go for great ends, and hold up the necessity of the Union, &c. &c.

DAN'L WEBSTER.

MR. WEBSTER TO MR. DUTTON.

Washington, March 8, 1830.

MY DEAR SIR,—I thank you for your friendly and flattering letter. Your commendation of my speech is measured less by its merits than by your bounty. If it has gratified my friends at home, I am rewarded for any little trouble it has cost me. The whole debate was matter of accident. I had left the court pretty late in the day, and went into the Senate with my court papers under my arm, just to see what was passing. It so happened that Mr. Hayne very soon rose in his first speech. I did not like it, and my friends liked it less; some of them reminded me, that some years ago a debate had happened in the House of Representatives, in which Mr. M'Duffie and myself had expressed opinions exactly the reverse of what was now ascribed respectively to the South and East. I had forgotten the circumstance, but promised to turn back to the debates to see how the matter was; I did so, and found it as stated, and referred tc it. This was one of the things that excited General Hayne; he found his narrow policy near home. Another was an allusion made by me, without any studied respect, I acknowledge, to their Carolina notions. He was very angry, and when he rose to oppose a day or two's postponement, as I wished to be in the court, talked perhaps a little too largely of what he was going to do. One thing is singular enough, and I can mention it to you without danger of your ascribing the remark to any wrong cause. I never spoke in the presence of an audience so eager and so sympathetic. The public feeling here was on our side almost universally. This is partly owing, no doubt, to the system of reform which has been brought to bear on so many individuals and so many families here. In the pamphlet I sent, some strange errors are corrected. In looking over the printed notes, I made them read, in one place, "There is no such thing as half allegiance and half rebellion; no treason made easy!" in allusion to books, you know, entitled "geometry made easy!" "logic made easy," &c. The printer put it "treason madcosy!" Twice I corrected the proof, and wrote, as I thought, plain enough, "made easy." But I could not make it easy, and so it has gone through the Union: "Treason madcosy!" Pray, what did you think that meant? Finally, I went to the press and had the whole sentence struck out.

Pray give my best regards to Mrs. Dutton. Mrs. Webster reciprocates your and her good wishes with all her heart. She has fully made up her mind, she says, to like New England, and is not quite certain, moreover, that it will require any great effort. I believe she is predestinated to be a good New Englander. Our excellent friend, Judge Story, is well and in good spirits. He seems to like his new associate, Judge Baldwin, quite well.

D. WEBSTER.

MR. MASON TO MR. WEBSTER.

Portsmouth, March 8, 1830.

DEAR SIR,—Not being on good terms with Mr. A., and not liking to write him on the subject you mention, I have requested Robert Means to make the desired inquiries. If any thing can be ascertained from him, I think it can be done better by conversation than by writing. When I know the result, I will inform you. I have no recollection of ever writing to him on the subject alluded to. I have read your last speech with great delight; it was sent me in pamphlet form from Boston. My expectation was highly raised, and I can truly say it has been fully satisfied. Your defence of New England is all that could be desired, and you have been most fortunate in effecting it, without polluting your own hands with any of the filth that was so abundantly collected round you. But the constitutional argument is of vastly greater importance. I have read that with great attention, and I think it unanswerable. If I mistake not, it cannot fail of producing a sensible effect even in South Carolina. If Colonel Hayne's answer is received as the true construction of the Constitution, our government is at an end. The sophistical Virginia resolutions of 1798, afford the only support of this wild doctrine. Mr. Madison, by adopting your gloss upon his resolutions, might atone for all his political sins, and confer a greater benefit on his country than he has done by the labor of a long life. But of his doing this I fear there is no hope.

This is our election day. Colonel Upham has a majority of about one hundred in this town; I do not know the exact number. We have succeeded in choosing five anti-Jackson representatives. Strong hopes are entertained of an anti-Jackson House of Representatives. This is important, as a senator of the United States is to be chosen. Upham's chance for governor is thought to be tolerable. The forged papers, lately returned by Hill, from Washington, have done much for him about here. If they have been as efficient in other parts of the State, he is elected. The papers were lately brought here, and pronounced to be forgeries by all who saw them, except I. W. and E. W. W. is supposed to have the promise of Decatur's place, in case he should be rejected by the Senate.

The suit of Mrs. Mellen against the Dover Manufacturing Company must, I believe, end in nothing. If there be any thing to argue in it, it must be a mere question of law, which I think cannot come on at the next term, which is to be held at Gilford. If you are inclined to come again to the old county of Strafford to argue a cause, you had best be engaged for the defendants, who are able and will be willing, if the case raises any question, to pay you good fees. The plaintiff has, I believe, spent all her money already. I think you had best not engage before I see you.

Affectionately yours,
J. Mason.

MR. MADISON TO MR. WEBSTER.

Montpelier, March 15, 1830.

Dear Sir,—I return my thanks for the copy of your late very powerful speech in the Senate of the United States. It crushes "nullification," and must hasten an abandonment of secession. But this dodges the blow by confounding the claim to secede at will, with the right of seceding from intolerable oppression.

The former answers itself, being a violation without cause, of a faith solemnly pledged. The latter is another name only for revolution, about which there is no theoretic controversy. Its double aspect, nevertheless, with the countenance received from certain quarters, is giving it a popular currency here, which may influence the approaching elections, both for Congress and for the State legislatures. It has gained some advantage also by mixing itself with the question, whether the Constitution of the United States was formed by the people or by the States, now under a theoretic discussion by animated partisans.

It is fortunate when disputed theories can be decided by undisputed facts. And here the undisputed fact is that the Constitution was made by the people, but as embodied into the several States who were parties to it, and therefore made by the States, in their highest authoritative capacity.

They might by the same authority and by the same process have converted the confederacy into a mere league or treaty, or continued it with enlarged or abridged powers; or have embodied the people of their respective States into one people, nation, or sovereignty; or, as they did by a mixed form, make them one people, nation, or sovereignty, for certain purposes, and not so for others.

The Constitution of the United States, being established by a competent authority, by that of the people of the several States, who were the parties to it, it remains only to inquire what the Constitution is, and here it speaks for itself. It organizes a government into the usual legislative, executive, and judiciary departments; invests it with specified powers, leaving others to the parties to the Constitution; it makes the government to operate directly on the people; places at its command the needful physical means of executing its powers; and finally proclaims its supremacy, and that of the laws made in pursuance of it, over the Constitution and laws of the States; the powers of the government being exercised, as in other elective and responsible governments, under the control of its constituents, the people and legislatures of the States, and subject to the revolutionary rights of the people, in extreme cases.

Such is the Constitution of the United States *de jure* and *de facto;* and the name, whatever it be, that may be given to it, can make it nothing more nor less than what it actually is.

Pardon this hasty effusion, which, whether according or not precisely with your ideas, presents, I am aware, none that are new to you.

With great esteem and cordial salutation,

JAMES MADISON.

MR. SULLIVAN TO MR. WEBSTER.

Boston, March 23, 1830.

DEAR SIR,—I have not done justice to you or myself in not having sooner acknowledged the favor conferred by you, in sending to me your speeches on Mr. Foote's resolution. The delay enables me to speak confidently of public opinion on your achievements; an opinion not formed under sudden impulses, but with good judgment and full means of using it. This opinion appears to me to be, that your speeches on this occasion not only excel all former ones, made by you, but by every other man in our own country; and that out of it, we must go back to the days of Burke, Chatham, &c. to find objects of comparison. This is the opinion of the club; and some of its members, you know, are judges, and very good ones. It seems to me, that the most valuable quality of these speeches is, that they teach the citizens in general what their relation to the Federal government is; and in a manner so comprehensible and satisfactory that every one not only assents, but is surprised that the doctrine should not have been familiar to him, and even that the same train of thought should not have occurred to his own mind. It is a pleasure to your friends here to be able to infer, from the effect produced in different parts of the Union, that an individual, even without the aid of war, and great public excitement, can raise himself to an elevation, on which he may be viewed from all parts of an extensive empire, with an honorable national pride. This is something to set off against military delusion.

I presume we have here as you have in Washington, many groundless assertions and items of news. Of late the rumors have turned on new coalitions; the latest is, I think, to this effect; that Mr. Van Buren and yourself have come to an understanding, but whether with the consent and approbation of Mr. Clay, or without consulting him, rumor seems not to know.

The election pending here is of considerable importance; but I do not find that any influential and discreet men are attempting to give it a proper direction. The representation of the county in the Senate is of much importance the coming year, on account of the valuation. The court are sitting, and will continue to sit about a fortnight longer. They have a great deal to do; and more than four men can possibly do. The subjects apart from home politics most spoken of here, are the discouraging state of things in England, and the want of talent in the public men there; some persons intimating that great changes must soon occur; and the continuance of similar embarrassments in this region. I do not hear any one speak of changes for the better, or even the hope of them.

As to mere town news, Mr. Thorndike is said to be much indisposed. Mr. Ritchie is to review Jefferson's works; Alex. E. is said to have become proprietor of the North American Review. Mr. Otis has been well enough to dine with the "Young Fish" lately. Mr. Sears and family are coming home in the spring. My own family are well; I noticed last evening that some of them were busy in making extracts from the poets, on small slips of paper, to be deposited in the cornucopia of the confectioners for future use.

It is a cold snowy day, the wind from the northeast; and one of those days in which one must plunge into business or pleasure within doors, to escape the misery of feeling what is going on without. An excellent day it might be made around a table, with six or eight congenial minds, with something fit thereon for use. Formerly, when the wind was damp and eastwardly, a small piece of salmon, and a brant apiece for six, in a snug room, with something liquid that could tell of the last century, had a tendency to make one forget which way the wind was. Whether the times are so bad that the like effects would not follow from such causes, is a point which I should be willing to test by actual experiment.

I beg leave to tender my best respects to Mrs. Webster; if you should know when the ladies of Boston may expect the pleasure of seeing her among them, and should tell me of it, I should be glad to be the medium of such news.

With great regard, respect, and thankfulness as your fellow-citizen, your obliged friend,

WM. SULLIVAN.

MR. WEBSTER TO MR. DAVIS.

Washington March 29, 1830.

MY DEAR SIR,—I perceive the booksellers are threatening to afflict the community with a book, made up of my Speeches. This offence is one for which they are answerable only to the public, and to their own pockets. But it seems further intended that I shall be compelled to lend my countenance to the undertaking; to this I demur. By an advertisement which happened to catch my eye in the National Intelligencer this morning, it would seem that the book is to have a head in it from Stuart's picture. This is without my consent; and I suppose it is only said subject to a tacit condition that such consent should be first had and obtained. I have written the proposed publishers on the subject. The object of this is merely to repeat to you the substance of what I have said to them. If they insist, first on making the book, which I suspect they had better not do; and, secondly, on having a head in it, which I do not at all desire they should, but prefer much they should not, I am willing to take the proper course to have a correct and handsome engraving from Stuart's picture, or from one to be made by Harding. I am against all lithographic things.

As yet I have not consented that any body should make an engraving from Stuart.

You will see the proposed publishers easily, and can learn from them their wishes more at large. I should like your opinion, whether to have an engraving from Stuart, or to give Harding a sitting for that purpose.

Mrs. Webster will leave me in about three weeks for New York. I shall hasten thither, and thence to Boston, the moment the session closes. I hope to be home by the 25th of May. If I should, we must once more wet a line together in Marshfield.

Remember me kindly to Mrs. Davis, and believe me truly yours,

D. WEBSTER.

MR. WEBSTER TO MR. DUTTON.

Washington, May 9, 1830.

MY DEAR SIR,—I thank you for your favor of April 19. To receive a letter at Washington which says nothing of business, little of politics, and gives a little honest Boston talk, such as the writer and the reader might hold together if they were taking a turn in the Mall, is quite refreshing. In general, when I open a letter, the silent question which I put to myself is, who is this that wants a cadetship or a midshipman's warrant, or an office, or an errand done at one of the departments? Now and then, it is true, there is a professional letter of rather more agreeable contents. My new wife ran away a fortnight ago, and took Julia with her. She is visiting her friends and leaving her P. P. C.'s in New York; so that when I catch up with her, as the boys say at school, she may be ready for transplantation to Boston. When that will be I cannot exactly tell. Nothing moves me but time, or rather, we all keep in motion without making progress; like that movement among soldiers which is called marking time, when they lift up their feet and put them down again, without going forward. We have been principally occupied in marking time since the first Monday in December.

For the next two weeks, we shall have a scene of confusion; some pressing to take up particular measures, some pressing to keep them off. "Indian Bill," "Tariff," "Massachusetts Claim," "Time of adjournment." A din will come from all these, and twenty more such, enough to split the ear.

The tariff bill—improperly so called—will pass the House and probably the Senate. Our Massachusetts delegation in the House have greatly distinguished themselves on that measure. They appear to me to have overcome the Southrons in the judgment of all the impartial. Mr. Gorham made an excellent speech; it was clear, strong, and manly. There was less of his peculiar ingenuity than I have witnessed in some former instances, but far more decision and force than in any other effort of his, within my knowledge. Davis had immediately preceded him, and necessarily occupied some of his ground. You know little probably of Davis. He is a singularly clear-headed man. You will read his speech with great pleasure, that is, if you can ever read with pleasure, speeches on questions of political economy, and connected with it. For my part, though I like the investigation of particular questions, I give up what is called the "science of political economy." There is no such science. There are no rules on these subjects so fixed and invariable as that their aggregate constitutes a science. I believe I have recently ran over twenty volumes, from Adam Smith to Professor Dew, of Virginia, and from the whole, if I were to pick out with one hand all the mere truisms, and with the other all the doubtful propositions, little would be left.

On Monday we propose to take up Kendall and Noah. My expectation is that they will both be confirmed by the casting-vote of the Vice-President, if the Senate should be full, as I think it will be. A week ago I was confident of their rejection, but one man who was relied on will yield, I am fearful, to the importunities of friends and the dragooning of party. We have had a good deal of debate in closed session, on these subjects, and sometimes pretty warm. Some of the speeches, I suppose, will be hereafter published, none of mine, however. Were it not for the fear of the out-door popularity of General Jackson, the Senate would have negatived more than half his nominations.

There is a burning fire of discontent, that must, I think, some day break out. When men go so far as to speak warmly against things which they yet feel bound to vote for, we may hope they will soon go a little further. No more of politics. We have now and then a Bostonian or two here. Your Jackson friends would not stay long enough to see or be seen. William Sawyer and Powell Mason are here, bound to Cincinnati. Mr. D. P. Parker is here also, with his daughter, and so is my countryman, that good citizen of the world, Mr. A. E. Belknap.

I am right down homesick; I want to go to Sandwich with I. P., first having had a look at you all. At any rate, I wish to shift this present scene; to get out of the Pennsylvania Avenue; to hear no more of bills, resolutions, and motions. I never felt more completely weary of a session. If it do not terminate soon, I shall run away and leave it.

I pray you to make my very best regards to Mrs. Dutton.

Yours ever truly, D. WEBSTER.

P. S. If, instead of a letter, I could send you peas and strawberries, which were very fine on our table yesterday, I think it would be a better offering.

MR. WEBSTER TO MR. WILLIAM SULLIVAN.

Washington, May 22, 1830.

MY DEAR SIR,—Your letter gives me an opportunity of talking freely on a subject which has been suggested to me from various quarters, and about which I have not said much. I am inclined to avail myself of this opportunity to talk right out, and give you the whole of my notions in regard to the matter.

1. I have heard that the good people of Boston would, some of them, like to show me some proof of kindness by a dinner, a ball, or something else. 2. That the mode or manner is not yet decided, and that all rests, as yet, in intention. Now I shall open my heart to you without reserve.

As to a dinner, there seem to me to be insuperable objections to it. I have received that compliment once, as you know, two years ago; it would, therefore, be nothing new. But what is more important, other persons' feelings might be injured. Our immediate representative has acquitted himself very ably in the House of Representatives, and done great honor to the State; so has Davis, and so has Everett. In truth, our whole delegation in the House of Representatives is uncommonly able, and all true. My colleague, too, though an unpretending man, has been entirely true, and very useful in more cases and ways than one. Now it would be invidious to select me alone, as the object of any particular expression of regard; I should, myself, feel that it would be in some measure unjust; I should think they would have a right to feel hurt.

And further, my friends know me, I know them; a public dinner would be no additional proof of regard; I am as sure of their good wishes and esteem as if they were to give me a dozen dinners, and ring all the bells for a fortnight. Then, would it do good elsewhere? I think not. It would necessarily have some political cast, and, however prudently it might be conducted, I suspect it could hardly do good abroad. I am, therefore, my dear Sir, against a dinner, and, indeed, against all ostentation and show, and parade. I believe the interest as well of my constituents as of myself, is likely to be better promoted by abstaining from all such things. I shall see all Boston, and much of the Commonwealth, in the course of the summer, and shall have an opportunity of seeing and shaking hands with most, or many, of those who take an interest in me, or would wish to give me congratulation.

As to a ball, the sun rides too high for that. Let us think of that in October.

And now I will tell you what may be done if you and others see fit. If fifty gentlemen are inclined to make a subscription for a piece of plate, say an urn or some such thing, let them do so. One single article, of size to bear an inscription, would probably be better than more and smaller ones. Yet even this last, which is your suggestion, would be perfectly well.

I have thus spoken to you in confidence, freely and unreservedly. Whatever you and others do, or omit, excepting always a dinner, and any thing else that is ostentatious, will be perfectly satisfactory to me. I know you will, some of you at least, be glad to see me, and that itself is high gratification. I owe my neighbors infinitely more than they can ever owe me; and I am satisfied, and gratified, and more than compensated a thousand times, for any labors or efforts of mine, by the consciousness that I am thought to have done some little good.

God bless you. Yours, D. W.

MR. CLAY TO MR. WEBSTER.

Ashland, June 7, 1830.

My dear Sir,—Your favor of the 29th ult. is duly received. The decision of my friends at Washington to stand still for the present, and to leave the first movement to Maryland, was best under all circumstances. Their opinion that I should go nowhere for political effect, is in conformity to my judgment and to my principles. I could not have gone every where that I was pressed to go, and dissatisfaction might have been given at places which I did not visit. I think further that you are right in supposing considerations of policy to be opposed to a nomination at present in Massachusetts. To me personally it would be highly gratifying, but then the question is not, what is most agreeable, but what is most expedient.

The exercise of the veto on the Maysville bill has produced uncommon excitement in Kentucky. I have not yet heard from other States. Prior to it, the public discontent with Mr. Bibb broke out in violent forms; and in the neighboring village of Lexington, most of the respectable, and some of the least worthy of Jackson's supporters have openly renounced their faith.

We shall attack the veto, by proposing an amendment of the constitution to restrict it, so as to require a majority of all the members elected to each branch of the Congress, instead of two thirds, subsequently, to pass the bill. I think such an amendment right, otherwise I would discountenance it. It is conformable to the analogy of many of the State constitutions, including our own; and it is in the spirit of our institutions.

The policy of such an attack is obvious. The other party will of course defend it, and we shall get the weather-gage of them. We will put them on the aristocratic bench, and more than balance the account of their proposition to amend the constitution in regard to the Presidential election.

You will consider how far it may be right and expedient, in proper time, to coöperate in this subject.

The Maysville road leads entirely across that third part of Kentucky that was most favorable to Jackson. You can imagine, then, what effect must be produced by this event. We were safe before. Now, I think, we may be considered as absorutely certain; and we shall send you some good and true man, I hope Crittenden or Letcher, in place of Rowan. From all other parts of the West information continues to be good.

I wish you were now in the House of Representatives, but I doubt whether you ought to return to it. You need make no change to advance your fame; you may rest entirely satisfied with what you have. The example to which you refer is not precisely in point; I had never served in the House of Representatives, and I was about thirty-two. You have served long there, and you are forty-eight.

I am happy to tell you that the very best effects have been produced by your vote, and that of our New England friends generally, for the Maysville road. It will not be forgotten.

To guard against the treachery of the post-office, if you write me, put your letters under cover to James Harper, Lexington. To whom should I address mine?

Ever yours cordially,

H. Clay.

MR. WEBSTER TO MR. DAVIS.

Washington, June 30, 1830.

Dear Sir,—I have received your letters, and am paying all due attention to the subject of cordage. I have drawn an amendment, like General Dearborn's in effect, and sent it to the committee, to whom the tariff bill is referred. I have spoken to four, out of five, of the committee, and I have no doubt they will report the desired amendment, and that it will pass. Depend upon it, I shall follow it up. It will not be either overlooked or overwhelmed by cries of "question," "question."

I am almost worn out, and am getting to be as thin as a hatchet. I sigh for the seaside, and for repose. The House of Representatives will probably go to work on the Bank to-day, and soon settle it, one way or the other. Probably they will pass it, and probably too, as I think, the President will place his negative upon it. Others think otherwise. We shall see.

Yours truly,

D. Webster.

MR. WEBSTER TO MR. JUSTICE STORY.

Salem, Wednesday, one o'clock, 11 August, 1830.

My dear Sir,—J. J. Knapp's trial commenced yesterday morning, and has made little progress. The A. M. yesterday was occupied in impanelling a jury; the P. M. mainly in debating whether the attorney-general had a right to bring in other counsel; on this question, their honors deliberated, and this morning agreed to let me in, I having stated to them that I appeared at the request of the attorney-general, and had not received, and should not receive, any fee in this case; which, of course, was and is true. This A. M. has been employed in discussing the admissibility of the confessions, and the court holds the point under advisement. I expect they will be ruled out. If they be not, I shall not send you this letter; if they be, then I shall find myself in such a situation, as that I shall be compelled to take some course, respecting the Rhode Island court. If the confessions be ruled out, there is no chance of finishing the cause, this week; and I must inevitably abandon it, unless I can make some disposition about the time of hearing the cause of Farnham *v.* The Blackstone Canal. My engagement in that cause is early, absolute, and indispensable. It will come on, I suppose, Monday or Tuesday; and the only question is, whether you can name a day next week for hearing it, at Providence, so late as to be certain of allowing me to be there. If not, I must leave this case on Saturday evening, at all events.

I write you thus early, because I know not what else to do; and because, if any thing is done, I must send off an express to Rhode Island. It is of great importance to the Messrs. Farnham, and I believe it is also the wish of the other party, to have the cause argued this term. Counsel on the other side do not consent to argue it in Boston, so I must go to Providence; and the only question is, whether you can, at all events, stay at Providence till I can come.

On reflection, I think it best to send this to you at once, because, even if the confession is admitted, the defendants' counsel may, under pretence of impeaching Frank Knapp's conviction, spin out the cause till Monday.

The bearer of this will bring an answer.

Yours always, D. Webster.

MR. A. LAWRENCE TO MR. WEBSTER.

Boston, October 23, 1830.

Dear Sir,—Permit me to request your acceptance of the accompanying small service of plate, as a testimony of my gratitude for your services to the country, in your late efforts in the Senate, especially for your vindication of the character of Massachusetts and of New England.

From your friend and fellow-citizen,

Amos Lawrence.

P. S. If by any emblem or inscription, on any piece of the plate, consisting of a pitcher, waiter, and two goblets, referring to the circumstances above mentioned, the whole will be made more acceptable, I shall be glad that you will designate what it shall be, and permit me the opportunity of adding it.

A. L.

MR. WEBSTER TO DR. PERKINS.

Boston, November 13, 1830.

My dear Friend,—I cannot tell you, indeed I cannot, how much I am distressed by the calamity which has fallen on you and your wife; of all others, it seemed the least likely to happen. So mighty a loss, and so unexpected, does indeed require of you both all the exercise of your patience and submission. It has made a very deep impression on all our household; and we all give you, in large measure, all we can give, our sympathy, and our participation in your grief. We can only pray God to succor and console you.

I returned but last evening from Salem, after near a week's absence. On Monday, if weather permits, Mrs. Webster and her sisters leave this place for New York. I go with them, as far as Providence, whence I expect to return, and to remain at home till about December. I am most anxious to see you, and to help soothe, if I can, your great affliction.

With the most fervent prayers for you both, I am, as ever, most sincerely and affectionately, yours,

DAN'L WEBSTER.

NOTE. Doctor Perkins's son, Henry, died while on a visit to his father's house in New York. He was married, and had come home from the West, to see his parents, and died very suddenly one evening.

MR. WEBSTER TO MR. C. B. HADDOCK.

Washington, February 6, 1831.

MY DEAR NEPHEW,—I heard from you, at the early part of the session, and have omitted to answer longer than I intended. I was at Salisbury after I saw you, and gave directions about the farm. I think it best to put an end to separate interests there as soon as convenient. I suppose you have by this time obtained your license to sell. My hope and expectation now are to be in Boston the first day of April; perhaps a little earlier. If you could arrange the sale for about the middle or 20th of April, I could conveniently attend it, as I propose to visit Salisbury in that month. In May and June, I doubt whether it will be in my power. If events come about according to my wishes, I hope to run away to Ohio, about the 1st of May.

Partly on my own motion, and partly at the request of friends, I have been putting into writing something of my early history, dates, incidents, &c., touching early years. I have not made much progress, nor is there indeed much to be said, but I have run over a few sheets of paper. It has occurred to me, in connection with this subject, to suggest to you the expediency, as of your own motion, of writing to Rev. Dr. Wood of Boscawen, who, I hope, is yet living. He may have few or no incidents to relate, but his general recollection may possibly be worth preserving. I need not enlarge; you will understand me. It may be well to tell him, that the object is to preserve materials, not to be used in his lifetime or mine. I wish he would say something of my brother, whom he knew so well, and so long.

The book,[1] I have seen. It is well enough except the awful

[1] A volume of Mr. Webster's Speeches.

face, which seems to be placed in the front of the volume, like a scarecrow in a cornfield, to frighten off all intruders.

Pray let me hear from you, and tell me all you have to say, *de omnibus rebus.* We have a most severe winter here; this is as frosty a morning as might become the neighborhood of Kearsarge. Mrs. Webster desires her regards, and I am,

Dear Charles, always truly yours,

DAN'L WEBSTER.

MR. WEBSTER TO MR. MASON.

New York, April 26, 1831.

MY DEAR SIR,—I came here Saturday, to bring my wife back to Boston, after spending a few days here with her friends. Having leisure this P. M. I incline to give it to the purpose of writing to you; but I am not about to speak on the subject of the resignation of our wise ministry at Washington, or any other public subject. It is to talk of yourself. Before I left home last fall, I had resolved to make one more effort to bring you up to Boston. For particular reasons, then existing, I was induced to postpone the mentioning of the subject. I write now, simply to execute that intention; and to entreat you, earnestly, to consider of the expediency of such a measure. I will not presume to enter into the consideration which recommended it, at least in my opinion; but I will say that my opinion is strong and decisive on the point. I am persuaded a removal will add to your happiness, and that of your family. You will find as much professional employment as you may wish to engage in; and you will find yourself surrounded by warm friends, who estimate you, as you deserve to be estimated. Your boys are now provided for. Your daughters are better at Boston than Portsmouth; at Boston, you will find associations, topics, congenial minds, and objects of greater interest than now surround you. New York, perhaps, might be still better. But Boston is something.

I am persuaded you dislike the idea of removal, and that that is the main obstacle. But that is a thing of a week. Once settled, and all that feeling is over.

My dear Sir, although it would add greatly to my happiness,

that you should come to Boston, I would not advise it, certainly, if I did not think it would promote yours, and promote it greatly. Indeed, I reproach myself for not having urged this point with you oftener. I wish to do it now, with earnestness; I am sure I do it with sincerity.

Ever truly and affectionately your friend,

DAN'L WEBSTER.

DANIEL WEBSTER TO MRS. EZEKIEL W. WEBSTER.[1]

Boston, June 14, 1831.

MY DEAR SISTER,—Your letter has come to hand quite apropos. It is our intention to set off on Thursday morning for Boscawen, by way of Nashua village. Weather being favorable, we may be expected Thursday afternoon at Nashua, and shall be happy to have you go north with us. I am under the necessity of being at Concord, at noon on Friday; so that I shall be obliged to put you to the distress of an early rising on that day. In addition to Mrs. Webster, Julia will come along. Edward begins to beg hard to go, and as his mother is on his side, he also may prevail. We shall have room for you. This is a great day with us, as Mr. Paige is to be married this evening.

"The dawn is overcast," &c.

The happy pair set out to-morrow or next day, for the Springs, the Falls, and other points of the grand tour.

Give my best regards to Mrs. Abbott.

Yours always affectionately,

D. WEBSTER.

P. S. Julia wrote you yesterday; so that, probably, your household will learn our intentions; that is to say, provided you have left a secretary to attend to your correspondence.

[1] Then at Nashua.

MR. E. A. CRAWFORD TO MR. WEBSTER.

September 7, 1831.

Dear Sir,—I will respectfully inform you, that we have had twice the number of visitors to the White Hills that we ever had in one season heretofore. I shall be at liberty in a short time, and I wish you would inform me at what time I should come down to Boston and see you, to make that contract with you and C. I will inform you that I have taken two bears last week, and the third one left his foot in the trap and made his escape; but I will take some more of these black rascals. I shall have to make an addition to my house another year.

Mrs. Crawford thinks that she will be my company to Boston. You will please write me, at what time I shall best see you at Boston. In so doing you will oblige your friend.

Respectfully your humble servant,

Ethan A. Crawford.

MR. WEBSTER TO MR. PAIGE.

December 23, 1831.

Dear William,—I am off to-morrow for Baltimore, thence to Annapolis on Monday, to spend the holidays at the Maryland court. The railroad and the canal have a controversy, and I am going down in aid of the railroad. My cold goes off slowly, but keeps going. Mrs. Webster and Julia were well at the last dates. I have a letter to-day from Fletcher; please give my love to him, and tell him I will answer it as soon as I return. I hear from Edward sometimes, through his mother, but he has not yet favored me with a line direct.

I pray my best love to Harriette; I hope she is by this time free from cold. I wish I could peep in at one of her little oyster suppers. Remember me also to Mr. White and the girls. Do they talk and laugh as usual, or has the cold weather sealed their lips?

Mr. Appleton, our partner, and I get on quite well. He is good company, and knows many things that I wish to learn. A month hence we shall be full of tariff debate.

Give my love to Edward, and ask him to favor me with a line, when his urgent engagements may allow him time.

Mr. Wirt is exceedingly sick at Baltimore.

Yours truly, ever. D. W.

MR. WEBSTER TO MRS. TICKNOR.

Washington, January 8, 1832.

My dear Mrs. Ticknor,—Although I hardly know what to say to you by way of condolence in your affliction, yet I cannot bear to say nothing; I am so desirous you should know how truly and deeply I sympathize with you, who have been near and most kind to me in my greatest trials.

Your last severe affliction a good deal resembles my last; except that Providence, in taking one brother, has left you another, and has left beloved sisters also. When my poor brother fell, I was bereft of everything near to me in blood, except the little saplings of my own household. But I know that in these cases the heart does not reconcile itself to its loss by recollecting what it retains, though sometimes it clings the closer to what remains. In the ordinary losses of life, in disappointed hopes, in loss of fortune, and the whole train of common ills, a firm and elastic spirit gathers consolation and new hopes from various sources. But for that anguish of the heart which the death of beloved objects creates, there is no solace but Christian resignation; no balm, but in the soft effusions of that spirit which can say, "Not as I will, but as thou wilt!" Affliction, I am persuaded, properly borne, not only purifies but elevates the mind. Its tendency is to strengthen religious feeling, and to bring into more vigorous exercise, and to increase by such exercise, that devout trust which teaches us that all is in His hand, and assures us the end will be right.

I pray you, my dear friend, to believe that, from the moment I first heard of Mr. Eliot's death, I have thought of you constantly and most affectionately, and I could not longer forbear some expression of my sympathy and regard. I implore for you and yours the best blessings of Heaven.

Perhaps Mr. Ticknor will sometimes write me; I shall be very desirous of hearing from some of you.

When a proper time comes, and you have a fit opportunity, I beg you to mention me to Mrs. Dwight, and tell her I share her sorrows.

My own health, which has at various times since I left home, suffered from the prevailing epidemic, is now good. The court commences to-morrow. Judge Story has not arrived, but is looked for soon. I feel anxious about him, only because the weather has been so severe, and the journey by land is so tedious.

With my most cordial regards to your husband, and love to your little ones, I am, dear Mrs. Ticknor,

Truly and affectionately yours,

DAN'L WEBSTER.

MR. WEBSTER TO MR. PAIGE.

Washington, Tuesday Evening, January 3, 1832.

DEAR WILLIAM,—You will be glad to hear that I am safe back from Annapolis; arrived at sunset this evening, having come across the country and not round by way of Baltimore. We were seven days, all of us, arguing our cause; I used only part of one. It is not yet decided, though we left the judges there, and shall know in a day or two. The controversy is about a narrow pass, which both companies have occasion to occupy on the banks of the Potomac River, at the foot of a perpendicular precipice, where the river breaks through the Catoctin Mountain, one of the ridges of the Alleghany, or part of the Blue Ridge, more properly. There is not room enough for both routes between the river and the foot of the mountain, and neither can take any other course without enormous expense. The canal has the oldest charter, but the railroad located first on this particular spot. The chances of the decision are thought to be about even; I incline to think they preponderate a little in our favor.

I pray you say to Mr. White, I thank him for his letter, and shall write him to-morrow. I see Mr. Worcester of Salisbury is dead. Love to Mrs. Paige and Edward.

Yours, ever truly, D. W.

MR. WEBSTER TO MR. PAIGE.

Washington, Friday P. M., March 5, 1832.

Dear William,—I give you great joy at the birth of a daughter! There is no event on which I could more sincerely congratulate you. A daughter is one of Heaven's best and sweetest gifts to man. It delights me to hear of her dark hair, dark eyes, and high forehead, although it costs me an involuntary tear, by the recollection of poor little Grace. My dear Sir, I share your feelings and partake your joy. May a thousand blessings hover over the little stranger! I beg to be most particularly remembered to Harriette. What a new world this has become to her by the events of a year! Pray give her my love.

I shall write a note forthwith to the Judge,[1] and send Charles off with it. I met Mr. Appleton between the House and my seat in the Senate, he bringing me the news, I carrying it to him. So you see the young lady makes a stir at Washington already. I thank you for your continued attention to my land matters, &c.

I would be glad to help poor Edward along with his hard lessons if I were at home. Tell him to keep good courage. Making Latin is hard work, but it will grow easier.

Yours most truly, always,

D. Webster.

MR. WEBSTER TO MR. PAIGE.

Washington, March 10, 1832.

Dear William,—I have been exceedingly glad to hear from you from day to day, with accounts of Harriette and Miss Paige. I rejoice to think, that by the time you receive this, Harriette will be at the head of her own table again; for

"What is a table, richly spread,
Without the lady at its head."

[1] Judge Story, uncle of Mrs. Paige.

Although not a passionate lover of children that I know nothing about, yet I really long to see this little specimen of humanity.

Mr. Appleton and Mr. Dutton seem much pleased with the result of the sales; they think it was better than was to have been expected. They both perused the catalogue, &c. many an hour, while I read the newspapers. Mr. and Mrs. Dutton leave us on Monday next.

I hear that Mrs. Webster was at Baltimore last night; and while I write this, I am expecting every moment to see her. Charles keeps watch at the door.

Pray dispatch Mr. White by the 15th. I want to see him, but do not let the girls suppose I am desirous of seeing them.

P. S. Six o'clock.—Mrs. Webster came into this great city at three, with Mrs. Edgar, Herman Newbold, and Mr. Hamilton Fish. All well.

I write to Mr. White by this post; if he shall have left you, you may either send it after him to New York, or put it into the fire, no matter which.

Yours, D. W.

MR. MERCER TO MR. WEBSTER.

Fredericksburg, April 10, 1832.

My dear Sir,—I have received with great pleasure the pamphlet, which you have been so good as to forward to me. The same mail brought me, from Judge John Pitman of Providence, R. I., an oration delivered by him on the same interesting occasion, "The Centennial Birthday of Washington."

I was associated with Judge Pitman some years ago on a board of visitors at West Point, and was much gratified in forming an acquaintance with a gentleman in all respects so estimable. This simultaneous proof of your regard and his is a very pleasing coincidence, and is much valued by me.

I will ask your acceptance of an Eulogium pronounced by Bishop Madison on the death of General Washington, under the resolution of Congress; which, as a profound statesman and

American patriot, will afford you pleasure. There is a beautiful and eloquent allusion made to my revered father, whose character and services belong to the nation, and I have endeavored to preserve the discourse to our country, by having it republished in Philadelphia during the last summer. I hope you will approve of my having in this manner discharged what I thought was a filial, pious, and patriotic duty to my country, whose adopted son I am.

Congress resolved in April, 1777, that monuments should be erected to the memory of General Warren and my father; that the eldest son of General Warren and the youngest son of General Mercer should be educated at the public expense. I am that son, and since I reached my years of discretion and reflection, have had a steady eye upon the responsibilities which the sacred connection imposed on me. I was but five months of age when my venerated parent sealed with his blood his devotion to the cause of our Independence. His adopted country has not been ungrateful; his memory is embalmed in the reverence and affection of the whole American people.

I had the honor of being introduced to you two years ago in the Senate Chamber; had my stay afterwards in Washington permitted, I should certainly, as I very much desired, have waited upon you at your lodgings, as you kindly invited me to do. In a short conversation I had with you, you spoke with touching and patriotic sensibility of having visited the house, still standing near Princeton, in which my father died under his wounds. In July last I was in Philadelphia; I made a visit to Princeton as privately as I could; visited the battle-field and house, and waited upon two very venerable and respectable Quaker sisters in the vicinity, but occupants of the house in January, 1777, who assisted in nursing my gallant and dying father. This visit was surely of the most sacred character, and I felt it to be so. The maiden name of those sisters, still living, no doubt, is Clarke; one a widow, the other never having changed her state; one eighty-two years of age, the other seventy-eight. What remarkable circumstances, and how closely allied with one of the most interesting epochs in our revolutionary history! They were much gratified upon my at length informing them who I was, and my object in visiting them; they gave me many interesting particulars of their attendance on my father. You are perhaps apprised that the body was removed under a military escort to Philadelphia. It was exposed one day in the coffee-house of that city to the army and people, and was then committed to the tomb in Christ churchyard, "followed by thirty thousand sympathizing mourners."[1] The monuments have not been reared, but the resolution of Congress, enrolled among the archives of the government, will endure with the republic, and will be more durable than monumental brass or marble.

When in Philadelphia, about eighteen years ago, I felt a wish to place some memorial over the grave. The venerable gentleman, Mr. Dalby, who was sexton of the church at the time of the funeral, was living, and still the sexton. This information was given me by Bishop White, one of the chaplains to the army. I ascertained the residence of Mr. Dalby, (now numbered among the dead,) called on him, made myself known, and told him the object of my visit. He said he recollected well and never could forget "the great funeral;" we met at Christ churchyard next morning at nine. Mr. Dalby pointed to a spot: "Underneath are the remains of your father." He called my attention to the letters G. M., rudely scratched on the brick wall immediately over the spot. They are intended, he said, for "General Mercer." Those letters were then plain, and easily seen; time has since obliterated them entirely. I directed a plain marble slab with a simple inscription to be placed over the spot, and the venerable and excellent Bishop White was so good as to see the work perfected upon my return home. In several visits to Philadelphia since, I have visited the sacred tomb, which now points out to the passing stranger the spot which contains the earthly remains of one who gloriously gave up his life in the holy cause of American Independence; before, there was no mound or stone, however rude, to designate the spot.

Your patriotism, Sir, pure and lofty as your country knows it to be, will excuse me with you for giving you these lengthy details. I have thought they might interest you, whilst I am

[1] Extract from a letter of Colonel James Innis of the Virginia line, then with the army and present at the funeral, to my grandmother, Mrs. Gordon. Colonel Innis was for many years after the Revolution one of the most eloquent and able gentlemen of the Virginia bar.

very sensible of the delicacy of such a communication coming from me; but I well know to whom I am writing. With high admiration of your distinguished and elevated character and virtues, I am, my dear Sir, with perfect esteem and respect,

Your friend and obedient servant,

HUGH MERCER.

MR. WEBSTER TO MR. PAIGE.

Washington, Tuesday morning, April 24, 1832.

DEAR WILLIAM,—I have received yours respecting the lining of the chaise. I do not like a dark lining; such linings look hot in summer, and in winter I go in a sleigh. I reject blue; therefore, the body and carriage being dark, I suppose a light drab would not answer, and dark drab looks dull. On the whole, I am for a brown, or a claret, though if I know what a claret is, it is rather darker than I should like, yet I think it will do very well. Please ask Harriette, whether it shall be a claret or a brown, and decide according to her response, as I hope she will sometimes do my new chaise the honor to take a drive in it.

I hear that Mr. White and daughters left Baltimore yesterday morning. Of course, Mr. A. and Mrs. White did not reach them there; they will, doubtless, overtake them this night, at Philadelphia. I am happy to say that my letters this morning, dated Sunday morning, represent Mrs. Jones as a good deal better.

Yours truly,

D. WEBSTER.

CHIEF JUSTICE MARSHALL TO MR. WEBSTER.

Richmond, June 6, 1832.

MY DEAR SIR,—I thank you very sincerely for the copy with which you have favored me of your speeches on the bill for renewing the charter of the Bank of the United States. I need not say that I consider an accommodation of the tariff question itself as scarcely more interesting to our country than the passage of that bill. Your argument presents the subject in its strongest point of view, and to me seems unanswerable. Mr. Ritchie, in his Inquirer, informs the people of Virginia that Mr. Tazewell has refuted you completely. This he may have done in the opinion of Mr. Ritchie. I have not seen Mr. Tazewell's speech, and do not understand from The Inquirer whether his refutation applies to your speech in favor of the bill or to that against the amendment offered by Mr. Moor. By the way, your argument against that amendment is founded in an idea which to me is quite novel. I had often heard it advanced that the States have no constitutional power to establish banks of circulation, but never that Congress might not introduce into the charter a restraining principle, which might prohibit branches altogether, or require the assent of a State to their introduction, or a principle which might subject them to State taxation. This may be considered not as granting power of taxation to a State, for a State possesses that power; but as withdrawing a bar which the constitution opposes to the exercise of this power over a franchise created by Congress for national purposes, unless the constitution of the franchise in its creation has this quality engrafted on it. I however am far from undertaking to dissent from your proposition; I only say it is new, and I ponder on it.

With great and respectful esteem, I am your obedient servant,

J. Marshall.

P. S. I only meant to express my obligation for your attention, and I have betrayed myself into the politics of the day.

MR. WEBSTER TO MR. WHITE.

Washington, June 28, 1832.

My dear Sir,—The tariff bill was engrossed yesterday, in the House of Representatives, and will probably pass to-day. It contains many good and some bad things, and was carried in the House by a strangely mixed vote. Many gentlemen south of the Potomac River voted for it, as did Mr. Adams, and Mr. Appleton, and others. John Davis, Mr. Choate, and others, voted against it. Its great objection is, that it leaves the broadcloths unprotected. In this respect we shall try to mend it; and I have hopes of success. One thing seems certain; if the bill passes, nullification is at an end. There are too many southern votes for it, to admit the idea of its being nullified by southern votes. If we can make the bill what it ought to be, in regard to woollen cloths, it will do much good. Some other things must be attended to. Say to Mr. I. P. Davis, that I do not draw back from attention to drawbacks; and that I am bound by strong cords to the interest of cordage. Lead goes very heavily, in the present bill; but my ever vigilant colleague will look out for Salem, and all its interests urban and sub-urban. In some other particulars we shall try our hand at amendments. Let us hope for the best and be prepared for the worst.

* * * * * * *

I suppose my wife is this day in Boston; I pray you take good care of her. Give my love to Mr. and Mrs. Paige, and show him this letter; and give my love also to the damsels.

Yours ever and a day,

D. Webster.

MR. WEBSTER TO MR. WHITE.

Marshfield, Sunday, August 2, 1832.

My dear Sir,—I did not write you, as I promised, on Friday, because, so soon as it ceased raining in the morning, there were certain flocks seen on the meadows, whose visits it was necessary to regard, and Mr. Blake came that evening, and took the field yesterday, so that I was occupied with him. We embarked in Mr. Hatch's boat, at the boat-house, head of South River, and went down to the mouth thereof, through the marshes, and returned the same way. We found some birds, though the meadows are not sufficiently mown to make them constantly plenty. Immediately after the rain, they were in great numbers, all round us. I have not followed the seas at all, since I saw you last. I reserve the pleasure of renewing that sort of life till you come again, and until The Calypso[1]

[1] A yacht presented to Mr. Webster by Mr. White.

makes her appearance on this coast. Meantime, Peterson takes care that we do not suffer for the want of a fish or two.

I have occasion to be in Boston on Wednesday, for a few hours; and now intend to send Peterson up, by one of the packets, on Tuesday, or else to get him along by the Hingham steamboat, on Wednesday morning, so as to be in Boston as soon as I am, say, Wednesday, twelve o'clock. If he has a fair chance to go by the packet, I shall let him take some man or boy with him, so as to have a full crew. If he goes in the other mode, he must ship a hand in Boston, unless you should feel inclined to take the helm yourself. Nothing happening, I hope to see you in Boston Wednesday, twelve o'clock; and bring you down with me on Thursday, unless you choose to come in the boat. From Thursday the 16th, to Monday the 28th, I wish you to be with us here, as much as you can; and on the last-mentioned day, viz: Monday, the 28th, we must go with our two boys to Chatham direct, and create a sensation among the curlews. I will stay with you at Cherry Hill, one week after our return from Chatham, at any time in September or October, as may be most convenient. I should like to hit on nearly the same period as last year, well recollecting how pleasant and agreeable every thing then looked. We will try to kill, not another horse, but another teal.

Yours very sincerely always,

DAN'L WEBSTER.

MR. WEBSTER TO MR. WHITE.

Boston, Sunday, twelve o'clock, at Mr. Paige's, 1832.

MY DEAR SIR,—I arrived here Friday noon, and was exceedingly sorry to find you had left, and more especially for the cause thereof. Yesterday, I despatched my little concern in court, and Mr. Paige and I had made arrangements to set forth this morning for Cherry Hill, when, lo! at five o'clock Mrs. Paige and little "h," and the two Carolines drove up. All this made it quite impossible to move Mr. Paige towards Cherry Hill, or in any other direction leading from the two "H's" to-day.

I saw your letter to him; you do quite right to keep still and quiet for some days, when I doubt not you will be well again. I shall not leave Boston till to-morrow, which will give me opportunity to see all attended to which you suggested touching the boat; your notions are all right and good. Commodore Morris and Mr. I. P. Davis insist that safety chests shall be placed under the thwarts, which the Commodore says will make it certain, in all cases, that if accident happen, the boat will still float. I know not much about the matter, but shall inquire to-morrow morning. Ought not a small axe to be put in a proper place, to cut a mast, in case of need, or carry on a quarrel with a shark, &c.? Notwithstanding that I shall give all needful directions to-morrow morning, I shall not let the ship be stirred till you see her, and pronounce all to be right. Commodore Peterson is very impatient to have his broad pennant flying at her mast's head. He says that her sails must of course have reefs, therefore he wishes not an inch of her masts to be taken off.

I hope, my dear Sir, you will be able to be in town in three or four days, and to take Mr. Paige over the waves to Green Harbor. Your arrival shall be duly honored.

I notice that the Nahant sales are absolutely fixed for Wednesday. As you said something of a partly-formed intention of buying one of the cottages, I take the liberty, which I hope you will excuse, of suggesting whether you might not safely postpone the execution of that intention.

I give the following reasons: 1. These cottages, or some of them, will be in the market, no doubt, and may be purchased whenever you please hereafter. 2. I want you to take a look at the south shore, from Quincy to Cohasset, inclusive. Come up by way of Hingham, and across the harbor in a boat, and look a little at certain localities which I wish you to see, before you fix on a spot for a marine villa.

Let me hear from you, my dear Sir, as soon as you are able; and remember that no fish will have the honor of being brought on board The Calypso, till you throw a line over her bulwarks.

Yours most faithfully always,

DAN'L WEBSTER.

P. S. I forgot to say that I expect to be in Boston about Wednesday, the 15th, to stay one night. If I should not see you before that time, I shall hope to meet you there, then. There are some matters of business which will call me up at that time, and though I shall not probably stay long, yet I hope to be able to find time to see you and other friends, as may be convenient.

MR. WEBSTER TO MR. WHITE.

Green Harbor, August 17, half-past twelve, 1832.

MY DEAR SIR,—I arrived at sunset yesterday, and found all well. Mr. Paige had been busily engaged all day, either shooting or driving out with the ladies. Mrs. Paige seems quite well; and as for the amiable and interesting Miss Paige, she is as gay as a lark and as fat as a plover.

The Calypso anchored in the inner roads last evening, before dark, out about seven or eight hours from Boston, and for some time becalmed off the cliffs; all well; spoke nothing. The Commodore speaks of her in the highest manner, as a sea boat. In her build and equipment he holds her unsurpassed. She will proceed on no cruise for halibut, cod, or haddock, until you shall be on board.

We look for you, of course, on Monday, rain or shine. I saw Mr. Blake after leaving you. He seemed disposed to return, and commissioned me to inquire him out some rooms. I think he can be accommodated at Captain Hewitt's, which you know is close by. I shall write him this post. You will, of course, arrange that Joseph shall rendezvous here by the end of next week, so as to be ready for a punctual departure for Chatham on Monday the 27th, at five A. M.

The shooting is fine this morning. Mr. Paige shot a dozen birds in the Captain's pond. I have made the number twenty without going far beyond the barn. He is now at Peterson's, and will be home to dine with a dozen more.

On reflection, I think Joseph ought to come down here, so as to have two or three days' shooting next week; I understand that the state of the tides and of the mowing on the meadows, will render that period auspicious. The shooting here is now good; the true way is, to hasten down, enjoy it, but not to proclaim it; don't speak too goldenly of it to Mr. Blake; it is not necessary to bring half the town into the Old Colony, by inflamed account of sports. Remember that this hint is not for yourself, for you have no tongue, except when tongues would be serviceable.

Give my love to the damsels.

Yours truly ever,

D. WEBSTER.

MR. WEBSTER TO MR. WHITE.

Green Harbor, Saturday evening, August 19, 1832.

MY DEAR SIR,—The foregoing[1] proposition has been duly talked over here, and meets with unanimous concurrence. We can find room for the two sprites somewhere, and if they can undergo Marshfield for a week, we shall be glad to see them. They will be beau-less, it is true; but a short abstraction from the world may cause their lights to appear more splendid when they reappear in it. Mr. Paige will talk over the matter with you and them.

Yours ever,

D. WEBSTER.

P. S. We look for you on Monday, and the weather being fine we will join the great fishing interest of the country on Tuesday.

MR. WEBSTER TO MR. WHITE.

Green Harbor, Marshfield, Wednesday afternoon.

MY DEAR SIR,—We only reached Quincy last night, nor did we accomplish that without a ducking. Nevertheless, we arrived here quite well, and without colds, at ten, A. M.

[1] A letter from Mrs. Webster, inviting Mr. White's two daughters to visit Green Harbor, with their father and brother Joseph, and to remain there during the contemplated visit to Chatham.

We have had a laugh at dinner, though we had to force it a little. We have found out that although we fobbed you off with some thin claret on Sunday, we were really rich, in various good wines, with which your kindness had supplied us. To prevent or alleviate extreme mortification, we have affected to make a joke of it, and tried hard to laugh. The truth is, I found a bottle of brandy, and two bottles of Sherry, in the cooler, neither seeing any more nor hearing of any more; and then, Mr. Paige having spoken of only a bottle or two, I thought I had seen all; and Henry, who knew all, being absent on Sunday, I was left to remain in my error. I pray you, in accepting thanks for your kindness, to accept also an apology for such a blunder. I assure you, it is not often that good wine is under any roof where I am without my knowing it.

Notwithstanding the copious shower which fell in Boston and its immediate vicinity, there was not a drop of rain here yesterday; nor hardly any as far on the road as Weymouth.

After I saw you, I was forced to agree to go to Boston, to argue a cause in the supreme court, for Messrs. Peters and Pond. I suppose it will be heard on Saturday next, though the time is not positively fixed. I pray you give my love to Mrs. Paige and the damsels, including Miss Paige. All have sent you the kindest remembrance. I am going over this P. M. to see Commodore Peterson.

Yours ever, truly and faithfully,

DANIEL WEBSTER.

MR. WEBSTER TO MR. WHITE.

Green Harbor, September 14, Friday evening, 1832.

MY DEAR SIR,—Mrs. Webster's health improves rapidly. She has had a drive to-day, and if she continues to improve and the weather should be fine, we shall set off for Cherry Hill Monday morning. We may probably cut Boston altogether, and dine at the Norfolk House, or elsewhere, and bring up at Cherry Hill at night. If we judge the day's drive too long, we shall of course stop by the way. From us to you, round Boston, is fifty-five miles, or thereabout, a pretty long drive for a convalescent lady.

As I was sitting down to dinner yesterday, I was told that five teal had sat down in the water just below the dike. I went out and shot three of them, and brought them in before the beefsteak had cooled. This afternoon I strayed down to the rock with Henry, just to look. We saw several small pods of coots go by; one of them came so near that I brought down one of the number composing it, with bird shot. But it fell in the sea, and we had no boat, and so we lost it.

Just at dusk this evening, a woodcock undertook to fly over our premises, but not steering well run afoul of the pig-pen fence and almost killed himself. He got off with difficulty. If he be a bird of any spirit, he must be mortified at the laugh which the bystanding unfeathered bipeds raised at this clumsy specimen of aerial navigation.

I believe I have now told you all the Marshfield incidents. To-morrow, if the weather should be fine, I intend to wet a line in the salt seas.

Mrs. Webster desires her best love to you and the girls.

I am, dear Sir, as always yours,

DANIEL WEBSTER.

MR. WEBSTER TO CHANCELLOR KENT.

Boston, October 29, 1832.

MY DEAR SIR,—Mr. Calhoun, as you are doubtless aware, has published a labored defence of nullification, in the form of a letter, to Governor Hamilton. It is far the ablest and most plausible, and therefore the most dangerous vindication of that particular form of revolution, which has yet appeared.

In the silence of abler pens, and seeing as I think I do, that the affairs of this government are rapidly approaching a crisis, I have felt it to be my duty to answer Mr. Calhoun, and, as he adopted the form of a letter, in which to put forth his opinions, I think of giving my answer a similar form. The object of this is, to ask your permission to address my letter to you. I propose to feign that I have received a letter from you calling my attention to Mr. Calhoun's publication; and then, in answer to such supposed letter, to proceed to review his whole argument at some length, not in the style of a speech, but in that of cool, constitutional, and legal discussion. If you feel no repugnance to be thus written to, I will be obliged to you for your assent; on the other hand if any reasons suggest themselves to your mind against such a form of publication, another can be readily adopted. I cannot complete the paper before the election, as I am at present a good deal pressed with professional affairs, but I hope to bring it into light in the course of the next month.

I have little to say to you, my dear Sir, upon political subjects. The whole ground is open to you. I trust you will be one of those who will have votes to give, and devoutly pray you may yet see some way of so uniting the well-disposed, as to rescue us from our peril.

I am, dear Sir, with most sincere and true regard, yours,

DANIEL WEBSTER.

CHANCELLOR KENT TO MR. WEBSTER.

New York, October 31, 1832.

DEAR SIR,—I have no objection that you should address in the form of a letter or letters to me your remarks on the Vice-President's scheme of nullification, and that you should assume it to be in answer to a letter from me relative to that subject. I shall deem it an honor to be addressed by you while engaged in the investigation of such an interesting subject. The Vice-President enclosed one of his pamphlets to me, and I read it attentively. It is ingeniously written; but such a construction of the constitution, and such principles as he deduces, are visionary and most unsound and sophistical. His repugnance to all solid constitutional principles would fix a deadly power of destruction in the very vitals of the government.

The crisis is indeed portentous and frightful. We are threatened with destruction all around us, and we seem to be fast losing our original good sense and virtue. The Democracy of this city require all their candidates to Congress to give another pledge to support all the measures of the administration. Can any thing be more degrading and monstrous? Is the proud House of Representatives and the grand inquest of the nation to be composed of such materials?

* * * * * * *

If we succeed in our election, I shall take the liberty of writing you again, and ask for a free communication of sentiments. If we fail, then indeed we may hang our harps upon the willows or on the witch hazel that shades Saint Fillan's Spring!

Your speech at Worcester was admirable for its logic as well as for its fervor and its force. If we are to be saved we shall be largely indebted to you. "*Si Pergama*," *&c.*

Adieu, yours most sincerely,

JAMES KENT.

MR. WEBSTER TO MR. WILLIAM SULLIVAN.

Washington, January 3, 1833.

MY DEAR SIR,—I am glad to receive your letter. We are surrounded with difficulties here, of various sorts; and it is not a little uncertain how we shall get out of them. At the present moment, it would seem that public opinion, and the stern rebuke by the executive government, had, in a great measure, suppressed the immediate danger of nullification. As far as we see the results of the legislation of South Carolina, her laws limp far behind her ordinance. For aught that appears, nothing will interrupt the ordinary collection of duties, after February 1, unless some individual chooses to try the nullifying remedy. If any importer should suffer a seizure to be made, and should endeavor to replevy, under the State process, the collector would probably not deliver up the goods to the sheriff; nor suffer his own goods to be taken in withernam. This, probably, would bring on a trial of strength.

But our more imminent danger in my opinion is, that, seizing on the occasion, the anti-tariff party will prostrate the whole tariff system. You will have seen the bill, reported by Mr. Verplanck. Great and extraordinary efforts are put forth, to push that bill rapidly through Congress. It is likely to be finally acted upon, at least in the House of Representatives, before the country can be made to look on it, in its true character. On the other hand, our friends will resist it, of course, and hold on to the last. A vigorous opposition will at least, it may be hoped, be made, and, as I believe, produce the necessity, on the part of the supporters of the measure, to make some beneficial amendments in it, before even it can get through the House of Representatives.

Under these circumstances, it seems to me it would be extremely useful that the legislature of Massachusetts should express its temperate but firm opinion, first, against the doctrine of nullification; secondly, on the violation of the public faith, which would be perpetrated by this thorough and sudden prostration of the protective system.

On this ground of vested interest, we can make, if well sustained at home, the most efficient stand against the threatened ruin. We mean to occupy this ground, and to make the most of it.

If the bill were now in the Senate, it would not pass; but how far individuals may be brought over by party discipline, in the drill of a month, it is impossible to say.

I do not believe the President himself wishes the bill to pass. *E contra*, I fancy he would prefer the undivided honor of suppressing nullification, now, and to take his own time, hereafter, to remodel the tariff. But the party push on, fearing the effect of the doctrines of the proclamation, and endeavoring to interpose, and to save Carolina, not by the proclamation, but by taking away the ground of complaint.

But against this, again, there is some degree of under current; because there are some who think that, surrendering the tariff to the menaces of nullification, would be voting a triumph to Mr. Calhoun, at the expense of Mr. Van Buren's expectations, &c.

I shall be glad to hear from you, and other friends; especially if you can give me any good advice.

Yours, ever truly,

DANIEL WEBSTER.

MR. WEBSTER TO CHIEF JUSTICE LIVERMORE.

Washington, January 5, 1833.

MY DEAR SIR,—Your letter of December 29 is received, and has given me pleasure. I regard you, my dear Sir, not only as an acquaintance of many years' standing, but also as one whose countenance and kindness were important to me in youth. I shall be sure to send you any thing which I may think you would like to receive, and I beg of you not to take the trouble to acknowledge receipts. It will be quite enough that I understand generally that such communications are welcome.

The impression here to-day, seems to be that nullification has assumed a less threatening aspect. At least the danger of immediate collision appears less. The act, passed by the legislature of South Carolina, to carry the ordinance into effect, does not come up to the ordinance. It may happen that, notwithstanding the ordinance and the act, things may go on much as they have done.

Nothing is more uncertain than the fate of the new tariff bill. It will pass the House, if the President desires it; but that is doubtful. If it were now in the Senate, it would be postponed from an indisposition to act again on that subject so soon; but I do not know what will be done with it, should it come to us a month hence.

It is sometimes said that, in so changing a world, if people will but stand still, others sooner or later will come to them. Were you not struck with this truth, in seeing the proclamation?

I am, dear Sir, with constant regard,

Yours,

DANIEL WEBSTER.

MR. WEBSTER TO MR. DUTTON.

Washington, January 15, 1833.

WE have little news, politically. In a day or two, the President is to send us a communication about nullification. It will probably bring on some debates. The House of Representatives seems to be pressing on the new tariff bill; but still there are suspicions that the bill will not get through that House, and this impression now daily gains strength. Look at Mr. Krebb's resolutions, in Pennsylvania. I hope Massachusetts will do something in the same way. Yours truly,

D. Webster.

MISS JULIA WEBSTER TO MR. WEBSTER.

Boston, March 3, 1833.

My dear Father,—I received your beautiful present a few days since, and was very much pleased with it. I think it contains some very fine faces, and I like the stories much better than those usually found in "Souvenirs," or "Annuals.' Your letter preceded it a few days, and I beg you, my dearest Father, to accept your little daughter's best thanks for them both.

I am staying with cousin Eliza, and am passing my time most pleasantly. I find it very convenient as regards my school, as I am never late now, which used sometimes to be the case. I have not commenced any new study since I last wrote you. I think I should like to study Italian very much, as I have not much to do.

I hope we shall soon see you in Boston, as Congress has risen, and we are very anxious to see you at home once more. Although spring has in reality begun, you would not imagine it to be so by the weather, which is intensely cold; the ground is covered with snow, and the thermometer last night was eleven degrees below zero. Fletcher dined with us yesterday, it being Saturday. I suppose you have heard he is to have a part at the next exhibition. Dr. and Mrs. Kirkland dined here to-day; the latter had, as usual, a good deal to say. I saw Edward yesterday, he was very well.

I went on Wednesday with cousin Eliza to hear a lecture on hieroglyphics, delivered by Mr. J. Pickering. It was very interesting, but he did not tell us as much upon the principal subject as I should have liked to have heard. A considerable part of it, was upon the necessity of attention, which he addressed principally to his younger hearers.

I heard two very good sermons to-day from Mr. Greenwood, one of which I shall make an abstract of, for my composition. It was upon the resignation of the Shunamitish woman, when she lost her only son. Cousin Eliza says she wishes you would come home, for she thinks if you were to, we should not think any more of the snow or the cold, for it would make sunshine in Boston. She also unites with me in a great deal of love to you, and believe me ever, dear father,

Your affectionate daughter,

JULIA WEBSTER.

MR. WEBSTER TO MISS JULIA WEBSTER.

Washington, March 9, 1833.

MY DEAR DAUGHTER,—I have this moment received your letter of the 3d instant. It is so kind and good a letter that I will not omit for a moment to answer it, although I am expecting a summons to go directly into court. Notwithstanding your mother's absence, I have felt quite easy about you, since I learned you were to spend your time at cousin Eliza's. Everybody is happy where she is.

I am quite glad to hear that Fletcher has a part at exhibition. You do not mention the time; I fear it will be before I get home.

We have the same cold weather here, at least in some degree, of which you speak. The last ten days have been the severest part of the winter. Some signs of relenting begin now to appear.

I heard yesterday from your mother in New York. I have written her, preferring that she should meet me in Philadelphia, as I shall be obliged to stay there on business, for a day or two.

The court will rise about the fifteenth, and by the end of next week, say by the sixteenth, I hope to take leave of Washington.

I must pray you to remember me most kindly to Mr. and Mrs. Lee. Give my love also to Edward, and to uncle Paige, and aunt Harriette, not forgetting the amiable Miss Paige.

Adieu! my dear daughter,

Ever your most affectionate father,

DANIEL WEBSTER.

MR. WEBSTER TO MR. TICKNOR.

Washington, April 8, 1833.

MY DEAR SIR,— * * * * * * I have read Tom Moore's first volume of Byron's Life. Whatever human imagination shall hereafter picture of a human being, I shall believe it all within the bounds of credibility. Byron's case shows that fact sometimes runs by all fancy, as a steamboat passes a scow at anchor. I have tried hard to find something in him to like, besides his genius and his wit; but there was no other likeable quality about him. He was an incarnation of demonism. He is the only man in English history, for a hundred years, that has boasted of infidelity and of every practical vice, not included in what may be termed, what his biographer does term, meanness. Lord Bolingbroke, in his most extravagant youthful sallies, and the wicked Lord Littleton, were saints to him. All Moore can say is, that each of his vices had some virtue or some prudence near it, which in some sort checked it. Well, if that were not so in all, who could 'scape hanging? The biographer, indeed, says his moral conduct must not be judged of by the ordinary standard! And that is true, if a favorable decision is looked for. Many excellent reasons are given for his being a bad husband; the sum of which is, that he was a very bad man. I confess I was rejoiced then, and am rejoiced now, that he was driven out of England by public scorn; because his vices were not in his passions, but in his principles. He denied all religion and all virtue from the house-top. Dr. Johnson says, there is merit in maintaining good principles, though the preacher is seduced into violations of them. This is true. Good theory is something. But a theory of living, and of dying too, made up of the elements of hatred to religion, contempt of morals, and defiance of the opinion of all the decent part of the public, when before has a man of letters avowed it? If Milton were alive to recast certain prominent characters in his great Epic, he could embellish them with new traits, without violating probability. Walter Scott's letter toward the end of the book, is much too charitable.

I find in one of Lord Byron's letters a suggestion, that part, or the whole of Robinson Crusoe was written while in prison, by the first Lord Orford, (Robert Harley,) and by him given to Defoe. Is there any such suggestion anywhere else? I do not believe it. Defoe's (his true name was Foe) other works show he could write Robinson Crusoe. Harley has left no proof of his capacity for such a work. While on the subject of books, whither I have strayed, I know not how, allow me to say there is one I want to see. It is Johnson's Shakespeare. I covet a sight of that book, just as Sam. Johnson left it. His first edition was about 1765 or 1766. Did he publish a second? You are not only a man for books in general, but for Shakespeare in particular, and can tell me. If you have the book, I shall get a reading of it; if you have it not, I wish you would order it on my account, the next time you write Mr. Rich. I suppose the first edition was folio, but know not.

* * * * * * *

I shall make no more speeches. What I have done, even, was not with malice prepense. Make our best regards to Mrs. Ticknor, and believe me always truly,

Yours, D. Webster.

MR. WEBSTER TO MR. PERRY.

Boston, April 10, 1833.

My dear Sir,—I was gratified by the receipt of your letter of the 1st of this month, and thank you for the favorable and friendly sentiments which you express in regard to an effort of mine, at the late session of Congress, in a cause which I deemed all-important to the country, and to which I had already learned you were as much devoted as myself. I am not at all surprised, my dear Sir, at the opinions you express, as to the ultimate object of those who have raised the flag of nullification. Circumstances, full of meaning, attracted my attention to it early; and in December, 1828, I became thoroughly convinced that the plan of a southern confederacy had been received with favor, by a great many of the political men of the South, especially of your State.

I agree with you also entirely in the opinion that the danger is not over. A systematic and bold attack, now but just begun, will be carried on, I apprehend, against the just and constitutional powers of the government, and against whatsoever strengthens the Union of the States.

For my own part I look forward to an animated controversy on these points, for years to come; and if we can sustain our side of the controversy, my dear Sir, with success, as I hope and believe we may, we shall transmit to posterity an inheritance above all price.

I do not apprehend any further difficulty with Georgia. There was not the slightest reference to the Georgia case, in my mind, or ever, as far as I know, in that of any other gentleman, in preparing and passing the bill for the better collection of the revenue. It is true that some of the provisions of the bill ought, in my judgment, to be permanent. If they had previously existed, the idea of putting the doctrines of nullification in practice, in the mode recently adopted at least, would probably not have been entertained. I have expected what I see now publicly announced, that the effort will be to repeal this law, so soon as Congress shall assemble.

It is probably expected that since the occasion has passed by many will be willing to repeal the law, although they were in favor of its passage at the time; and it is hoped that, by the repeal of this act, it may be considered as decided, that Congress is hereafter to take no step to execute any laws which are resisted by State authority.

The high regard I feel for the patriotic gentlemen with whom you act in your own State, and the respect which I have been led to entertain for yourself, induces me, my dear Sir, to express a wish to hear from you, on the interesting subjects which at present occupy the public attention, whenever your convenience may allow.

With friendly salutations, I remain your obedient servant,

DAN'L WEBSTER.

MR. CASS TO MR. WEBSTER.

Washington, April 17, 1833.

My dear Sir,—I have just received your kind letter, and sincerely thank you for your recollection of me. I think the President will visit New England this season; if he does, he will leave here about the first of May, and he is desirous that I should accompany him. I shall accordingly do so; and I presume we shall be in Boston not far from the 20th of June. I cannot ask you to postpone your intended journey till after this time, as it might expose you to much inconvenience. Still, I will confess to you, that the hope of meeting you and of revisiting with you the scenes and friends of our youth, has dwelt upon my mind, since we first conversed together on the subject. Nothing could give me greater pleasure than such an occasion; and if more pressing engagements should require your absence, at the time I have mentioned, I shall still look forward at a future day to realize this hope.

With sincere regard, I am, my dear Sir, truly your friend,

Lewis Cass.

MR. WEBSTER TO MR. CASS.

My dear Sir,—I have received your letter of the 17th instant. A journey to the West has long been in contemplation by me, but I have not yet been able to accomplish it. Every other year the session of Congress has been so far protracted as to forbid the undertaking for that season, and professional duties have allowed me no leisure, hitherto, in the intervening years. In addition to these causes, the political state of things has, for some time been such, that the motive and objects of such a tour would have been very likely to be misinterpreted and misunderstood.

In this last respect, the present moment seems favorable; and as I have found myself able to make the necessary arrangements with my professional engagements, I have thought it not well to defer, longer, the execution of that which has been already a good while postponed.

Nevertheless, I am very unwilling to miss your visit to New England; and although I might even make that sacrifice in the hope that you would, as you suggest, hereafter repeat your visit, I still feel great reluctance in being from home, when the President comes to Massachusetts. In the first place, it would give me pleasure to see him, and to extend to him and his party the hospitalities of my house, as well as to unite with my friends and neighbors in such manifestations of respect as are due to him. And in the next place, my absence on such an occasion, when it was known that a visit from him to this part of the country was intended, may be liable to much misconstruction.

I am inclined, therefore, at all events, to be at home by the time the President reaches Boston. My plan has been to return by the first of July, if I shall not be able to accomplish all I intend, and return earlier than that day. But under present circumstances, I shall abridge the extent of my travels, so as to be able to return to Boston by the 20th of June.

D. W.

MR. WEBSTER TO MR. WILLIAM SULLIVAN.

Friday, April 19, 1833.

My dear Sir,—I must thank you for your kind and friendly note of the 15th. I have passed an arduous winter, but am richly repaid for all my labors, if those, whose esteem I value, think I have done any thing for the good of the country. All things have not happened as I could wish; but on the whole, I think the events of the winter have tended to strengthen the union of the States, and to uphold the government. But it has many and powerful enemies, not easily subdued, and never to be reconciled.

Your prophecies, or hopes, for certain future events, are a good deal influenced, I suspect, by your private friendship. I do not indulge in any expectations; nevertheless, I thank you for all your favorable sentiments and kind wishes. We must one day, a warm one, take a walk round the Common, and talk over matters.

Yours, always truly,
Dan'l Webster.

DANIEL WEBSTER TO FLETCHER WEBSTER.

Steubenville, July 1, 1833.

My dear Son,—I am at last arrived at the borders of Ohio, though, it is true, at a very late period. I have found it absolutely impossible to get on further, without giving offence. I cross the river this morning, go down to Wheeling, stay there a part of to-morrow, and then go East. My purpose is to get to New York as soon as possible. If it be within the reach of possibility, I will be home before July 15, so as to hear your oration. At present there is no doubt of it, provided I find your mother at New York.

I pray you, spare no pains in regard to that effort. Consider how much depends on it, and how much you owe to those who elected you. Make it long; you will be likely to err on the other extreme. Do not omit a few flowers and flourishes; they become young orators. Let not your taste be too severe. Above all things, be sure to have it perfectly committed, and rehearse and practise it till you feel that you can deliver it perfectly well.

My health is entirely good, but I long to get home. Give my love to Uncle's and Mr. A's family. It is a long time since I heard from Boston, or from mother and Julia.

Your affectionate father,

D. Webster.

FRAGMENT OF A JOURNAL OF MR. WEBSTER.

(UNFINISHED.)

Tuesday, May 28.

ARRIVED at Avon, evening of 27th. On 28th A. M. visited Mr. E. Le Roy's farm; it lies on the Genesee River, north of the road, leading from Avon Bridge, and consists of eighteen hundred acres. The land is of three characters. 1. Flats. This is purely alluvial, low, and level. It is subject to be overflowed. When the country was settled, much of it was prairie. It has great depth of loose soil, vegetable mould, and other deposits. On the bank of the river, where the roots of trees are exposed, they are near six, eight, or ten feet from the surface. The trees still remaining are fine, especially elm and white oak, some of them very large. The land is adapted to grazing, but uncertain for wheat. In very dry seasons, wheat has succeeded on it. 2. The hazel flat. This is a table of land rather higher than the last mentioned. It is flat, well covered with wood, undoubtedly, I think, alluvial, but an earlier formation. It is not usually overflowed, and is, perhaps, more valuable than the lower flats, as adapted to wheat, as well as grazing. 3. Upland. This seems a peculiar soil. It is full of small stones, and the ground covered with a growth of oaks, of no great size. To the eye, it does not seem to be extraordinary land; but its fertility is very great, especially for wheat and clover. When ploughed, little pebbles, stones, as they would seem, are turned up in great plenty; but these crumble or dissolve by exposure to the air, and seem to be marl or a mixture of lime and clay, or some such thing, which I do not exactly know about. This land grows better by cultivation. It will yield two crops of wheat, then one of clover, then one year pasturage, and then wheat again, all without manure. The only rotation seems to be, from wheat to pasturage, sometimes cropping with the scythe, the first after wheat.

The lands up and down the river seem much like Mr. Le Roy's. I saw no difference between his flats and those at Geneseo. The highland, or upland, near Geneseo, was higher, and seemed to have a heavier original upland growth.

Mr. Le Roy cuts, on his lower flats, two hundred or two hundred and fifty tons of hay. This is housed in small barns or barracks, standing round on the flats, and is fed out, thence, to the cattle. The cattle lie on the meadows through the winter, except working oxen, milch cows, &c., and so do the sheep. Mr. Le Roy winters one hundred, or one hundred and fifty head of cattle, and feeds out to them two tons of hay a day. This is carried and spread over the field, by a sled, or wagon, so that the growth of the flats is consumed on them. These flats are sometimes ploughed, but some of them have not been ploughed for forty years, and yet bear good grass. The feed is abundant.

END OF VOLUME I.

www.ingramcontent.com/pod-product-compliance
Lightning Source LLC
LaVergne TN
LVHW021258110826
845150LV00003B/416